高等院校经济管理类专业应用型系列教材

城市管理学双语教程

Introduction to Urban Administration

王 波 主 编

叶兴艺 副主编

中国财经出版传媒集团

经济科学出版社

Economic Science Press

·北京·

图书在版编目（CIP）数据

城市管理学双语教程 / 王波主编；叶兴艺副主编 .
北京：经济科学出版社，2024.6. —— （高等院校经济
管理类专业应用型系列教材）. —— ISBN 978 – 7 – 5218
– 5994 – 2

Ⅰ. F293
中国国家版本馆 CIP 数据核字第 2024BL1028 号

责任编辑：杜　鹏　张立莉
责任校对：徐　昕
责任印制：邱　天

城市管理学双语教程

CHENGSHI GUANLIXUE SHUANGYU JIAOCHENG

王　波　主　编

叶兴艺　副主编

经济科学出版社出版、发行　新华书店经销

社址：北京市海淀区阜成路甲 28 号　邮编：100142

编辑部电话：010 – 88191441　发行部电话：010 – 88191522

网址：www. esp. com. cn

电子邮箱：esp_bj@ 163. com

天猫网店：经济科学出版社旗舰店

网址：http：//jjkxcbs. tmall. com

固安华明印业有限公司印装

787 × 1092　16 开　18.5 印张　430000 字

2024 年 6 月第 1 版　2024 年 6 月第 1 次印刷

ISBN 978 – 7 – 5218 – 5994 – 2　定价：52.00 元

（图书出现印装问题，本社负责调换。电话：010 – 88191545）

（版权所有　侵权必究　打击盗版　举报热线：010 – 88191661

QQ：2242791300　营销中心电话：010 – 88191537

电子邮箱：dbts@ esp. com. cn）

前　言

　　城市管理作为一个源远流长且异彩纷呈的研究领域，它不仅跨越了历史的长河，更遍布全球各个角落。对于渴望深入探索这一领域广度与深度的教师和学生而言，城市管理无疑带来了一系列独特的挑战。因为在本科教育阶段，学生们常常需要通过零散的途径来接触这一领域，他们尝试将不同学科的理论碎片拼凑起来，却往往缺乏一个统一的框架来整合和应用这些知识，特别是对于中国学生，城市管理领域与中国本土经验的联系以及城市管理者可能面临的具体问题很少得到充分探讨。这不仅限制了他们对城市管理全貌的理解，也影响了他们将理论应用于实践的能力。为了应对这些挑战，本教材精心设计，旨在提供一个全面的视角。我们不仅整合了城市管理的多学科理论，更特别关注了中国在这一领域的实践和挑战。我们希望本教材能够激发学生的兴趣，促进他们对城市管理的深入理解，并鼓励他们探索与本土实践相结合的创新解决方案。

　　首先，本教材采用双语编写，既适合以英语授课的课程，也适合以汉语授课的课程。对于中国大学生而言，以英语进行学习不仅具有独特的优势，而且至关重要。随着中国在全球经济和治理中的日益融入，英语已成为帮助中国学生提升全球竞争力的关键工具。我们鼓励学生超越简单的记忆，积极参与到对所学内容的深入理解中。双语教材正是提供了这样一个平台，要求学生在语言学习的同时，也能够与全球知识体系进行互动。通过用英语学习，学生们不仅能够提升语言能力，还能够拓宽视野，增强跨文化交流的能力，为未来参与国际舞台做好准备。

　　其次，本教材不仅回顾了城市管理的历史，更注重历史与现实的联系。我们的目标是让学生通过了解不同地区城市化的不同阶段，对城市管理有一个全面而深入的了解，这不仅为他们未来的学术研究打下坚实的基础，也为那些希望在城市政府工作的学生提供了必要的知识储备。此外，本教材特别强调比较视角，使学生能够洞察中国城市化进程与其他国家的差异。这种对比不仅有助于学生认识到中国在城市化和管理方面的独特性，而且鼓励他们思考如何在全球化背景下，借鉴国际经验，发展适合中国国情的城市管理模式。

　　再次，本教材汇集了多种理解城市环境的方法，涵盖了政治、经济、行政和社会学等多个框架。这种跨学科的视角为学生提供了丰富的工具和理论，帮助他们深入理解城市如何有效运作。对于有志于在城市政府工作的学生来说，这种全面的观点将极大地增强他们解决问题的能力，提高他们成为高效管理者的潜力。即使对于那些不打算从事城市政府工作的学生，这种多角度的学习方法也同样重要。因为城市是现代生活的中心，大多数学生将在未来居住在城市地区。通过本教材的学习，他们将更好地准备面对城市生活中的各种挑战，提升自己作为城市公民的责任感和参与度，为建设更加和谐、可持续的城市社区作出贡献。

最后，本教材深入探讨了中国城市政府面临的实际问题，并提供了具体的案例。这种案例驱动的方法不仅赋予了理论以生命，而且展示了如何将知识应用于实际问题的解决中。通过这种方式，本教材超越了纯粹的理论探讨，成为了一本实用的指导手册，帮助学生理解并应对城市管理中的复杂挑战。我们相信，通过案例分析，学生能够更深刻地认识到理论的力量，以及如何将这些理论应用于提升我们对世界运作方式的理解。在当今世界，超过半数的人口居住在城市之中，城市问题已经成为全球性的关注焦点。通过深入了解城市的发展和挑战，我们能够为改善未来的生活质量和推动社会进步作出贡献。

在本教材的写作过程中，我们深感荣幸能够获得众多人士的宝贵支持和贡献。首先要特别向李钟烈教授、吉尔·陶以及柴德·安德森表达我们深深的谢意，他们不仅在文本的构思和初稿阶段提供了宝贵的反馈，而且在完善和深化内容方面发挥了不可或缺的作用。李钟烈教授以其深厚的学术造诣和丰富的经验，为本教材的理论框架和实践应用提供了关键的指导，吉尔·陶和柴德·安德森则以其敏锐的洞察力和创新的思维，对文稿进行了细致的审阅和建设性的批评，极大地丰富了本教材的深度和广度。最后还要对余来文老师致以最诚挚的感谢和崇高的敬意。

王波　叶兴艺

南宁，2024 年 6 月

Preface

Urban administration is a study with a long and colorful history that spans the globe through time. Such a study provides unique challenges, however, to professors and students who seek an introductory text that can capture this breadth and depth together. Undergraduate students must approach the field in piecemeal fashion, pulling together theories from different disciplines with little integration and less application. Additionally, for Chinese students, there is a discussion about how it relates to experiences within China or the issues that urban administrators may face. This can prove frustrating for all concerned, and does little to encourage further study within the field.

This book attempts to address these challenges in the following ways. First, it is written in both Chinese and English for classes that are taught in both English and Chinese. For Chinese university students, studying in English offers unique advantages. As China integrated more into the global economy and governance, English becomes an indispensable tool which could help Chinese students become competitive on a global level. Moving beyond mere memorization to engage with the world at large requires a text that asks students to become active participants in their own comprehension of the material they study. Studying in English provides just such an opportunity.

Second, it offers an introduction of the history of urban administration in a simple way. In this way, students can become familiar with the different periods of urbanization in different parts of the world, so that they may be better prepared to further study or work in urban governments. Additionally, this approach allows students to see how the process of urbanization in China differs from the process in other countries, and therefore better understand some of the unique components of Chinese urbanization and administration.

Third, it pulls together multiple approaches to understand the urban environment, including political, economic, administrative, and sociological frameworks, so that students have multiple ways of seeing what makes a city function well. For students who are planning to pursue a career in a municipal government, this kind of perspective will help them addrey problems in a more comprehensive manner, thus increase their chances of being effective administrators. And even if students do not pursue a career in urban government, they are likely to live in an urban area. With this kind of approach, they will be better prepared for the lives they will face, and improve their chances to be better urban citizens.

Finally, it offers student's examples of issues that urban governments face in China, and illustrations of how problems can be addressed in concrete ways. In this regard, it is more than a list of theories; there are cases that demonstrate the theory, and how knowledge can be applied to improve our understanding of the way the world works. More than half of the world's population now lives in cities. Understanding the problems that cities create and face improves our chances of making our future lives better.

We would like to acknowledge the people who were essential to the book. Our colleagues, and friends have provided much support. Here, we would especially like to thank Prof. Lee Jong Youl and Jill Tao as well as Chad Anderson who have provided essential feedback on ideas and drafts of this book.

Bo Wang   XingYi Ye
Nanning, June 2024

目　录

Contents

第1章 导 论

1.1 城市的概念及内涵

"Urban"一词通常指城市或城镇，而城市地区是指与周边地区相比，建筑密度更高的地区，城市地区通常是在城市化进程中形成和发展起来的。计算城市化地区的规模有助于评估城市人口密度和城市蔓延指数，区分城市和农村地区以及简单地确定各自的人口规模。

在过去的五十年，中国经历了快速的城市化进程——一个压缩的城市化，这意味着是在短时间内密集发生的。韩国和日本等国的城市化地区通常是人口密集的毗连地区。在法国，城市地区被称为 unités urbanités，法语是"城市单元"的意思。美国有两类城市地区："城市化的地区"是指 50000 人及以上的城市化地区（urbanized Area）；50000人以下的城市地区称为组团式城市群（urban cluster）。

我国的城市体系由 23 个省份、5 个自治区（内蒙古、广西、西藏、宁夏、新疆）、4 个直辖市（北京、上海、天津、重庆）和 2 个特别行政区（香港和澳门）构成，城市人口超过了 9 亿人。根据第七次全国人口普查数据显示，截至 2020 年底，我国有 14 个特大城市（城区常住人口在 500 万人以上 1000 万人以下），17 个超大城市（城区常住人口在 1000 万人以上）。我国的城市化水平从 1978 年的 17.9% 上升到 2012 年的 52.6%，2020 年达到 63.89%，目前我国城市数量有 687 个。

1.1.1 城市管理学研究

城市管理学之所以成为一门学科，主要有以下几个原因。首先，最重要的是 20 世纪的快速城市化，使得大多数人成为城市居民。这意味着城市管理涵盖更多的人。其次，由于城市的发展历程比较漫长，城市的快速发展也伴随着许多旧有城市的相对和绝对衰落。可持续的城市发展是 21 世纪人类社会面临的较严峻的挑战。与此同时，在城市化进程中，环境污染、交通拥挤、资源的过度开发与使用、城市暴力犯罪等问题日益凸显，而要解决这些问题，需要了解城市发展及其运行规律，加强城市管理研究。

城市管理不同于政治学等其他学科，它是一个包括公共管理、政治学、城市规划、经济学、社会学和地理学等领域的跨学科的知识体系。这种多样性意味着需要来自许多不同领域的研究人员和从业者的合作，在一个动态的环境中工作，吸收人们从多个角度看待城市问题的见解。例如，社会学研究社会结构和当地社会行动者在塑造环境的同时也被环境塑造，政治学研究治理制度和政策选择的权力维度，经济学研究城市发展和再发展问题，而公共行政学则指政策的制定和执行，以及对地方政府及其服务的管理。

城市管理是一门专门的应用科学。虽然学术界确实在理论问题上花费了大量时间，但该科学的总体主旨仍然是实际应用。我们考虑与城市化相关的理论观点，城市地区的现实发展更为重要。这包括如何提高城市服务质量，特别是公共服务质量的问题。理论和实践之间的联系在预算这样的问题上是显而易见的，预算理论是研究预算的，但仍需要着眼于将其应用于现实问题的解决中，如财政压力。另一个例子是城市规划理论，其中的决策是为了影响城市无限扩张和交通拥堵的实际问题。

城市管理学研究内容在其发展过程中也在不断变化，早期侧重于城市化进程及其特点、城市决策者和政府结构等。对城市化进程进行研究，以便于把握其动态和影响，强调决策者、城市领导层和其他城市行动者的关键作用。研究政府结构是为了了解游戏规则，并了解大部分活动发生的舞台。新近的研究趋势发生改变并超出本学科的范围。虽然旧有的话题仍然在讨论中，但现在城市管理更加注重解决现实问题。这是由于城市问题的数量和严重性不断增加，以及由于日益严重的财政压力，越来越需要优先考虑资源配置。解决更多更严重问题所需的资源越来越有限，就更加需要积极地解决问题的技能，以便为财政压力较大的城市地区制定和实施政策选项。

1.1.2　对城市空间的认识

美国城市规划学家林奇描述了个人对城市元素感知的心理地图以及如何定义对城市场所的感知。五个因素构成了一个城市留给公民、居民或游客的印象：道路、边界、区域、节点、地标。林奇提出了两个对比鲜明但可以强化用于产生对城市感知的维度。第一个是可读性，意味着人们容易辨认出城市景观的构成，并能在脑海中将其抽象为一种连贯可理解的形态。第二个是形象性，这意味着城市基于其独特的特征所唤起的形象是很强烈的。他假设最可读的城市也是最具形象性的，因为强烈的形象基于对清晰图像中的元素进行排序和理解的能力。

道路

道路是人们或频繁、或偶然、或有潜在可能沿之运动的轨迹，可以是街道、步道、运输线、河道或铁路。人们沿着道路运动，同时观察城市，并靠这些道路将其余的环境因素组织联系起来。纽约的百老汇和北京的长安街是两条著名的道路。

边界

边界是一种线性元素，是两个片段之间的界线，是连续体上的线性裂纹：海滨、铁道断口、城市发展的边缘、墙体，等等。它们只是附加的脚注，而不是对等的轴线。这种边界可以是将一个地区与另一个地区相隔的，具有一定可渗透性的屏障，也可以是两个地区互相联系、互相结合的接缝线。这些边界元素具有重要的组织特征，特别是在将更广阔的区域连接在一起的时候，如通过水或墙勾勒出的城市轮廓，比如纽约的第五大道。

区域

区域是城市中等尺度或大尺度的组成单元，代表着两个不同尺度的范围。观察者们在精神上深入它们"内部"，它们由于具有一些个性鲜明的共有特征而易于被人们感知。从内部看，它们总是易于辨认的；如果从外部可见的话，它们也常被用作外部空间的参照物。尽管在道路或地区是主导要素方面存在个体差异，大多数人是以这种方式在一定范围内来构想他们心目中的城市的，这似乎不仅取决于个人，还取决于城市的特征。纽约的格林威治村和成都的春熙路就是这样两个著名的区域。

节点

节点就是标识点，是城市中观察者所能进入的重要战略点，是旅途中抵达与出发的聚焦点。它们主要是一些联结枢纽、运输线上的停靠点、道路岔口或会合点，以及从一种结构向另一种结构转换的关键环节。另外，节点也可以只是简单的汇聚点，只因为是某种功能或物质特性的中心而显得举足轻重，比如，街角空间或是围合的广场。也有些中心节点是一个地区辐射影响力的焦点，并作为整个地区的缩影，成为一种象征标志，我们可以将他们称作"核心"。当然，许多节点既是连接点又是集中点。节点的概念与道路的概念有关，因为交叉点通常是道路的汇聚点。节点与区域概念类似，因为核心通常是区域的集中焦点。首尔的钟路 Sageori 就是一个很好的节点的例子。

地标

广州的广州塔（昵称小蛮腰）、伦敦的大本钟和巴黎的埃菲尔铁塔都是著名的地标性建筑。这些是另一种类型的参照点。在这种情况下，观察者身处它们外部，而不进入其中。它们通常是一些简单定义的实物，如建筑、标识牌、商店或山峰，作用是从一堆可能的对象中挑选并凸显出一个单独的元素。一些地标很遥远，从不同的角度和距离来看，位于顶部的较小元素用作参考点。它们可能位于城市内部或很远的地方。这些无以计数的标识、店面、树木和其他城市细节填补了大多数观察者对城市的印象。

批判

对这个理论的一个批评是，它假设人们可以沿着地图的线条组织他们的城市印象，但它没有考虑人们可能会加入诸如颜色、质地、气味、美学或视觉吸引力等的可能性。另一个批评是草图方法的可靠性。许多人可以制作一张心理地图，但无法将这些信息转换为地图的形式。此外，不同的人会有不同的侧重点，会在同一地点绘制不同的地图，比如，游客可能会更加注重交通节点和路径，但居民可能会制作出同一空间的截然不同的地图。由于这种可变性，在聚合不同个体的地图中归纳出有意义的共享参考时也存在问题。

1.2 城市发展的历史

城市有着悠久的历史，可以追溯到史前时代。简·雅各布斯（1969）认为，第一批城市是在黑曜石等可开采和交易的资源附近发展起来的，那些开采资源的人以其他人愿意与其交易的资源开采为生。工人及其家人，以及开采和贸易剩余部分形成了第一个永久定居点。

这些定居点看起来与我们认为的任何城市都不太一样。对于不同的特定地点是否应被视为城市，学术界的观点各不相同。最早的城市中心是位于现代以色列的杰里科镇，其废墟可追溯到公元前3000年之前（芒福德，1961）。其他较早的城市遗址发现于中东和小亚细亚。

戈登·柴尔德在1950年发表的论文《城市革命》中，从考古学的角度设立了识别最早城市的十条标准：较大的规模与高密度的人口、人口构成与功能的分化、赋税、纪念性的公共建筑、庙宇与神职人员、记录系统与实用科学、文字的发明、艺术表达、长距离贸易，以及专职工匠的存在。从这些史前定居点发展出古代世界、中世纪、近代早期、工业时代以及后工业时代兴起的城市。

1.2.1 古代至公元5世纪的城市（古代～公元5世纪）

第一批被认可的城市出现在底格里斯河和幼发拉底河沿岸的美索不达米亚、埃及的尼罗河流域、印度的印度河流域，以及古代中国。在这些文明摇篮中的城市兴起之前，很少有规模巨大的定居点。最早的最大城市人口不足数万人，但仍有一些城市发展出城市政府、规划、排水系统和废物管理系统以处理垃圾和污水等创新。

城市是大多数人活动的中心，也成为袭击的目标。城市也成为宗教和政治的中心，储存了过剩的粮食，用于在经济不景气的年份养活人口。城市中心是一个市场、象征性的宗教和政府机构包括司法中心。作为这些重要的中心，城市开始受到保护，并用城墙包围起来，这些城墙通过坚固的防御工事来对进出的交通进行疏导。

城市通常在靠近资源丰富且交通便利的地方。贸易路线先是通过天然的小路，然后是人工道路，也沿着河流和港口，因为与人力和畜力相比，水路是一种相对快速的交通工具，因此，丰富的水资源附近往往会产生大而繁荣的城市。四大古典文明中心以尼罗河、印度河、黄河和幼发拉底河为中心，形成了古埃及、古印度、中国和古巴比伦四大文明。

自给自足的城邦城市如希腊城邦证明了一个城市可以自给自足。雅典、斯巴达和底比斯等城市在周边相对较小的农业区的支持下得以幸存。城市政府是国家生活的中心，古"城邦"一词的含义除了城市本身之外，还包括以城市生活为中心的政府形式。在辅助帝国建立之前，这些独立的城市就能够实现这一目标。

大的城市与古代世界的主要帝国一起成长为首都城市和贸易工业中心。与帝国有关的主要古城，如亚历山大城，作为其帝国的中心而建立，以及随后的印度的巴特那、中国的西安、北非的迦太基、意大利的罗马和土耳其的君士坦丁堡，都是早期数十万人口的城市。

在帝国的支持下，城市得到了更大的发展，帝国越强大，城市规模越大。罗马帝国在公元 32 年进行了一次人口普查，所以古罗马世界的许多城市都有完整的数据保留下来。随着布匿战争期间罗马帝国的发展（摧毁了敌对帝国的中心迦太基），大约在公元前 1 世纪末，罗马已成为一个人口接近百万的城市，亚历山大和巴格达等其他主要城市在古代也达到了同样的规模。罗马人通过在被征服的领土上建立殖民地来扩大他们的影响，这些城市以典型的罗马城市为原型，拥有一批遵循罗马语言、法律和习俗的公民，为受其支配的民族融入罗马社会提供了城市生活模式。

古代中国也产生了许多城市。最早起源于公元前 2000 年左右的黄河流域。

1.2.2　中世纪的文艺复兴时期的城市（公元 5 世纪～公元 15 世纪）

中世纪后期，南京、北京成为中国明朝的首都。当日本天皇决定迁往京都时，京都成为城市中心并在附近建立了一座城市。中东古城巴格达在许多不同帝国和国家的统治下继续得到发展和繁荣。到了公元 8 世纪，巴格达的人口已经超过 100 万人，是世界上已知的第一个人口达到这个规模的城市。

再来看欧洲，罗马的衰落导致了权力的分散化，并回归到较小规模且相对独立的城市。在罗马帝国统治下的德国境内，除了理论上效忠天皇外，一些城市保持了所有权力的独立。有些城市有独立的立法机构，城市通常存在于封建秩序之外，或者至少在封建秩序中占有特殊地位。许多西欧城市与教堂联合起来，围绕大教堂建造的城市本身就成为重要的中心。意大利也被划分为多个小国，这些小国通常由一个单一的城邦式城市主导。在德国和意大利，一些城市发展成为大国，威尼斯成为一个统治亚得里亚海的帝国，并将其势力扩展到地中海。

1.2.3　近代早期到工业革命时期的城市（公元 15 世纪～公元 18 世纪）

这是一个城墙作为城市重要特征逐渐消失的时期。在某些情况下，如在法国，国家建设和权力集中的过程意味着政治因素导致城墙倒塌，削弱了相对独立的城市权力，增强了国家政府的权力。一个更大且更重要的原因是，随着火药和火器的出现，城墙在现代战争中的作用逐渐减弱。坚固到足以抵挡炮弹的墙变得太昂贵了，无论如何都需要用新的战术来克服。停止修建新城墙并保留旧城墙，开始定义城墙外快速增长的新的大城市与旧城的区别。

贸易增加、海外殖民地的进贡以及伴随资本主义兴起的更具活力的城市化进程为其提供了支持，欧洲城市在近代早期繁荣发展（Heilbrun，1981）。许多欧洲的首都和港口城市在新的贸易路线（如大西洋贸易路线）进一步发展。工业革命初期，伦敦有一百多万人口，成为当时世界上人口最多的城市。海峡对岸英国的竞争对手巴黎紧随其后，一些欧洲城市已经发展成为与中东的巴格达德、土耳其的伊斯坦布尔、中国的北京和日本的京都等历史悠久的古老城市规模相当的城市。

在西半球，阿兹特克人建立的墨西哥城仍是世界上最大的城市之一。西班牙殖民遵循罗马模式，在被征服的领土上建立新城市，传播西班牙语、习俗和法律，同时为行政管理、区域发展和资源开发提供基础。西班牙人带来了现代技术、罗马法律和天主教。此外，他们经常奴役土著人民，实行野蛮的原始积累，通过应用当时最现代最可怕的军事技术来征服当地居民。他们将大量的农业和矿产财富转移到西班牙，使其成为世界强国。

尽管伦敦、北京、巴格达和其他几个城市达到了新的高度，但与工业化的加速发展相比，大多数城市仍然规模较小。在此期间，只有几十个城市的居民超过10万人，其中数万个城镇被认为是大城市。尽管如此，这些大型城市与工业时代后期的城市有所不同，因为它们缺乏大规模生产和机械化生产等特点，而即将到来的水和蒸汽动力为特征的大量手工艺品的生产代替了大部分人力。

1.2.4 公元18世纪工业革命至今的城市（公元18世纪至今）

这个时期既是历史的，也是当代的。从18世纪的英国开始，欧洲经历了工业化，此后世界其他地区也相继开始了工业化进程。现在世界上许多城市仍在沿用工业化模式，许多发展中国家仍在经历工业化进程。工业化的兴起是一个真正的世界经济的兴起，核心国家通过生产来主导整个体系，而外围国家则为核心国家提供劳动力和原材料以及无法在国内消费的剩余消费品的市场。

资本主义和工业化的兴起使商业被制造业取代，主导经济活动。这从几个方面改变了城市。除了城墙的消失，还有其他新的发展。城市中心的宗教元素被淡化，取而代之的是股票交易所等商业元素。在中心市场依然存在的地方，一个处理现代商业的新市场出现了。

工业不再分散在城市的小手工商店中，而是集中在位于特殊地区的大型工厂中，这些工厂将劳动力安置在附近的工人阶级社区。人口的集中产生了新的阶级，包括由中世纪城市工匠演变而来的拥有和管理大型工厂的城市资产阶级。产业和人口的快速集聚导致污染和拥堵成为新问题。使得这一过程合理化的一种方法是为城市开发一个网格系统，以取代旧的有机或星形布局。随着城墙的消失，促进了城市超越旧的边界得到快速扩展。

新兴经济惊人的生产力将大批人吸引到城市，在商业、工业、文化、教育和政府的新中心和集中地的城市寻找新机会。这一进程导致了大规模的城市化和新城市的兴起，其中许多城市迅速超越了旧城市，大量农村移民进入城市。科技的不断进步发明了新的交通工具，虽然城市仍位于河流和天然港口附近，但许多新城市围绕十字路口、公路出口、铁路站以及机场发展，这些新的快速的大众运输方式也促进了快速城市化。除了污染和拥堵之外，前所未有的人口集中使得城市容易受到传染病、压力和环境污染造成的健康问题的影响。主要产业的大量集中使得城市在经济衰退期间容易受到干扰，大量闲置工人聚集在一起也带来社会的不稳定。

1.2.5　后工业化的城市

此时，世界人口已经城市化，至少一半以上的世界人口生活在城市地区。在发展中国家，每年有数百万人从农村迁徙到城市，而在其他地方，这一进程则相对缓慢。后工业城市是以 IT 和服务业（如金融、房地产和保险）为核心的经济组织。根据萨森的说法，最大的城市通常是全球控制中心和产业集聚中心。

一些之前的"核心"国家的产业秩序的转变带来了后工业城市的发展。快速的城市化导致了城市空间的扩张，这些空间往往超出了城市政府的边界和控制范围。这种增长是由全球化趋势推动的，全球化趋势可能会挫败政府为应对这些趋势所做的任何努力（Judd，2011）。大城市地区有时不再包括单一的城市中心，而是有多个中心，一起发展起来的旧城市中心，则需要新的政府间协调与合作手段来获得新的发展。

中国的京津冀都市圈是这种协作的典范之一。尽管司法管辖区之间有明确的界限，但许多资源需要共享，合作与协调对于解决交通等基本问题也是必要的。城市区域在城市边界上有许多共同的特点，例如，流域、水资源、共同的基础设施、共享文化设施和共享经济。这一地区的通勤情况错综复杂，通常可能人们居住在一个城市，却在另一个城市学习或工作。

为了解决城市中心区的问题，人们开始转向郊区，在旧城市中心的外围形成了新的城市中心。郊区在形式上与城市中心不同，但又与城市中心有相互依赖的关系。郊区为城市中心提供劳动力，城市中心为郊区提供资源。

一些人提出了这样的论点，即由于技术和组织变革，经济基础对城市发展而言已不再那么重要（Florida，2002）。萨维奇（1988）将这些新发展描述为后工业化，得益于这些趋势的权力结构推动了后工业城市的创建。后工业城市不再以制造业为基础，而是以银行、房地产、保险等服务业和时尚等文化产业为基础。全球化促进了城市作为休闲空间和文化产业集中的兴起，作为部分国际旅游业兴起的商业区（Judd and Fainstein，1999）。同时城市的发展也存在压力，一方面，推动人们更加关注多样性；另一方面，更大的压力是要融入一个同质化的"熔炉"，这个熔炉可能是标准化或"麦当劳化"的，以便在城市按照新的后工业化进程发展的同时，无论走到哪里都能找到为人们所熟悉的东西（Ritzer，2008）。

1.3　基于不同视角的城市定义

城市涵盖各种各样的大量或密集人群。像北京、东京、伦敦、纽约或巴黎这样的大城市让人想起人口众多、设施现代化、摩天大楼、交通繁忙、公共交通、体育场馆、博物馆和繁忙的生活模式。城市被定义为大且人口稠密的城市地区。这可能包括一个或几个不同的合并的政治行政单位，这些政治行政单位界定了边界和法定权力。同时，城市是人口、商业和文化的中心，具有重要的规模和意义，其重要性和规模不同于城镇。城市也可以定义为具有特殊行政、法律或历史地位的地方。

更多的技术上的定义可能包括最小规模、特定的政治或法律地位或特定的人口密度。城市也可以通过其基础设施和活动来定义。例如，城市人口主要从事非开采性工作，即工人不参与采矿或其他类型的资源开采。城市拥有基础设施：下水道、交通系统、废物处理系统、学校、图书馆、医院和其他公共服务。城市有财富的象征和唤起城市形象的场所，如巴黎的埃菲尔铁塔、纽约的自由女神像、北京的紫禁城。城市也有一种与众不同的生活方式，这将它们与农村区别开。人们移居城市是为了参与快节奏且令人兴奋的不同于传统的生活方式。

1.3.1 不同视角的城市定义

除了这些对城市的一般定义之外，还有来自构成城市研究的不同学科特有的观点，本节介绍了这些视角的一部分，包括社会学、政治学、经济学和管理学的视角。

社会学视角

马克斯·韦伯（1958）提出了一个被人认为与系统的城市主义理论相近的城市理论，以大都市的形式对现代城市进行批判性反思（Wirth，1938；Mumford，1961）。他研究不同城市间社会、政治、经济、宗教和法律基础以及社会秩序的其他方面，从结构主义的视角看待城市。韦伯从消费城市、生产城市、工业城市和商业城市的分类来定义城市，认为现代城市代表着资本主义统治下的一种日益恶化的生活形式。理想的城市需要在理性而不是在魅力或传统的基础上授予权威。法律应是普遍适用的，而不是个人的，群体认同应依据社会阶层而不是亲属关系。

罗伯特·帕克和欧内斯特·伯吉斯（1984）创立了城市生态方法，将城市视为类似的生物体，有着成长与衰退、疾病与健康、相互依存与竞争的过程。芝加哥学派基于生活的视角研究城市，并研究城市生命周期中的各种市场因素。即便如此，在研究城市的诞生、兴起、活力、衰落和重建时，他们发现没有必要否认对人类价值的关注，从流浪汉到出租车司机都表现出对整体和个人的同时关注。例如，一个城市可能会经历资源繁荣，如淘金热，城市繁荣一段时间，然后衰落，匹兹堡和韩国的浦项就处于钢铁产业生命周期的不同阶段。

路易·沃思（1938）将城市化视为一种生活方式。他根据规模、密度和多样性来定义城市化。简·雅各布斯（1969）同样将城市定义为多样性之地，因为城市是充满陌生人的地方。在现代城市，甚至居民不认识他们的邻居都很常见。城市生活是匿名的，具有讽刺意味的是，这也可能意味着社区的消失，尤其是传统意义上的社区，例如，在银行，是通过号码而不是名字被呼叫的。城市在教育、工作、收入和生活方式方面都具有异质性。

马克思主义者和其他批判性社会学家（以及其他学科的科学家）使用资本主义生产模式和阶级冲突来描述城市的特征，认为其在资本主义制度下是不可避免的，城市土地按收入划分——所有权决定租金和土地使用结构。大多数人口作为劳动力从事生产，而少数人控制着这些劳动力及其产品。统治阶级和被统治者之间的这种关系是一种冲突，使城市成为一个无休止的斗争场所（Harvey，1985，1996）。曼努埃尔·卡斯特尔（1996）将城市的抗议运动定义为结合集体消费斗争与文化和政治自决斗争的运动。这些分歧和斗争可能是基于阶级的，在多民族和多种族社会中，城市的分裂也可能以种族隔离和族裔分裂为标志。

近年来，特里·克拉克（2004）专注于城市行动者在确定城市生活和城市外观方面的作用。一种新的政治文化取代了阶级政治，城市不再仅仅是一个生产场所，而是一个"娱乐机器"。马克思主义者之前对阶级的关注，由与生产资料的关系来定义，现在已经被基于消费的新关注取代。城市居民和游客可以通过他们的生活方式和消费选择来定义自己，而不是仅仅由他们无法控制的力量决定。

政治学视角

有组织的政府和精细的管理可以将城市与较小的城镇和其他非城市地区区分开。有正式领导的正式政治进程、税收和法律支持政府和政治议案。政治科学关注政治领域、法律、法规、控制系统，以及谁掌权、如何获得权力以及如何利用权力的问题。

自古以来，亚里士多德就把国家看作城邦。公民是居住在城邦中的人，通过担任政治、行政、立法或司法职务，更充分地参与城市生活。他以古希腊实践为基础的城市公民观，不仅比现代代表性的公民模式更具排他性，而且要求更高，因为公民更直接地参与城邦治理。无论宪法如何规定城邦的治理形式，城邦的存在都是因为人们是政治动物，希望共同生活。亚里士多德来自民主政治的摇篮雅典，雅典实行直接民主，城市规模小，有资格参加的人数有限（仅限于公认的成年男性公民），这意味着所有公民都可以作为一个集体机构直接作出决定。雅典卫城和开放市场等特色设施通过允许公民以较大团体的形式集会，甚至在审议过程之外，促进了民主讨论，这是许多欧洲城市中心大广场的起源，它既是市场交易的场所，也是市民聚集和讨论城市重要问题的场所。

新近的政治科学家，如丹尼斯·贾德，研究了政治制度、权力体系和城市权力竞争的性质（贾德，2011）。政党在城市政治中的作用是什么？学者们研究了空间政治以及在城市空间中发挥作用的政治和权力动态，也有大量政策文献研究政治行为者在获得权力时做什么或提出什么。例如，保罗·彼得森（1981）在他的《城市极限》中研究了导致不同城市推行不同类型政策的因素，并得出结论：与政府高层（如国家）的行动者相比，城市的权力有限。因此，城市推行的政策将使那些最多拥有房地产和企业的人受益。约翰·莫伦科普夫（1983）等政治学家也从城市地区不同性别、种族、民族和民族群体之间的关系的角度来看待城市，认为城市是经常发现冲突的和"有争议的城市"。

政治学观点的关键是"谁统治"的问题（Dahl，1961）。有时，政府代表一个城市中的许多不同群体，但有时某些群体比其他群体拥有更大的权力。这就是精英主义与多元主义之争的实质。那些用精英主义解释城市政治的人认为，大多数决策都是由一个小团体或精英做出的，精英的意见不需要一致，但决策通常需要精英的一致意见，或者是至少精英可以接受的意见。洛根和莫洛奇（2007）提出的"增长机器"的概念，表明城市中的精英群体因其增长愿望而团结在一起。城市有时是由政治"机器"组织起来的，随着时间的推移，它主导着城市的政治。在这种情况下，政治精英通过一种客户管理制度与其支持者联系起来，通过这种制度，系统中的一些利益可以与外部团体分享，以换取维持机器运转的权力。该机器管理者之间的冲突，并将其控制在范围内。来自机器外部的竞争通常不会成功，因此，参与城市生活的前提是接受既定秩序。相反，多元化的概念认为城市中有许多不同的群体，城市政治是这些群体为满足他们的利益而竞争的过程。在城市的政治舞台上，这些团体之间的冲突可以在不打乱日常生活秩序的情况下得到解决。如果政治舞台无法解决这些冲突，那么一个城市可能会在政治和经济两方面均受到影响（Stone，2008）。

经济学视角

经济学家将城市视为一个市场，它既是生产也是消费的来源，因为它创造了大量的购买力。城市还可以在更广泛的经济活动中提供某些专门的经济功能，包括商品和服务的专业组合以及特殊的需求和问题。海尔布伦用城市表示居住在大型市政实体政治边界内的人口，这是经济学中常见的观点，在这里，城市是一个具有一定独立性和自主性的经济体系，商品和服务向企业和家庭高度集中。

城市经济学研究城市地区的经济性质、经济结构和市场经济的运作。经济发展是城市经济的重要组成部分。这包括通过市场或计划过程形成城市的经济学和所涉及的经济激励，以及提高城市生活质量的不同选择。城市经济学家也在很大程度上关注城市政策和政策选择的经济分析。他们用标准化的方法来评估和比较不同交通系统、土地使用选择、住房政策、税收政策和总体经济政策的成本、效率和影响。将政策视为解决方案的关键因素并检验其对问题的解决是外部性的概念。外部性是指在自愿经济交换中，对不同意这种影响的人或群体产生的影响。污染和交通拥堵是城市问题的负外部性的例子，旅游景点增加附近企业销售额的效应则是一种正外部效应。

许多非经济学家从事与经济学有关的城市研究。社会学家约翰·洛根和哈维·莫洛奇（2007）撰写了一部关于地方政治经济的有影响力的著作。此外，政治学家保罗·彼得森（1981）也分析了导致不同经济发展政策的选择的原因。洛根和莫洛奇明确了生长机器的概念——这是一群城市精英，他们可能在各种问题上存在分歧，但会联合起来支持和推动有利于增长的政策，对增长联盟的反对可能会被追求增长的城市精英的统一战线压制。

管理学视角

管理学同政治学对城市的看法有点相似，但其重点在于如何管理城市及其服务提供。较小规模的城市可能更依赖市场、非正式协议、互助和自愿社会合作，但大城市是复杂的实体，需要专业的管理和领导、法规和税收等。就政治和专业领导层与城市内外的其他团体联合行动而言，城市的公共管理具有政治和权力方面的关切。它还有经济因素的考量，因为城市是一个经济舞台，政府需要作出具有经济影响的政策选择。管理的边界和定义甚至在经济领域也占主导地位，因为许多积极的外部性在政治和管理边界之间没有太大的溢出效应。对管理的定义通常来自行政法，包括非农业人口的百分比、建成区的环境 、人口和密度等，城市的管理更为复杂。

城市作为向居民提供服务的场所，需要重点关注这些服务的提供和管理以及政策的实际执行。城市政策可能侧重于许多领域，如城市的增长和发展、衰落地区的再生、为就业提供良好的经济环境、解决城市问题以及为城市居民提供高质量的健康生活环境等。管理观是一种管理城市的观点，管理是为了实现公共目的而对人和资源进行高效和有效的管理。因此，在地方一级，城市管理部门负责将有效提供服务视为一个管理问题。

城市管理作为一门学科，在 20 世纪初，在美国一些主要城市寻求反腐、提供更好服务和反对大城市机器的城市改革者的影响下迅速发展起来。与此同时，市政府是管理人员将新思想付诸实践并在当地"民主实验室"进行测试的好地方（奥斯本，1988）。这段历史和强有力的对政策的强点都意味着，城市管理更具实践性。

1.3.2　与城市相关的概念

大都市区

大都市区是由一个大城市（或多个城市）组成的区域，位于与城市核心经济一体化的更大区域的中心，一个较大的城市从中心开始城市蔓延的过程，大都市区往往超越其政治和行政边界。整个系统共享共同的基础设施、住房和产业等。交通系统的发展和蔓延都沿着系统的主要路径进行，系统也随着更新的发展集中而扩展。多个城市可能会沿着一条主要的交通走廊发展，尤其是连接主要城市的交通走廊，城市之间的空间发展表现为现有城市的链接，该地区通常以区内最大的城市命名，不同的国家有不同的定义。首尔大都市区包括首尔、仁川和京畿道大部分地区，是韩国最著名的大都市区；加拿大有多伦多和温哥华大都市区。欧盟国家的大都市区指的是基于通勤量增加和相互依存的大型城市区（LUZ）。法国使用"市区"表示城市核心周围的区域，例如，巴黎和马赛周边地区。日本使用 toshiken（都市圈）一词，意思是东京周边地区的一组"城市"。如上所述，美国使用基于大都市和核心统计区的方法，如纽约大都市区包括纽约市、纽约州部分地区、康涅狄格州部分地区和新泽西州北部大部分地区。

城市与农村

与周边地区相比，城市地区的人口密度更高。城市和城镇等较大的定居点被称为城市，而村庄等较小的定居点则被称为农村。虽然农村地区可以定居，但人口稀少，不发达，缺乏基础设施。城市通常集中了制造业和服务业。另外，农村地区通常涉及自然资源开采或管理。他们可能从事采矿和伐木等，甚至可能基本上无人居住。随着越来越多的人离开农村迁往城市，城市化进程伴随着农村地区人口的减少。在这个过程中，随着城市变得越来越像农村，农村也越来越像城市——人们移居城市带来了乡村风俗，城市得到了绿化，而农村则引进了城市技术和便利设施，城乡二元对立变得模糊了。

全球城市

沙森因在同名书中创造了"全球城市"一词而闻名。全球城市与一个国家内的其他城市不同,彼此之间的共同点比国内城市更多。北京、上海、纽约、东京和伦敦等地在质量和人口数量上都与其他城市不同。他们通常规模巨大,在世界舞台上的竞争比在国家层面上更激烈,因为其在国家舞台上几乎没有竞争对手。全球城市是国际经济中的一个专门指挥和控制中心。

全球城市有着前所未有的权力和经济资源的集中,主要基于经济和人力资本。它们可以利用这些资源来影响世界,也是全球娱乐和旅游业的战略地点。全球城市可能是金融、房地产、保险、信息和 IT、交通、时尚以及任何其他产业的中心,尤其是服务业。全球城市有时是按等级排名的,2021 年北京在全球城市指数中排名第六,在全球城市实力指数中名列第三。

科技城

科技城一词来源于希腊词根,意为技术和城市,也被称为科技园、科技城邦或研究园。无论是来自公共部门还是私营部门,这是一个研究和技术相关机构高度集中的区域,公共部门的参与通常来自公立大学的研究机构。这些领域的重点是创新和新产品的开发以及新技术和新产业的孵化。

科技城提供了广泛的基础设施以满足科研机构的特殊需求,如特殊的电网以保证不间断供电,先进的电信、管理和安全设施,以及各种支持服务体系和便利设施。这些特殊研究园区通常受到地方政府的鼓励,地方政府不仅招募机构,为其提供特殊服务,而且常常提供土地补贴和税收优惠。

美国硅谷是随着斯坦福大学技术和人力资源开发而成长起来的。美国北卡罗来纳州也有大量的技术中心,特别是在制药方面。日本有著名的筑波科学城,拥有 240 多个私人研究机构和来自 90 个国家的 3000 名外国学生。

花园城市(田园城市)

花园城市的概念起源于 19 世纪末英国的埃比尼泽·霍华德(Ebenezer Howard)。他的想法是使用一种非常有规律的城市规划形式将生活注入城市乌托邦的愿景。这座城市的结构是一个独立的经济体,通勤时间短,对乡村自然美景的破坏最小。这些城市经过高度规划,并由公园的常规绿化带和城市周围的绿地组成。规划将特定比例的土地用于制造业、住房、公园和农业,较小的卫星城市将围绕拥有 50000 人口的中心城市。随着卫星城市的发展,当旧的卫星城市达到理想的 32000 人并自给自足时,就会形成新的卫星城市,这些城市将通过高效的铁路和公路网络与中心城市彼此相连。

新城(新区)

新城是通过规划而非有机增长创建的新城市地区,旨在通过为居民提供住房、就业、教育、娱乐和购物来实现自给自足。新城通常建设在未开发地区,并经过高度规划，同时规划过程严格定义土地使用，避免了与现有社区典型的土地使用发生冲突。新城之所以成为热门发展项目，主要有几个原因：新城实现让过度拥挤的人口分散，也有助于缓解城市核心区的拥堵；新城还为城市的重要参与者（城市开发商）提供了经济利益，更不用说随着房地产升值带来的新的税收。雄安新区是中国许多新城中的一个例子。

创意城市

英国城市规划师查尔斯·兰德里（Charles Landry）提出了创意城市的概念，并撰写了《创意城市：如何打造都市创意生活圈》，书中概述了他对城市规划的看法。这一概念现在已成为国际创新城市规划运动的热门词汇，也催生了联合国教科文组织国际创意与可持续发展中心的创立，并激发了其他一些有影响力的城市发展理念，如理查德·佛罗里达的创意阶层理念，为城市成功提供核心人才（Florida，2002）。

创意城市的概念要求在城市运营中融入并在城市利益相关者中培养创意和想象力文化。这扩大了解决城市问题的可能方案的范围，赋予创意城市更多的灵活性和弹性。与注重物质基础设施的传统城市规划不同，创意城市概念通过人力资源等软件包括城市运营中的创意氛围和态度来增强作为硬件的物质基础设施，这需要一支灵活、熟练、充满活力的人才队伍，能够设想、计划、实施和贯彻解决困难问题的创造性解决方案，这就要求创意城市寻找、吸引、发展并留住有创意的人，通过其自身的创造力，超越关于居民、劳动力和工作人员的常规想法，通过城市场景的营造、居民和游客的生活体验以及地方的独特性对城市进行改造。

无处不在的城市

无处不在的城市，也称 u-city，是与所谓无处不在信息技术相连的城市或地区，通过无线网络等技术建立普遍连接的信息系统。电子服务创造出无所不在的服务，如智能停车、智能交通调度和智能犯罪预防等。所有主要的信息系统都与计算机系统共享数据，这些计算机系统内置于房间和建筑物中，通过这一过程将家庭生活与街道生活联系起来。通过高技术媒介，城市扮演信息流枢纽。

无处不在的城市概念是 1998 年施乐帕洛阿尔托研究中心首席技术员马克·韦瑟（Mark Weiser）在加利福尼亚州帕洛阿尔图提出的一个想法（Chung，2009）。这在韩国已成为现实，韩国 2007 年开始在华城市东滩开始建设 u 型城市——仁川松岛新区，2014年竣工时成为世界上最大的 u 型城市。

1.4　现代城市问题及成因

城市作为集中的生活和工作场所，为居住的人们提供各种福利。值得注意的是，这种相互作用既有积极影响，也有消极影响。当城市的收益大于成本时，城市就会发展。上面提到了几个城市发展带来的好处，包括降低交通成本，扩大市场，创造性地交流思想，更有效地共享自然资源、教育、就业以及城市生活的所有基本便利设施，如污水和废物处理。然而，并非所有的影响都是积极的，城市发展也带来了许多问题，如更高的犯罪率、死亡率、生活成本、污染和交通拥堵等。可以确定的是所有城市都可能面临着一系列共同的城市问题，包括：

- 不平等
- 政治问题
- 管理问题
- 经济问题
- 土地使用
- 住房

- 贫困
- 交通
- 环境问题
- 自然和人为的灾害
- 犯罪
- 冲突

这份清单与 1997 年联合国开发计划署关于城市问题的报告基本一致，该报告将失业列为最大的问题，其次是固体废物处理、城市贫困、住房不足、固体废物收集、交通拥堵、卫生服务差、民间社会参与不足、教育资源不充分、空气污染、犯罪和城市暴力以及歧视等。

发展中国家的城市和发达国家的城市之间存在一些差别。发展中国家往往负担不起城市外来人员的住房，他们最终生活在棚户区。棚户区曾经在很多国家很常见，通常是用废旧材料临时建造的，但最终作为城市贫民的永久住房解决方案，棚户区往往缺乏自来水、卫生设施和电力。在较发达的国家中，棚户区可能在很大程度上已经不存在了，但在发展中国家如菲律宾、孟加拉国和印度尼西亚，仍有大量贫民居住在大型棚户区，给城市管理带来了严峻挑战。

发达国家的城市问题更有可能以发展早期未解决问题的形式继续存在。在一些发达国家，经济不平等和贫困可能会持续存在，城市蔓延可能会吞噬土地，而政府却不准备作出艰难的土地使用选择，增长的影响可能会体现在环境影响上，如污染和城市居民的健康状况不佳，甚至交通便利可能会变为拥堵、空气和噪声污染等。此外，大多数国家都面临着种族、民族、宗教和阶级隔离的问题，这导致了大规模的抗议活动。全球化、经济下滑、经济危机和经济衰退导致了反对政府的活动，这些活动反对削减公共部门，私营企业因纳税不足或占领华尔街而受到批评，希腊和西班牙的抗议反对一小部分有影响力经济精英和绝大多数群体之间的利益差距。

城市问题形成的原因各不相同，但许多可以被视为由快速城市化、市场化、市场失灵以及公共和私人规划的失败造成的。在某种程度上，城市问题的性质是由看问题的视角来界定的。例如，以生态学或芝加哥学派的视角来看，人们可能会从城市生命周期的阶段寻找原因，而那些采用批判、新马克思主义或纽约学派观点的人可能会认为冲突和阶级差异是城市问题的根源。

综上所述，城市管理学需要综合来自不同学科的研究，不同学科可能强调问题的不同方面，可能被视为政治、社会、管理或经济问题等。然而，大多数城市问题并没有很好地解决，需要从多个学科视角进行理解和关注。即便如此，这些问题也可能仍然难以理解和解决。

【思考题】

1. 如何定义城市?
2. 为什么说公共管理是交叉学科?
3. 如何看待城市空间?
4. 城市在什么时期发展成为制造业和工业中心? 这些城市与早期的城市相比有何不同?
5. 后工业城市与早期城市的区别是什么?
6. 今天城市面临的主要问题是什么? 问题的成因是什么?

【关键术语】

中心地理论	花园城市
城市意象	增长机器
创意城市	熔炉
去工业化	新城
外部性	都市主义

参考文献

［1］Bluestone, Barry, Stevenson, Mary Huff, Williams, Russell (2008). *The Urban Experience*：*Economics*, *Society*, *and Public Policy*. New York：Oxford University Press.

［2］Castells, Manuel (1996). "The Information Mode of Development and the Restructuring of Capitalism" pp. 23 – 60, *in* Fainstein, Susan, Cambell, Scott (eds) (1996). *Readings in Urban Theory*. Oxford, U. K.：Blackwell.

［3］Childe, V. Gordon (2008). "The Urban Revolution", *Town Planning Review*, 21 (1)：3 – 19.

［4］Clark, T. N. (ed) (2004). *The City as an Entertainment Machine* Amsterdam：Elsevier.

［5］Florida, Richard (2002). *The Rise of the Creative Class*. New York：Basic Books/Perseus.

［6］Harvey, David (1985). *The Urbanization of Capital*. Baltimore, MD：Johns Hopkins University Press.

［7］Jacobs, Jane (1969). *The Economy of Cities*. Random House, New York.

［8］Mark, M., Katz, B., Rahman, S., and Warren, D. (2008). *MetroPolicy*：*Shaping A New Federal Partnership for a Metropolitan Nation*. Brookings Institution.

［9］Pacione, Michael (2001). *The City*：*Critical Concepts in the Social Sciences*. New York：Routledge.

［10］Ritzer, George (2008). *The McDonaldization of Society*, 5*th ed*. Los Angeles：Pine Forge Press.

［11］Smith, Michael E. (2002). "The Earliest Cities", In Gmelch, George, and Zenner, Walter (eds). *Urban Life*：*Readings in Urban Anthropology*. Prospect Heights, IL：Waveland Press：3 – 19.

［12］Squires, Gregory (ed) (2002). *Urban Sprawl*：*Causes*, *Consequences*, *& Policy Responses*. Baltimore：Urban Institute Press.

［13］Stone, Clarence (2008). "Urban Politics Then and Now", in *Power in the City*：*Clarence Stone and the Politics of Inequality*. Marion Orr and Valerie Johnson, eds. ：267 – 316.

［14］Weber, Max (1958). *The City*. New York：Free Press.

Chapter 1   Introduction

1. 1   Definition and Connotation of Urban

The term urban is usually applied to a city or a town, and an urban area is often referred to as a city or town. An urban region is a region that has a higher density of man-made structures as compared to the surrounding area. Urban areas are usually shaped and grown through urbanization. Calculating the size of urbanized areas helps in evaluating population density and urban sprawl, differentiating urban from rural areas, and in simply determining population.

The urbanization process in China has taken place mostly during the last forty years and is an unusually rapid case of urbanization. China has undergone a compressed urbanization, meaning that it has happened intensively over a very short period. Urbanized regions in countries like Korea and Japan are contiguous regions that are thickly populated. In France, urban areas are known as unités urbanités, which simply means "urban units" in French. There are two categories of urban areas in the United States. The term *urbanized area* denotes an urban area of 50000 or more people. Urban areas under 50000 people are called *urban clusters*.

In China, there are 23 provinces, 5 autonomous regions (i. e. Inner Mogolia Autonomous Region, Guangxi Zhuang Autonomous Region, Xizang Autonomous Region, Ningxia Hui Autonomous Region, Xinjiang Uygur Autonomous Region), 4 municipality directly under the Central Government (i. e. Beijing, Shanghai, Tianjin, and Chongqing), and 2 special administrative regions (Hongkong and Macao). Chinese cities are defined as having a population of more than 0. 9 billion. According to the date from the 7th National Population Census, 14 megacities with a population of more than 5 – 10 million, 17 megalopolises with a population of 10 million by the end of 2020 in China. The level of urbanization in China has risen from 17. 9% in 1978 to 52. 6% in 2012. By 2020, the level of urbanization in China has reached 63. 89% , and the number of cities in China has reached 687.

1. 1. 1   Urban Administration as a Discipline

Urban administration has emerged as discipline for several reasons. Foremost is the rapid urbanization of the 21st century that has led to the consequent fact that most people are city dwellers. This means that urban administration covers most people where they live. Next, due to the long historical time span of cities, there is the need to manage the growth of cities as well as the relative and absolute decline of many older cities. Sustainable urban development is one of the most serious challenges of human society in the 21st century. At the same time, in the process of urbanization, environmental pollution, traffic congestion, excessive development and use of resources, urban violent crime and other problems are increasingly prominent. To solve these problems, it is necessary to understand urban development and its operation rules, and strengthen the research on urban administration.

Urban administration is different from other academic disciplines like political science in that it is interdisciplinary. It incorporates public administration, political science, urban planning, economics, sociology, and geography, among other fields. This diversity means that researchers and practitioners from many different fields collaborate to work in a dynamic environment that draws on the insights of people looking at urban issues from multiple perspectives. For example, sociology looks at social structures and at how local social actors act to shape their environment while being shaped by it, political science looks at governing systems and the power dimensions of policy choice, economics considers issues of urban development and redevelopment, while administration points to the formulation and implementation of policy and the management of the local government and its services.

Urban administration is specifically an applied science. While academics do spend a great deal of time with theoretical issues, the overall thrust of the science is towards practical application. Theoretical perspectives related to urbanization are considered but the reality of urban areas is more important. This includes issues of how to improve the quality of urban services, particularly public ones. The connection between theory and practice is apparent in an issue like the budget, where budget theory is studied, but with an eye towards applying it to real-world problems like fiscal stress. Another example is urban planning theory, where decisions are made to affect the practical issues of urban sprawl and traffic congestion.

Urban administration has undergone dramatic changes over its history in terms of scope. The traditional focus was on the process of urbanization and its characteristics, urban decision makers, and government structure. The process of urbanization was studied to facilitate the management of its dynamics and effects. The key role of decision makers, urban leadership, and other urban actors was highlighted. The structure of government was studied to understand the rules of the game and to understand the arena in which much of the action takes place. Recent trends have shifted the scope of the discipline. Although the old topics are still addressed, urban administration now focuses more on problem solving. This has stemmed from the rising number and severity of urban problems as well as from the increasing need to prioritize resources due to rising financial stress. Fewer resources for solving more problems that are more serious requires active problem-solving skills for generating and implementing policy options for stressed urban areas.

1. 1. 2　Perceptions of Urban Place

Lynch described how the mental map of individual perception of the elements of a city defined the perception of urban place. Six factors form the image of a city for the citizen, resident, or visitor. These are paths, edges, districts, nodes, and landmarks. Lynch came up with two contrasting but reinforcing dimensions that are used to produce the perception of a city. The first is legibility, which means how easily people can organise the elements of a city into a mental representation. The second is imageability, which means how strong an image the city evokes based on its distinctive features. He hypothesised that the most legible cities were also the most imageable in that the strong image would be based on the ability to order and understand the elements in a clear image.

Paths

Paths are the places through which people travel. They may be streets, walkways, transit lines, canals, railroads, among others. These are the predominant elements in their image for many people as they observe the city while moving through it. The other environmental elements are arranged and related along these paths. Broadway in New York and Chang'an street in Beijing are two well-known paths.

Edges

Edges are line breaks in the continuity of the city. They are linear elements not used or considered paths by the observer that form boundaries. These include things like shores, railroad cuts, edges of development, and walls. They are lateral references rather than coordinate axes. Such edges may be barriers that close one region off from another. Alternately, they may be lines along which two regions are joined together. These edge elements are important organizing features, particularly in the role of holding together generalized areas, as in the outline of a city by water or wall. The Fifth Avenue in New York is a good example of edges that bind parts of the city.

Districts

Districts are the larger sections of the city, conceived of as two-dimensional. These are places where observer mentally enters and that possess a common, identifying character. Always identifiable from the inside, they are also used for external reference if visible from the outside. Most people structure their city in this way to some extent, with individual differences as to whether paths or districts are the dominant elements. It seems to depend not only upon the individual but also upon the nature of a city. Greenwich Village in New York and Chunxi Road in Chengdu both are two famous districts.

Nodes

Nodes are focal points. They are strategic spots in a city that an observer can enter, and are the intensive places to and from which the observer travels. They may be junctions, places of a break in transportation, crossing of paths, or shifts from one structure to another. On the other hand, nodes may simply be concentrations that attain their importance from being the condensation of some use or physical character, such as a street-corner hangout or an enclosed square. Some of these concentration nodes are the focus of a district, over which their influence radiates and of which they stand as a symbol. They may be thus called cores. Many nodes, of course, are both junctions and concentrations. The concept of node is related to the concept of path, since junctions are typically the convergence of paths, which are events on the journey. Nodes are similarly related to the concept of district, since cores are typically the intensive foci of districts. Jongno Sageori in Seoul is a good example of a node.

Landmarks

Canton Tower in Guangzhou, Big Ben in London, and the Eiffel Tower in Paris are famous landmarks. These are another type of point-reference. In this case the observer does not enter them. They are external. They are usually a simple physical object like a building, sign, store, or mountain. Their use involves the singling out of one element from many possibilities. Some landmarks are distant, seen from many angles and distances, over the tops of smaller elements, and are used as reference points. They may be within the city or at a great distance that for all practical purposes they symbolize a constant direction. These are the innumerable signs, store fronts, trees, and other urban details that fill in the image of most observers.

Criticisms

The first criticism of this idea is that it assumes that people may organize their image of the city along the lines of a map, but it does not consider the possibility that people may consider qualities like color, texture, smells, esthetics, or visual appeal. A second criticism is the reliability of the sketch map approach. Many people can make a mental map, but some people cannot convert this information into a map form. Further, different people would have different emphases and would construct different maps of the same place, as where a tourist might put much more emphasis on transportation nodes and paths while a resident may put more emphasis on the familiar to produce two very different maps of the same space. Due to this variability, there is a problem in aggregating maps from different individuals and in generalizing from them to produce a meaningful shared reference.

1. 2   History of the City

Cities have a long history, dating from prehistoric times. Jane Jacobs (1969) argued that the first cities grew up near resources, like obsidian, that could be extracted and traded. Those who extracted the resource came to live off what others were willing to trade for it. The workers, their families, and the surplus from extraction and trade were housed in the first permanent settlements.

These settlements did not look much like anything we would recognize as a city. Scholarly opinion varies as to whether different particular sites should be considered cities. The earliest urban center is the town of Jericho located in modern Israel, with its ruins dating from long before 3000 BC (Encyclopedia Britannica; Mumford, 1961: 33). The other earliest city ruins have been found in the Middle East and Asia Minor.

Gordon Childe (1950) created a set of ten criteria to apply specifically to cities in history in ways that show how different cities have become today. His historic "cities" had greater population and higher population density, differentiation of labor, payment of taxes, public monuments and public buildings, royal support for those who were not self-sufficient in food, practical science, a system of writing and recording, symbolic art, trade in raw materials, and specialists coming from outside of kinship networks. From these prehistoric settlements developed the cities of the ancient world, the Middle Ages, the early modern period, the Industrial Age, and those involved in the rise of the post-industrial era.

1. 2. 1   Cities in the Ancient World to the Fifth Century

The first cities that have been recognized arose in Mesopotamia on the banks of the Tigris and Euphrates Rivers, in the Nile River Valley in Egypt, in the Indus River Valley in India, and in modern China. Prior to the rise of cities in these cradles of civilization, there were few settlements of significant size. The largest of the earliest cities had populations in the low tens of thousands, but some still developed such innovations as city government, planning, drainage systems, and waste management systems for dealing with refuse and sewage.

The city was a center of most human endeavors and became an attractive target for raids. The city also became the center of religion and politics and housed the surplus that was stored for feeding the population in bad years. At the center of the city was a marketplace and symbolic religious and government structures, including centers of justice. As such important centers, cities came to be protected and surrounded by walls that would funnel incoming and outgoing traffic through strong fortifications.

Cities were located near resources, first, and then near means of transportation. Trade routes were on natural trails and then on man-made roads, but also along rivers and through ports that often gave rise to large and prosperous cities as the water provided a relatively fast means of transportation compared to human and animal power. The first four major centers of civilization were centered on the Nile, Indus, Yellow, and Euphrates rivers. These were the great cities of ancient Egypt, ancient India, China, and ancient Babylon.

The Greek *polis*, the independent city-state, demonstrated that a city could be self-sufficient. Cities like Athens, Sparta, and Thebes survived with the support of a relatively small surrounding agricultural area. The urban government was at the center of the life of the state and the very word *polis* had a meaning that included the form of government centered on city life in addition to the city itself. These independent cities were able to achieve this prior to the creation of a supporting empire.

Great cities grew along with major empires of the ancient world as capital cities and centers of trade industry. Major ancient cities associated with empires like Alexander the Great's Alexandria, founded as a center of his empire and the successor states that followed, Patna in India, Xi'an in China, Carthage in North Africa, Rome in Italy, and Constantinople in Turkey were among the early cities that had populations in the hundreds of thousands.

Cities with the support of an empire saw more dramatic growth and the greater the empire, the greater the size of the city. Due to an advanced census under the Roman Empire in 32 AD, there were good data for many cities in the ancient Roman world. Following the growth of the empire during the Punic Wars (that destroyed Carthage, the center of a rival empire), Rome emerged as a city estimated to have a population close to a million around the end of the First Century BC. Other major cities like Alexandria and Baghdad reached similar size during the ancient period. The Romans extended their influence by setting up colonies in conquered territory. These cities were modeled after typical Roman cities and had a core population of citizens following Roman language, law, and customs and providing a model of urban life for subject peoples to emulate to integrate into Roman society.

The ancient period gave rise to many cities in China. The earliest dated from about 2000 BC, and came from the Yellow River Valley.

1. 2. 2   Cities in the Middles Ages and Renaissance from the 5th Century BC to the 15th Century BC

Later in the Middle Ages, In China, the cities of Nanjing, Beijing served as capitals of the Ming Dynasty. Kyoto became an urban center when the Emperor of Japan decided to relocate there and a city grew up in the vicinity. In the Middle East, the ancient city of Baghdad continued to grow and prosper under many different empires and states. By the 8th Century BC, Baghdad had surpassed the one-million mark in terms of population, the world's first city known to have reached that size.

Back in Europe the decline of Rome led to a decentralization of power and a return to smaller, relatively independent cities. Within Germany, under the Holy Roman Empire, some cities maintained independence of all authority except for the theoretical allegiance to the emperor. There were cities with independent legislatures, and cities generally existed outside of the feudal order or at least occupied a special status within the order. Many Western European cities were united by the church and cities built around large cathedrals became important centers. Italy was also divided into small states that were often dominated by a single *polis*-like city. In both Germany and Italy, some of these cities grew into major powers, with Venice becoming an empire that dominated the Adriatic Sea and extended its power to the Mediterranean.

1.2.3 Cities in the Early Modern Era to Industrialization from the 15th to 18th Centuries BC

This was a period when the town wall gradually disappeared as an important feature of cities. In some cases, as in France, the process of nation-building and centralization of power meant that political factors caused the walls to come down, reducing the power of the relatively independent cities and enhancing that of the national government. A larger and more-universal factor was the decline of the usefulness of city walls in a period of modern war with the advent of gunpowder and firearms. Walls strong enough to withstand cannon balls became too expensive to build and could be overcome by new tactics in any case. New walls stopped being built and where the old walls remained, they came to define the difference between and old city and a new larger city based on rapid growth outside the walls.

The cities of Europe flourished in the early modern era, supported by increased trade, tribute from overseas colonies, and a more dynamic urbanism accompanying a rising capitalism (Heilbrun, 1981). Many of Europe's capitol and port cities further developed from new trade routes like those of the Atlantic trade. By the end of this period, at the dawn of the Industrial Revolution, London had a population of more than a million, making it the largest in the world at the time. Britain's rival across the Channel, Paris, was not too far behind and some European cities had grown to equal older cities of longer standing like Bahgdad in the Middle East, Istanbul in Türkiye, Beijing in China, and Kyoto in Japan.

In the Western Hemisphere, the Aztecs founded the city that would become Mexico City, now one of the largest in the world. Spanish colonizationfollowed the Roman pattern here by founding new cities in conquered territories to promulgate Spanish language, customs, and law while providing a basis for administration, regional development, and resource exploitation. The Spanish brought with them modern technology, Roman Law, and the Catholic Church. In addition, they often enslaved indigenous peoples and practiced brutal forms of primitive accumulation whereby they subjugated local populations with terrible applications of the most modern military technologies of the time. They transferred massive agricultural and mineral wealth to

Spain, catapulting it into a world power.

Although London, Beijing, Baghdad and a few other cities reached new heights, most cities remained smaller during the run-up to industrialization. There was only a couple dozen cities with more than 100000 residents during this period, with towns in the tens of thousands considered large. These massive cities were nonetheless distinct from the later cities of the industrial era, as they lacked features like mass production and mechanized production, instead featuring large concentrations of handicrafts and mostly muscle power in place of the water and steam power to come.

1. 2. 4　Cities in the Industrial Era from the 18th Century BC to the Present

This period is both historical and contemporary. Starting with Great Britain in the 18th Century, Europe underwent industrialization and other parts of the world industrialized in turn after that. Many of the world's urban centers are still following an industrial pattern and much of the developing world is still going through the process of industrialization. Predating and accompanying the rise of industrialism was the rise of a true world economy with the core countries coming to dominate the system through production while the peripheral countries supplied labor and raw materials and markets for surplus consumer goods that could not be consumed at home in the core countries.

The rise of capitalism and industrialization saw commerce displaced by manufacturing as the dominant economic activity. This transformed the city in several ways. Apart from the disappearance of the walls, there were other newer developments. The religious elements at the center of the city came to be downplayed, replaced by commercial elements like stock exchanges. Where the central marketplace remained, a new marketplace for handling modern commerce emerged in its place.

Instead of being dispersed through the city in small artisanal shops, industry was now concentrated in large factories that were quartered in special districts that also housed the workforce in special working-class neighborhoods nearby. The concentration of population gave rise to new classes, including the urban working class that worked in the large factories that were owned and administered by the bourgeoisie that had evolved from the artisans of the medieval city. This rapid concentration of industry and population led to pollution and congestion as new issues. One means for rationalizing this process was developing a grid system for cities in place of the old organic or star-shaped layouts. In concert with the disappearance of walls, this facilitated the rapid expansion of the city beyond old boundaries.

The fantastic productivity of the new economies pulled large numbers of people to cities for new opportunities in commerce, in industry, and in the new centers and concentrations of culture and education and government. This process led to massive urbanization and the rise of new cities, many of them quickly outpacing old ones, from the large numbers of migrants from rural areas into urban areas. The continual increase in technology developed new means of transportation. While cities were still located near rivers and natural ports, many new cities grew around crossroads, highway exits, at railroad stops, and now around the major transit airports. These new means of rapid mass transportation also facilitated fast urbanization. In addition to the pollution and congestion, the unprecedented concentrations of people made cities vulnerable to communicable disease, health problems from stress and environmental contaminants. The large concentrations of major industries made cities susceptible to disruptions and social instability during economic downturns with large concentrations of idle workers.

1. 2. 5　Post-industrial Cities

At this time the world's population has become urbanized. A little more than half of the world's population now lives in urban areas. Millions make the in-migration every year from the countryside into cities in the developing world, with the process continuing more slowly elsewhere. Post-industrial cities are economically organized around IT and services, such as finance, real estate, and insurance. As per Sassen, the largest cities are often global centers of command and control and concentrated industry.

The passing of the industrial order in some of the former "core" countries has led to the development of the postindustrial city. Rapid urbanization has led to sprawling urban spaces that have often flowed beyond the boundaries and control of urban governments. This growth is driven by globalization trends that may foil any efforts governments make to counter those trends (Judd, 2011). Large metropolitan areas sometimes include no single city center as such anymore, but may have multiple centers representing older city centers that have grown together, requiring new means of intergovernmental coordination and cooperation.

The Chinese capitol area is an example with Beijing, Tianjin, and Hebei run together. Despite clear boundaries between the jurisdictions, many resources need to be shared and cooperation and coordination is necessary for addressing even basic issues like transportation. The urban region shares many common features across municipal borders such as the watershed, water resources, common infrastructure, shared cultural facilities, and a shared economy. There is an intricate commuting crisscrossing the region, with people living in one city and studying or working in another.

There has also been a shift to suburbs to avoid problems of urban areas, multiplying these new urban centers on the periphery of the older urban centers. Suburbs are distinct in form from the central city, but have a mutually dependent relationship with the central city. The suburb provides labor for the city and the city provides resources for its suburbs.

Some have advanced the argument that the city has become irrelevant as an economic base due to technological and organizational changes (Florida, 2002). Savitch (1988) has described these new developments as deindustrialization. The creation of postindustrial cities has been driven by the power structures that benefit from these trends. Postindustrial cities are no longer based on manufacturing but on service industries like banking, real estate, insurance, and cultural industries like fashion. Globalization has contributed to the rise of the city as leisure space and concentration of culture, contributing to the commodification of place as part of the rise of international tourism (Judd and Fainstein, 1999). Simultaneous pressures exist, pushing greater celebration of dynamic diversity and variety as unique factors of space on the one hand and greater pressures to fit into a homogenized "melting pot" that may be standardized or "McDonaldized" to provide the familiar to people wherever they go while cities develop according to new postindustrial processes (Ritzer, 2008).

1. 3   Defining Cities

In common usage, a city is a general word that covers a wide variety of large or dense concentrations of people. Large cities like Beijing, Tokyo, London, New York, and Paris brings to mind a large population, the modern facilities, skyscrapers, heavy traffic, public transportation, stadiums, museums, and a busy pattern of life. Cities have been defined as large and densely-populated urban areas. These may include either a single or several different incorporated political-administrative units that have defined boundaries and legal powers. A city is a center of population, commerce, and culture that is of major size and significance. The level of significance and size differentiates it from a town. Cities may also be defined as places with special administrative, legal, or historic status.

More technical definitions may include a minimum size, a specific politicalor legal status, or a population density. Cities may also be defined by infrastructure and activities that take place there. Cities, for example, have primarily non-extractive employment, that is workers are not involved in mining or other kinds of resource extraction. Cities have a infrastructure: sewers, transportation systems, waste disposal systems, schools, libraries, hospitals, and other public services. Cities have symbols of wealth and sites that evoke an image of the city. Paris has the Eiffel Tower, New York has the Statue of Liberty, and Beijing has the Forbidden City. Cities also have a distinctive lifestyle that set them apart from their rural counterparts. People move to cities to participate in a fast-paced and exciting lifestyle that is at odds with traditional ways of doing things.

1. 3. 1   Definition of City from Different Perspectives

Beyond these general definitions of city, there are more specific perspectives coming from the different disciplines that make up urban studies. This section presents a slice of these views, with a look at the sociological view, the political science view, the economic view, and the administrative view.

Sociological Perspective

Max Weber (1958) presented a theory of the city that has been seen by others as close to a systematic theory of urbanism that amounted to a critique of the modern city in the form of a metropolis (Wirth, 1938, Mumford, 1961). He looked at cities from a structural perspective by examining all the social, political, economic, religious, and legal foundations of the city relative to other cities and other aspects of the social order. Weber defined cities based on an archetypal typology of consumer city, producer city, industrial city, and merchant city. Weber saw the modern city as representing a deteriorated form of urban life under capitalism. The ideal city would vest authority on a rational basis rather than a charismatic or traditional basis. The law would be universal instead of personal. Group identification would be according to social class instead of kinship.

Robert Park and Ernest Burgess founded the ecological approach to cities, seeing them as analogous to living organisms. This analogy extends to the processes of growth and decay, sickness and health, and interdependence and competition. This Chicago School looked at cities in living terms and looked at various market factors in the life cycle of the city. Even so, they did not find it necessary to deny a concern with human values, showing simultaneous concern with the whole and the individual, from the hobo to the taxi driver in investigating the birth, rise, vitality, and decline and redevelopment of cities (Park and Burgess, 1984). For example, a city may go through a resource boom, like a gold rush, where the city flourishes for a time and then declines. Pittsburgh and Pohang are at different stages in the life cycle of the steel industry.

Louis Wirth (1938) invented the concept of urbanism, seeing it as a way of life. He defined urbanism based on size, density, and diversity. Jane Jacobs (1969) likewise defines a city as a place of diversity, as cities are places that are full of strangers. In modern cities, it is common that residents do not even know their next-door neighbors. Life in the city is anonymous and ironically may also represent a loss of community, particularly as it has been traditionally understood. For example, you are called by a number in the bank, not by your name. the city is marked by heterogeneity in terms of education, jobs, income, and lifestyle.

Marxist and other critical sociologists (as well as scientists from other disciplines) use the capitalist mode of production and class conflict to describe the features of the city as inevitable under a capitalist system. Urban land is divided in terms of income and ownership also determines rent and land use structure. Most of the population engages in production as labor, while a minority controls that labor and the products of that labor. This relationship between the ruling class and the ruled is one of conflict, making the city a site of endless struggle (Harvey, 1985, 1996). Manuel Castells (1996) defines urban protest movements as movements that combine struggles over collective consumption with struggles over cultural and political self-determination. These divisions and struggles may be class-based. In multi-ethnic and multiracial societies, divisions in the city may also be marked by racial segregation and ethnic divisions.

More recently, Terry Clark (2004) has focused on the agency of urban actors in determining the contours of the city and urban life. A new political culture has replaced the politics of class. The city is no longer predominantly just to be a site of production, but as an "entertainment machine". The previous Marxist focus on class, defined by relationship to the means of production has given way to a new focus based on consumption. Urban residents and visitors may define themselves by their lifestyles and consumption choices rather than being determined solely by forces beyond their control.

Political Science Perspective

Organized government and elaborateness of administration may distinguish a city from smaller urban and non-urban forms. There is a formal political process with formal leadership. Taxation and laws support the government and political projects. Political science concerns itself with the political field, the laws, regulations, systems of control, and the question of who is in power, how they attain power, and what they do with it.

Aristotle, from ancient times, focused on the state as a *polis* or city-state. The citizen was someone who inhabits the city and has certain rights to participate more fully in the life of the *polis* through holding a political, administrative, legislative, or judicial office. His view of urban citizenship, based on ancient Greek practice, is both more exclusive than modern representative models of citizenship, and more demanding, as citizens participated more directly in governing the city-state. The *polis*, regardless of the constitution that defines its governing form, exists because people are political and want to live together. Aristotle was from Athens, the cradle of democracy, which practiced a form of direct democracy. The small size of the city and the limited number of people eligible to participate (limited to free adult males recognized as citizens) meant that direct decision making by all citizens as a collective body was possible. Features like the acropolis and open markets facilitated democratic discussions by allowing citizens to gather and meet in large groups, even outside of the deliberative process. This is the origin of the large square at the center of many European cities. It is a place for market transactions, but also for citizens to gather and discuss issues of import to the city.

More recent political scientists such as Dennis Juddhas looked at the nature of political institutions, systems of power, and the contest for power in cities (Judd, 2011). What is the role of political parties in urban politics? They also investigate the politics of space and the dynamics of politics and power as they play out in an urban space. There has also been the extensive policy literature looking at what political actors do or propose to when they achieve power. Paul Peterson (1981), in his *City Limits*, examines what factors lead different cities to pursue different types of policies, for example, and concludes that cities have limited powers when compared to actors at higher levels of government (e. g. national). Thus, cities pursue policies that benefit those who own property and businesses the most. Political scientists such as John Mollenkopf (1983) have also viewed the city through the lens of the relations between different gender, ethnic, racial, and national groups in urban areas, often finding conflict and a "contested city".

Key to the political science view is the question of "who governs" (Dahl, 1961). Sometimes, the government represents the many different groups that can be found in a city, but occasionally certain groups have more power than others. This is the essence of the debate between elitism and pluralism. Those who argue for an elitist explanation of urban politics suggest that a small group, or elite, does most of the decision making. Elites need not be unanimous, but decisions usually involve an elite consensus or are at least acceptable to elites. The concept of the "growth machine" of Logan and Molotch (2007), mentioned below suggests that elite groups in the city are united by their desire for growth. Cities are sometimes organized by a political "machine", that dominates the city's politics over time. In such a case, political elites connect to supporters through a system of clientelism whereby some of the spoils of the system are shared with outside groups in return for maintaining the machine in power. Competition from outside the machine is not usually successful so participation in city life is premised on acceptance of the established order. In contrast is the concept of pluralism. This is the idea that there are many different groups in the city and that urban politics is the process of these competing to meet their interests. The city's political arena is where conflicts between such groups can be resolved without disturbing the order of daily life. If the political arena fails to resolve these conflicts, then a city may suffer in both political and economic ways (Stone, 2008).

Economic Perspective

Economists concern themselves with the city primarily as a marketplace. It is a source of production, as well as of consumption through its massive concentrations of purchasing power. The city may also provide specialized economic functions within the broader economy, with specialized bundles of goods and services as well as specialized needs and problems. Heilbrun used the term city to mean the population residing within the political boundaries of a large municipal entity, a view that is common in economics. The city is an economic system that has some independence and self-determination, and a heightened concentration of flows of goods and services, both to businesses and households.

Urban economics investigates the nature of the economy in urban areas, their economic structures, and the working of market economies in cities. Economic development is an important element in urban economics. This includes the economics of how cities are formed, through market or planned processes and the economic incentives involved, as well as the different options for increasing the quality of urban life. Urban economists also concern themselves to a great degree with economic analysis of urban policies and policy options. They have standardized methods for evaluating and comparing the cost and efficiency and impact of different transportation systems, land use options, housing policies, revenue policies, and overall economic policies. A key factor in viewing policies as solutions and in viewing the issues they address is the concept of externalities. Externalities are effects that fall on people or entities that did not agree to the effect in a voluntary economic exchange. Pollution and traffic congestion are examples of negative externalities that are major urban issues. The effect of tourist attractions increasing the sales of nearby businesses is a positive externality.

Many non-economists have pursued work on urban studies related to economics. The sociologists John Logan and Harvey Molotch (2007) wrote an influential work on the political economy of place. In addition, the political scientist Paul Peterson (1981), noted above, has analyzed choices leading to different economic development policies. Logan and Molotch identified the concept of the growth machine. This is a collection of urban elites who may disagree on various issues but combine to support and push pro-growth policies. Opposition to the growth coalition may be steamrolled by the united front of city elites pursuing growth.

Administrative Perspective

Administratively, a city is similar to a city under the view of political science, but the emphasis is on what is done to manage the city and its services. Smaller urban forms may be able to rely on markets, informal agreements, mutual aid, and voluntary social cooperation, but large cities are complex entities that require professional administration and leadership, regulations and taxation. The administration of a city has political and power concerns in terms of the political and professional leadership acting in alliance with other groups both within and outside of the city. It also has economic impacts as the city is an economic arena with the administration needing to make policy choices that have an economic impact. Administrative boundaries and definitions predominate even in the economic realm, as many positive externalities do not have much spillover across political and administrative boundaries. Such administrative definitions often come from administrative law and include things like the percentage of non-agricultural jobs, and extent of built-up environment, population, and density. The administration is more complicated in cities.

The formation of cities as places that offer services to residents necessitates a focus on the provision and management of these services, as well as on the actual implementation of policies. Urban policies may focus on many areas such as the growth and development of the city, regeneration of decaying areas, providing a good economic climate for jobs, resolving urban problems, and providing a healthy environment with a good quality of life for urban residents. The administrative view is a view towards managing the city. Administration is the efficient and effective management of personnel and resources to accomplish public purposes. Therefore, at the local level, urban administration is charged with the question of providing services efficiently as a management issue.

Urban administration, as a discipline, grew dramatically in the early 20th Century under the influence of urban reformers seeking to fight corruption, provide better services, and oppose big city machines in some of the major American cities. At the same time, municipal government was a good place for administrators to put new ideas into practice and test them in the local "laboratories of democracy" (Osborne, 1988). Both this history and the strong policy emphasis have meant that urban administration has had a more practical approach than some of the other views.

1. 3. 2　Different Concepts related to City

Metropolitan Area

A metropolitan area is a region comprised of a large city (or cities) at the center of a larger area economically integrated to the urban core. One larger city starts at the center and the process of urban sprawl spreads out. Metropolitan areas often extend beyond their political and administrative boundaries. The entire system shares common infrastructure, housing, and industry. A transportation system develops and the sprawl both follows the main paths along the system and the system extends to follow the newer concentrations of development. Multiple cities may grow up along a main transportation corridor, particularly one that connects major cities where the spaces between cities develops to connect the existing cities. The area is usually named for the largest city within the area. Different nations have different official definitions. The Seoul Metropolitan Area, including Seoul, Incheon, and most part of Gyeong-gi Province, which is the most famous Korean metropolitan area. Another example is Toronto and Vancouver in Canada. The European Union refers to Larger Urban Zones (LUZ) that are based on an increased volume of commuting and interdependence. France uses the term La Ville for the area around an urban core, such as around Paris and Marseilles. Japan uses the term *toshiken*, meaning a "group of cities" as in the area around Tokyo. As noted above, the US uses metropolitan and *micropolitan* core based statistical areas. The New York metropolitan area includes New York City, parts of New York State, parts of Connecticut, and much of northern New Jersey.

Urban versus Rural

Urban areas have higher population density compared to surrounding regions. Larger settlements like cities and towns are referred to as urban, but smaller settlements like villages are called rural. While rural areas may be settled, they are sparsely populated, not highly developed, and lacking in infrastructure. Cities generally contain concentrations of manufacturing and services. Rural areas, on the other hand, generally involve natural resources extraction or management. They may be agricultural, involved in extractive industries like mining and logging, or may even be largely uninhabited. The process of urbanization proceeds with the decline of rural areas as more people leave the countryside to move to cities. In the process the urban-rural dichotomy has become blurred as cities become more like the countryside and the countryside becomes more like cities as people moving to the city bring country mores and cities are greened while the countryside imports city technology and conveniences.

Global City

Saskia Sassen is known for coining the term global city in her book of the same name. Global cities are differentiated from other cities within a nation and share more in common than with their national counterparts. Places like Beijing, Shanghai, New York, Tokyo, and London are qualitatively and quantitatively different from other cities. They are usually huge and compete more on a world stage than on a national one, where they have little competition. The global city serves as a specialized command and control center within the international economy.

Global cities are unprecedented concentrations of power and economic resources, largely based on economic and human capital. They can marshal these resources to influence the world. They also serve as strategic sites in global entertainment and tourism. Global cities may be centers of finance, real estate, insurance, information and IT, transportation, and fashion, as well as any other, particularly service-oriented industries. Global cities are sometimes measured in hierarchical rankings, with Beijing listed as number six in the Global Cities Index, number three on the Global Power City Index in 2021.

Technopolis

The word technopolis comes from the Greek roots meaning technology and city, and is also known as a science park, a technology park, or a research park. It is an area that has a large concentration of research and technology-related institutions, whether from the public or private sector. Public sector participation often comes from public university research institutions. These areas are focused on innovation and the development of new products and the incubation of new technologies and new industries.

The technopolis offers an extensive infrastructure oriented to the particular needs of scientific and research institutions like special power grids to guarantee an uninterrupted supply of electricity, as well as advanced telecommunications, management and security, as well as a variety of support services and amenities. These special research parks are often encouraged by local governments, which not only recruit institutions, provide special services, but often even provide land subsidies and tax incentives.

Silicon Valley in the US grew up as business extension of technological and human resource developments coming out of Stanford University. The US state of North Carolina also has substantial techno centers, in particular in relation to pharmaceuticals. Japan has the famous Tsukuba Science City, host to more than 240 private research facilities and 3000 international students from 90 countries.

Garden City

The idea of the garden city originated with Ebenezer Howard in England at the end of the nineteenth century. His idea was to use a very disciplined form of urban planning to breathe life into urban utopian visions. The city would be structured to have an independent economy with short commutes and minimal disruption to the natural beauty of the countryside. The cities would be highly planned and would be circular and broken up with regular green belts of parks and with green space surrounding the city. Planning would devote specific proportions of land for manufacturing, housing, parks, and agricultural use. Smaller satellite cities would surround the central city of 50000 people. As satellite cities grew, new satellites would be formed when the older ones reached the ideal size of 32000 and became self-supporting. The cities would be linked by an efficient rail and road network to the central city and to each other.

New Town

A new town is a new urban community created through planning instead of through organic growth and is designed to be self-sufficient by providing housing, employment, education, entertainment, and shopping for its residents. A new town is usually constructed in an undeveloped area and is highly planned, avoiding land use conflicts typical of organic communities, as the planning process defines the land use. New towns have been a popular development for several reasons. First, they allow for the dispersion of overcrowded populations, and they also help ease congestion at the urban core. Second, they also provide economic benefits for urban developers who may be among the important actors in the city, not to mention providing for new tax revenue as property values rise. Finally, they provide new sources of housing. Xiong'an New Area in Hebei Province is one recent example of many new towns in Chinese.

Creative City

Charles Landry, a British urban planner, came up with the idea of the creative city and wrote *The Creative City: A Toolkit for Urban Innovators* outlining his ideas about urban planning. The concept has now become the center of an international movement for innovative urban planning that has spawned the UNESCO Creative Cities Network, and inspired other influential urban concepts like Richard Florida's idea of the creative class that provides the talent at the heart of urban success (Florida, 2002).

The concept of the creative city calls for a culture of creativity and imagination to be embedded in urban operations and cultivated among urban stakeholders. This expands the universe of possible solutions to urban problems, giving creative cities more flexibility and resilience. In contrast to traditional urban planning that focuses on physical infrastructure, the creative cities concept augments the physical infrastructure hardware with personnel software, including the creative atmosphere and mindset in operation in the city. This requires a flexible, skilled, and dynamic labor force able to envision, plan, implement, and follow-through on creative solutions to difficult problems. This demands that the creative city finds, attracts, develops, and retains the talent that makes up this creative labor force. This may require its own creativity in going beyond the usual ideas about residents, the labor force, and personnel to reengineering the city to be the sort of place that does this through the creative feel of the city scenes, the lived experience of residents and visitors, and the uniqueness of the place.

Ubiquitous City

A ubiquitous city, also known as a u-city, is a city or area connected with so-called ubiquitous information technology. The area is to have universally-linked information systems through technologies like wireless networks. Electronic services are coined as u-services such as u-parking control, u-traffic coordination, and u-crime prevention. All major information systems share data with computer systems are built into houses and buildings to facilitate the process, linking life at home to life on the street. Cities play the role of information flow hubs through high-tech media.

The concept of the u-city is an idea that started in Palo Alto, California with Mark Weiser, the chief technologist for the Xerox Palo Alto Research Center in 1998 (Chung, 2009). However, it has become a reality in Korea. The first Korean u-city to start construction was Hwaseong Dongtan, which was begun in 2007. New Songdo in Incheon became the world's largest u-city when it was completed in 2014.

1.4 Urban Problems and Causes

Cities function as centralized locations for living and working for the benefit of people living in close proximity. This close proximity generates interactions of all kinds that have both positive and negative effects. Cities grow when their benefits outweigh their costs, and there are many benefits. Several benefits have been noted above, including reduced transportation costs, larger markets, creative exchange of ideas, more efficient sharing of natural resources, education, employment, as well as all the basic amenities of urban life like clean water and waste disposal. Not all the effects are positive, however, and cities also come with many problems. The cities of the world may have higher rates of crime, higher mortality rates, higher cost of living, pollution, and traffic congestion. Usually it can be identified a common set of urban issues that all cities may face, including:

- Inequality
- Political issues
- Administrative problems
- Economic issues
- Land use
- Housing

- Poverty
- Transportation
- Environmental problems
- Natural and man-made disasters
- Crime
- Conflict

This list is broadly consistent with the 1997 United Nations Development Program report on urban problems that ranked unemployment as the biggest problem, followed by solid waste disposal, urban poverty, inadequate housing, solid waste collection, traffic congestion, poor health services, insufficient civil society participation, inadequate education, air pollution, crime and urban violence, and discrimination.

There are some divides between the cities in the developing world and in developed countries. Developing nations frequently cannot afford to house migrants, who end up living in shantytowns. Once common in many countries, shantytowns are usually made in a makeshift fashion from scrap materials, but end up being a permanent housing solution for the urban poor, who often lack running water, sanitation facilities, and access to electricity. Squatters and shanty towns may be largely a vision of the past in more developed economies, but developing economies such as the Philippines, Bangladesh, and Indonesia, a large number of civilians reside in Large shantytowns that present major challenges to urban administration.

Urban problems in developed nations are more likely to take the form of the effects of unresolved issues from earlier stages of development. Economic inequality and poverty may persist in otherwise wealthy countries, sprawl may eat up land for a regime not prepared to make difficult land use choices, the impact of growth may be seen in environmental effects like pollution and poor health among urban residents, and even the conveniences of transportation may be transformed into congestion and air and noise pollution. Further, most countries face issue of racial, ethnic, religious, and class segregation that lead to major protests. Globalization, economic decline, economic crisis and recession have led to anti-government movement that fight against public sector cuts where private businesses are criticized for not paying enough in taxes or Occupy Wall Street and the uprisings in Greece and Spain that criticize the gap between a tiny economic elite and the overwhelming majority whose interests and influence have diverged.

The causes of urban problems vary, but many can be seen as being caused by rapid urbanization, marketization and market failure, and the failure of public and private planning. In part, the nature of urban problems is defined by the perspective being employed. For example, someone looking from an ecological or Chicago School perspective is likely to look to the stage of a city's life cycle for causes whereas those employing a critical or NeoMarxist or New York School perspective are likely to see conflict and class difference at the root of urban problems.

As noted above, urban administration comes from an interdisciplinary approach; different disciplines may emphasize different aspects of a problem. Some problems may be seen as political, social, administrative, or economic. However, most urban problems are not solved and require understanding and input from multiple disciplines. Even then, they may be difficult to be understood and solved.

Questions

1. How to define "urban"?

2. Why is urban administration considered interdisciplinary?

3. How do people perceive urban place?

4. In what era did cities develop as centers for manufacturing and industry? How did these kinds of cities differ from those of earlier periods?

5. What makes post-industrial cities different from cities in earlier periods?

6. What are some of the major problems facing cities today? What has caused these problems?

Key Terms

central place theory	*garden city*
city image	*growth machine*
creative city	*melting pot*
deindustrialization	*new towns*
externality	*urbanism*

References

［1］ Bluestone, Barry; Stevenson, Mary Huff; Williams, Russell (2008). *The Urban Experience: Economics, Society, and Public Policy.* New York: Oxford University Press.

［2］ Castells, Manuel (1996). "The Information Mode of Development and the Restructuring of Capitalism" pp. 23 – 60*in* Fainstein, Susan, Cambell, Scott (eds) (1996). *Readings in Urban Theory.* Oxford, U. K. : Blackwell.

［3］ Childe, V. Gordon (2008). "The Urban Revolution" . *Town Planning Review* 21 (1): 3 – 19.

［4］ Clark, T. N. (ed) (2004). *The City as an Entertainment Machine* Amsterdam: Elsevier.

［5］ Florida, Richard (2002). *The Rise of the Creative Class.* New York: Basic Books/Perseus.

［6］ Harvey, David (1985). *The Urbanization of Capital.* Baltimore, MD: Johns Hopkins University Press.

［7］ Jacobs, Jane (1969). *The Economy of Cities.* Random House, New York.

［8］ Mark, M. , Katz, B. , Rahman, S. , and Warren, D. (2008). *MetroPolicy: Shaping A New Federal Partnership for a Metropolitan Nation.* Brookings Institution.

［9］ Pacione, Michael (2001). *The City: Critical Concepts in the Social Sciences.* New York: Routledge.

［10］ Ritzer, George (2008). *The McDonaldization of Society*, 5*th ed.* Los Angeles: Pine Forge Press.

［11］ Smith, Michael E. (2002). "The Earliest Cities" . In Gmelch, George, and Zenner, Walter (eds). *Urban Life: Readings in Urban Anthropology.* Prospect Heights, IL: Waveland Press: 3 – 19.

［12］ Squires, Gregory (ed) (2002). *Urban Sprawl: Causes, Consequences, & Policy Responses.* Baltimore: Urban Institute Press.

［13］ Stone, Clarence (2008). "Urban Politics Then and Now" in *Power in the City: Clarence Stone and the Politics of Inequality.* Marion Orr and Valerie Johnson, eds. : 267 – 316.

［14］ Weber, Max (1958). *The City.* New York: Free Press.

第 2 章 城市化

2.1 概念及内涵

1997 年，联合国开发计划署（UNDP）前任署长詹姆斯·古斯塔夫·斯佩斯宣称："世界历史上第一次有一半以上的人口居住在城镇而不是农村地区。因此，城市问题及其解决办法现在是世界的首要议题。"同年 7 月，在纽约举行的一次会议上，联合国开发计划署公布了来自全球主要城市 151 名市长的调查结果，确定了 14 类严重的城市问题（详见 1.4 节）。

然而，正如 2007 年联合国人口基金（UNFPA）的报告所述，"城市化——城市在总人口中所占比例的增加是不可避免的，但也可能是积极的……工业时代没有一个国家在没有城市化的情况下实现显著的经济增长。城市集中了贫困，但也代表了摆脱贫困的最佳希望。虽然城市体现了现代文明对环境造成的破坏，然而专家和政策制定者越来越认识到城市长期可持续性发展的潜在价值"（UNFPA，2007）。

城市化给人类带来的问题令人担忧，但城市地区也为城市移民提供了更好的生活。世界各地的人们将继续迁往城市地区，随着城市化进程的推进，城市管理研究变得更加重要。城市化程度与发展水平有着普遍的联系，也就是说，随着城市化程度的提高，发展趋势也在增加，反之亦然。图 2.1 显示了中国城市化率与人均国民收入增加的趋势。

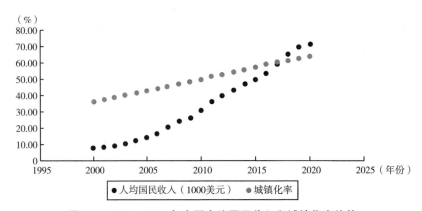

图 2.1 2000～2020 年中国人均国民收入和城镇化率趋势

资料来源：《中国统计年鉴》（2000～2020 年）。

据联合国开发计划署称，当今世界大多数人口生活在拥有 100 多万居民的大都市地区。在过去的 30 年里，随着 400 多个人口集中在如今被称为"城市地区"的城市中，城市的形式和功能、城市政治经济的组织方式、人口的文化构成以及城市化作为一种生活方式的本质都发生了许多变化。这些变化反过来又刺激了研究城市和城市化进程的新方法的出现（Soja，2005）。图 2.2 是世界城乡人口趋势。

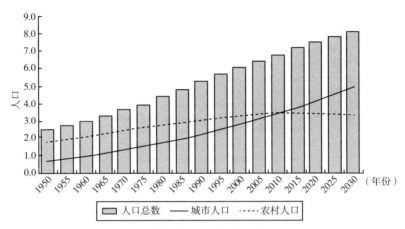

图 2.2　世界城乡人口趋势（1950~2036 年）

资料来源：联合国经济和社会事务部人口司，《世界城市化展望：2005 年更新版》，2006.

《世界城镇化展望》的 2014 年更新版显示，在 1990 年，全世界有 10 个人口上千万的超大城市，到 2014 年，全球有 28 个这样的城市，一共居住着 4.5 亿人，相当于世界城市人口的 12%。在超大城市中，16 个在亚洲，4 个在拉丁美洲，3 个在非洲和欧洲，2 个在美洲。位于世界超大城市之首的是东京，拥有 3800 万人，德里有 2500 万人，上海有 2300 万人，墨西哥城、孟买和圣保罗分别有 2100 万人。

城市化是越来越多的人口居住在城市而不是农村地区的过程（Kendall，1998：374）。城市是人们的空间聚集地，他们的生活围绕着非农业活动进行，其基本特征是城市意味着非农业。因此，一个社区可能在面积和人口上都比另一个社区大，但如果它以农业为导向，就不被视为城市地区，相反即使较小的社区也可被视为城市地区。

城市化可以描述某一特定时间的特定情况，即城市或城镇中总人口或总面积的比例，或者可以用来描述该比例随时间的变化。因此，城市化一词可以代表城市人口相对于总人口的比例，也可以代表城市化的增长率。例如，中国的城市化率很高，随着越来越多的人从农村地区迁移到城市，预计未来几年将继续保持高水平。然而，工业化和后工业化国家，如美国或德国，城市化水平较高，但城市化增长率较低。这意味着，这些国家的大多数人口已经生活在城市地区，因此，人们迁移到城市的速度开始放缓。

城市也是一个复杂的概念，定义城市的标准可以包括人口规模、空间、密度和经济组织等。然而，通常城市只是由一些基线规模来定义的，比如 10000 人。由于全球变化，城市化也代表了城市地区的实际增长。城市化的定义如下：

- 一个国家居住在城市或城市地区的总人口百分比的逐渐增加。
- 消除一个地区的农村特征，这是一个与文明和技术发展相关联的过程。从人口统计学角度来看，表示人口从农村迁移到城市。

- 人类向城市和城市地区迁移和集中的过程，伴随着相应的工业化、城市蔓延和都市生活方式的变迁。
- 城市人口日益集中，土地利用向城市用地模式转变。
- 居住在城市地区的人口比例的增长。

因此，城市化程度可能因国家而异，但通常反映了各个国家的财富。发达的工业化国家往往是城市化程度最高的国家，例如，在荷兰，几乎89%的人口生活在城市地区，而埃塞俄比亚是一个贫穷的国家，只有22.2%的人口居住在城市地区（CIA世界概况2021）。

2.2 城市化的成因

城市化可以定义为大城市的快速大规模增长和移民，城市化可能会产生积极和消极的后果。个人和集体努力减少通勤时间和费用，同时改善工作、教育、住房和交通的机会，城市生活使个人和家庭能够充分利用邻近、多样性和市场竞争的机会，这种机会通常被称为"拉动"因素——将个人吸引到城市地区。

人们移居城市寻求经济机会，但也有其他一些因素可以"推动"人们进入城市。一个主要因素是农村人口主动迁往城市。在农村地区，通常是在小型家庭农场，除了维持基本生计之外，很难提高生活水平。农村生活依赖于不可预测的环境条件，在干旱、洪水或瘟疫期间，生存变得极为困难。在现代，农业工业化对中小型农场的经济产生了一定的负面影响，大大缩小了农村劳动力市场的规模。

相比之下，众所周知，城市是资金、服务和财富集中的地方，是创造财富和社会流动的地方，创造就业和资本的企业通常位于城市地区。无论来源是贸易还是旅游，外国资金流入一个国家都是通过城市，所以很容易理解为什么生活在农村的人可能希望抓住机会搬到城市，在那里他们可以努力挣足够的钱，然后寄钱回农村困难的家庭。

农村地区没有更好的基本服务和其他专业服务，城市有更多的工作机会和更多种类的工作。健康是另一个主要因素，尤其是老年人，常常被迫搬到有更好医疗条件的城市，那里可以满足他们的健康需求。其他因素包括更多的娱乐活动（餐馆、电影院、主题公园等）和更好的教育质量，特别是高等教育。由于人口众多，城市地区也可以有更多样化的社会社区，让人们可以找到其他有相似兴趣的人，农村地区则可能不存在这样的机会。

在近代史上，与欧洲和北美相比，非洲和亚洲的城市化程度相对较低。然而，由于来自农村地区的大规模移民和城市人口本身的自然增长，发展中国家的城市人口一直在迅速增长。例如，开罗的人口在过去50年中增长了两倍，预计到2030年，一半以上的非洲人口将居住在城市。同样，中国城市人口比例从1960年的19.75%左右上升到今天的一半以上（64.7%）。图2.3是1950~2030年按主要地区划分的城乡总人口。

Major area	Population (millions)					Average annual rate of change (percentage)	
	1950	1975	2000	2005	2030	1950-2005	2005-2030
Total population							
Africa	224	416	812	906	1 463	2.54	1.92
Asia	1 396	2 395	3 676	3 905	4 872	1.87	0.88
Europe	547	676	728	728	698	0.52	-0.17
Latin America and the Caribbean.......	167	322	523	561	722	2.20	1.01
Northern America	172	243	315	331	400	1.19	0.76
Oceania	13	21	31	33	43	1.72	1.01
Urban population							
Africa	33	105	294	347	742	4.29	3.04
Asia	234	575	1 363	1 553	2 637	3.44	2.12
Europe	277	443	522	526	546	1.17	0.16
Latin America and the Caribbean.......	70	197	394	434	609	3.31	1.35
Northern America..........................	110	180	249	267	347	1.62	1.05
Oceania	8	15	22	23	31	1.96	1.18
Rural population							
Africa	191	310	518	559	721	1.95	1.02
Asia	1 162	1 820	2 313	2 352	2 236	1.28	-0.20
Europe	271	232	206	203	152	-0.53	-1.16
Latin America and the Caribbean.......	97	125	129	127	113	0.49	-0.45
Northern America..........................	62	64	66	64	53	0.05	-0.73
Oceania	5	6	9	10	11	1.25	0.58

图 2.3　1950 ～ 2030 年按主要地区划分的城乡总人口

资料来源：联合国经济和社会事务部人口司，《世界城市化展望：2005 年更新版》，2006.

表 2.1　　　　　　　　2015 ～ 2050 年主要地区城市人口和百分比

地区	城市人口（百万）								市区百分比							
	2015	2020	2025	2030	2035	2040	2045	2050	2015	2020	2025	2030	2035	2040	2045	2050
世界	3981	4378	4774	5167	5555	5938	6312	6680	53.9	56.2	58.3	60.4	62.5	64.5	66.4	68.4
更发达地区	979	1003	1027	1049	1070	1090	1108	1124	78.1	79.1	80.2	81.4	82.7	84	85.4	86.6
欠发达地区	3002	3375	3747	4117	4485	4847	5204	5556	49	51.7	54.3	56.7	59	61.3	63.4	65.6
非洲	491	587	698	824	966	1125	1299	1489	41.2	43.5	45.9	48.4	50.9	53.6	56.2	58.9
亚洲	2119	2361	2589	2802	2998	3176	3335	3497	48	51.1	54	56.7	59.2	61.6	63.9	66.2
欧洲	547	556	565	572	580	587	593	599	73.9	74.9	76.1	77.5	79	80.6	82.2	83.7
拉丁美洲和加勒比地区	505	539	571	600	626	649	669	685	79.9	81.2	82.4	83.6	84.7	85.8	86.9	87.8
北美洲	290	304	319	334	349	362	375	386	81.6	82.6	83.6	84.7	85.8	86.9	88	89
大洋洲	26	28	30	32	34	36	39	41	68.1	68.2	68.5	68.9	69.4	70.2	71.1	72.1

资料来源：《2022 年世界城市报告：展望城市未来》。

　　即使是一个几百万人口的城市，和人口超过 1000 万的城市相比也会相形见绌。根据各种估计，这些巨大的大都会地区可能已经有 20 个或更多，其中大多数在亚洲，比如东京、首尔、大阪、上海、孟买、北京、加尔各答、雅加达、天津、卡拉奇、德里和马尼拉；其他还包括纽约、圣保罗、墨西哥城、洛杉矶、莫斯科、布宜诺斯艾利斯、里约热内卢和开罗。在未来几年，发展中国家的城市如拉各斯和圣菲波哥大的爆炸性增长几乎可以肯定他们会在不远的将来加入这个群体。图 2.4 为 1950～2015 年 1000 万居民及以上城市人口。

	1950			1975			2000			2005			2015	
	City	Population (millions)		City	Population (millions)		City	Population (millions)		City	Population (millions)		City	Population (millions)
1	New York-Newark	12.3	1	Tokyo	26.6	1	Tokyo	34.4	1	Tokyo	35.2	1	Tokyo	35.5
2	Tokyo	11.3	2	New York-Newark	15.9	2	Ciudad de México (Mexico City)	18.1	2	Ciudad de México (Mexico City)	19.4	2	Mumbai (Bombay)	21.9
			3	Ciudad de México (Mexico City)	10.7	3	New York-Newark	17.8	3	New York-Newark	18.7	3	Ciudad de México (Mexico City)	21.6
						4	São Paulo	17.1	4	São Paulo	18.3	4	São Paulo	20.5
						5	Mumbai (Bombay)	16.1	5	Mumbai (Bombay)	18.2	5	New York-Newark	19.9
						6	Shanghai	13.2	6	Delhi	15.0	6	Delhi	18.6
						7	Kolkata (Calcutta)	13.1	7	Shanghai	14.5	7	Shanghai	17.2
						8	Delhi	12.4	8	Kolkata (Calcutta)	14.3	8	Kolkata (Calcutta)	17.0
						9	Buenos Aires	11.8	9	Jakarta	13.2	9	Dhaka	16.8
						10	Los Angeles-Long Beach-Santa Ana	11.8	10	Buenos Aires	12.6	10	Jakarta	16.8
						11	Osaka-Kobe	11.2	11	Dhaka	12.4	11	Lagos	16.1
						12	Jakarta	11.1	12	Los Angeles-Long Beach-Santa Ana	12.3	12	Karachi	15.2
						13	Rio de Janeiro	10.8	13	Karachi	11.6	13	Buenos Aires	13.4
						14	Al-Qahirah (Cairo)	10.4	14	Al-Qahirah (Cairo)	11.5	14	Al-Qahirah (Cairo)	13.1
						15	Dhaka	10.2	15	Osaka-Kobe	11.3	15	Los Angeles-Long Beach-Santa Ana	13.1
						16	Moskva (Moscow)	10.1	16	Al-Qahirah (Cairo)	11.1	16	Manila	12.9
						17	Karachi	10.0	17	Lagos	10.9	17	Beijing	12.9
						18	Manila	10.0	18	Beijing	10.7	18	Rio de Janeiro	12.8
									19	Manila	10.7	19	Osaka-Kobe	11.3
									20	Moskva (Moscow)	10.7	20	Istanbul	11.2
												21	Moskva (Moscow)	11.0
												22	Guangzhou, Guangdong	10.4

图 2.4　1950～2015 年 1000 万居民及以上城市人口

资料来源：联合国经济和社会事务部人口司，《世界城市化展望：2005 年更新版》，2006.

如此大规模的人口聚集造成了巨大的环境问题。例如，墨西哥城位于一个山谷中，因此，该市受到机动车空气污染的严重影响，市中心必须定期关闭交通。墨西哥城的问题在发展中世界的大多数其他大城市（如开罗、北京和天津）都存在，在工业化国家的大城市（洛杉矶）也有轻微存在。

大都市区成长的另一个特征是，曾经分离的城市合并为一个连续的建成区。随着交通的改善，人们可以通勤更远的距离，城市向外蔓延。虽然建成区内的每个城市都有自己的政府，但从实际情况来看，各个城市城府融合为一个政府。"大都市"（megalopolis，希腊语意为"大城市"）一词是用来描述美国东北部大西洋沿岸从波士顿到普罗维登斯、哈特福德、纽约市、纽瓦克、费城和巴尔的摩再到华盛顿，绵延约 800 公里（约500 英里）的几乎连续的城市区域，该词后来扩展到城市蔓延连接曾经分离的城市的其他地区，如荷兰的兰斯塔德、德国的鲁尔河谷和日本的东京—横滨—川崎地区。

2.3　城市化的特征

20 世纪见证了世界人口的快速城市化，全球城市人口比例从 1900 年的 13%（2.2亿人）急剧上升到 1950 年的 29%（7.32 亿人），2005 年上升到 49%（32 亿人）。据联合国的报告，预计到 2030 年，这一数字可能会上升到 60%（49 亿人）。20 世纪以来，随着城市化的稳步发展，美国成为城市移民趋势的典范。1890 年，只有 39% 的美国人口居住在城市，而在 20 世纪末，这一数字已增长到近 80%（Glaeser，1998）。

世界各地的城市化率各不相同。美国和英国的城市化水平远高于中国或印度，但每年的城市化率增长要慢得多，因为居住在农村地区的人口要少得多。墨西哥城的大规模城市化引发了环境改革，以改善其周围对流层和生态的状况。当一个城市达到一定规模，并开始吸引比周边地区更多的物质资源进入城市时，这个城市就达到了"灵长类"的地位。灵长类城市有时需要超越国界的资源，在日益全球化的经济中，这可能导致大规模的劳动力迁移。虽然城市化率通常是在国家内部衡量的，但有时可能包括来自东道国以外的移民人口（UNFPA，2007），这使得与城市化相关的问题变得更糟，因为它会给基础设施和公共融资带来意想不到的压力。

城市化预测

根据联合国人居署 2006 年年度报告，2007 年年中的某个时候，我们经历了"城市千年"的到来。就未来趋势而言，预计 93% 的城市增长将发生在亚洲和非洲，拉丁美洲和加勒比地区的增长幅度较小。到 2050 年，将有超过 60 亿人即全人类的 2/3 生活在城镇中。对于经历了城市化及其影响的大城市来说，这些预测可能不会太难，另外，此类预测对缺乏此类经验的较小城市则构成了一系列真正的挑战。根据联合国人口活动基金会的说法，城市可能面临一定的机遇和负面影响：随着小城市人口的增加，其薄弱的管理和规划能力将面临越来越大的压力。必须找到新的方法，使他们能够对蔓延加以规划，可持续地使用资源，并提供基本服务（UNFPA，2007 年）。

积极影响

城市化通常被视为一种负面趋势，但事实上，它是个人和企业努力减少通勤和交通费用，同时改善就业、教育、住房和交通机会的自然结果。城市生活使个人和家庭更能够利用邻近、多样性和市场竞争带来的机会。

经济影响

随着农业、传统的地方服务业和小规模工业让位给现代工业，城市和与城市相关的商业将利用不断扩大的地区的资源来维持生计，用于交易或加工成制成品的货物。城市生态学研究发现，较大的城市可以为当地市场和周边地区提供更多的专业化的商品和服务，充当较小地区的交通和枢纽，积累更多的资本、金融服务和受过教育的劳动力，并经常集中所在地区的行政职能。不同规模的地方之间的这种关系称为城市等级。城市等级的概念来源于中心地理论，在中心地理论中，城市区域根据从生产点到市场的货物运输成本发展。

随着城市的发展，其影响可能包括土地成本的急剧增加，通常会将当地工人（包括当地市政当局的雇员等官员）排除在市场之外。例如，埃里克·霍布斯鲍姆（Eric Hobsbawm，1996）表示，"在英国的工业时期（1789～1848 年），城市发展是一个巨大的阶级隔离过程，将新的劳动力推到了政府、商业中心和资产阶级新的专门居住区之外的巨大苦难沼泽。在这一时期，欧洲几乎普遍将大城市划分为'好'的西端和'差'的东端"（Hobsbawm，1996：208－209）。"这是因为盛行的西南风将煤烟和其他空气污染物带到下风口，使得城镇的西部边缘比东部边缘更受欢迎。"

根据约翰·胡辛（John Husing，2005）的说法，将城市以外的农业用地重新划分为住宅用地的土地成本会以新的方式影响城市化。由于城市地区对集中空间内的土地需求很高，胡辛提出了一种"污垢理论"来解释居民迁出城市地区的原因——一个城市达到特定的规模，并且住宅物业的成本对于普通工人的工资来说太高，工人就会迁移到城市核心区以外的土地上，有时会迁移很远，因为这些土地的价格在其工资承受范围内。在非常现代化的城市中，经济发展增加了生活成本，周围的农业用地成为住宅开发的目标，小农场主经常要求地方官员重新划分他们的土地。如果再加上良好的公路系统，这些条件可能会导致城市蔓延或新城区的发展。

2.4　逆城市化

逆城市化是布莱恩·贝里首次使用的一个术语，用于描述居民从中心城市向农村地区迁移。他将其定义为"人口分散的过程，意味着从一个更集中的状态转移到一个不太集中的状态"（Bervy，1976：17），可以通过几种不同的方式发生。如果逆城市化是城市化的反义词，城市化指城市生活方式和价值观遍布一个地区，那么逆城市化可以指"农村生活方式的传播"或反城市化（Hosszu，2009：20）。可能包括价值观的转变，以支持更少的高密度住宅、更多的开放空间、更少的交通或可用的基础设施，如高速公路或大型道路。还强调简化生活方式，居民使用更少的现代便利设施，变得更加自力更生。

逆城市化比郊区化更激进，因为比郊区居民远离中心城市的距离更远。如果取消对人员流动的限制，将现有工作转移到更多农村地区可能会导致逆城市化。在东欧和苏联的计划经济中，农村地区被认为是人们居住的低效场所，因此，对居住在城市以外的地区实行了限制。随着苏联的解体，这些限制被解除，许多人选择回到农村地区，那里的就业机会可能比中心城市更多（Hosszu，2009）。

逆城市化对大城市的影响已通过几种方式得到证明。城市认识到，移居到农村地区的人，特别是那些寻求更清洁环境和更简单、更少依赖技术的生活方式的人，都在寻求生活质量的提高，作为回应，城市将开放空间和"绿地"纳入其新区规划。首尔市前市长李明博利用这一假设提出了修复清溪川并将"自然带回到市中心"的计划，虽然成本很高（最终花费3860亿韩元，约19亿人民币），但改造后的清溪川现已成为居民和游客的热门目的地，每天约有90000名行人前往，尤其是在炎热的夏季，因为清溪川沿岸的温度比周围地区低要5摄氏度（Revkin，2009）。

城市化的规划

对城市化的规划即新城或花园城市运动，基于预先规划，可出于军事、美学、经济或城市设计的原因进行准备。从历史上看，规划的原因是不同的，许多古代城市都有这样的例子，征服意味着许多被入侵的城市会呈现出占领者所期望的规划特征。例如，罗马人以在被征服的领土上创建有规划的城市、修建沟渠和道路而闻名，这些沟渠和公路是以直线布置的，很少考虑当地地形。这种对城市基础设施的苛刻规划导致了"条条大路通罗马（古罗马帝国的首都）"的说法。

　　在更现代的经验中，城市规划已被用于应对城市快速发展出现的许多问题，如无限蔓延、道路拥堵、空气质量差以及不健康的生活方式（以汽车为中心而非以人为中心）。规划协会强调以问题为基础的规划方法，城市规划者开发旨在发现解决城市环境恶劣的原因和症状的技术。我们将在下一章继续这个话题，但由于它与城市化密切相关，因此，在此提及。

2.5　关于城市化的讨论

　　传统的城市化表现为人类活动集聚在市中心周围，当居住区向外转移时称为郊区化。一些研究人员和学者认为，郊区化迄今已在市中心以外形成了新的集中点，这种网络化、多中心的集聚形式被一些新兴的城市化模式所考虑，被称为各种各样的远郊、边缘城市、网络城市或后现代城市，洛杉矶是后现代城市最著名的例子。随着城市的快速增长，出现了许多问题，这些问题可能会为城市管理人员的技能带来挑战。

发展不平衡

　　当城市快速发展时，当城市的某些地区增长过快或其他地区的发展随着居民迁移到更新的地区而下降时，问题就可能会出现，如可能会导致发展不平衡，居民可能聚集在一些提供他们能够负担得起的便利设施和服务社区或地区。因此，富有的居民可能居住在提供高档服务的高租金地区，可能需要额外的公共支出用于基础设施的维护和发展。由于城市预算是固定的，这样的资源集中可能意味着贫困地区没有得到同样的重视。对城市化特别是无规划的城市化的批评者经常将发展不平衡作为解释规划是实现城市基本功能的关键因素。如果发展不平衡继续并得不到遏制，城市管理者可能会发现他们的资源被随意要求，从而难以以有效和公平的方式提供服务。随着郊区的发展，发展不平衡的问题将成为一个紧迫的问题。

案例：首尔城市地区与农村地区

　　韩国的经历在农村地区和城市之间形成了戏剧性的对比，尤其在过度发达的首尔形成了更鲜明的对比。首都地区面临过度拥挤、交通问题、污染和增长问题。即使在城市内部，汉江以南的繁荣地区和北部不太富裕的地区之间仍然存在着很大的差距。尽管存在着工业、文化中心和政府集中在首都的问题，但人口仍在继续流动，进而使得其他地区的人口减少。历史上向首都的集中使得首都的发展以牺牲其他地区为代价，让首尔成为最理想的教育和就业目的地。另外，随着年轻人移居城市，农村地区人口减少，在农村地区，近一半的婚姻是当地男子和外国新娘之间的婚姻。农村地区也在迅速老龄化，这既是因为年轻人的离开，也是因为退休人员正在返回对老年人更友好的地区。与此同时，便利设施发展缓慢，如农村地区引入高速互联网的时间要比大城市晚得多。

郊区化

郊区化是"大都市区内非中心城市的任何地方"（Oliver，2003）。这意味着郊区在人口、经济、阶层和密度方面可能非常多样化。郊区围绕中心城市发展，通常是因为中心城市不断上涨的土地价格和人口密度将负担得起的生活场所推到了中心城市边界之外，郊区开始成为居住社区，但一些郊区随着规模和多样性不断扩大，成为中心城市。然而，一般来说，郊区是在居民能够进出中心城市、就业地和周围地区交通更便利的地方发展起来的，汽车或公共交通（公共汽车或火车）的可达性可以促进郊区的发展。

如果郊区超出了城市的政治管辖范围，那么通常会创建一个新的政治管辖区。这意味着郊区将成为一个独立的城市，拥有自己的规则、行政办公室和政治代表权。在美国，郊区的政治通常与中心城市大不相同，也可能与其他郊区不同。因此，不可能对郊区政治或行政的性质作出一般性的陈述。郊区各不相同，正是这种多样性使其发展成为城市管理者的挑战。

伪城市化

伪城市化是指在没有功能性基础设施支持的地区形成大城市的情况。随着城市化地区人口的增长，城市的基础设施必须随之增长，否则就会出现服务短缺，尤其是住房、教育、交通、饮用水和废物处理等服务，或其他服务如执法。城市地区人口过剩的特点往往是棚户区的服务不足或完全没有。如果一个城市在缺乏足够基础设施的情况下实现了显著增长，那么它将被视为"伪城市化"。

第三世界的城市化倾向于主要由伪城市化组成。这在很大程度上是因为所谓的"农村推动"因素，这些因素把人们从农村推向城市，而城市却没有准备好接受他们。正如多根和卡萨达所指出的那样，第三世界的农村—城市移民通常由于与贫困有关的因素而迁入城市。

大多数发展中国家农村地区死亡率的下降并没有与相应的生育率下降相匹配，由此导致的人口增长无法通过停滞的农村经济来维持，这导致农村人口就业机会失衡加剧，人口迁移成为缓解这种不平衡的唯一机制（Dogan and Kasarda，1988）。

这导致人口激增，贫困的迁移人口逐渐向城市迁移，由于基础设施和可用资源有限，一个城市只能容纳这么多人，城市服务负担过重的额外压力可能带来不健康的生活条件、易受疾病传播、犯罪和自然灾害（如季节性洪水）的影响，或受地震等自然灾害影响的地区，住房和基础设施的崩溃（Quarantelli，2003）。

这类问题突出表明，需要在预测这些推动因素的情况下进行城市规划。对于公共资源稀缺的发展中国家来说，这种规划往往被视为一种奢侈，但是没有规划的成本可能会更高。后面将讨论伴随这些问题而来的对城市化的批评，以及各种形式的规划城市的兴起。

【思考题】

1. 城市化有哪些特征？
2. 城市化如何影响世界各地的总体生活水平？

3. 城市化与工业化之间的关系是什么?

4. 构成城市迁移人口结构中的"推动"和"拉动"因素有哪些?

5. 与城市化相关的问题有哪些?

6. 解决城市化带来的问题的方法有哪些?

【关键术语】

农业社会	拉动因素
污垢理论	推动因素
大都市	郊区
多中心的	城市蔓延
伪城市化	

参考文献

[1] Anselin, Luc (2010). "Thirty Years of Spatial Econometrics". *Papers in Regional Science*, 89 (1): 3 – 25.

[2] Batten, D. F. (1995) "Network Cities: Creative Urban Agglomerations for the 21st Century". *Urban Studies*, 32: 313 – 327.

[3] Berry, Brian J. L. (ed) (1976). "*Urbanization and Counter-urbanization*. Beverly Hills, CA: Sage.

[4] Dogan, Mattei and Kasarda, John (1988) eds. *The Metropolis Era: Megacities*. Beverly Hills, CA: Sage.

[5] Kendall, Diana (1994). *The New Urban Sociology*. New York: McGraw-Hill.

[6] United Nations (2006). *World Urbanization Prospects: The 2005 Revision Paper No. ESA/P/WP/200*. Population Division, Department of Economic and Social Affairs.

Chapter 2   Urbanization

2. 1   Definition

In 1997, according to James Gustave Speth, the former UNDP Administrator, "For the first time in world history, more than half of the world's population now live in cities and towns rather than in rural areas. Urban problems and their solutions, therefore, now top the world's agenda. " At a meeting in New York in July of that year, the UNDP unveiled the results of a survey of 151 mayors of major cities around the globe. The mayors identified fourteen categories of urban problems as severe (see 1. 4 for more information).

However, as a 2007 United Nations Population Fund (UNFPA) report states, "Urbanization—the increase in the urban share of total population—is inevitable, but it can also be positive…no country in the industrial age has ever achieved significant economic growth without urbanization. Cities concentrate poverty, but they also represent the best hope of escaping it. Cities also embody the environmental damage done by modern civilization; yet experts and policymakers increasingly recognize the potential value of cities to long-term sustainability" (UNFPA, 2007, Introduction).

The problems facing humanity because of urbanization are troubling, but urban areas also offer a standard of living not possible to previous generations of migrants to the city. Because of this, people around the globe will continue to move to urban areas, and the study of urban administration becomes more important as urbanization continues. The degree of urbanization has a general relationship with the level of development. That is, as urbanization increases, there is a tendency for development to increase and vice versa. Figure 2. 1 shows the trend of increasing income as the percentage of urbanization increases.

According to the UNDP, today most of the world's population lives in large metropolitan regions of more than one million inhabitants. This concentration of population in 400 or so sprawling "city-regions," as they are now called, has been accompanied over the past thirty years by many dramatic changes in the form and functioning of cities, in the ways the urban political economy is organized, in the cultural composition of the population, and in the very nature of urbanism as a way of life. These changes have, in turn, stimulated new approaches to

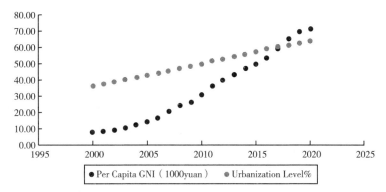

Figure 2. 1   Per Capita GNI versus Urbanization in China, 2000 – 2020

Source: *China Statistical Yearbook* (2000 – 2021).

studying cities and the urbanization process (Soja, 2005). Figure 2. 2 shows the urban and rural population of the world.

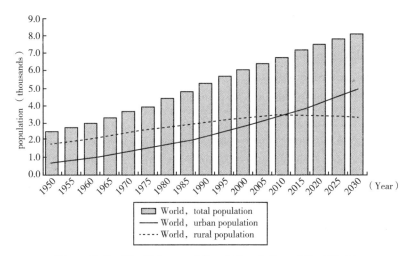

Figure 2. 2   The Urban and Rural Population of the World

Source: UN Department of Economic & Social Affairs, Population Division (2006). *World Urbanization Prospects*: *The 2005 Revision.*

World Urbanization Prospects: *The 2005 Revision* showed there were 10 mega cities with a population of more than 10 million in the world in 1990. By 2014, there were 28 such cities with a total population of 450 million, equivalent to 12% of the world's urban population. Among the megacities, 16 are in Asia, 4 in Latin America, 3 in Africa and Europe, and 2 in the Americas. The largest megacity in the world is Tokyo, with a population of 38 million, followed by Delhi, 25 million, Shanghai, 23 million, Mexico City, Mumbai and Sao Paulo, with 21 million respectively.

Urbanization is the process by which an increasing proportion of a population lives in cities rather than in rural areas (Kendall, 1998: 374). An urban place is a spatial concentration of people whose lives are organized around non-agricultural activities. The essential characteristic here is that urban means non-agricultural. It is possible, therefore, to have one community that is larger than another, both in area and perhaps, population, but because it is agriculturally oriented, it is not considered urban, while the smaller community is considered urban.

Urbanization can describe a specific condition at a set time, i. e. the proportion of total population or area in cities or towns, or the term can describe the increase of this proportion over time. So, the term urbanization can represent the level of urban relative to overall population, or it can represent the rate at which the urban proportion is increasing. For example, the rate of urbanization in China is quite high, and is expected to continue at high levels for several years into the future as more people migrate from rural areas to cities. However, industrialized and post-industrial countries, such as the U. S. or Germany, have high levels of urbanization, but low rates of urbanization. This means that most of the population in each country already lives in an urban area. As a result, the rate at which people migrate to cities is low.

Urban can also be defined as a complex concept. Criteria used to define urban can include population size, space, density, and economic organization. Usually, however, urban is simply defined by some base line size, like 10000 people.

Urbanization also represents the physical growth of urban areas because of global change. Urbanization can be defined as follows:

● The gradual increase in the overall percentage of a country's population living in urban or city area.

● The removal of the rural characteristics of an area, a process associated with the development of civilization and technology. Demographically, the term denotes the redistribution of populations from rural to urban settlements.

● The process of human movement and centralization towards and into cities and urban areas, with the associated industrialization, urban sprawl and lifestyle of urbanism.

● An increasing concentration of the population in cities and a transformation of land use to an urban pattern of organization.

● The growth in the proportion of a population living in urban areas.

The degree of urbanization, therefore, can vary from country to country, but generally reflects the wealth of individual countries. The industrialized countries tend to be the most highly urbanized. For example, in the Netherlands, almost 92. 2% of the population lives in urban areas, compared to Ethiopia, a much poorer country, where only 13% of the population lives in urban areas (CIA World Factbook 2021).

2. 2   Causes

Urbanization can be defined as the rapid and massive growth of, and migration to, large cities. Positive and negative consequences can result. It occurs naturally from individual and collective efforts to reduce time and expense in commuting and transportation while improving opportunities for jobs, education, housing, and transportation. Living in cities permits individuals and families to take advantage of the opportunities of proximity, diversity, and marketplace competition. Such opportunities are often referred to as "pull" factors, since they draw individuals into an urban area.

People move into cities to seek economic opportunities. But there are factors that can "push" people into cities as well. A major contributing factor is known as rural flight. In rural areas, often on small family farms, it is difficult to improve one's standard of living beyond basic subsistence. Farm living is dependent on unpredictable environmental conditions, and in times of drought, flood or pestilence, survival becomes extremely problematic. In modern times, industrialization of agriculture has negatively affected the economy of small and middle-sized farms and strongly reduced the size of the rural labor market.

Cities, in contrast, are known to be places where money, services and wealth are centralized. Cities are where fortunes are made and where social mobility is possible. Businesses, which generate jobs and capital, are usually located in urban areas. Whether the source is trade or tourism, it is also through the cities that foreign money flows into a country. It is easy to see why someone living on a farm might wish to take their chances and move to the city where they can try to make enough money to send back home to their struggling family.

There are better basic services as well as other specialist services that aren't found in rural areas. There are more job opportunities and a greater variety of jobs in the city. Health is another major factor. People, especially the elderly are often forced to move to cities where some doctors and hospitals can cater to their health needs. Other factors include a greater variety of entertainment (restaurants, movie theaters, theme parks, etc.) and a better quality of education, especially at the university level. Due to their high populations, urban areas can also have much more diverse social communities, allowing people to find others with similar interests. Such opportunities might not exist in rural areas.

In recent history, the degree of urbanization has been relatively low in Africa and Asia compared to Europe and North America. However, because of large-scale migration from rural areas and a natural increase in the urban populations themselves, the populations of cities in the developing world have been growing rapidly. The population of Cairo, for example, has tripled in the last 50 years, and more than half of Africa's people are expected to be living in cities by 2030. Similarly, the urban share of the population in China has risen from about 19.75% in 1960 to more than half today. Figure 2.3 shows total urban and rural population by major area, 1950 – 2030.

Major area	Population (millions)					Average annual rate of change (percentage)	
	1950	1975	2000	2005	2030	1950-2005	2005-2030
Total population							
Africa	224	416	812	906	1 463	2.54	1.92
Asia	1 396	2 395	3 676	3 905	4 872	1.87	0.88
Europe	547	676	728	728	698	0.52	-0.17
Latin America and the Caribbean	167	322	523	561	722	2.20	1.01
Northern America	172	243	315	331	400	1.19	0.76
Oceania	13	21	31	33	43	1.72	1.01
Urban population							
Africa	33	105	294	347	742	4.29	3.04
Asia	234	575	1 363	1 553	2 637	3.44	2.12
Europe	277	443	522	526	546	1.17	0.16
Latin America and the Caribbean	70	197	394	434	609	3.31	1.35
Northern America	110	180	249	267	347	1.62	1.05
Oceania	8	15	22	23	31	1.96	1.18
Rural population							
Africa	191	310	518	559	721	1.95	1.02
Asia	1 162	1 820	2 313	2 352	2 236	1.28	-0.20
Europe	271	232	206	203	152	-0.53	-1.16
Latin America and the Caribbean	97	125	129	127	113	0.49	-0.45
Northern America	62	64	66	64	53	0.05	-0.73
Oceania	5	6	9	10	11	1.25	0.58

Figure 2. 3　Total Urban and Rural Population by Major Area, 1950 – 2030

Source: UN Department of Economic & Social Affairs, Population Division (2006). *World Urbanization Prospects*: *The 2005 Revision*.

Table 2. 1 shows estimated urban population and percentage urban by region 2015 – 2050.

Table 2. 1　　　　Estimated Urban Population and Percentage Urban by Region 2015 – 2050

Region	Urban Population (million)								Percentage Urban							
	2015	2020	2025	2030	2035	2040	2045	2050	2015	2020	2025	2030	2035	2040	2045	2050
World	3981	4378	4774	5167	5555	5938	6312	6680	53. 9	56. 2	58. 3	60. 4	62. 5	64. 5	66. 4	68. 4
More developed	979	1003	1027	1049	1070	1090	1108	1124	78. 1	79. 1	80. 2	81. 4	82. 7	84	85. 4	86. 6
Less developed	3002	3375	3747	4117	4485	4847	5204	5556	49	51. 7	54. 3	56. 7	59	61. 3	63. 4	65. 6
Africa	491	587	698	824	966	1125	1299	1489	41. 2	43. 5	45. 9	48. 4	50. 9	53. 6	56. 2	58. 9
Asia	2119	2361	2589	2802	2998	3176	3335	3497	48	51. 1	54	56. 7	59. 2	61. 6	63. 9	66. 2
Europe	547	556	565	572	580	587	593	599	73. 9	74. 9	76. 1	77. 5	79	80. 6	82. 2	83. 7
Latin America and the Caribbean	505	539	571	600	626	649	669	685	79. 9	81. 2	82. 4	83. 6	84. 7	85. 8	86. 9	87. 8
North America	290	304	319	334	349	362	375	386	81. 6	82. 6	83. 6	84. 7	85. 8	86. 9	88	89
Oceania	26	28	30	32	34	36	39	41	68. 1	68. 2	68. 5	68. 9	69. 4	70. 2	71. 1	72. 1

Source: *World Cities Report 2022*: *Envisaging the Future of Cities*.

One of the most noticeable features of urban growth in the 20th century has been the rapid increase in the number of very large cities. Before 1800, cities with more than a million inhabitants were rare. Since then, however, the number of such cities has risen steadily. In 1900 there were at least 13 cities with more than a million inhabitants, and by 1950 the number had grown to 68. By 2000 there will be at least 250 cities of more than a million, many of which will be in Asia, especially in India and China (130 in 2021).

Even a city of a few million people is dwarfed by the urban giants with populations exceeding 10 million. According to various estimates, there may be 20 or more of these gigantic metropolitan areas already. Most are in Asia: Tokyo, Seoul, Osaka, Shanghai, Mumbai (Bombay), Beijing, Calcutta, Jakarta, Tianjin, Karachi, Delhi, and Manila. The other giants are New York, São Paulo, Mexico City, Los Angeles, Moscow, Buenos Aires, Rio de Janeiro, and Cairo. In coming years, explosive growth in cities of the developing world such as Lagos and Santa Fe de Bogotá will almost certainly propel them into this group. Figure 2. 4 shows population of cities with 10 million inhabitants of more, 1950 – 2015.

	1950		1975		2000		2005		2015	
	City	Population (millions)	City	Population (millions)	City	Population (millions)	City	Population (millions)	City	Population (millions)
1	New York-Newark	12.3	Tokyo	26.6	Tokyo	34.4	Tokyo	35.2	Tokyo	35.5
2	Tokyo	11.3	New York-Newark	15.9	Ciudad de México (Mexico City)	18.1	Ciudad de México (Mexico City)	19.4	Mumbai (Bombay)	21.9
3			Ciudad de México (Mexico City)	10.7	New York-Newark	17.8	New York-Newark	18.7	Ciudad de México	21.6
4					São Paulo	17.1	São Paulo	18.3	São Paulo	20.5
5					Mumbai (Bombay)	16.1	Mumbai (Bombay)	18.2	New York-Newark	19.9
6					Shanghai	13.2	Delhi	15.0	Delhi	18.6
7					Kolkata (Calcutta)	13.1	Shanghai	14.5	Shanghai	17.2
8					Delhi	12.4	Kolkata (Calcutta)	14.3	Kolkata (Calcutta)	17.0
9					Buenos Aires	11.8	Jakarta	13.2	Dhaka	16.8
10					Los Angeles-Long Beach-Santa Ana	11.8	Buenos Aires	12.6	Jakarta	16.8
11					Osaka-Kobe	11.2	Dhaka	12.4	Lagos	16.1
12					Jakarta	11.1	Los Angeles-Long Beach-Santa Ana	12.3	Karachi	15.2
13					Rio de Janeiro	10.8	Karachi	11.6	Buenos Aires	13.4
14					Al-Qahirah (Cairo)	10.4	Rio de Janeiro	11.5	Al-Qahirah (Cairo)	13.1
15					Dhaka	10.2	Osaka-Kobe	11.3	Los Angeles-Long Beach-Santa Ana	13.1
16					Moskva (Moscow)	10.1	Al-Qahirah (Cairo)	11.1	Manila	12.9
17					Karachi	10.0	Lagos	10.9	Beijing	12.9
18					Manila	10.0	Beijing	10.7	Rio de Janeiro	12.8
19							Manila	10.7	Osaka-Kobe	11.3
20							Moskva (Moscow)	10.7	Istanbul	11.2
21									Moskva (Moscow)	11.0
22									Guangzhou, Guangdong	10.4

Figure 2. 4   Population of Cities with 10 Million Inhabitants or More, 1950 – 2015

Source: UN Department of Economic & Social Affairs, Population Division (2006). *World Urbanization Prospects: The 2005 Revision.*

Such large concentrations of people pose immense environmental problems. Mexico City, for example is in a valley, as a result, the city suffers so badly from air pollution from motor vehicles that the city center must periodically be closed to traffic. Mexico City's problems are replicated in most other large cities in the developing world (like Cairo, Beijing, and Tianjin), and to a lesser degree in the large cities of industrialized countries as well (Los Angeles).

Another characteristic of the growth of urban giants is the coalescence of once separate cities into a continuous built-up area. As transport improves, people can commute longer distances, and cities have sprawled outwards. Although each town within the built-up area maintains its government, in physical terms the individual cities blend into one. The term megalopolis (Greek for "great city") was coined to describe the nearly continuous urban area that stretches about 800 kilometers (500 miles) along the Atlantic Coast of the northeastern United States from Boston to Providence, Hartford, New York City, Newark, Philadelphia, and Baltimore to Washington, D. C. The term has since been extended to other areas in which urban sprawl links once separate cities, such as Randstad in the Netherlands, the Ruhr Valley in Germany, and the Tokyo-Yokohama-Kawasaki region in Japan.

2. 3 Characteristics

The 20th century witnessed the rapid urbanization of the world's population, as the global proportion of urban population rose dramatically from 13% (220 million) in 1900, to 29% (732 million) in 1950, to 49% (3. 2 billion) in 2005 and it projected that the figure is likely to rise to 60% (4. 9 billion) by 2030 according to a report of UN. The United States exemplifies this trend of urban migration, as urbanization increased at a steady pace over the 20th century. In 1890, only 39% of the US population lived in cities, while at the close of the 20th century, the figure had grown to almost 80% (Glaeser, 1998).

Urbanization rates vary across the world. The US and UK have a far higher urbanization level than China or India, but a far slower annual urbanization rate, since much less of the population is living in a rural area. The massive urbanization of Mexico City has invoked environmental reforms to improve the status of its surrounding troposphere and ecology. When a city reaches a certain size and begins to draw more resources into the city than can be produced by surrounding areas, the city has reached "primate" status. Primate cities can sometimes demand resources that go beyond national boundaries, and in an increasingly global economy, this can lead to labor migrations of massive proportions. Although urbanization rates are generally measured within nations, these may sometimes include migrant populations from outside the host country (UNFPA, 2007). This can make the problems associated with urbanization worse, since it can put unanticipated pressure on infrastructure and public financing.

Urbanization Projections

According to the UN-HABITAT 2006 Annual Report, sometime in the middle of 2007 we experienced the arrival of the "Urban Millennium". Regarding future trends, it is estimated 93% of urban growth will occur in Asia and Africa, and to a lesser extent in Latin America and the Caribbean. By 2050 over 6 billion people, two thirds of humanity, will be living in towns and cities. For larger cities that have become experienced with urbanization and its effects over time, these projections may not be too troubling. On the other hand, such projections pose a real set of challenges for smaller cities that lack such experience. According to the UNFPA, there are opportunities as well as negative consequences that cities may face: as the population of smaller cities increases, their thin managerial and planning capacities come under mounting stress. New ways will have to be found to equip them to plan for expansions, to use their resources sustainably, and to deliver essential services (UNFPA 2007: Introduction).

Positive Aspects

Urbanization is often viewed as a negative trend, but in fact, it occurs naturally from individual and corporate efforts to reduce expense in commuting and transportation while improving opportunities for jobs, education, housing, and transportation. Living in cities permits individuals and families to take advantage of the opportunities of proximity, diversity, and marketplace competition.

Economic Effects

As agriculture, more traditional local services, and small-scale industry give way to modern industry, the urban and related commerce with the city will draw on the resources of an ever-widening area for its own sustenance and goods to be traded or processed into manufactured goods. Research in urban ecology finds that larger cities provide more specialized goods and services to the local market and surrounding areas, function as a transportation and wholesale hub for smaller places, and accumulate more capital, financial service provision, and an educated labor force, as well as often concentrating administrative functions for the area in which they lie. This relation among places of different sizes is called the urban hierarchy. The idea of an urban hierarchy is drawn from central place theory, where an urban area develops according to the cost of transportation of goods from points of production to markets.

As cities develop, effects can include a dramatic increase in the cost of land, often pricing the local working class out of the market, including such functionaries as employees of the local municipalities. For example, Eric Hobsbawm (1996) stated urban development "during the industrial period in England (1789 – 1848) was a gigantic process of class segregation, which pushed the new laboring poor into great morasses of misery outside the centers of government and business and the newly specialized residential areas of the bourgeoisie. The almost universal European division into a 'good' west end and a 'poor' east end of large cities developed in this period" (Hobsbawm, 1996: 208 – 209). "This is likely due the prevailing south-west wind which carries coal smoke and other airborne pollutants downwind, making the western edges of towns preferable to the eastern ones."

According to John Husing (2005), the cost of land that is rezoned from agricultural to residential use outside of urban areas can affect urbanization in new ways. Since urban areas create a high demand for land in a concentrated space, Husing developed a "dirt theory" to explain residential migration out of urban areas. Once a city reaches a particular size and the cost of residential property becomes too much for the average worker's wages, the worker will migrate, sometimes great distances, to land outside of the urban core that is priced within his or her wage limits. In very modern cities where growth has driven up the cost of living, surrounding agricultural land becomes a target for residential development, and small farmers often ask that their land be rezoned by local officials. When coupled with good highway systems and easy access to vehicle ownership, these conditions can lead to urban sprawl, or the development of new urban areas.

2.4　Counter-urbanization

Counter-urbanization is a term first used by Brian Berry to describe migration of residents from central cities to rural areas. He defined it as "a process of population deconcentration; it implies a movement from a state of more concentration to a state of less concentration" (Berry, 1976: 17). However, this can happen in several different ways. If counter-urbanization is the opposite of urbanization, where city lifestyles and values are spread throughout an area, then counter-urbanization can refer to "the spread of the rural lifestyle" or anti-urbanization (Hosszu, 2009: 20). This may include a shift in values to favor fewer high-density dwellings, more open space, less traffic or visible infrastructure, such as highways or large avenues. There is also an emphasis on simplifying lifestyles, where residents use fewer modern conveniences and become more self-reliant.

Counter-urbanization is more radical than suburbanization, where residents move greater distances away from a central city. Shifts to more rural areas of available jobs can cause counter-urbanization, as well as the lifting of restrictions on the movement of people from place to place. In the planned economies of Eastern Europe and the former Soviet Union, rural areas were considered inefficient places for people to live, so restrictions on residing outside of urban areas were imposed. With the fall of the USSR, such restrictions were lifted, and many people chose to move back to more rural areas where job opportunities might be more numerous than in the central cities (Hosszu, 2009: 4).

The impact of counter-urbanization on large cities has been demonstrated in a few ways. Cities recognize that there is quality of life issues sought by those who migrate to rural areas, especially those in search of a cleaner environment and simpler, less technologically dependent lifestyle. In response, cities have incorporated open spaces and "greenbelts" within their plans for new areas. In central Seoul, former mayor Lee Myungbak used this reasoning to put forward his plan to restore the Cheonggyecheon and bring "nature back to downtown". Although very costly (eventually it cost 386 billion won), it has become a popular destination for residents and tourists, visited by an estimated 90000 pedestrians a day. This is especially true during the warm summer months, when temperatures along the stream can be up to five degrees cooler than the surrounding areas (Revkin, 2009).

Planning for Urbanization

Planned urbanization, i. e., the new town or the garden city movement, is based on an advance plan, which can be prepared for military, aesthetic, economic or urban design reasons. Historically, reasons for planning have differed. Examples can be seen in many ancient cities, where conquest meant that many invaded cities took on the desired planned characteristics of their occupiers. The Romans, for example, were well known for creating planned cities in conquered territories, building aqueducts and roads which were laid out in straight lines with little regard for local topography. This rigid planning of city infrastructure led to the saying that "all roads lead to Rome (the capital of the ancient Roman Empire)".

In more modern experience, urban planning has been used to combat many of the undesirable characteristics of rapid urban growth, such as sprawl, congestion on roadways, poor air quality, and environments that promote an unhealthy lifestyle (car-centric rather than people-centric). Planning associations emphasize the problem-based approach to planning, where urban planners will develop techniques meant to address the causes as well as the symptoms of a poor urban environment. We will return to this topic in a later chapter, but it should be mentioned here because of its close association with urbanization.

2.5   Issues

Traditional urbanization exhibits a concentration of human activities and settlements around the downtown area. When the residential area shifts outward, this is called suburbanization. A few researchers and writers suggest that suburbanization has gone so far to form new points of concentration outside the downtown. This networked, poly-centric form of concentration is considered by some an emerging pattern of urbanization. It is called variously exurbia, edge cities, network cities, or postmodern cities. Los Angeles is the best-known example of this last type of urbanization. With rapid growth come many problems that can challenge the skills of urban administrators.

Uneven Development

When cities grow rapidly, problems may develop when some sections of a city grow too fast or others decline as residents move to newer areas. This can cause uneven development, where residents may cluster in neighborhoods or areas that either offer amenities and services that they can afford. Thus, wealthy residents may live in high rent areas, offering upscale services that may require extra public expenditures on infrastructure, maintenance, and development. Since city budgets are fixed, such resource concentration can mean that poorer areas go without the same level of attention. Critics of urbanization, especially unplanned urbanization, often cite uneven development as a key reason why careful planning is an essential urban function. If uneven development continues unchecked, urban administrators may find that their resources are being requested in haphazard ways, making it difficult to respond with services in an efficient and equitable manner. As suburbs develop, the issue of uneven development becomes a pressing concern.

Case : The Seoul Area versus Rural Areas

The experience in Korea has featured a dramatic between the rural areas and cities, with a particularly stark contrast drawn between overdeveloped Seoul. The capital area suffers from overcrowding, traffic problems, pollution, and the problems of growth. Even within the city there remains a major division between the prosperous area south of the Han River and the less-affluent areas to the north. Despite the problems associated with the concentration of industry, culture, and government in the center of the capital, people continue to flow there, depressing the population elsewhere. Historic concentration on the capital has left the capital developed at the expense of other regions, leaving it the most desirable destination for education and employment in most fields. On the other hand, life in rural areas, have featured a decline in population as young people move to the city. Almost half of marriages in rural areas are between a local man and imported foreign brides. The rural areas are rapidly graying as well, both because young people are going, but also because retires are returning to areas that are more hospitable for senior citizens. At the same time, amenities are slow to develop, with high-speed internet introduced much later to rural areas than to the big city.

Suburbanization

Suburbanization is "any place within a metropolitan area that is not a central city" (Oliver, 2003). This means that suburbs can be very diverse in population, economic class, and density. Suburbs develop around central cities, generally as rising land prices and population density in central cities push affordable living places outside the central city's boundaries. Suburbs generally begin, therefore, as residential communities, but some grow in size and diversity to become central cities themselves. In general, however, suburbs develop in places where residents have access to transportation in and out of the central city, where they are employed, and the surrounding areas. Car ownership or the availability of public transportation (buses or trains) can facilitate the development of suburbs.

If a suburb develops outside of a city's political jurisdiction, then a new political jurisdiction is usually created. This means that the suburb becomes an independent city in its own right, with its own rules, administrative offices, and political representation. In the United States, the politics of suburbs usually differ substantially from those of the central city, but their politics may also differ from those of other suburbs. Therefore, it is not possible to make general statements about the nature of suburban politics or administration. Suburbs can be very different from one to the next, and it is this diversity that makes their development a challenge for urban administrators.

Pseudo-urbanization

Pseudo-urbanization is the condition in which a large city has formed in an area without a functional infrastructure to support it. As the population of an urbanized area grows, the city's infrastructure must grow with it, or else shortages will develop, typically in housing, education, transportation, clean water and waste removal services, or other services such as law enforcement. Overpopulation in urban areas is often characterized by shanty towns, where such services are inadequate or wholly absent. A city in which significant growth in the absence of adequate infrastructure has taken place will be deemed "pseudo-urbanized".

Urbanization in the third world tends to consist primarily of pseudo-urbanization. This happens largely because of so-called "rural push" factors which push people from the countryside into the cities, without the city being prepared to accept them. Rural-urban migrants in the third world usually move into the cities due to poverty-related factors, as noted by Dogan and Kasarda:

Declining mortality rates in rural areas of most developing nations have not been matched with corresponding fertility declines. The resulting increase of population cannot be sustained by stagnating rural economics, which leads to growing demographic-employment opportunity imbalances in the countryside. Migration becomes the only mechanism to relieve this imbalance. (Dogan and Kasarda, 1988: 19).

This leads to a demographic explosion and a progressive concentration of poor migrants in the cities. Since one city can only hold so many people due to limited infrastructure and available resources, the additional pressures placed upon city services that are already overly burdened can lead to unhealthy living conditions, populations that are vulnerable to the spread of disease, crime, and natural disasters, such as seasonal flooding, or in earthquake-prone regions, the collapse of housing and infrastructure (Quarantelli, 2003).

These kinds of problems highlight the need for planning in anticipation of such push factors. For developing nations where public resources are scarce, such planning is often considered a luxury. But the costs associated with no planning can be very high. The next section will look at the criticism of urbanization that has grown along with these problems, and the rise of planned cities in many forms.

Questions

1. What characteristics are associated with urbanization?
2. How has urbanization affected overall living standards worldwide?
3. What is the relationship between urbanization and industrialization?

4. What are some of the "push" and "pull" factors that structure migration to cities?

5. What are some of the problems associated with urbanization?

6. What are some methods for addressing the problems of urbanization?

Key Terms

agrarian societies

dirt theory

megalopolis

poly-centric

pseudo-urbanization

pull factors

push factors

suburbanization

urban sprawl

References

[1] Anselin, Luc (2010). "Thirty Years of Spatial Econometrics". *Papers in Regional Science*, 89 (1): 3 – 25.

[2] Batten, D. F. (1995). "Network Cities: Creative Urban Agglomerations for the 21st Century". *Urban Studies*, 32: 313 – 327.

[3] Berry, Brian J. L. (ed) (1976). "*Urbanization and Counter-urbanization.* Beverly Hills, CA: Sage.

[4] Dogan, Mattei and Kasarda, John (1988) eds. *The Metropolis Era: Megacities.* Beverly Hills, CA: Sage.

[5] Kendall, Diana (1994). *The New Urban Sociology.* New York: McGraw-Hill.

[6] United Nations (2006). *World Urbanization Prospects: The* 2005 *Revision Paper No. ESA/P/WP/* 200. Population Division, Department of Economic and Social Affairs.

第3章　国内外市政体制

3.1　概　　况

城市政府采取多种形式影响和塑造公共管理。谁在地方政府任职是政治问题。例如，在韩国实行地方自治之前，地方官员是由中央政府任命的，尽管市长和议员现在不是任命制了。然而，无论是任命还是选举，本章的主要问题是塑造地方行政制度的管理框架。本章还讨论了城市治理的主题，以及政府应如何构建以实现创新和高绩效。虽然政府和官僚机构的传统结构很容易在组织结构图上体现出来，但这一趋势正在从政府转向治理，表现出快速灵活的形式，允许管理适应高度竞争和不断变化的环境，要求创新、效率、回应能力，以及公民满意度，以完成新时代政府的职能。本章包括与政府体制相关的问题——公民参与和公民在地方管理中发挥作用的讨论，社会资本在地方政府中的作用，以及城市背景下分权的政府。

3.2　国外市政体制类型

本节讨论了议会市长制和市长议会制的主要形式以及一些其他形式，包括议会经理制，这是美国最常见的形式之一（Lorch，2000）。本节还考虑了两种不太常见的形式——市委员会制和城镇（市民）大（议）会，这两种形式在美国部分地方存在，但在其他地方很少或根本不存在，但代表着地方政府中的少数群体。市委员会制在美国中西部和西部农村地区最为常见，城镇会议只限于东北部。

3.2.1　市长议会制

地方政府的市长议会制是美国大城市中最常见的形式（Ahn，2005）。这种形式的结构是行政部门（市长）和立法部门（市议会）之间的权力分离和制衡制度，分权意味着市长和市议会有不同的职责，议会制定法律，表达选民的意愿，而市长执行法律，履行选民的意愿，制约是对政府部门权力的限制。市长通常负责编制预算，但由议会审查并通过预算。市长通常任命市政府各部门的负责人，但这些任命必须得到议会的批准。

在这种体制下，议会在讨论地方问题和通过地方法令时履行立法职能，市长履行行政职能，负责有效执行法律以及规章制度，提供地方领导，并监督地方行政。然而，市长在这些角色中的实际独立程度和参与程度的差异很大。市长议会制有两种模式，强市长制和弱市长制。顾名思义，强市长制在行政领域发挥着更广泛的作用，而弱市长制的作用更为有限，尤其是与议会相比。

强市长制是美国采用的形式，在这里的市长议会制下，市长拥有更广泛的权力。议会负责立法职能，但是立法部门的作用相对有限，他们对行政权力的制约更加有限。市长"强大"的关键力量在于否决权制度，市长有权否决议会通过的法令。这种模式的目的是防止政府分裂，并提供更有效和更果断的行政行动。另外，市长对地方政府的管理具有直接权力，除了象征性和一般性的领导职能外，市长还任命地方政府机构和部门的负责人，就像总统任命部门和部委的负责人一样。城市管理对选民的责任由市长承担，市长最终负责所有城市管理。市长在制定和执行地方议程方面具有强大的政治和行政影响力。

城市越大，市长就越有可能雇用更多对市长办公室负责的行政人员。市长还可以聘请一名城市经理协助完成复杂的行政工作，使市长能够更多地关注政治和担任更广泛的决策角色，行政人员对市长负责，韩国城市市长由中央政府提供两名助理或副市长担任这一角色，一位是由市长任命的副市长，另一位是中央政府任命的行政副市长。尽管行政副市长对中央政府负责，但由于与市长合作困难，副市长的职业生涯又不会通过频繁的职位变动而得到提升，因此该职位具有与市长密切合作的强烈动机。图 3.1 为强市长制。

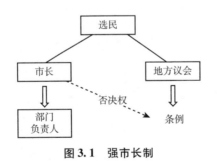

图 3.1　强市长制

例如，首尔著名的市长与议会之战中，反对议会藐视市长，带来福利政策的冲突，导致吴世勋市长下台。与此相反，韩国大多数地方议会都非常尊重当地的行政人员，即使大多数地方议会和市长来自不同的党派（Ahn，2005）。对此的解释包括地方行政部门的强势地位、儒家道德中领导角色的重要性、公众缺乏参与的兴趣，以及缺乏强有力的立法人员等资源来对抗地方官僚机构对市长的权力。

3.2.2　议会市长制（弱市长制）

在美国，这与早期美国人对行政权力集中的不信任有关，这是许多美国人特别关注

的问题，因为英国国王领导下的行政权力集中引发了美国革命（Karlen，1975；Lorch，
2000）。在美国历史早期，弱市长制形式更为常见，它可能最适合不需要特别大或复杂
管理的相对较小的城镇。在这种市政体制下，预算控制和官僚机构被分割，市长的作用
要弱得多。虽仍然存在着制衡和分权，但行政权力受到更多限制，议会的权力更加突
出，对行政权力的制约也更多，此外，对行政权力的一个关键限制是缺乏市长否决权。
议会负责制定选民的意愿，但市长和议会共同负责执行选民的意愿。

　　市长主持议会，但不直接领导对议会负责的官僚机构或预算，这将政策制定和预算
编制的官僚角色划分为几个部分。例如，在强有力的市长制度下，市长办公室的责任由
个别议会成员和市长，或市长和整个议会负责。因此，如果一个人不承担责任，就要承
担更广泛群体的共同责任。图 3.2 所示为弱市长制。

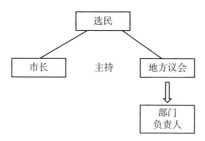

图 3.2　弱市长制

　　这一制度有效地解决了行政权力集中的问题，它旨在解决和管理更广泛的行政参与
问题，然而，这使得控制政府服务更加困难。随着服务和策略实施的权力分散，不同服
务间的协调变得困难，或者至少更成问题，即阻碍了投票公众对地方政府服务的质量、
效率和有效性的问责制，当出现问题时，可能会出现对由谁负责的问题的争议。

　　如果不是技术或行政问题，可能会涉及更多的政治问题，因为更多的服务更直接地
由政治行动者控制，这让管理者有动力提供优质服务，毕竟这会帮助他们推进自己的政
治生涯。它还为选民提供了一条非常直接的途径，让他们与当地决策者交流意见。另
外，这一制度可能会给政客们提供不正当的动机，让他们相互拒绝对方的资源。在政治
分区的情况下，行政资源也可能不太倾向于根据需要分配，而更倾向于支持由更强大或
更受尊敬的地方官员控制的部门。这一制度的优势随着较小的行政管辖区而得到放大，
在行政管辖区内，当选人员可以取代对专业人员的需要，并可以以选民容易理解的方
式，对其决定的成败承担个人责任。但是，在更大或更复杂的管辖范围内，其弱点会被
放大，尽管这可能会被聘用的行政人员的素质部分抵消。

3.2.3　议会经理制

　　议会经理制是一种试图将政府管理从政府政治中移除的制度。这与美国 20 世纪早
期伍德罗·威尔逊、伦纳德·怀特以及公共行政学者和实践者提出的政治与行政二分法
的观点相类似。市长和市议会组成地方政府的政治部门，并聘请一名专业的管理人员，

通过执行地方政策或监督地方政府来接管城市管理。与弱市长制一样，议会经理制也与美国的问题有关，其兴起与19世纪末20世纪初进步运动提出的问题特别相关，议会经理制旨在使地方政府非政治化和专业化。

一方面，著名的政治机器控制着许多大城市的市政府，并以腐败闻名，许多是由新近移民投票支持的，这些移民被本地中产阶级改革者所憎恨。此外，许多较小的城市已经被民粹主义者和社会党等少数激进党派所接管，当时民主党派和共和党派分裂严重，这促使改革者质疑地方政府的中立性和专业性，因为地方政府是由不熟悉的党派以不熟悉的方式治理的。另一方面，随着工业化和城市化进程的加快，技术和社会发展也不断加快，地方政府的职能变得更加复杂。城市人口规模的爆炸性增长进一步给城市政府带来了新的复杂性。除了增加城市官僚机构的规模外，地方政府的理事会管理机构还试图通过雇用专业管理人员监督城市管理来提高城市管理的技术能力。

城市经理由市议会雇用或任命，他们具有特殊的专业管理知识。最初，管理者往往是工程师（随着科学管理运动的盛行）或业务经理。目前，除了私人或公共机构的管理经验外，大多数城市管理者还拥有工商管理硕士（MBA）或公共管理硕士（MPA）学位。图3.3所示为议会经理制。

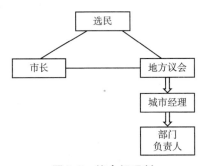

图3.3　议会经理制

如果市长在行使地方政府的行政职能时通常控制行政管理，那么城市经理将接管这一角色——城市经理编制预算——这通常是市长的职责。此外，城市经理直接或通过监督部门主管监督城市正式员工的正常运营，并监督人事决策。城市经理就运营事宜向市议会提出建议，并根据需要或要求出席议会和其他公开会议。最后，城市经理还可以发挥公共领导作用，在由公众或外部团体和组织（如潜在商业投资者或州政府和国家政府）代表城市时，可以加强市长的公共领导作用。

实际上，议会经理制在较小的城市中最为常见。在强有力的市长制度下，美国较大的城市通常是市长办公室扮演同样的政治和行政角色，市长负责监督大型专业行政管理，但大部分时间用于政治和公共领导问题。

3.2.4　城市委员会（议会委员会制）

城市委员会是一种相当独特的形式，它将政府的行政和立法职能结合在一个单独的机构中，即委员会。委员会形式过去在城市中更为常见，原因与议会经理制相同，现在城市委员会很大程度上被议会经理制取代了，尽管在一些州，特别是在农村地区，城市委员会形式仍在继续。

　　城市委员会由地区或全体选举产生，该委员会的作用与市议会相同，负责该市的立法职能，如通过法令和制定税率。作为一个集体机构，该委员会还担任行政主管，负责政治领导和行政职能，行政职责由不同的专员对不同部门的职责进行划分，可以是固定的或轮换的。尽管在小的司法管辖区，委员会可以集体负责行政，其中一名委员可能被选为委员会名义上的负责人，但该职位通常除了主持会议之外没有其他作用，因此，即使这个职位被称为主席或市长，也主要是一个礼仪职位。就一般行政职责而言，委员会是代替市长的行政机构。图 3.4 所示为城市委员会。

图 3.4　城市委员会

3.2.5　城镇大会（乡镇议会）

　　美国历史早期，东北部新英格兰地区有许多地方人口稀少，不涉及常设政府，甚至不涉及民选官员，而是通过一种称为城镇会议的直接民主形式进行管理。这些社区的公民聚集在一起，直接就政策和立法进行投票（Karlen，1975，Lorch，2000）。这符合亚历克西斯·德·托克维尔（1835）时期平等和参与性民间社会组织兴起的传统，当时德·托克威尔来到美国，见证了广大中产阶级的崛起，他们以积极的方式加入组织并参与民主社会活动。

　　这种形式在美国新英格兰的几个州延续至今，目前，以不同的形式存在。例如，市镇会议可以广泛地直接立法并规定执行某些职能，它可以立法并选择一个董事会作为行政部门或会议之间的管理者，可以是一个为更专业和为有限的目的而召开会议的机构，如决定特殊问题或修改市镇章程（相当于本地宪法）。

3.3　城市治理的概念内涵

3.3.1　定义

　　广义上的治理并不是新概念，尽管近年来它变得更加普遍，也有了新的含义，所以它对不同的人意味着不同的含义。因此，这一概念的含义取决于治理水平、遵循的目标和采取的方法。长期以来，这个概念指的是管理政府或其他组织的一般任务，新的治理形式使各个政府和组织能够贡献自己的力量和才能，履行职责，保持和加强组织和机构的独特性（Koliba，Meek and Zia，2011）。

治理是一个比政府更广泛的概念。政府的主要组成部分包括宪法、重要法律和政府的正式组成部分。治理涉及这些正式机构与民间社会组织之间的互动，治理是指社会要素行使权力、权威和影响力的过程，是公共和私人组织制定有关公共生活以及经济和社会发展的政策和决定的过程。治理包括国家，但通过将私营部门和民间组织纳入这一进程，治理超越了国家。政府的作用是创造一个鼓励创新和绩效的政治和法律环境，私营部门应该创造就业机会并提供收入，而民间组织促进政治和社会互动，动员团体参与经济、社会和政治活动。治理的重要目标之一是促进三个行动者之间的所有有效和建设性互动，因为每个部门都有自己的优缺点，其他部门可以从互动中受益并实现互补。

3.3.2　治理的维度

治理没有必然的规范内涵，然而在某种情况下评估治理的典型标准可能包括合法性、代表性、公众问责制和公共事务执行效率的程度，治理是公共领导的艺术，公共部门借此协调社会所有部门以实现有效绩效。治理的三个不同维度包括：政治制度的形式，在管理城市经济和社会资源方面行使权力的过程，政府设计、制定、实施政策及履行职能的能力（Koliba，Meek and Zia，2011）。

构成善政的标准也是从这三个方面得出的。它们包括合法性、问责制、能力和对基本权利的尊重。政府的合法性意味着行使民主的程度以及被统治者的同意和参与程度。问责制是指政府和官方部门的反应能力，包括媒体自由、透明决策以及正式和非正式问责机制等要素。城市政府的能力是其制定政策和提供服务的效率和有效性。尊重人权和法治包括个人和群体权利、公共安全、经济和社会活动框架，以及民众参与制度的形式和状态。

3.3.3　治理的特征

治理的特征是参与、透明度、法治、回应性、共识、公平、有效性、效率、问责制和战略愿景（奥斯本和盖布勒，1993）。参与是公民和居民在决策过程中其呼声的表达，只要是合法的，无论是直接参与还是通过议会和理事会等中间代表机构，这需要言论和结社自由，以及以具体和建设性方式参与的实际能力。法治是对法律制度公平和公正的要求，在执行基本权利方面尤其重要。透明度和公开性规定了信息自由和信息自由流动，意味着最关切的人可以直接获得城市政府和治理进程和机构以及理解、解释和监测这些进程和机构所需的信息。回应性意味着治理过程和机构试图以代表性的方式为每个受影响的人服务，尽可能公正地平衡相互间竞争的利益。共识是推迟决策和执行的过程，直至实现城市的最佳利益，特别是达成广泛甚至压倒性的协议的总体目标，可能还包括可行的政策和程序。

公正是对公平和平等待遇的关注，这样城市里的每个人都有机会遵守可识别的规则，并能够维护或改善自己的福祉。效率是相对于所产生的结果，尽量减少资源使用的要求。有效性是要求产生结果，并根据结果对方案、过程和机构进行评估。问责制意味着决策者必须对公众负责，而不仅仅是对机构利益相关者负责。具体情况不同，这取决于任何特定决策的内部和外部性质及影响。最后一个特点，即战略愿景，要求领导人和公众采取与治理相关的长远观点，将个人和社会发展纳入城市环境，这样的愿景需要考虑城市中独特的文化、社会和历史因素，而不仅仅是影响城市的更广泛的力量。

3.3.4　走向善治

善治具有透明度和问责制的要素，也是参与性的。如上所述，它还遵循了行政的基本管理目的，即有效、公平和高效，努力促进法治。善治应致力于促进上述共识，将所有部门（或绝大多数）达成共识的不同政治、社会和经济优先事项汇集在一起，关键是要确保弱势的人或群体在分配和其他重要决策中拥有充分的发言权。城市社会价值观和实践应该鼓励并赋予公民和居民权力，让他们更多地实现自己在城市中的利益诉求。这些是善治的条件，这种发展是在尊重所有人基本权利的前提下进行的。

任何一个城市，无论多么一致，都是极其多样化的，因此，如果不努力达成共识，就无法从长远来改善大多数人生活的城市，协作和集体行动对善治至关重要，善治要求个人和机构，无论是公共部门、私营部门还是第三部门，共同努力实现共同利益和共同目标，善治本身就是协调不同的利益冲突以成功解决冲突的过程。正式机构和政府制度是必要的，非正式协议和安排也是如此，需要不同的人、团体、利益集团和机构聚集在一起以实现共同利益。

城市管理的质量往往是决定一个城市或城市地区发展和进步的重要因素，民主政府形式可能会有所帮助，但无论正式安排如何，只有积极的公民参与才能真正提供并保持良好的治理。在公共部门，服务质量是一个关键问题，开放性和回应性对于提供创新和创造力非常重要，这些创新和创造力可以提供解决城市问题的新思路，并以回应和知情的方式满足公民的需求，以积极的方式寻求更好的表现，而不是被动地接受他们的命运。

善治的要素指标构成

被治理者接受的民主理念以及管理理念构成了治理背景下问责制的基础，可以通过使用既定标准来实现，通过估计城市或市政当局的经济和财政状况来考察城市官员的问责制和绩效。这些标准可能包括效率、公民参与、与选民的有效沟通、分散的规划和规划的实施、城市金融交易的规律性、严格遵守法律和行政程序和政策，以及使用标准化方法定期评估城市经济绩效（Koliba，Meek and Zia，2011）。

回应是一种特殊类型的问责制，公民认为政府领导人和其他参与治理的公众人物和机构会倾听并回答他们的问题。回应性指标包括确定公众愿望和需求的制度、公民参与规划和实施规划的制度、评估有关是否实现了既定目标的政策有效性的制度、对公众建议和意见采取公平和迅速的行动以及信息的公共可用性，让人们可以向城市政府提供知情反馈。

管理创新包括在地方政府公共管理中成功实施的促进地方治理的改革。指标包括制定措施方面的创新、处理城市问题的创新概念和做法、改进的官僚结构和程序、满足公众需求的创新和创造性手段，以及使用全面质量管理和信息技术等新的管理技术。

公私伙伴关系是地方政府和私营部门之间积极的合作安排。指标包括鼓励私营部门参与发展的激励计划、商业部门提高地方官僚机构效率的举措、公共和私营部门共同参与规划、资助和实施方案/项目，以及酌情私有化或外包地方政府服务。

公民与政府之间的互动表明政府、非政府组织和整个社区之间的公开沟通。指标可能包括地方政府和非政府组织之间的合作努力，地方政府和选民之间就各种地方问题进行协商，以及公民/非政府组织/非营利组织与地方政府合作的实施。

分权管理涉及当地管理层界定和授权责任以及确保准确报告和监测的能力。指标可以是明确的授权指导方针、涵盖授权任务执行情况的反馈系统、官员就授权任务作出的决定以及组织层级结构与实际授权任务之间的一致性。

联网是城市政府与其他地方政府和实体建立合作关系以建设基础设施建设能力的地方。指标包括市政府网络、区域（地方内）网络、国际网络、网络中的补充资源、技术交流与合作、共同利益和议程以及专门知识交流和培训。

人力资源开发建议持续实施一项计划——以招聘、培训、激励和发展当地劳动力，使其成为更高效、专注和有效的公共服务人员。指标涵盖旨在改善人力资源管理各个方面的政策——基于业绩和能力的充分且持续的招聘和甄选方案，提高地方政府工作人员能力的培训方案，可行的和快速的人员分工，以及同工同酬的薪酬制度。

这些要素在地方治理结构中的社会等级与在地区或国家政府一级有所不同。事实上，由于重塑政府的概念在很大程度上是从地方一级政府的改革和创新中得来的，可以说，这种形式的治理理念可能最适用于城市治理。当然，由于规模相对较小，参与人数较少，因此，有可能在此背景下建立公民参与制度更有意义。还应指出，治理的理念与任何特定的治理结构无关，但与上面提到的任何或所有结构相兼容。

3.4　城市治理的功能

政府履行两类一般职能（班菲尔德和威尔逊，1963）：第一类是公共产品和服务的供应。城市地方政府履行多种服务职能，如垃圾回收、提供警察和消防、维护街道和其他城市基础设施等，这些类型的服务将在下一章中介绍。第二类职能是通过政治和其他制度管理解决相互竞争的利益，这涉及解决城市中有关政府绩效、回应能力和代表性的争议，尤其是与服务职能相关的争议。

几乎政府所做的任何事情都可能引发某种冲突。人事决定常常导致城市政府和群体之间的纠纷，群体觉得自己没有得到公平的工作分配，或者与其他群体相比没有被公平考虑。为资助和支持不同级别的政府服务而征收的税收是另一个经常发生冲突的根源，特别是在税收或服务发生变化的时候。即使是一些普通的问题，比如，哪条街道应该首先得到维护、公交服务的频率和时间，以及图书馆和公园等新基础设施的位置选择，也可能引发不同城市群体之间的冲突。这些冲突都必须得到解决，否则不断恶化的冲突可能会爆发更严重的争端，甚至暴力，这两项功能同时执行（班菲尔德和威尔逊，1963），即服务和冲突管理同时进行。无论何时作出决定，政府和非政府行动者都应作出回应，政府行动者通常会通过法律或政策作出回应，尽管他们也可能根据决策如何影响该政策领域提供反馈或回应。另外，非政府行为者将根据认为决定将如何影响他们及所在群体而作出反应。当对城市政府决策有不同的反应时，就会产生冲突，从而需要冲突管理功能。决策者可以直接和立即参与这一过程，根据反馈修改计划，大部分职能由市政府和议会履行，这些官员拥有批准、资助和执行有争议的决定的最终权力。

3.5　关于城市治理的讨论

本章重点介绍了地方政府的市政体制，这些制度构成了决定地方政策和地方利益争夺权力的游戏场。最后一节将讨论与地方政府市政体制有关的一些令人感兴趣的问题。

本节讨论的第一个问题是公民参与问题。考虑到当代所有市政制度至少都涉及某种形式的代议制政府，那么公民在地方政府中发挥的直接作用是什么？社会资本、社交网络和网络之间的联系在地方公共管理中扮演什么角色？故本节讨论的最后一个问题是分权的政府。在美国政治体制下，地方行政机构和地方议会可能由不同的政党控制，这是如何发生的，为什么会发生，对城市管理又意味着什么？

3.5.1　公民参与

除了本章前面提到的少见的城镇会议形式外，本章中的所有地方市政体制都是代表性的制度，代表权和直接参与之间持续存在着紧张关系。韩国 1948 年《宪法》没有要求建立民主制度，而是要求建立共和国。从日本独立后的这段时期，一直保持着威权制度的连续性，直到 20 世纪 80 年代末和 90 年代初的民主运动迫使其进行变革，代表制在很长一段时间内都不民主（Ahn，2005）。

同样，美国宪法的制定者也并不认为它是一个民主文件，仅是一个代表性规则体系，他们倾向于认为民主类似于暴徒统治（Possiter，2003）。在美利坚共和国成立时，"多数统治"由拥有财产的成年白人男性公民选出的代表组成分权统治，并将大多数人排除在外，这一制度只是逐渐扩大到包括现在获准参与民主进程的所有团体。

公民参与的重要性

只要存在民主制度，民主进程的一部分，公民参与至少在理论上就是可取的。因此，无论是通过一般的城市政治进程，还是作为社区发展进程的一部分，还是作为参与城市服务的手段，公民参与都应该在城市管理中发挥重要作用。《明镜周刊》（德国）将公民参与称为"将项目与人联系起来的过程。这样，公民就有了额外的机会可以朝着公众问责的方向微调行政程序"。

布里奇斯（Bridges）明确指出了公民积极参与地方社区事务的五个好处。第一，公民可以通过个人和集体行动作出他们想要的改变。第二，公民可以了解这一过程以及如何在民主社会中进行变革。第三，公民了解他们的社区以及社区中所有不同群体的需求和利益。第四，公民学习如何解决利益冲突，以利于实现公众福利。第五，公民了解社区中的群体和个人行为。除了由此产生的积极变化外，公民和居民通过参与的过程获得了作为公民的权利。

在基本层面上，公民通过遵守法律和纳税来参与的程度最低，但参与的程度更深，特别是参与通常是指超出公民参与最低限度的自愿参与方式。阿恩斯坦建立了公民参与项目开发的途径，从不参与到象征性参与，到合作项目开发、规划合作、授权，最终到公民控制和对社区项目的完全所有权。

公民参与社区事务也是对政治权力的制约，它可以让政治和经济精英对人民负责，让人民更全面地享受民主社会的利益，更多的公民参与可以通过提供更多的信息来源和官员可能不具备的专业知识来改善决策过程。来自不同背景的公民的存在可能会限制政治庇护、裙带关系和选民不认可的利益交易。腐败可能在公众视线之外的地方滋生，但公民参与可以成为防止或揭露腐败的聚光灯，也减少了公众与任命和选举官员之间的隔阂，并改进了代表程序，以减少作出自利决定的可能性。

传统的公民参与途径（方法）

西门森和罗宾斯（Simonsen and Robbins，2000）认为，公民参与是政治与行政、专业知识与准入、代表权与参与之间张力的中心。威尔逊和怀特认为，政治和行政是两分的，政治是为了表达选民的意愿，而行政是服务这种意愿的表达。这一概念虽然不具有排他性，但与通过调查和电子治理等方法让公民参与行政管理的努力形成鲜明对比。

专业知识和获取途径是专业人员和训练有素的专家与公民之间的分界线，怀特（2004）对现代行政的复杂性与美国公民通过社会合作参与历史的讨论概括了这一分界线。现代政府在多大程度上是一个需要专业公务员作出独立决策的技术问题，这些专业公务员在多大范围内不受公众影响？公民如何直接或通过其代表了解政府的内部工作？公务员如何对当选官员和人民作出回应，在决策过程中仍然不受政治的影响？代表与参与是现代代议制政府的核心张力，公民在多大程度上会坐视不管，如何让他们选出的代表作出决定，又在多大范围内可以提供指导并直接表达意见，进而游说自己的偏好？

西门森和罗宾斯（Simonsen and Robbins，2000）确定了政府资助（自上而下）和基层（自下而上）的参与方法。他们为每种类型确定了最有效的问题、管辖权和利益级别。政府支持的参与对于影响整个司法管辖区的问题最为有效，在这些问题上，司法管辖区范围内的接受是重要的，并且存在高度的社区分歧或低水平的公共利益。基层参与在影响同质或当地的群体内最有效，在这些群体中，邻里接受度很重要，社区分歧程度低或兴趣程度高也很重要。他们以公众听证会和咨询委员会（政府赞助）、公民机构或社区行动计划（政府赞助的促进基层式参与）作为参与的方式。

佐恩和安（Sohn and Ahn，2005）讨论了自韩国实施地方自治以来所采用的几种方法，它们分别是直接参与和间接参与、个人参与和集体参与、动员公民主导或合作参与、机构参与和非机构参与。他们确定的制度形式包括披露行政信息、委员会和邻里会议、公开听证会、上诉、公民咨询、请愿、检查要求（公民可以要求行政部门对不公平或不公正待遇进行直接调查）、地方公民投票和社区中心，非机构形式包括地方民间团体和公民运动。他们的结论是，需要大力推行机构参与，因为机构参与没有得到充分利用，而非体制形式却很常见，似乎反映了地方政府未能在地方管理中充分反映公民的意见。

线上公民参与的方法

科格利安（Coglianese，2004）指出，许多人预测互联网将带来更多的公民参与，因为技术进步使公民更容易向当选官员表达自己的意见。最近的这些变化也使得新的管理方法更为可能，让公民和居民更容易参与地方治理进程。公民有新的方式与当选或任命的官员交流和互动，也有新的手段来监督和追究政府的责任。

电子政务的概念涵盖这一领域。根据雷利亚（Relyea，2002）的说法，电子政务最初用于指政府应用不同信息通信技术的融合，这也意味着当前的 IT 应用于政府管理，以及更有效和成本更低的政府职能的应用。库克等（Cook et al.，2002）将电子政务定义为利用信息技术支持政府运营、提供政府服务和吸引公民参与。电子服务是通过互联网和其他电子手段以电子方式交付信息和服务，电子管理是利用信息技术改进政府管理，电子民主是利用电子通信来加强公民参与。雷利亚认为，电子政务仍然是一个动态的概念，其核心是利用技术更好地为公民服务，实现民主制度。

莱恩和李（Layne and Lee，2001）制定了电子政务的四阶段流程。第一阶段是编目，即为政府建立在线存在的过程，在线呈现政府信息和可下载的表格。第二阶段是交易，政府开始将内部政府系统连接到在线接口，允许公民直接与政府在线交易（更新许可证、纳税等）。第三阶段是纵向一体化，地方和中央政府层面的类似政府实体相互联系并进行职能合并。第四阶段是横向整合，将同级机构联系起来，让公民在与政府打交道时有一个地方可以满足他们的所有需求（如一个连接所有城市政府机构的单一网站）。莱恩和李建议，由于不同级别的类似部门所共有的共性比同一级别的不同职能所面临的要大，因此，应首先考虑垂直性的职能关联。

参与的电子政务系统包括在线社交网络系统（SNS）。社交网络可以复制离线参与方式，可以进行在线请愿、在线获取信息、在线呼吁等，然而在线参与的主要领域一直停留在在线讨论和在线组织。从韩国反自由贸易协定运动，到中东的阿拉伯之春民主运动，再到美国的占领华尔街运动，近年世界各地的运动很多都通过在线组织得到了推动。

电子参与和在线社交网络有一些局限性。一方面是有机会利用新技术的人与受教育者之间的数字鸿沟，穷人可能难以负担 IT 费用，而老年人在使用新技术方面可能会遇到问题。另一方面是互联网上信息的不可靠性，特别是与传播的容易程度相比，在线交流尤其容易受到难以发现的谣言的影响，因为如果线下广播和出版物传播错误信息，责任很容易被追究，但发布没有经过仔细审查的信息的网站现实中可能与符合更严格新闻或学术标准的网站声誉一样良好。

3.5.2 社会资本

资本是用于投资的资金，人力资本是投资于人们的知识、技能和能力使他们能够用自己的劳动生产更多的东西。社会资本是社会网络、社区和组织中持有的价值，虽然它通常强调社会关系、合作和社区带来的好处，但它是一个具有不同定义的通用术语，在社会科学中有很大差异，它可能包括将一个群体联系在一起的社会资本或将不同群体联系在一起并提供信息的社会资本（或者弱联系）。

普特南（Putnam，2000）注意到美国社会资本在下降时，将其下降与各种社会问题联系起来，并对其所带来的后果发出警告。他的定义包括通过共同利益解决问题，因此，社会资本的下降会让问题的解决更加困难。涉及社会资本下降的问题包括选民投票率的下降、会议出席率的下降以及对政府的信任度下降等。从这个角度来看，社会资本低可能构成公民参与的障碍。

公民组织、志愿协会和其他非市场、非政府组织在鼓励公民参与行政和政治事务方面发挥着重要作用，公民社会是健康民主的重要组成部分。我国有许多积极参与政治和社会的非政府组织和公民组织，许多人在地方一级这样做，试图向地方政府施加压力，并与之谈判，以实现其目标。佐恩和安（Sohn and Ahn，2005）指出，公民团体的参与是更多参与地方政府的趋势的一部分。

3.5.3 分权政府

分权政府是指不同政党控制不同政府部门的情况。2010 年，首尔地方选举后的情况就是这样，大国家党的吴世勋赢得了连任，但反对派赢得了市议会的多数席位。在某些地方政府体制下，政府不可能实行分而治之。韩国的市长委员会制度允许市长或其他地方行政人员获得多数支持，即使他们的政党在地方委员会中可能并不占多数，在多党制下尤其可能出现这种情况，在大多数地区，三个或三个以上的政党可能会定期进行投票。

这可能会导致僵局，党派竞争对手间可能不愿意妥协，这阻碍了选民们通常希望其政党代表能够采取强有力的行动。因此，分权政府使变革更加困难，因为他们更愿意维持现状，毕竟分权是美国宪法的意图，尽管这可能会让想要采取行动的选民感到沮丧。分权的意义在于引导人民在民主方面达到不同的目的，以便集中执法权力，同时分散制定法律的权力，这是一种检查选民中不明智的一时冲动的方法，这种冲动几乎是普遍存在的。从这个意义上说，分权政府仅仅代表了当公众舆论存在分歧时所设计的制度的运作。

分权政府也可能鼓励对无法强制执行其意愿的当选官员进行妥协，这会增加达成广泛共识的机会，大多数公民更愿意接受这种共识，而不是主要选民不接受的狭隘治理。至少这会降低信任，也可能使政策更难实施，效率更低，因为公民需要其发挥作用，而不是反对并试图挫败他们所反对的政策。

【思考题】

1. 地方自治实现的障碍是什么？
2. 市长议会制和市长议会制的利弊是什么？
3. 善治的主要特征是什么？
4. 为什么公民参与在城市管理中很重要？
5. 是什么促成了社会资本的形成？它扮演着什么角色？
6. 社交网络对城市政策有何影响？

【关键术语】

制约与平衡	电子政务
城市经理	善治
委员会	市长议会制
数字鸿沟	社会资本
分权政府	否决权

参考文献

［1］Ahn, Chung-si, (ed) (2005). *New Development in Local Democracy and Decentralization in East Asia.* Seoul：Seoul National University Press.

［2］Coglianese, Cary (2004). "E-Rulemaking：Information Technology and the Regulatory Process", *Administrative Law Review* 56.

［3］Goodnow, Frank (2004). "Politics and Administration", pp. 35-37 in Shafritz, Jay; Hyde, Albert; and Parkes, Sandra (eds) *Classics of Public Administration*, 5th ed. Belmont, CA：Wadsworth.

［4］Harrigan, John J., and Vogel, Ronald K. (2002). *Political Change in the Metropolis*, 7th ed. Upper Saddle River, NJ：Longman.

［5］Ketcham, Ralph (ed) (2003). *The Anti-Federalist Papers and the Constitutional Convention Debates.* Signet Classic；New York.

［6］Koliba, Christopher, Meek, Jack W. and Zia, Asim. (2011). *Governance Networks in Public Administration and Public Policy.* Boca Raton, FL：CRC Press.

［7］Layne, Karen, and Lee, Jungwoo (2001). "Developing Fully Functional E-government：A Four Stage Model", *Government Information Quarterly*, Vol. 18, No. 2, pp. 122 – 136.

［8］Lorch, Robert S. (2000). *State and Local Politics：The Great Entanglement* 6th Edition. Upper Saddle River, NJ：Prentcie-Hall.

［9］ Putnam, Robert （2000）. *Bowling Alone: The Collapse and Revival of American Community*. New York: Simon and Schuster.

［10］ Relyea, Harold （2002）. "E-Gov: Introduction and Overview", *Government Information Quarterly*, Vol. 19, No. 1, pp. 9 – 35.

［11］ Rossiter, Clinton （ed） （2003）. *The Federalist Papers*, Signet Classic: New York.

［12］ Simonsen, William, and Robbins, Mark D. （2000）. *Citizen Participation in Resource Allocation*. Boulder, CO: Westview Press.

［13］ White, Leonard （2004）. "Introduction to the Study of Public Administration", pp. 56 – 63 in Shafritz, Jay; Hyde, Albert; and Parkes, Sandra （eds） *Classics of Public Administration*, 5th ed. Belmont, CA: Wadsworth.

［14］ Wilson, Woodrow （2004）. "The Study of Administration", pp. 22 – 34 in Shafritz, Jay; Hyde, Albert; and Parkes, Sandra （eds） *Classics of Public Administration*, 5th ed. Belmont, CA: Wadsworth.

Chapter 3   Municipal Systems

3. 1   Overview

Urban government takes several forms that influence and shape administration. There are purely political issues of who serves in local government. Prior to local autonomy in Korea, for example, local officials were appointed by the central government, although mayors are not now. However, whether they are appointed or elected, the main issue of this chapter is the administrative framework that shapes the local administrative system. This Chapter also addresses the topic of urban governance and how government should be structured to deliver innovation and high performance. While government and the bureaucracy have had traditional structures that are easily captured on organizational charts, the trend has been shifting away from government and towards governance, representing rapid and flexible forms that allow for the adaptation of administration to a highly competitive and changing environment that demands innovation, efficiency, responsiveness, and citizen satisfaction to accomplish the old tasks of government for a new era. Finally, this chapter includes issues related to the government forms, including a discussion of citizen participation and the role citizens must play in local administration, the role of social capital in local government, and divided government in the urban context.

3. 2   Types of Foreign Municipal Forms

This section considers the main forms of council-mayor and mayor-council as well as a few other forms, including the city manager form, which is one of the most common in the United States (Lorch, 2000: 278). This section also considers two less common forms that are present in the US, but rare or non-existent elsewhere. These are the city commission and the town meeting, which do exist, but represent very small minorities of local governments. The city commission is most common in the Midwest and West in rural areas and the town meeting is almost exclusive to the Northeast.

3. 2. 1 Mayor-Council

The mayor-council form of local government is the most common form in the United States in large cities (Ahn, 2005). This form is structured with a system of separation of powers and checks and balances between the executive branch (the mayor) and the legislative branch (the council). Separation of powers means that the mayor and the council have different responsibilities. The council makes the law, expressing the will of the voters, whereas the mayor executes the law, carrying out the will of the voters. Checks are limitations on the power of a branch of government. The mayor is generally responsible for preparing the budget, but the council may review the budget and must approve it. The mayor generally appoints heads of the city departments, but the council must approve the appointments.

Under this model, the council carries out the legislative functions as it debates local issues and passes local ordinances. The mayor carries out the executive functions, implementing and enforcing ordinances, providing local leadership, and overseeing local administration. However, the actual level of independence and engagement the mayor has in these roles varies considerably. There are two versions of the model, the strong mayor and the weak mayor. As the names imply, the strong mayor plays a more expansive role within the executive realm, whereas the weak mayor is much more limited, particularly in comparison to the city council.

The strong mayor form is the form adopted by the United States. Under this version of the mayor-council form, the mayor assumes more expansive powers. The council is responsible for legislative functions while the role of the legislative branch is relatively limited and they have more limited checks over executive power. The key power that makes the mayor "strong" is the institution of the veto. The mayor has the power to veto ordinances passed by the council. The purpose of this model is to forestall government fragmentation and provide for more efficient and resolute executive action. On the other hand, the mayor has direct authority over administration of the local government. In addition to symbolic and general leadership functions, the mayor appoints the heads of local government agencies and departments much as the president appoints heads of departments and ministries. Accountability of urban administration to the voters goes through the mayor, who is ultimately responsible for all urban administration. The mayor has a strong political and administrative hand in setting the local agenda as well as in carrying it out.

The larger the city, the more likely a mayor will hire administrative staff personally accountable to the office of the mayor. The mayor may also hire a city manager to assist with the complicated job of administration, allowing the mayor to focus more on political and broader administrative policy roles. This kind of administrator is accountable to the mayor. The mayor of Korean cities has two assistant or vice mayors provided by the central government to assume this role. One is a vice mayor who is appointed by the mayor and the other is the administrative vice mayor appointed by the central government. Although the administrative vice mayor is responsible to the central government, the position carries strong incentives for working closely with the mayor as a vice mayor's career does not advance through frequent changes of post due to a difficulty in working with a mayor. Figure 3. 1 shows strong mayor-Council.

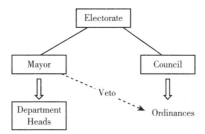

Figure 3. 1   Strong Mayor-Council

For example, in contrast to the famous mayor-council battles in Seoul, where an opposition the council was able to defy the mayor, resulting in the conflict over welfare policy that brought down Mayor Oh Sehoon, most local councils have been very deferent to the local executive in Korea, even where the council majority and the mayor come from different parties (Ahn, 2005). Explanations for this include the strong position of the local executive, the importance of the leadership role in Confucian ethics, the newness of local councils and lack of widespread interest or involvement with them, and the lack of resources like strong legislative staff to counter the power of the local bureaucracy accountable to the mayor.

3. 2. 2   Council-Mayor (Weak-Mayor)

In the United States, it is related to early American distrust of concentrated executive power, which was a particular concern of many Americans following the negative experience of concentrated executive power under the British King that spurred on the American Revolution (Karlen, 1975: 408; Lorch, 2000: 278). The weak mayor form was more common earlier in American history. It is probably most compatible with relatively small cities and towns that do not require particularly large or complicated administration. Under this form, control over the budget and bureaucracy are divided, with the mayor playing a much weaker role. There are still checks and balances and separation of powers, but the powers of the executive are more constrained, those of the council accentuated, with more checks on executive power. Furthermore, a key limitation to executive power is the lack of a mayoral veto. The council is responsible for enacting the will of the voters, but the mayor and the council share responsibility for carrying out the will of the voters.

The mayor presides over the council but not directly over the bureaucracy or the budget, which are responsible to the council. This divides bureaucratic roles of policy-making and budgeting into several parts such that individual council members and the mayor, or the mayor and the council as a whole are responsible for what would be the sole responsibility of the mayor's office under a strong mayor system. Thus, what a single person would otherwise be held accountable for is the joint responsibility of a broader group. Figure 3. 2 shows weak Moyor-Council.

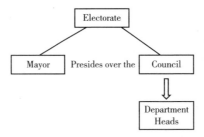

Figure 3. 2   Weak Mayor-Council

This system effectively solved the problems of concentrated executive power, it was designed to solve and manage a broader system of participation in administration. However, it results in more incredible difficulty in controlling government services. With diffused authority for services and policy implementation, coordination of different services becomes difficult, or at least more problematic. This hinders accountability to the voting public for the quality, efficiency, and effectiveness of local government services. The question may arise as to who is responsible when there is a problem.

What would otherwise have been technical or administrative issues may come to involve more politics as more services are more directly controlled by political actors. This gives politician-administrators incentives to provide superior services as that will help them advance their political career. It also gives voters a very direct path to exercise voice with local policymakers. On the other hand, this system may provide perverse incentives for politicians to deny each other resources. It is also possible that administrative resources, under the circumstances of political division could be less inclined to distribute resources according to need and more inclined to favor departments controlled by more powerful or esteemed local politicians. The strengths of this system are magnified with smaller administrative jurisdictions where elected personnel can replace the need for professional personnel and may take personal responsibility for the success or failure of their decisions in a way that may be very easy for voters to hold to account. The weaknesses are conversely magnified under larger or more complicated jurisdictions, although this may be at least partially offset by the quality of hired administrative personnel.

3. 2. 3   Council-Manager

The council manager form is a system that attempts to remove government management from the politics of government. This is parallel to the idea of the politics versus administration dichotomy associated with Woodrow Wilson, Leonard White, and other public administration academics and practitioners in the early 20th Century in the United States. The mayor and the city council would make up the political arm of the local government and a professional manager would be hired to take over the urban administration, either through implementing local policy or supervising the local government. Like the weak-mayor form, the council manager form of local government is also associated with issues in the United States. The rise of the council manager in local government was particularly connected to issues raised by the progressive movement in the late 19th and early 20th century. The council manager system was designed to depoliticize and professionalize local government.

On the one hand political machines famously controlled city governments in a number of major cities and had a reputation for corruption. Many of the machines were supported by the votes of recent immigrants who were resented by native-born middle-class reformers. In addition, many smaller cities had been taken over by minor radical parties like the Populists and the Socialists with a plurality when the Democratic and Republican parties were closely divided prompting reformers to question the neutrality and professionalism of local government as it was governed in unfamiliar ways by unfamiliar parties. On the other hand, increasing technological and social developments in the wake of industrialization and increasing urbanization made the tasks of local government far more complicated. Explosive increases in the size of urban populations further created new complications for urban governments. In addition to increases in the size of the urban bureaucracy, the council manager form of local government tried to raise the technical, managerial capacity of the city by hiring managerial professionals to oversee city management.

The city manager is hired or appointed by the city council and has special managerial expertise. Initially, managers tended to be engineers (following the popularity of the Scientific Management Movement) or business managers. Presently, most city managers have a Master's of Business Administration (MBA) or a Master's of Public Administration (MPA) in addition to management experience in private or public bureaucracies. Figure 3.3 shows Council Manager.

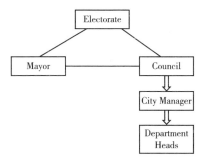

Figure 3.3　Council Manager

Where the mayor, in occupying the executive function of local government usually assumes control over administration, the city manager takes over this role. The city manager prepares the budget, which is usually a mayoral responsibility. In addition, the city manager supervises the regular operations of regular city employees, either directly, or through supervising department heads and oversees personnel decisions. The city manager advises the city council concerning operations and attends council and other public meetings as required or requested. Finally, the city manager may also have a public leadership role that may augment that of the mayor in representing the city to the public or to outside groups and organizations such as with potential business investors or state and national governments.

In practice, the council-manager form is most common among smaller cities. Larger American cities usually have the political and administrative roles likewise combined in the office of the mayor under the strong mayor system, with the mayor overseeing a large professional administration, but devoting much of her or his time to political and public leadership issues.

3. 2. 4　City Commission

The city commission is a fairly unique form that combines the executive and legislative functions of government in a single body, the commission. The commission form used to be more common among cities, for the same reasons as the council-manager form, which has largely displaced it, although it continues in some states, particularly in rural areas.

A city commission is elected, by district or at-large. The commission serves the same role as a city council and is responsible for the city's legislative functions, like passing ordinances and setting tax rates. As a collective body, the commission also serves as the executive in taking charge of both political leadership administrative functions. The administrative duties may be handled by divided responsibility for different departments among different commissioners, which may be fixed or rotated, although in small jurisdictions the commission may act collectively in charge of administration. One of the commissioners may selected as the nominal head of the commission, but usually has no other role than presiding over meetings and is thus mostly a ceremonial position, even when this position is referred to as the chairperson or the mayor. In terms of general executive duties, the commission serves as the executive in place of the mayor. Figure 3. 4 shows City Commission.

Figure 3. 4　City Commission

3. 2. 5　Town Meeting

Early in the history of what would become the United States there were many localities in the New England portion of the Northeast that were sparsely populated and did not bother with permanent administration or even with elected officials but governed through a form of direct democracy known as the town meeting. Citizens of these communities would gather and vote directly on policy and legislation (Karlen, 1975: 408, Lorch, 2000: 278). This is in line with the traditions of equality and rising participatory civil society in Alexis de Tocqueville's (1835) time when de Tocqueville came to America and witnessed the rise of the broad middling classes that joined organizations and participated in democratic society in such an active way.

This form continues in the United States in a few states in New England. At present, the town exists in different forms. For example, the town meeting may broadly legislate directly as well as provide for the execution of some functions, it may legislate and choose a board to serve as the executive branch or as administrators between meetings, or it may be a body that is convened for more specialized and limited purposes like deciding special issues or changing the town charter (the equivalent of the local constitution).

3.3 Urban Governance

3.3.1 Definition

As a broad concept, governance is not new, though it has become much more common in recent years. It has also taken on new meanings, so it means different things to different people. Therefore, the meaning of the concept depends on the level of governance, the goals followed, and the approach taken. The concept has been used a long time to refer to the generic task of running a government or other organization. New forms of governance allow individual governments and organizations to contribute their strengths and talents, to carry out responsibilities and to preserve and enhance the distinctiveness of organizations and institutions (Koliba, Meek, and Zia, 2011).

Governance is a broader notion than government. The main elements of government include the constitution, important laws, and the formal parts of government. Governance involves interaction between these formal institutions and those of civil society. Governance refers to the process where elements in society exercise power, authority, and influence. It is the process where organizations, public and private, enact policies and decisions concerning public life, as well as economic and social development. Governance includes the state, but goes beyond it by including the private sector and civil society in the process. The role of government is to create a political and legal environment that encourages innovation and performance. The private sector is supposed to create jobs and provide income. Civil society facilitates political and social interaction and mobilizes groups to participate in economic, social, and political activities. One of the most important objectives of governance is to promote an effective and constructive interaction among all three actors because each sector has its own strengths and weaknesses that the others can benefit from and compensate for.

3. 3. 2　Dimensions of Governance

Governance has no automatic normative connotation. However, typical criteria for assessing governance in a context might include the degree of legitimacy, representativeness, popular accountability and efficiency with which public affairs are conducted. Governance is the art of public leadership, whereby the public sector is coordinating all sectors of society to achieve effective performance. The three distinct dimensions of governance include, first, the form of political regime, secondly, the process by which authority is exercised in the management of a city's economic and social resources and, lastly, the capacity of governments to design, formulate, and implement policies and discharge functions (Koliba, Meek, and Zia, 2011).

The criteria that constitute good governance have been drawn from these three dimensions. They include legitimacy, accountability, competence, and respect for basic rights. Legitimacy of government means the degree of democracy exercised and the level of consent and participation by the governed. Accountability refers to the responsiveness of political and official elements of government and includes elements such as media freedom, transparent decision making, as well as formal and informal accountability mechanisms. Competence of the urban government is how efficiently and effectively it formulates policies and delivers services. Finally, respect for human rights and the rule of law cover individual and group rights, public safety, the framework for economic and social activity, and the forms and state of popular participation in the system.

3. 3. 3　Characteristics of Governance

Governance is characterized by participation, transparency, rule of law, transparency, responsiveness, consensus, equity, effectiveness, efficiency, accountability, and strategic vision (Osborne and Gaebler, 1993). Participation is the expression of the voice of citizens and residents in decision-making processes, whether directly or through intermediate representative institutions like assemblies and councils, provided that they are legitimate. This requires free speech and freedom of association, and the practical ability to participate in concrete and constructive ways. Rule of law is the requirement that legal systems be fair and impartial. This is particularly important in the enforcement of basic rights. Transparency and openness provide freedom of information and the free flow of information. This means that urban government and governance processes and institutions and the information necessary to understand, interpret and monitor them are directly accessible to those most concerned. Responsiveness means that governance processes and institutions try to serve everyone affected in a representative way that balances competing interests as impartially as possible. Consensus is the process of deferring decisions and implementation until broad or even overwhelming agreement is achieved as to the best interests of the urban area, particularly regarding general goals. This may also include policies and procedures where practical.

Equity is the concern for fairness and equal treatment so that everyone in the city has to opportunity to follow identifiable rules and can maintain or improve their well-being. Efficiency is the requirement to minimize use of resources relative to results produced. Effectiveness is the requirement that results are produced and that programs and processes and institutions are evaluated based on results. Accountability means that decision makers must answer to the public and not just to institutional stakeholders. This will be different on a case by case basis and depends on the internal and external nature and impact of any given decision. The final characteristic, strategic vision, calls on leaders and the public to adopt long-term perspectives relating to governance that incorporate individual and social development in the urban context. Such a vision needs to consider the unique cultural, social, and historical factors in the municipality, above and beyond the broader forces that impact it.

3. 3. 4   Towards Good Governance

Good governance has the elements of transparency and accountability, and is also participatory. As noted above, it also follows the basic management purposes of administration in being effective and fair, and efficient. It should also be working to promote the rule of law. Good governance should be working to promote the consensus noted above by bringing together different political and social, and economic priorities that all sectors (or the overwhelming majority) can agree on. Key to this is making sure that the most alienated and vulnerable, and disadvantaged have a full voice in allocative and other important decisions. Urban social values and practices should encourage and empower citizens and residents and give them more control over their stake in the city. These are the conditions of good governance, provided that this development takes place in an environment where the basic rights of all are respected.

Any city, no matter how unified, is incredibly diverse, so there is no way to improve the city for most people in the long run without working for a consensus. This requires collaboration and collective action. This is essential for good governance, which entails individuals and institutions, whether public or private or third sector, working together to achieve common goals for the common good. Good governance is itself the process whereby these diverse interests in conflict are brought together to a successful resolution. Formal institutions and government regimes are necessary, as are informal agreements and arrangements where different people, groups, interests, and institutions have come together to meet the common good.

The quality of municipal governance is often the single most significant factor in determining the development and progress of a city or urban area. Democratic governmental forms may help, but only active citizen participation, regardless of the formal arrangements, can really provide for and keep good governance alive. In the public sector, where quality of service is a key concern, this is particularly obvious. Openness and responsiveness are important for delivering the innovation and creativity that provide the new ideas that will solve urban problems and meet the needs of citizens in a responsive way for and informed citizenry that seeks better performance in an active way rather than passively accepting their fate.

Indicators of Good Governance Elements

The democratic concept of the consent of the governed along with the idea of stewardship, forms the basis of accountability in the context of governance. This may be done by using established criteria to demonstrate the accountability and performance of urban officials by estimating the economic and financial state of the city or municipality. These criteria may include things like efficiency, citizen participation, clear communication to constituents, decentralized planning and implementation of plans, regularity in city financial transactions, strictly following legal and administrative procedures and policies, and regular evaluation of urban economic performance using standardized means (Koliba, Meek, and Zia, 2011).

Responsiveness represents a specific type of accountability where the broad citizenry feels that the government leaders and other public figures and institutions involved in governance listen to and answer their concerns. Indicators of responsiveness include things like systems for determining the public's desires and needs, systems of citizen participation in planning and implementation of plans, systems for evaluating the effectiveness of policies regarding whether stated goals have been achieved, equitable and rapid action on public suggestions and comments, and public availability of information so that the people have the knowledge to provide informed feedback to the municipal government.

Management innovation consists of reforms successfully implemented in local government administration in furthering local governance. Indicators include innovations in generating measures, innovative concepts and practices that deal with urban problems, improved bureaucratic structures and procedures, innovative and creative means for meeting public needs, and the use of new management techniques such as total quality management and information technology.

Public-private partnerships are active joint working arrangements between local government and the private sector. Indicators include incentive schemes that encourage the private sector to participate in development, the presence of business sector initiatives to improve the efficiency of local bureaucracy, the joint involvement of the public and private sectors in the planning, funding and implementation of programs/projects, and the privatization or contracting out of local government services where appropriate.

Interaction between citizens and the government indicates open communication between the government, non-government organizations and the community as a whole. Indicators may include cooperative efforts among local governments and nongovernmental organizations, consultation between the local government and the constituents on various local concerns, and implementation of citizen/NGO/NPO collaboration with local government.

Decentralized management concerns the ability of the local management to delineate and delegate responsibilities and to ensure accurate reporting and monitoring. Indicators are clear-cut delegation guidelines, feedback systems covering the implementation of delegated tasks, decisions made by officials on delegated tasks, and the consistency between the organizational hierarchical structure and the actual delegation of tasks.

Networking is where urban governments forge cooperative relationships with other local governments and entities to build infrastructure capacity. Indicators are municipal government networks, regional (intra-local) networks, international networks, complementary resources in networks, technological interchange and collaboration, common interests and agenda and exchange of expertise and training.

Human resource development suggests the sustained implementation of a program to recruit, train, motivate, and develop a local work force to be more efficient, dedicated, and influential members of the public service. The indicators are coverage of policies designed to improve the different aspects of human resource management, an adequate and sustained program of recruitment and selection based on merit and fitness, training programs to improve the capabilities of local government personnel, a workable and responsive classification and pay based on equal pay for equal or comparable work.

These elements take on a somewhat different caste in the context of local governing structures than they do at a regional or national government level. In fact, as the concept of reinventing government was drawn to a large extent form reforms and innovations taking place at the local level, it can be said that the idea of governance in this form may be most applicable to urban governance. Certainly, with the relatively small scale and smaller numbers of people involved, it is possible to construct more meaningful systems of citizen participation in this context. It should also be noted that the idea of governance is not linked to any particular governing structure, but is compatible with any or all of the structures mentioned earlier in the chapter and has been applied in all of these contexts.

3. 4   Government Functions

Governments perform two general types of functions (Banfield and Wilson, 1963). The first is the supply of public goods and services. Urban local governments perform numerous services such as collecting garbage, providing police and fire protection, and maintaining streets and other urban infrastructure. These types of services will be covered in the next chapter. The second type of function is the management of competing interests through political and other systems. This involves the resolution of disputes in the city over government performance, responsiveness, and representation, particularly as related to service functions.

Almost anything that a government does can provoke some kind of conflict. Personnel decisions frequently lead to disputes between the municipal government and groups that feel they are not being given a fair share of available jobs or are not being fairly considered compared to other groups. The level of taxation levied to finance and support different levels of government services is another frequent source of conflict, especially at the point at which the taxes or the services change. Even mundane questions like which streets get maintenance first, how frequent and when bus service is offered, and the location of new infrastructure like libraries and parks may spark conflict between different urban groups. Any of these conflicts must be resolved or festering conflict may erupt into more serious disputes and even violence. These two functions are performed at the same time (Banfield and Wilson, 1963). Services and conflict management take place at the same time. Both governmental and non-governmental actors will respond whenever a decision occurs. The governmental actors will often respond based on law or policy, although they may also provide feedback or a response based on how the decision will affect their policy area. On the other hand, non-governmental actors will respond depending on how they perceive a decision will affect them and their group. There is conflict when there are diverse reactions to an urban government decision, giving rise to the need for the conflict management function. The decision-maker may participate in this process directly and immediately by revising plans in reaction to feedback. Most of the function is performed by the municipal executive and council. These are the officials with the ultimate authority to approve and fund, and implement a controversial decision.

3. 5 Issues

To this point, this chapter has focused on the administrative-political systems of local government. These systems make up the playing field where local policy is determined, and local interests compete for power. This final section addresses some issues of interest related to the administrative forms of local government.

The first issue in this section is the question of citizen participation. All the contemporary systems under consideration involve at least some form of representative government, but what is the direct role played by citizens in local government? The next issue is social capital. What role do the social networks and connections between networks have to play in local administration? The final issue addressed in this section is the question of divided government. Under American political systems, it is possible for the local executive and the local council to be controlled by different political parties. How and why does this happen and what does it mean for urban administration?

3. 5. 1   Citizen Participation

Apart from the rare town meeting form of local government mentioned earlier in the chapter, all the local systems in this chapter are representative systems. There is a continuing tension between representation and direct participation. The 1948 Constitution of the Republic of Korea did not call for a democratic system, but for a republic. The period following independence from Japan maintained the continuity of an authoritarian system with a system of representation that was not democratic for any great length of time until the pro-democracy movement forced changes in the late 1980s and early 1990s (Ahn, 2005).

Likewise, the framers of the American Constitution did not perceive it as a democratic document, but as a system of representative rule. They tended to consider democracy as akin to mob rule (Rossiter, 2003). At the founding of the American republic, "majority rule" constituted divided rule by representatives chosen by adult white male property-owning citizens and excluded most of the population of the early United States. This system only gradually expanded to include all the groups who are now allowed to participate in the democratic process.

The Importance of Citizen Participation

As long as there is a democratic system, citizen participation is at least theoretically desirable as part of the democratic process. Therefore, it should also be valuable in urban administration, whether through general urban politics, as part of the community development process, or as involvement in urban services. *Spiegel* refers to citizen participation as "the process that can meaningfully tie programs to people. In this way citizens have an extra opportunity to fine-tune the administrative process in the direction of popular accountability".

Bridges specified five benefits of active citizen participation at the local community level. First, citizens can make changes they want through individual and collective action. Second, citizens can learn about the process and how to make change in a democratic society. Third, citizens learn about their community and the needs and interests of all the different groups in the community. Next, citizens learn how to resolve interest conflicts in favor of the general welfare. Finally, citizens learn about group and individual behavior in their community. Apart from any positive changes that result, citizens and residents therefore gain in capacity as citizens through the very process of participating.

At a very basic level, citizens participate minimally through obeying the law and paying taxes, but there are deeper levels of participating. In particular, participation usually refers to voluntary means of participation that go beyond minimum levels of civic involvement. Arnstein developed a ladder of citizen involvement in program development that ranged from non-involvement to tokenism, to cooperative program development, partnership in planning, delegated power, and ultimately to citizen control and full ownership of a community project.

Citizen participation in the community also serves as a check on political power. It may hold political and economic elites accountable to the people and allows the people more complete access to the benefits of a democratic society. More citizen participation may improve decision making process by providing greater access to information sources and expertise that officials may not possess. The very presence of citizens from diverse backgrounds may limit political patronage, nepotism, trading of favors that voters would not endorse. Citizen participation may serve as a spotlight to prevent or reveal corruption that may flourish where the public's business take place out of view of the public. This reduces the separation between the public and appointed and elected officials and refines the representative process to reduce the likelihood of self-serving decisions.

Traditional Methods of Citizen Participation

Simonsen and Robbins (2000) identify citizen participation as taking place at the center of tensions between politics and administration, expertise and access, and representation and participation. Wilson and White identified politics and administration as dichotomous, with politics serving to express the will of the electorate and administration serving that will. This concept, although not exclusive, is in contrast with more recent efforts to involve citizens in administration through methods like surveys and e-governance.

Expertise and access are the divide between professionals and trained experts versus the citizens, and is encapsulated by White's (2004) discussion of the complications of modern administration versus the history of citizen involvement in the United States through social cooperation. To what extent is modern government a technical matter requiring insulated decisions by professional civil servants and to what extent are these professionals insulated from the public? How can citizens access the works inside the government directly and through their representatives? How can civil servants be responsive to elected officials and the people and still be insulated from politics in their decision-making process? Representation and participation are the tension at the center of modern representative government. To what extent do the citizens sit back and let their elected representatives make decisions and to what extent do they provide guidance, express opinions directly, and lobby for their preferences?

Simonsen and Robbins (2000) identified government-sponsored (top-down) and grassroots (bottom-up) methods of participation. They identified the most effective issues, jurisdiction, and level of interest for each type. Government-sponsored participation was most effective for issues affecting an entire jurisdiction, where jurisdiction-wide acceptance is important, and where there are high levels of community disagreement or low levels of public interest. Grassroots participation is most effective when it affects homogeneous or very local groups, where neighborhood acceptance is important, and where there are low levels of community disagreement or high levels of interest. They gave public hearings and advisory committees (government sponsored), and citizen agencies or community action programs (government sponsored but facilitating grassroots-style participation) as examples of participation.

Sohn and Ahn (2005) discussed several methods that have been employed since the implementation of local autonomy in the Republic of Korea. They divide between direct and indirect participation, between individual and collective participation, between mobilized or citizen-led or cooperative, and as institutional or non-institutional. The institutional forms they identified included disclosure of administrative information, committees and neighborhood meetings, public hearings, appeals, citizen consultations, petitions, claims of inspection (where a citizen may request a direct investigation by the executive of unfair or unjust treatment), local referenda, and community centers. Non-institutional forms included local civic groups and citizen campaigns. They concluded that the institutional methods needed to be invigorated as they had been underutilized while the non-institutional forms had been common, but seemed to reflect a failure on the part of local government to reflect the opinions of citizens in local administration.

Online Methods of Citizen Participation

Coglianese (2004) noted that many people have predicted the internet will lead to more citizen participation due to recent advances in technology that make it easier for citizens to make their voices heard to elected officials. These recent changes have also made it more possible for new administrative practices that make the process of governing locally more accessible to citizens and residents. There are new means for citizens to communicate and interact with elected and appointed officials. There are also new means for citizens to observe and hold their governments accountable.

The concept of e-government covers this territory. According to Relyea (2002), e-government was initially used to refer to the confluence of different information technologies (IT) as applied to the government. It also means current IT applied to government as well as for more effective and less costly government functioning. Cook et al. (2002) define e-government as the use of IT to support government operations, engage citizens, and provide government services. E-service is the electronic delivery of information and services via the internet and other electronic means. E-management is the use of IT to improve the management of government. E-democracy is the use of electronic communications to increase citizen participation. E-commerce is the internet exchange of goods and services. Relyea argues that e-government has remained a dynamic concept, but that at its core is the idea of using technology to better serve the citizenry and fulfill the guarantees of the democratic system.

Layne and Lee (2001) developed a four-stage process of e-government. The first stage was cataloguing, the process of establishing an online presence for government, with online presentation of government information and downloadable government forms. The second was transacting, the stage where the government starts connecting internal government systems to online interfaces to allow citizens to transact directly with government online (renewing licenses, paying taxes). The third was vertical integration, where analogous government entities at the local and central government levels link up to combine functions. The fourth stage was horizontal integration that connects agencies at the same level, giving citizens one place to meet all their needs when dealing with government (such as a single website connecting all city government agencies). Layne and Lee suggest verticality linked by function would come first as the commonalities shared by similar departments at different levels are greater than those faced by different functions at the same level.

Systems of e-government for participation include online social networking systems (SNS). Social networks may replicate offline means of participation, with the potential for online petitions, online access to information, online appeals, etc. However, the major areas for online participation have been promoting online discussions and in online organizing. Recent campaigns around the world have been facilitated by online organizing, from anti-KORUS FTA movements in Korea to the Arab Spring democracy movements in the Middle East to the Occupy Wall Street movement in the United States.

E-participation and online social networking has some limitations. The first issue is the digital divide between those who have the access and education to make use of new technologies. The poor may have trouble affording IT, while senior citizens may have problems in using new technologies. A second issue is the unreliability of information on the internet, particularly as compared to the ease of spread. Online communications are particularly susceptible to rumors that are difficult to debunk. While offline broadcasts and publications are easily held accountable for spreading misinformation, websites that do not carefully check information may look just as reputable as those that meet more rigorous journalistic or academic standards.

3.5.2 Social Capital

Capital is money used for investment. Human capital is the knowledge, skills, and abilities invested in people that allow them to produce more with their labor. Social capital is the value held in social networks, communities, and organizations. It is a general term that has different definitions that vary greatly among the social sciences, though it usually emphasizes the benefits that flow from social relations, cooperation, and community. It may include both bonding social capital (or strong ties) that holds a group together and bridging social capital (or weak ties) that connects different groups together and provides for the flow of information.

Putnam (2000) noted a long decline in social capital in the United States and warned of the consequences, relating the decline to various social problems. His definition includes problem solving through mutual interests. A decline in social capital would therefore make problem solving more difficult. Problems involving declining social capital include declining voter turnout, declining meeting attendance, and decreased trust in government. In this view low social capital may be an obstacle to citizen participation.

Civic organizations, voluntary associations, and other non-market, non-governmental organizations are playing an important role in democracy and in encouraging civic participation in administration and politics. This civil society is an essential ingredient in a healthy democracy. China has many NGOs and citizen organizations that take an active part in politics and society. Many do so at the local level and try to apply pressure on and negotiate with local governments to achieve their goals. Sohn and Ahn (2005) point to the participation of civic groups as part of the trend towards more participation in local government.

3. 5. 3 Divided Government

A divided government is a situation where different political parties control different branches of government. This was the case in Seoul following the 2010 local elections, where Oh Sehoon from the Grand National Party won reelection to office, but the opposition won a majority on the City Council. Divided government is not possible under some systems of local government. In the Republic of Korea, the strong mayor-council system allows for the possibility that a mayor or other local executive may have majority support even though their party may not have a majority on the local council. This is particularly likely under multi-party systems where the vote may be regularly divided by three or more parties in most districts.

This may produce deadlock where partisan rivals may be unwilling to reach compromise. It does stymie the kind of strong action that voters often hope representatives of their party will deliver. Thus, divided government makes change more difficult and favors the *status quo*. Although this may be frustrating to voters wanting action, separation of powers is the intention of the constitutions in the United States. The point of separation of powers is to channel different democratic aspects of the people into achieving different ends so that power to execute law would be concentrated while the power to make law would be more dispersed. This was a method of checking ill-advised momentary passions among the electorate that were not almost universally held. In this sense, divided government merely represents the working of the system as designed when public opinion is divided.

Divided government may also encourage compromise on elected officials who are not able to force their will. This increases the chance of forging broad consensus that most citizens will accept in the place of a narrow governance that is not accepted by major constituencies. At the least, this reduces trust, but it may also make policy more difficult to implement, less efficient as citizens needed to make it work instead oppose and try to frustrate policy they oppose.

Questions

1. What are the dysfunctions of local autonomy?
2. What are the pros and cons of the two mayor-council forms?
3. What are the main features of good governance?
4. Why is citizen participation important in urban administration?
5. What contributes to the formation of social capital? What roles does it play?
6. What is the impact of social networks on urban policies?

Key Terms

checks and balances

city manager

commission

digital divide

divided government

e-government

good governance

mayor-council

social capital

veto power

References

[1] Ahn, Chung-si, (ed) (2005). *New Development in Local Democracy and Decentralization in East Asia*. Seoul: Seoul National University Press.

[2] Coglianese, Cary (2004). "E-Rulemaking: Information Technology and the Regulatory Process", *Administrative Law Review* 56.

[3] Goodnow, Frank (2004). "Politics and Administration", pp. 35-37 in Shafritz, Jay; Hyde, Albert; and Parkes, Sandra (eds), *Classics of Public Administration*, *5th ed.* Belmont, CA: Wadsworth.

[4] Harrigan, John J., and Vogel, Ronald K. (2002). *Political Change in the Metropolis*, *7th ed.* Upper Saddle River, NJ: Longman.

[5] Ketcham, Ralph (ed) (2003). *The Anti-Federalist Papers and the Constitutional Convention Debates*. Signet Classic: New York.

[6] Koliba, Christopher, Meek, Jack W. and Zia, Asim. (2011). *Governance Networks in Public Administration and Public Policy*. Boca Raton, FL: CRC Press.

[7] Layne, Karen, and Lee, Jungwoo (2001). "Developing Fully Functional E-government: A Four Stage Model", *Government Information Quarterly*, Vol. 18, No. 2, pp. 122 – 136.

[8] Lorch, Robert S. (2000). *State and Local Politics: The Great Entanglement 6th Edition.* Upper Saddle River, NJ: Prentcie-Hall.

[9] Putnam, Robert (2000). *Bowling Alone: The Collapse and Revival of American Community*. New York: Simon and Schuster.

[10] Relyea, Harold (2002). "E-Gov: Introduction and Overview", *Government Information Quarterly*, Vol. 19, No. 1, pp. 9 – 35.

[11] Rossiter, Clinton (ed) (2003). *The Federalist Papers*. Signet Classic: New York.

[12] Simonsen, William, and Robbins, Mark D. (2000). *Citizen Participation in Resource Allocation*. Boulder, CO: Westview Press.

[13] White, Leonard (2004). "Introduction to the Study of Public Administration", pp. 56 – 63 in Shafritz, Jay; Hyde, Albert; and Parkes, Sandra (eds), *Classics of Public Administration*, *5th ed.* Belmont, CA: Wadsworth.

[14] Wilson, Woodrow (2004). "The Study of Administration", pp. 22 – 34 in Shafritz, Jay; Hyde, Albert; and Parkes, Sandra (eds), *Classics of Public Administration*, *5th ed.* Belmont, CA: Wadsworth.

第4章 城市公共服务

4.1 概念及内涵

城市政府将大部分时间用于为居民提供服务，但城市应该提供什么样的服务？这个问题的答案取决于许多因素，如城市的规模、发展阶段和工业化水平，等等。然而，总的来说，城市服务是由政治、经济和规划力量共同决定的，这些力量对公民的需求达成了一些共识。

威廉·C. 贝尔（William C. Baer）将城市公共服务定义为"通过实现以下一个或多个目的实现公共利益的服务：保护生命、自由和财产安全，提高公众生活质量，为其参与公共事务提供保障等，由一个或多个经济部门通过政府监管、合作生产或直接提供的"（Baer, 1985）。对城市政府来说是非常重要的，城市政府应该提供许多服务，让城市生活既便捷又愉快，如果政府做不到，那城市生活对许多居民来说可能是非常艰难的生活。因此，了解城市公共服务是了解城市管理者所做工作的重要组成部分之一。

4.2 政府参与的理由

为什么城市政府应该提供服务，应该提供哪些服务？一般来说，城市政府应提供城市居民所需（政治回应）且市场不会或无法提供的服务，在经济方面，在市场失灵的条件下会发生。对于经济学家来说，市场失灵有非常具体的定义和条件，在城市管理中，该定义略有不同，因此，下面将对这两种定义加以介绍。此外，城市政府可能试图解决公共问题，结果要么使问题变得更糟，要么产生其他意料之外的问题。公共问题的解决需要政府干预，但有时候也是因为政府失灵才带来一些问题，我们将在以下章节中单独讨论。

4.2.1 市场失灵：经济学的视角

要理解经济学家对市场失灵的看法，必须先了解经济学家对人类行为的三个基本假设：第一，当人们作出决策时，是作为个人作出的决策。第二，每个人的决定都是由利益驱动的，利益可以是一个人所看重的任何东西：金钱、爱情或幸福都可以发挥这样的作用。第三，当一个人作出决定时，会合乎逻辑地作出自身利益最大化的选择。例如，如果我的效用是金钱，那么我的决定将是基于我可以通过这个选择获得的金钱最大化的选择。经济学家将个人称为理性和利益最大化，这种行为普遍存在的假设是大多数经济模型的基础。

经济学中有几种市场失灵，但一般来说，市场失灵可以用帕累托效率来定义：当个人（或公司）在竞争的市场中进行自愿交易（买卖）时，供求力量将找到一个点，在这个点上，任何人都无法在不使其他人的境况恶化的情况下使自己境况好转，这一点被称为商品的帕累托有效配置（Weimer and Vining, 2005）。当违反了其中一个或多个条件，并且无法实现帕累托有效的商品配置时，就会出现市场失灵。换言之，不同的选择可以让更多的人在不伤害别人的情况下变得更好。在经济学家看来，这是低效的，因此，也是社会无法接受的，当此类失灵发生时，市场外部的权威机构进行干预并试图纠正失灵是合乎逻辑的。

不同类型的市场失灵：垄断

垄断是市场正常运行时可能产生的，但垄断的存在会导致市场效率低下。当一家公司或一组公司拥有足够的市场力量来影响一种商品或服务的价格时，就会出现垄断。一般来说，当一家公司或一组公司缺乏足够的有效竞争来提供价格控制时，就会发生这种情况。这会导致商品或服务的定价效率低下，所以参与市场的人可能不会这样做。简单来说，垄断通常意味着价格高于应有的水平，消费者为某种商品或服务支付的费用比在竞争激烈的市场上要高。

解决垄断问题的工具

垄断发生时，政府最常用的工具是一种称为反垄断的监管，这是一种通常超出城市政府能力范围的工具，它要求有权解散一家规模过大的公司，在大多数国家，这种权力只存在于国家一级（如果有的话）。然而城市政府也面临着与垄断有关的问题，因为城市往往是一个或多个有影响力的企业或产业的所在地，它们的存在对城市居民的经济福祉至关重要。因此，即使一个城市可能没有法律权力来影响垄断行为，但如果中央政府决定解散一家规模太大又没有竞争力的公司，那城市会受到影响。如果一个产业为了打击垄断而缩小规模，那么即使国民经济得到改善，该产业所在的城市在地方一级仍会感受到这种影响。

外部性

外部性是一种成本，它没有反映在商品的价格中，因为它被转移到不参与买卖双方交易的第三方。例如，假设你有一家生产纸张的公司（A）和一家销售办公用品的公司（B）。公司B想以特定的、尽可能便宜的价格购买纸张，公司A以公司B愿意支付的价格生产纸张，所以B公司从A公司购买纸张，每个人都会很满意吗？

当然不完全是。公司A以这个价格生产纸张，因为它需要对生产过程中产生的废水在排向当地河流前进行处理，因为生产过程中使用了漂白剂（白纸价格较高），不处理的话河流中的所有鱼类都会被废水杀死。现在，住在河边的人们没有鱼可吃，河流也被污染了，居民也没有饮用水。为了生存，他们必须购买昂贵的设备来去除饮用水中的有害化学物质。公司 A 通过将生产成本（废水的安全处理）转移给不属于公司 A 和公司 B 之间交易的人，以低于竞争对手的价格出售纸张。该成本现在由住在河边的人支付，不属于交易范围，因此，公司 B 为纸张支付的价格其实不包括真实的全部生产成本。

这种外部性被称为负外部性，因为它们会给第三方带来成本。然而，外部性也可能是正面的。当交易为第三方提供的利益未反映在价格中时，就会发生这种情况。例如，如果你买了漂亮的花放在你的窗前，让你的家更加赏心悦目，你为此支付了成本。但是，从你窗前经过的人也可以看到并欣赏这些鲜艳的花朵而无须参与交易，在这种情况下，利益已经转移给第三方（路人），因此，此时的外部性是正面的。

解决外部性的工具

政府处理负外部性（通常比正外部性更令人担忧）通常是使用监管工具对带来问题的公司或企业施加成本。一般来说，政府试图施加足够高的成本，使得企业自身吸收外部性比支付政府施加的成本要便宜。成本可以是货币性的（如罚款或费用），也可以是惩罚性的（处罚，如监禁或公开曝光），但一般来说，成本是为了改变产生外部性的一方的行为。政府还可以利用激励措施让某人承担外部性的成本。如果一家公司使用了一种更善于控制负外部性的流程，那么其动机可能带来减税，进而提高公司的声誉，例如，政府将公司指定为良好的企业代表。

然而，有时居民的行为会给其他居民带来成本，这时候也需要外部干预。大多数城市在出现这种情况时都会通过法令或规则的执行来实现。因此，当居民有这样的一些行为（深夜举行喧闹的聚会，在门外堆放垃圾以至于引来害虫）时，通常有相关法律由城市警察或卫生和环卫人员执行。

城市政府用于解决外部性问题的最有力的监管工具是分区。城市可以在其管辖范围内控制其发展，并可以根据土地用途划分土地使用区域。这样，对可能会产生冲突的活动用地加以区分，这样居民就不会被其他居民的活动所困扰。因此，城市可能会将一个地区划为重工业区，然后再将另一个更远的地区划为住宅区。这样，重工业产生的一些成本（例如，空气质量降低、噪声大）将被控制在远离城市居民活动的区域内，这有助于保持城市环境的和谐，同时保证社区繁荣所需的多样性。

信息不对称

需要政府干预的第三种市场失灵是信息不对称。这是买方和卖方能够进行交易的条件（买方有足够的钱支付货物，卖方愿意以买方支付的价格提供货物），但买方对货物是否值得卖方提供的价格存在疑问，当怀疑强烈到足以阻止交易进行时，就发生了市场失灵。在这种情况下，市场失灵是由于卖方掌握的有关商品的信息与买方确定的价格是否公平所需的信息之间的不平衡，这也是为什么被称为信息不对称。

对于买方和卖方来说，这种失败可能令人沮丧。例如，一个人想买一辆二手车，因为它比新车便宜，而且买方也能买得起状况相对较好的最新车型，所以买方寻找一辆自己喜欢并且买得起的车。买方找到了一个非常便宜又合适的里程数和车况的车。买方问卖方，为什么愿意以比其他相似状况的汽车便宜得多的价格出售。卖方说因为不再需要这辆车，所以愿意以较低的价格迅速处理它。然而，买方并不确定这辆车是出了事故，还是发动机出了什么问题，买方又无法确定，买方认为自己对这辆车的了解程度不足以相信卖方的解释，所以买方会继续寻找另一辆车。

解决信息不对称的工具

这里的部分困难在于，买方不知道如果买了这辆车会发生什么，它的性能有没有达到自己的预期。如果将车还给卖方，卖方会将钱还给买家吗？由于缺乏信息，交易无法进行。这正是需要政府干预的地方，在信息不对称的情况下，政府用来解决这个问题的工具通常是要求卖方披露更多信息，并执行买方和卖方之间签订的合同，其他常见工具是消费者保护法。在二手车的例子中，可以通过"柠檬定律"（在美国许多地区很常见）来实现。此类法律规定，当车辆所有权（说明谁拥有车辆的官方文件）转让给新车主时，新车主在购买车辆后有一定的时间（通常为三个月）来确定车辆是否按照卖方承诺的条件出售，如果出现问题，柠檬法案允许买方将车辆退还给卖方，并全额退款。这种保证有助于交易顺利进行，因为买方和卖方都有第三方（政府）帮助他们执行交易条款。

对于城市管理者来说，信息不对称可能出现在许多地方，并可能导致效率低下，给居民带来问题。这些问题与居民所掌握的关于他们可能希望购买的商品或服务的信息量有关，但不确定所提供的价格是否合理，当怀疑某一特定产品或服务的安全性时，就会发生这种情况。例如，有许多维生素、能量饮料和草药声称具有多种健康功能被出售给消费者，但这些说法是真实的吗？需要有法律要求公司在生产产品时列出所包含的成分，以便消费者更好地了解他们购买的产品。如果没有这样的法律，通常人们购买的产品不会像他们预期的那样对他们有利，有时甚至会造成严重的伤害。政府作为信息提供者发挥监管的角色，因为它给信息提供者带来了成本。

道德风险

最后一种通常被视为需要政府干预的市场失灵是道德风险。当产品定价基于不确定或不完整的信息时，就会出现道德风险，此类问题最常见的例子是购买保险。例如，在对美国驾驶人进行的精算研究中，年龄在16岁（大多数州的法定驾驶年龄）至24岁之间的年轻男子最有可能发生高速/高损伤车祸，因此，保险公司对属于这一年龄段的男性收取更高的费率。然而，由于风险较低而不属于较高保险价格的人可能会选择不购买保险，因为他们认为事故风险较低。这意味着保险费用由那些支付更高费率的人承担，并且随着支付保险的人数减少，平均费用上升得更快。这将保险负担转移到高风险人群，并允许那些选择不购买保险的人"搭便车"。"搭便车"是指个人的行为，他们知道如果不支付服务费用也不会被惩罚，因为接受服务的人太多，服务提供商无法监控所有人。这是一个通常与公共物品提供有关的问题（Weimer and Vining，2005）。

对于城市管理者来说，当提供某种保证时，道德风险可能会发生，这种保证可能会扭曲人们感知风险的方式。如果低估了风险成本，人们可能会愿意从事风险行为。例如，有些人可能会在靠近海洋的地方建造自己的家，因为多年来没有发生台风带来的洪水灾害，所以当建造房子时，他们不考虑如果遇到台风，带来的成本会是多少，他们不仅会失去房子，而且由于台风造成的洪水也会失去房子里面的东西。因此，他们为自己的房子投保，但却低估了更换房屋的价值，如果出现洪水，那么重建的成本将远远超过保险价值。

解决道德风险的工具

由于道德风险同样可以由信息缺乏引起信息不对称，因此，解决道德风险的工具是相似的。如果消费者低估了他们的风险和潜在损失，那么政府可以要求最低限度的恢复，如对在百年一遇洪水区内建造房屋的业主实行强制性洪水保险。城市政府还可以利用分区来建立某些活动风险较小的区域以更适合某些公共用途，例如，托儿所或为老年人提供锻炼设施的公园。

然而，道德风险提出了一个相当独特的问题，即在试图纠正市场失灵的过程中，可能会造成政府失灵。例如，2008 年末，当美国政府介入并为几家大型银行和贷款机构的债务提供担保时，布什政府从根本上降低了作出高风险贷款决定的银行的风险。当时给出的理由是，需要这样一种保障来稳定市场，防止普遍的经济自由落体状态。然而，这让许多主流经济学家极度紧张，因为它增加了道德风险，而不是减少了道德风险。

对于城市管理者来说，纠正道德风险通常与提高公众可用信息的质量联系在一起。提高信息质量可以让公民更容易正确评估与某些行为相关的风险，从而更好地采用保护措施。例如，如果孩子的父母认为他们的孩子感染麻疹等需要接种疫苗的疾病的风险很低——因为所有其他孩子都接种了疫苗——那么他们可能会选择不给孩子接种疫苗。然而，如果有太多的父母作出这样的决定，那么在弱势人群中爆发麻疹的真正风险就会增加。为此政府可以确保让父母了解，如果他们不给孩子接种疫苗会带来什么风险，或者政府可以强制接种疫苗用于公共服务，如作为入学的要求。

4.2.2　政府失灵

有时，由于政府执行政策产生了意想不到的结果而出现了问题，当这种情况发生时，被称为政府失灵。政府失灵不像市场失灵那样经常被讨论，但政府失灵也可能带来政府干预的需要，因此，应将其纳入城市政府采取行动的理由的考量中。一般来说，政府失灵被定义为一种妨碍公共资源最佳配置的情况，这可以通过三种不同的方式实现（Weimer and Vining，2005）：直接民主、代议制政府和分权政府。将个人偏好传达给政府提供的集体行动和服务方面，每一种形式都有一定的缺陷，这些缺陷导致了政府失灵。

直接民主

当人们在选举中投票时，投票过程本身可能会产生问题，将人们期待的政策与政府制定政策联系起来。诺贝尔经济学奖得主肯尼斯·阿罗是第一个证明在公平选举中投票不会导致任何人获得最高优先权，并且会在连续选举中缺乏连贯一致的政策的人。他在他的一般可能性定理（Arrow，1951）中概述了这个问题，该定理说明了投票的悖论。综上所述，即使在一次选举中大多数人投票支持某项特定政策，也无法保证所选政策实际上是选民最喜欢的政策，这给了控制政策议程的人即处于统治地位的人很大的优势，这种情况在议会制政府（内阁制政府）中不太明显，但仍然适用。

直接民主的另一个问题是多数人的暴政，当那些在社会中占据更有利地位、比穷人更多的人投票维持资源分配的现状时，就会发生这种情况，因为大多数人可以通过投票支持少数公民的私人利益而对多数公民施加成本。在其他情况下，如公民投票，大多数公民可以通过法律，允许对少数群体实行歧视性做法，在这种情况下，多数人统治并不意味着一个公正的社会。因此，对于多数人统治的民主国家，通常必须维持某种平衡来保护少数人，否则就会导致暴政。

因此，当赢得大多数选票的政治家声称他们的政策代表人民所期待的政策和价值观时，这种说法并不成立。在一个真正民主的社会中，必须始终保持平衡，以最好地适应价值观间的相互竞争并解决社会冲突。今天的多数可能不是明天的多数，因此决策者必须不断调整思维以赢得选举。

代议制民主

在民主政体中，选民通常会选举他们认为会在政府中代表自己观点的候选人。然而，代表们除了为他们的选民服务，还会受动机的驱使。一般来说，这些动机被描述为代表必须扮演的两个有时相互竞争的角色：代表和受托人。

代表力求尽可能忠实地代表其选民，并相信这种忠诚正是他当选所要实现的目标。例如，如果选民强烈反对在选区内设置核电站，那么代表应尽一切可能确保核电站不建在其选区内。另外，受托人认为公众信任他的判断，这项工作要求代表作出符合其选民和社会最大利益的决定。如果受托人认为在其选区内安置核电站确实是解决超出投票选区边界的问题的最佳方案，那么他可能不会认为这是一项糟糕的政策。因此，受托人的治理方式可能与代表的截然不同。

这两种情形都可能出现各种各样的问题，如寻租行为、互相吹捧和猪肉桶政策制定等。每一种行为都会让选民感到满意，但也会给政府带来问题，这通常是国家一级政府的问题，在国家层面，此类决定的影响很难让各个选区看到，但在不同地区争夺共享资源的大城市中也可能发生这种情况。例如，在强有力的市长制度中，市长可能会支持由市长所在政党代表的地区，或者市长可以决定，无论绩效或需求如何，每个地区都有权获得相同的资源。这种情况下，公民可能会认为这种行为是不公平的，并可能对由此产生的政策作出负面反应。

分权政府

当地方政府有权自行决定如何充分利用其管辖范围内的资源时，就会出现权力下放。对于中央政府而言，这可能是一种更有效的资源配置方式，因为资源分配的决策者更了解地方一级的情况，因此可以作出更高质量的决策。然而，由于政策的实施可能因地方政府而异，因此监管政策在实现其目标方面的有效性变得更加复杂和困难。因此，权力下放会增加政策执行产生意外后果的可能性，意外后果是特定政策带来的结果，因此可能需要额外的政府干预。

4.3　公共服务类型

定义服务类型的一个标准是它是必需的还是可选择的，地方政府必须提供的必要的服务称为基本服务，这是支持和维护城市发展所必需的，包括垃圾收集、路面和道路维修等。另外，可选服务也称为便利服务，意味着为提高公民生活质量提供的服务，包括公共图书馆和娱乐设施等。

强制性与自由裁量

第二种类型是基于城市政府提供哪些服务的自由裁量权，城市政府必须提供某些服务，法律规定此类服务是强制性服务，警察和消防服务是典型的强制性服务，在任何情况下都必须提供。其他服务，即自由支配服务，可由地方政府选择或自行决定提供，自由支配服务包括娱乐和文化服务。

空间分布

划分公共服务的第三种类型是基于服务在物理空间如何分布。点模式设施系统基于固定设施，如图书馆和医院，居民需要前往一个固定地点接受服务。另一种选择是网络设施系统，在该系统中，服务广泛分布于整个城市，并在空间上进行连接，使居民无论身在何处都可以使用服务。污水处理和饮用水提供是通过网络设施系统提供服务的两个例子。然而，有些服务同时具有这两个特点，如警务服务以固定的警察局为基础，但包括以定期巡逻和警察派遣的形式进行的点间连接。有些服务需要跨广泛领域的政府间合作，如消防和警察服务需要区域间协调，提供此类服务需要覆盖广泛领域的大都市组织形式。

城市政府提供的一般服务

一般来说，这些是城市政府定期提供的服务类型：公共交通、交通基础设施、发展规划、执法、消防、教育、公园建设和维护、卫生服务、饮用水、污水处理系统、供电、电信基础设施（电缆或无线系统）等。此外，根据城市规模和人口，政府还可以为贫困人口提供福利服务，或为企业提供发展服务，以促进增长，这些服务可以由不同类型的服务提供商提供。在下一节中，将介绍三种一般类型的服务供给，并讨论服务类型和服务提供商类型之间的联系。

4.4 公共服务供给

城市政府提供的服务种类可以根据提供者和服务的性质而有所不同。一般来说，有三大类：完全由公共部门提供，公私合营（也称为共同生产），完全由私有部门提供。完全由公共部门提供的服务完全由政府提供，通过公私伙伴关系提供的服务通常是政府决定应为公共利益的服务，但私营部门（企业）组织可能比政府组织更有效地提供部分服务，完全私有的服务通常是政府通过与能够提供全部服务的企业签订合同来完成且没有公共部门的参与（Ostrom et al.，1978）。

不同类型的服务通常与不同种类的服务提供商相关联。例如，可以根据使用情况向个人提供的服务收费，这类服务通常是通过公私伙伴关系或与私营供应商签订的合同提供的。这是因为所提供的商品不是纯公共物品，纯公共物品是指不能根据用途划分为单个单位的物品，不能排除个人使用该物品（非排他性），并且一个人对该物品的使用不会剥夺另一个人对物品的使用（非竞争性）。例如，公园被认为是纯公共物品，因为它们向所有人开放，一个人使用公园并不会阻止其他人使用。

一般来说，如果一个城市提供公共物品，那么提供者应是完全公共的提供者。如果城市提供的服务或商品不是公共物品，那么有时私人供应商如企业可能能够以比公共机构更具成本效益的方式提供该商品或服务，公共交通、水、污水和废物处理，这些服务依赖于公私伙伴关系的结合，或者由城市政府与私营供应商签订合同来提供服务。

私有化和外包：利与弊

私有化一直存在争议，服务一旦由国家提供，公众就会将该服务与国家联系起来，并抵制对该服务提供方式的更改，政府工作人员的工作依赖于这些服务的提供，选民越来越成熟去保护服务的公共提供（政府免费地向消费者提供产品和服务），政治家甚至可能会参与对各种服务的赞助。因此，即使私有化和外包以前由国家提供的服务背后有坚实的逻辑基础，这种决定仍然受到来自倡导者和批评者的争议。

赞成意见

私有化的倡导者认为，市场在提供商品和服务方面实际上比政府更有效率。这些主张私营部门优越性的人将把政府的论点局限于市场失灵的一个非常狭隘的例外。人们认为，政府缺乏良好经营企业的激励，也缺乏利润动机作为推动绩效和效率的激励。

在没有这种利润动机的情况下，政府机构的绩效以内部控制和环境合理化为导向，公共部门的绩效包含多个目标，因此牺牲了对私营部门而言至关重要的因素。效率是公共部门的众多目标之一，却是私营部门的盈利之路，对私营部门至关重要，也推动其成本的降低和生产力的提高，从而使利润成为可能，预期从公共部门向私营部门的转移将提高效率并促进业绩。

理论上，通过追求纯粹的经济目标而非政治目标，也可以加快业绩的提升，这是市场约束的过程。在公共部门花费大量资源来实现非经济目标的情况下，私营部门可以专注于纯利润和效率，对利润的需要要求企业服从市场规则，否则就会亏损。根源于私营部门非常不同的激励机制，私营部门对选民的民主问责机制与公共部门截然不同，导致从纯粹的经济角度来看，这种评估更加合理和有效。有了以利润为导向的问责机制，改进和投资完全是根据业务需要进行的，而不是根据政治或官僚因素进行的。

根据这一问责制，公共部门在理论上更容易腐败和受到外部影响。缺乏市场约束意味着政治影响力可能会因赞助人而受到影响，出现委托代理问题，即政治家可能会试图通过更适合经济目的的组织来实现其政策目标，最终，政府可能会出于纯粹的政治考虑介入并投资或纾困效率低下、不合理的政府实体。由于主要经济实体掌握在国家手中，相对狭隘的政治利益集团有可能夺取当地的部分资源，以实现自己的经济利益。除了采取政治行动保护自己的权力外，大量的公共精英还可能通过对政治制度的影响保护他们实际上控制的财富的集中。此外，经济模型倾向于假定对信息的自由控制，但市场扭曲的另一个来源是政府对信息的控制，因为国家有独特的信息获取渠道，并且可能根据其他经济行为体无法获取的信息采取行动。

提高绩效的另一个因素是专业化。地方政府所需的规模和普遍或接近普遍的覆盖面意味着私营实体可以将任务划分得更专业化，通过专门调整其工作以满足特定需求，进而更好地服务于特定利益。

当经济实体与市场约束隔绝时，也存在其他问题。政府在筹集资金方面具有不公平的竞争优势，因为政府有权征税和支出，这在地方政府中可能是一种更受限制的权力，因为中央政府通常会限制地方税收政策。然而，即使在相对薄弱的地方政府中，由于政府投资的安全性，进入资本市场也相对容易，这样地方政府就可以像私人公司一样更容易筹集到同等数量的资金，这意味着债券发行有可能带来资本市场的扭曲。另外，尽管地方政府可能没有为筹集资金支付任何经济溢价，但可能在筹集资金时必须支付政治溢价，特别是在经济不稳定或企业不倾向于看好政府举措的项目中，可以通过将这些决策转移给市场来消除这种可能性。

最后，私有化可能会限制国家的规模，降低税收，使更多的经济体受制于有效的市场。尽管可能是出售时的一次性收益，但私有化过程本身可以为国家筹集资金。这种市场化可能会产生一种全面的变革效应，在提高经济效率的同时，就业水平也可能会全面提高。

反对意见

私有化的反对者持有不同的关注点和论点，在某些情况下，甚至对评估的影响也有所不同。基本区别之一是，反对私有化的人往往会质疑政府领域缺乏激励机制，他们认为，官僚机构缺乏盈利动机，但对环境非常敏感，不一定是市场信号和市场压力，而是政府更适合应对的压力，如选民和重要选区的要求。

从这个角度来看，缺乏市场约束是一种优势，而不是一个问题。问责制主要是民主的，因此优先事项和政策可以由选民决定，而不是由未经选举的金融行动者决定，这些行动者除了作为投资者之外，甚至可能在当地没有个人利益。市场通常不允许对经济进行太多的协调和控制，特别是在满足最容易成为市场失灵受害者的服务不足的社区的需求方面。政府有权制定灵活且符合当前形势的民主目标，而私人目标可能不会通过施加政治影响来实现公共目标。例如，当裁员以降低成本、减少需求、进一步减少销售额时，响应市场信号的私人投资可能会加剧市场问题，从而形成恶性循环。此外，裁员会增加提供失业福利、职业培训和安置的成本。当成本较低且整体经济乘数效应可能最大时，公共实体可以战略性地忽略市场信号，并参与计算周期性投资。

此外，政府可能更有能力实现企业由于财政压力而无法或不愿意做的改进，即使这些改进可能用于公共福利或其他无法实现的共同目的。这种设定灵活目标的能力，加上政府负责的各种绩效目标，甚至可能意味着政府绩效优于私人绩效，这是因为私营部门在效率方面表现出色，而公共部门必须在另外的领域表现出色。

另一个优势是尊重法律。国家更有可能遵守法律，通常有更高的法律责任标准，公民自由问题可以从公共利益的角度加以解决，而无须考虑市场压力。总而言之，许多公共部门工作的管理与企业私营部门经常出现的短期利润最大化背道而驰。

私有化最基本的问题之一是实际进程本身，私有化进程很难管理，而且经常有腐败交易的可能性，如内幕信息泄露，在竞标公共财产时给特定的私人利益带来不公平的优势等。尽管政府官员通常受到严格的道德标准的约束，但当政府签订合同时，操纵投标始终是一种潜在的腐败形式，并且可能存在强大的地方商业利益集团可能通过这种方式施加有效的政治压力来实现其经济目标。

虽然利润动机对私有化的支持者来说是可取的和有价值的，但它可能会通过增加额外费用来降低绩效。公共实体不需要盈利，可以以成本或低于成本的价格提供服务，而私人部门必须提高价格以增加利润。这可能会导致基本服务的削减，因为私营部门试图将利润添加到成本组合中，可能会在这个过程中增加贫困等问题，因为向目标群体提供的资金较少，由于类似的原因，这也可能导致失业和裁员。或者出于政策原因，比如在经济衰退期间和经济需求不足时，一个公共部门可以负担得起更多人的工资。

最后，在任何私有化过程中都必须谨慎，因为自然垄断或公共产品的生产可能被不适当地转移到私营部门。然而，不存在真正的竞争，市场竞争的理论利益也不会实现。

4.5 关于公共服务的讨论

居民通常根据五个标准来判断服务提供情况：服务提供是否有效率？服务提供是平等的还是公平的？服务提供有效果吗？服务是否能满足公民和居民的需求？是通过中央政府在民主制度下提供的服务吗？

第一个标准与居民认为提供特定服务水平的合理成本有关，换言之，作为交换，他们的税款是否获得了公平的价值？效率通常是服务的质量或数量与其成本之间的比较，单位成本的质量或数量越高，服务提供的效率越高。当服务价格上涨时，居民通常会考虑服务成本是否是公平的成本。例如，如果乘坐公共汽车的费用增加1角，一些乘坐公共汽车的公众可能会认为这一增加表明服务提供效率降低了。由于公共服务通常是根据投入来判断的（在服务上花了多少钱，而不是人们每次乘坐多少钱），因此很难确定乘坐公交车的价格是否公平，毕竟，没有其他公交车服务可以进行价格比较，因此没有有效的定价机制来确定合理的成本，这使得很难反驳"服务提供效率降低了"的结论。但城市政府可以做很多其他的事情，如向公众提供信息，说明为什么需要增加成本。

第二个标准涉及总体公平问题。由于城市的服务提供是通过政治手段决定的，因此，在资源分配方面经常会出现问题。例如，如果一个城市决定将其收入用于在新社区的基础设施建设以促进增长，这意味着用于现有社区的收入减少，在负担不起迁入新社区的居民眼中，这种政策决定可能被视为不公平或不公正的，这种提供服务的方式可以称为再分配，因为城市从所有居民那里收取税款，并将其重新分配给某一特定群体。服务提供的再分配方法也可能引起高度争议，因为这种做法是从全体纳税人那里获取资源，并将其用于一个较小的群体或企业。

第三个标准是有效性。一个城市解决问题的情况如何？服务质量如何？这些是通过有效性标准来判断的。如果城市政府在一项旨在增加旅游业和城市收入的活动上花费了大量资金，那么这个政策决定的有效性将受到密切关注。如果没有人来参加活动，或者出席人数远低于预期，那么城市政府的努力将被视为无效，这会给城市官员带来很大的困难，因为对有效性的看法往往与城市领导人的看法以及他们维持一定服务水平的能力相联系。

第四个标准是回应性。服务提供如何满足公民需求？换言之，这一标准与公民满意度有关。尽管可以有效地提供服务，并且可能有效地解决问题或需求，但公民仍然可能对服务不满意。

第五个标准是内部控制问题。这是服务组织内的个体如何与监管部门联系并在其监督下工作的问题。真正的服务提供商将大部分时间花在远离主管的领域，从而造成不受欢迎、腐败、适得其反和浪费的可能性。一个典型的例子是警察服务，在警察服务中，他们的主管无法直接监测到正在巡逻和回应报警电话的警官的工作情况。

【思考题】

1. 为什么政府要干预当地市场以提供城市服务？
2. 为什么会存在政府失灵？
3. 在提供地方公共服务方面，效率和公平哪个更重要？
4. 私有化或外包的利弊各是什么？
5. 判断服务提供的标准是什么？

【关键术语】

便利设施服务	投票悖论
基本服务	市场失灵
共同生产	道德风险
外部性	网络设施

搭便车	点模式设施
政府失灵	猪肉桶
互相吹捧（互投反对票）	委托代理问题
强制性服务	多数人暴政
公用事业	

参考文献

［1］ Peters，B. Guy（2001）. *The Politics of Bureaucracy*，5th ed. New York：Routledge.

［2］ Weimer，David and Vining，Aidan（2005）. *Policy Analysis：Concepts and Practice.* 4th ed. Upper Saddle River，NJ：Pearson/Prentice-Hall：54 – 191.

Chapter 4   Urban Public Services

4. 1   Definition

City governments spend a substantial portion of their time providing services to their residents. But what kinds of services should a city provide? The answer to this question depends on many factors, such as the size, age, and level of industrialization a city may have achieved. In general, however, urban services are decided by a mix of political, economic and planning forces that come to some consensus about what citizens both want and need.

William C. Baer defines urban public services as "one which serves the public interest by accomplishing one or more of the following purposes: preserving life, liberty and property; promoting enlightenment, happiness, domestic tranquility and the general welfare. It is provided by one or more of the sectors in the economy through government regulation, co-production, or direct provision" (Baer, 1985: 886). This is asking quite a lot of an urban government, but urban governments are expected to provide many of the services that make life in a city both convenient and enjoyable. If the government fails in this respect, city life can be a very hard life for many of its residents. Therefore, understanding urban public services is an important part of understanding what urban administrators do.

4. 2   Rationale for Government Intervention

Why should urban governments provide services, and which services should those governments provide? Generally, urban governments are expected to provide services that are required by city residents (political responsiveness) and that the market will not or cannot provide. In economic terms, this happens under conditions of market failure. For economists, market failure has very specific definitions and conditions. In urban administration, the definitions are somewhat different, so both will be covered below. Additionally, city governments may attempt to solve a public problem, and end up either making the problem worse, or creating other, unanticipated problems. These also may require government intervention, but the rationale is due to conditions of government failure. This will be treated separately in the following sections.

4. 2. 1 Market Failure: The Economist's View

To understand the economist's view of market failure, one must first understand some basic assumptions economists make about human behavior. There are three basic assumptions: first, when people make decisions, they make decisions as individuals. Second, each person's decision is driven by that person's utility. A utility is anything that a person values: money, love, or happiness can all play this role. Third, when a person makes a decision, therefore, he or she will logically make choices that maximize his or her utility. For example, if my utility is money, then my decisions will be based on the choice that maximizes the amount of money that I can gain through that choice. Economists refer to individuals as rational and utility-maximizing, and the assumption that this behavior is universal underlies most economic models.

There are several kinds of market failure in economics, but generally market failure can be defined in terms of Pareto efficiency: when individuals (or firms) are engaged in voluntary transactions (buying and selling) in a competitive market, the forces of supply and demand will find a point at which no person can be made better off without making someone else worse off. This point is known as a Pareto-efficient allocation of goods (Weimer and Vining, 2005: 71). A market failure occurs when there is a violation of one or more of these conditions, and a Pareto-efficient allocation of goods cannot occur. In other words, a different set of choices could make more people better off without harming anyone. In the eyes of the economist, this is inefficient and therefore, socially unacceptable. When such failures occur, it is logical for an authority external to a market to intervene and try to correct the failure.

Different Kinds of Market Failure: Monopolies

A monopoly is something that markets may create when functioning normally, but the presence of a monopoly can cause inefficiencies in the market. A monopoly occurs when a firm or a group of firms have enough market power to influence the price of a good or service. In general terms, this happens when a firm or group of firms lack enough effective competition to provide a check on price. This leads to inefficient pricing of the good or service, and therefore people who might otherwise participate in the market do not. In simple language, a monopoly generally means that prices are higher than they should be, and consumers are paying more for a good or service than they would in a competitive market.

Tools for Addressing Monopolies

If a monopoly occurs, the government tool most commonly used is a kind of regulation called anti-trust regulation. This is a tool that is usually beyond the scope of what a city government can do. It requires the authority to break up a company that has grown too large, and in most countries, that authority only exists at the national level (if at all). However, city governments do face problems related to monopolies, since cities are often where one or more in-fluential businesses or industries based, whose presence is central to the economic well-being of the city's residents. So even though a city may not have the legal power to influence the behavior of a monopoly, it could certainly be affected should the national government decide to break up a corporation that they considered too large and uncompetitive. If an industry were downsized to combat monopoly tendencies, cities that house that industry would feel the effects at the local level, even if the national economy improved as a result.

Externalities

An externality is a cost that is not reflected in the price of a good because it is shifted to a third party who is not involved in the transaction between a buyer and a seller. For example, let's say you have a company that produces paper (Firm A) and a company that sells office sup-plies (Firm B). Firm B wants to buy paper at a particular price, preferably as cheaply as pos-sible. Firm A produces paper at a price that Firm B is willing to pay. So Firm B buys its paper from Firm A, and everyone fees happy?

Well, not quite. Firm A produces paper at that price because it disposes of the wastewater created during production in the local river. Since bleach is used in the process (white paper sells at higher prices), all the fish in the river are killed by the wastewater. The people who live alongside the river now have no fish to eat, and a polluted river with water they cannot drink. To survive, they must buy expensive equipment to remove harmful chemicals from their drinking water. Firm A has been able to sell paper at a lower price than its competitors by shift-ing a production cost (safe disposal of wastewater) to people who were not part of the transac-tion between Firm A and Firm B. That cost is now being paid by the people who live alongside the river, and is therefore external to the transaction. So, the price that Firm B paid for the pa-per did not include the actual cost of production.

Externalities like this one are called negative because they impose a cost on the third party. However, externalities can also be positive. This happens when the transaction provides a benefit to a third party that is not reflected in the price. For example, if you buy bright flowers to put in your front window to make your home more cheerful, you have paid for flowers that you think will achieve that goal. But people who pass by your window on the street can also see and enjoy the bright flowers, without having participated in the transaction. In this case, a benefit has been shifted to the third party (the passersby), so the externality is positive.

Tools for Addressing Externalities

The tools that governments use to deal with negative externalities (which are generally of more concern than positive ones) are regulatory tools that impose a cost on the firm or entity that is creating the problem. Generally, the government tries to impose a cost that is high enough so that it will be cheaper for the firm to absorb the externality itself than it will be to pay the cost imposed by the government. A cost can be monetary (like a fine or fee) or it can be punitive (punishment, such as incarceration or public spectacle), but generally, the cost is meant to change the behavior of the party that is creating the externality.

The government can also use incentives to get someone to absorb the cost of the externality. An incentive might be a tax reduction if a company uses a process better at containing negative externalities. It can also be something that improves the reputation of a company, such as the government offering a designation to the firm as an excellent corporate citizen. City governments may confront externalities in many ways. For example, disputes often arise between city residents who use their property for conflicting purposes. One resident may wish to sleep well during the day because they work night shifts, and their neighbor may want their child to practice the trumpet in the afternoons when she returns from school. Clearly these uses will not combine well. When the conflict arises one-on-one, usually the parties involved may try and negotiate some sort of agreement between themselves (the girl's mother agrees to have her practice the trumpet an hour and a half later, after the neighbor has woken up from his nap).

Sometimes, however, the behavior of one resident can impose costs on many residents. Then there is a need for outside intervention. Most cities use ordinances, or rules, that they enforce when such situations arise. So, when one resident is engaging in undesirable behavior (loud parties late at night, garbage piled outside their door that attracts bugs or vermin), there are usually laws that can be enforced by the city police or health and sanitation workers.

The most powerful regulatory tool that city governments have for addressing externalities is zoning. Cities can control development within their jurisdictions, and can zone land according to its use. In this way, conflicting uses can be separated, so that residents or workers will not be troubled by the activities of other residents. So, a city may zone one area for heavy industry, and then zone another area further away for residential use. This way, some of the costs created by heavy industry (e. g. lower air quality, loud noise) will be contained within that area of the city—residents will be far removed from such activities. This helps keep the city's environment harmonious while allowing the diversity necessary for a thriving community.

Informational Asymmetry

The third kind of market failure that demands government intervention is informational asymmetry. This is a condition where a buyer and a seller are both able to engage in a transaction (the buyer has enough money to pay for the good, and the seller is willing to offer the good at a price the buyer will pay), but there is doubt in the buyer's mind as to whether the good is worth the price the seller is offering. When the doubt is substantial enough to prevent the transaction from going through, then a market failure has occurred. In this case, the market failure is due to an imbalance between the information that the seller has about his or her sound and the information that the buyer requires to determine whether the price is fair. This is why it is called informational asymmetry.

For a buyer and a seller, this kind of failure can be frustrating. For example, a man would like to buy a used car because it is cheaper than a new car, and he can afford a car of recent model in relatively good condition, so he searches for a car he likes and can afford. He finds one that is remarkably cheap for the mileage and the condition. He asks the owner why she is willing to sell her car at a price that is much cheaper than other cars with similar mileage and in similar condition. The owner says that she no longer needs the car, so she is willing to take a lower price to get rid of it quickly. Still, the man is not sure. He wonders if the car has been in an accident, or if there is something wrong with the engine that he cannot determine on his own. He decides that he does know enough about the car not to trust the owner's explanation, so he continues to look for another car.

Tools for Addressing Informational Asymmetries

Part of the difficulties here is that the man doesn't know what will happen if he buys the car and it does not perform as he expects. Will the owner return his money if he returns the car to her? The lack of information has made the transaction impossible. This is where government intervention could be quite helpful. In cases of informational asymmetry, the tool governments use to address the problem is usually to require the disclosure of more information by the seller, and to enforce contracts that are struck between buyer and seller. Other common tools are consumer protection laws. In the used car example, this could be done by passing a "Lemon Law" (common in many parts of the US). This kind of law states that when a title for a vehicle (the official document stating who owns the vehicle) is transferred to a new owner, the new owner has a certain amount of time after buying the vehicle (usually three months) to determine whether the vehicle has been sold in the condition promised by the seller. If a problem arises, the Lemon Law allows the buyer to return the vehicle to the seller and be fully reimbursed. This kind of assurance helps the transaction go through because both the buyer and the seller have a third party (the government) to help them enforce the terms of the transaction.

For urban administrators, informational asymmetry can surface in many places, and can cause inefficiencies that create problems for residents. Such problems are related to the amount of information residents have about goods or services they may wish to buy, but are unsure about whether the price offered is reasonable. This can happen when there is suspicion about the safety of a given product or service. For example, there are many vitamins, energy drinks, herbal remedies that are sold to consumers claiming to have a wide variety of health benefits. But are these claims genuine? There are laws that require companies to list the ingredients they use when making a product so that consumers are better informed about what they are buying. Without such laws, people often bought products that did not benefit them in the ways they anticipated, and sometimes could cause serious harm. The government's role as a provider of information is a regulatory role, since it imposes a cost on those who produce the information.

Moral Hazard

The last kind of market failure generally seen as requiring government intervention is moral hazard. A moral hazard occurs when the pricing of a product is based upon uncertain or incomplete information. The most common example of this kind of problem arises with the purchase of insurance coverage. In actuarial studies done of drivers in the US, for example, young men between the ages of 16 (the legal driving age in most states) and 24 are the most likely to be involved in high speed/high damage crashes. Therefore, insurance companies charge higher rates for men who fall into this age category. However, people who do not fall into the higher price categories because they are lower risks may choose not to buy insurance, since they perceive the risk of an accident as low. This means that the cost of insurance is being covered by those who pay higher rates to begin with, and with fewer people paying for insurance, the average cost rises even more. This shifts the burden of coverage to the high-risk population, and permits *free riding* for those who choose not to purchase insurance. Free riding refers to the behavior of individuals who know that they will not be caught if they do not pay for a service because the number of people receiving the service is too high for the service provider to monitor payment. This is a problem often associated with the provision of a public good (Weimer and Vining, 2005: 120-124).

For urban administrators, moral hazards may occur when there is some sort of guarantee offered that may skew the way people perceive risk. People may be willing to engage in risky behavior if they have underestimated the cost of risk. For example, someone may build their home close to the ocean because there have been several years without flooding from typhoons. When they build the house, they do not consider what the cost will be to them if they lose not only the building but its contents in flooding due to a typhoon. As a result, they insure their house but undervalue replacing its contents. If flooding does occur, then the cost of replacement will far exceed the value of insurance.

Tools for Addressing Moral Hazards

Since moral hazards can be caused by the same lack of information that generates informational asymmetry, the tools for addressing moral hazards are similar. If consumers are undervaluing their risk and potential loss, then the government can require minimum thresholds for recovery, such as instituting mandatory flood insurance for owners with homes built within a 100-year flood zone. City governments can also use zoning to establish areas within which certain activities carry less risk, and are therefore more suitable for certain public purposes, such as childcare facilities or public parks with exercise facilities for the elderly.

However, moral hazard poses the rather unique problem of potentially creating government failure in attempts to correct a market failure. For example, when the U S government stepped in and guaranteed the debt owed by several large banks and lending houses in late 2008, the

Bush Administration essentially lowered the risk to banks that had made risky lending decisions. The rationale given at the time was that such a guarantee was needed to stabilize markets and prevent widespread economic freefall. However, it made many mainstream economists extremely nervous because it increased, rather than reduced, the risk of moral hazard.

For urban administrators, correcting moral hazard is usually tied to improving the quality of information available to the public. Improving the quality of information can make it easier for citizens to correctly assess the risk associated with certain behaviors, and therefore better avail themselves of the necessary level of protection. If a child's parents, for example, believe that their child's risk of contracting a disease that requires vaccination, such as measles, is low because all other children are vaccinated, then they may choose not to have their child immunized. However, if too many parents make this kind of decision, then the real risk of an outbreak of measles in a vulnerable population increases. Government can make sure that parents understand what the risk is to their child should they not get the vaccination. Or, the government can make vaccination mandatory for use of public services, such as enrolling in school.

4. 2. 2   Government Failure

Sometimes a problem arises because a government has implemented a policy with unanticipated outcomes. When this occurs, it is referred to as a government failure. Government failures are not as commonly discussed as market failures, but they can result in a need for government intervention, so they should be included in this examination of reasons for urban governments to act. In general, a government failure is defined as a condition that prohibits the best allocation of public resources. This can happen in three separate ways (Weimer and Vining, 2005: 157). These are direct democracy, representative government, bureaucratic supply, and decentralized government. Each of these forms holds certain imperfections in relaying individual preferences to the collective action and services provided by government. These imperfections form the basis for government failure.

Direct Democracy

When people vote in elections, the process of voting itself can create problems in relating what people want as policies to those who make policies in government. Kenneth Arrow, a Nobel-prize winning economist, was the first to demonstrate that voting in fair elections can result in no one getting their top preferences, and a lack of coherent policies over consecutive elections. He outlined this problem in his general possibility theorem (Arrow, 1951), which illustrates the paradox of voting. To sum up, even if a majority votes for a particular policy in one election, there is no guarantee that the policy selected is actually the policy most preferred by voters. This gives a great advantage to whoever controls the policy agenda, which means those who are in a ruling position. This condition is somewhat less pronounced in parliamentary systems of government, but can still hold true.

Another problem with direct democracy is known as tyranny of the majority. This can happen when people who occupy a more advantaged position in society and have greater numbers than those less well off vote to keep the distribution of resources as it is. Thus, the majority can impose a cost on a minority of citizens simply by voting in favor of its private interests. In other instances, such as the voting on referenda, most citizens can decide to pass laws that allow discriminatory practices to be put in place against minorities. Under these conditions, majority rule does not equal a just society. Thus, for democracies with majority rule, there must usually be some sort of balance to protect minorities, or tyranny will result.

Thus, when politicians who have won most votes claim that their policies represent the people's policies and values, such claims do not hold true. In a truly democratic society, there is always a balance that must be struck to best accommodate competing values and resolve social conflict. A majority today may not be a majority tomorrow, so policy makers must constantly adjust their thinking to move beyond winning elections.

Representative Government

In a democracy, voters generally elect candidates who they believe will represent their views in government. However, representatives can be motivated by incentives other than simply serving their constituencies. In general, these motivations have been described as two sometimes competing roles that representatives must play: the delegate and the trustee.

The delegate seeks to represent his constituents as faithfully as possible, and believes that this faithfulness is what he was elected to demonstrate. If constituents, for example, are strongly opposed to locating a nuclear power plant in their district, a representative behaving as a delegate does everything possible to make sure the power plant is not located in his district. The trustee, on the other hand, believes that the public has trust in his judgment, and that the job requires that the representative make decisions that are in the best interests of both their constituents and society. As a result, a trustee might not see the placing of the nuclear power plant within his district as a bad policy if he believes that such placement is really the best solution for a problem that goes beyond the borders of the voting district. A trustee's approach to governing, therefore, can be quite different from that of a delegate.

There are all sorts of problems that can arise with either approach. Rent-seeking behavior, log-rolling and pork barrel distributive policymaking are some examples. Each of these behaviors can make constituents happy, but can create problems for the government. This is generally an issue at national levels of government, where the impact of such decisions is difficult for individual constituencies to see, but it can happen in large cities where different districts are competing for shared resources. In a strong mayor system, for example, the mayor may favor districts that are represented by representatives from the mayor's political party. Or, a mayor may decide that every district, regardless of performance or need, may be entitled to the same resources. In each of these situations, citizens may not perceive such behavior as equitable, and may respond negatively to the resulting policies.

Decentralized Government

Decentralization occurs when local governments are given the discretion to make decisions about how to best use resources within their jurisdictions. For national governments, this can be a more efficient way to allocate resources, since the people making decisions about resource allocation know more about the situation at the local level, and can therefore make better quality decisions. However, since implementation of a policy may vary from local government to local government, monitoring the effectiveness of a policy in achieving its goals becomes more complicated and more difficult. Thus, decentralization can increase the likelihood of unintended consequences arising from policy implementation. Unintended consequences are unexpected results from a particular policy, and therefore may require additional government intervention.

4. 3　Types of Services

Basic versus Amenity Services

One standard for defining types of service is whether it is necessary or optional. Necessary services that local governments must provide are known as basic services. These are the fundamental services required to support and maintain the city. These include basic essentials such as garbage collection and pavement and road repair. On the other hand, optional services are called amenity services. These mean services to improve citizen quality of life. These include public libraries and entertainment facilities.

Mandatory versus Discretionary Services

The second typology is based on the discretion of what services are provided by urban government. There are certain services that an urban government must provide. Such services, as mandated by law, are mandatory services. Police and fire services are typical mandatory services that must be provided in every case. Other services, known as discretionary services, may be provided at the choice or discretion of local government. Discretionary services include entertainment and cultural services.

Spatial Distribution

The third typology for dividing public services is based on how services are concentrated in physical space. A point-pattern facility system is based on fixed facilities, like libraries and hospitals. Residents need to go to one of the fixed locations to receive services. The other option is a network facility system, where the services are broadly dispersed throughout the city and connected spatially, allowing the residents to access the service wherever they are. Sewage and drinking water are two examples of services delivered through a network facility system. However, some services have both traits simultaneously. For example, policing services are based around police stations that are fixed, but include the inter-point connections in the form of regular patrols and police dispatch. Some services require intergovernmental cooperation across a broad area. For example, fire and police service require interregional coordination. Metropolitan forms of organization covering broad areas are necessary to provide such services.

Common Services Provided by City Government

Generally, these are types of services that city governments provide on a regular basis: public transportation, transportation infrastructure, planning for development, law enforcement, fire protection, education, public park creation and maintenance, sanitation services, provision of clean water, sewage treatment systems, provision of electricity, and occasionally, telecommunications infrastructure (cables or wireless systems). Additionally, depending on the city size and population, the government may also provide welfare services for the poor, or development services for businesses and to promote growth.

Each of these services may be provided through different kinds of service providers. In the next section, three general kinds of service provision will be introduced, and then the link between the type of service and the kind of service provider will be discussed.

4. 4　Service Provision

The kinds of services that city governments provide can range according to the nature of the provider and the nature of the service. Generally, there are three broad categories: fully public; public-private partnerships (also known as coproduction); fully private. A service that is fully public is provided entirely by government employees. A service provided through a public-private partnership is usually one that government has decided should be a public benefit, but private sector (business) organizations may be able to provide the service in part more efficiently or effectively than government organizations. A service that is fully private is generally done through a contract with a business that can provide the service in full, with no involvement from public sector employees (Ostrom *et al.* , 1978).

Different types of services are often associated with different kinds of service providers. For example, services that can be offered to individuals for a fee based on usage are generally provided through either a public-private partnership or through a contract with a private provider. This is because the good being provided is not a pure public good. A pure public good is one that cannot be divided up into individual units according to usage and cannot exclude individuals from using the good (non-excludable), and one individual's use of the good does not take away from another individual's use of the good (non-rivalrous). Public parks, for example, are thought of as public goods because they are open to all, and if there are not too many people using the park, one person's use of the park does not keep someone else from using it as well.

Generally, if a city is providing a public good, the provider is a fully public provider. If the city is providing a service or good that is not a public good, then sometimes a private provider, such as a business, may be able to provide that good or service in a more cost-effective manner than a public agency. Public transportation, water, sewage and waste disposal are all examples of city services that rely on a combination of public-private partnerships or where city governments contract with private providers to provide the service.

Privatization and Contracting Out: Pros and Cons

Privatization has been controversial. Once a service is provided by the state, the public associates that service with the state and resists changes to how that service is provided. Government employees come to depend on the provision of those services for their jobs. Constituencies grow up to protect the public provision of services. Politicians may even become involved in patronage regarding various services. Therefore, even when there is solid logic behind privatization and contracting out of previously state-provided services, such decisions remain controversial with both advocates and critics.

Pros

Advocates for privatization argue that markets are *de facto* more efficient in delivery of goods and services than government. Such advocates for the superiority of the private sector would limit the argument for government to a very narrow exception for market failure. There is the belief that governments lack incentives to run enterprises well with the lack of the profit motive as an incentive to drive performance and efficiency.

In the absence of this profit motive, bureaucratic performance is oriented towards internal controls and rationalization with the environment and public-sector performance incorporates multiple goals, sacrificing what is of paramount importance to the private sector. Efficiency is the road to profit in the private sector. Where it is one of many goals in the public sector, it is of primary importance in the private sector, driving the reduction of costs and the increase in productivity that make profit possible. It is expected that a transfer from the public sector to the private sector will increase efficiency and give a boost to performance.

This boost to performance is also theoretically sped along through the pursuit of purely economic and not political goals. This is the process of market discipline. Where the public sector expends substantial resources to accomplish non-economic goals, the private sector organizations can afford to focus on pure profit and efficiency. The need for profit demands that the firm be subjected to the requirements of the market or lose money. This very different incentive structure is the source of accountability in the private sector, unlike the democratic accountability to the electorate in the private sector. This will lead to outcomes that, in pure economic terms, may be evaluated to be more rational and efficient. With profit-oriented accountability structures in place, improvements and investments are made purely according to business need, and not according to political or bureaucratic factors.

According to this system of accountability, the public sector is theoretically prone to corruption and outside influences. The lack of market discipline means that political influence may be brought to bear for patronage reasons, principal-agent issues may arise, politicians may try to follow other policy goals with organizations better suited to economic purposes and, ultimately, the government may step in and invest or bail out inefficient and irrational government entities for purely political considerations. With major economic entities in state hands, it is possible for relatively narrow political interests to capture parts of the local state and twist it to their economic benefit. In addition to acting politically to protect their power, substantial public elites may act politically to protect the economic concentrations of wealth they *de facto* control through their influence over the political system. Further, economic models tend to assume free control of information, but another source of economic market distortion is government control of information as the state has unique access to information and may be able to act on information that other economic actors do not have access to.

Another factor boosting performance is specialization. The required scale and universal or near universal coverage in local government means that private entities can divide the tasks into narrower specializations, all the better to serve particular interests by specially tailoring their work to meeting particular needs.

When economic entities are insulated from market discipline, there are other problems as well. Government has an unfair competitive advantage in raising capital as governments have the power to tax and spend. This may be a more restricted power in local government as the national government usually places limits on local revenue policy. However, even in relatively weak local governments, access to capital markets tends to be relatively easy due to the security of government investments so that government may have an easier time raising an equal amount of money as a private firm would. This means that there is the possibility that bond issues may distort capital markets. On the other hand, though there may not be any economic premium paid by the government for raising capital, there may be a political premium government may have to pay in raising capital, particularly for projects in unstable economies or where businesses do not tend to look favorably on a government initiative. This possibility is eliminated by shifting these decisions back to the market.

Finally, privatization may limit the size of the state, lowering tax revenues, and subjecting more of the economy to the efficient market. The privatization process itself raises money for the state, although this may be a one-time benefit at the time of sale. This marketization may have an overall transforming effect whereby, in making the economy more economically efficient, there may be an overall rise in employment levels.

Cons

Opponents of privatization have a different set of concerns and arguments and even, in some cases, apply similar concerns with a different assessment of the impact. One of the fundamental differences is that anti-privatizers tend to question the lack of incentives in the government sphere. They acknowledge the lack of profit motive, but see the bureaucracy as very environmentally sensitive, just not necessarily to market signals and market pressures, but to pressures that are more appropriate for government to address, such as the demands of the electorate and key constituencies.

In this view, the very lack of market discipline is an asset instead of a problem. Accountability is primarily democratic so that priorities and policies may be determined by the electorate instead of by unelected financial actors who may not even have a personal stake in the locality, other than as an investor. The market does not generally allow for much coordination and control over the economy, particularly in meeting the needs of underserved communities most prone to being the victims of market failure. Government has the power to set democratic goals that are flexible and correspond to current situations in a way that private goals may not through applying political influence to achieve public goals. For example, private investment in responding to market signals may intensify market problems when layoffs to reduce costs reduce demand further reducing sales, creating a vicious cycle. In addition, layoffs will increase the costs of providing for unemployment benefits and job training and placement. Public entities can strategically ignore market signals and engage in count-cyclical investments when costs are low, and the overall economic multiplier effect may be the greatest.

Moreover, the government may be better positioned to deliver on improvements that businesses may be unable or unwilling to do due to financial pressures, even though they may provide for the public welfare or other common purposes that would not otherwise be accomplished. This ability to set flexible goals, plus the variety of performance goals government is held accountable for may even mean, in this view, that government performance is superior to private performance. That is because the private sector excels at efficiency whereas the public sector must perform on several dimensions.

Another advantage is respect for law. The state is more likely to obey the law, is generally held to higher standards of legal accountability, and civil-liberties concerns can be addressed in the public interest without necessarily having to consider market pressures. All-in-all, this results in something of a stewardship attitude towards many public sector endeavors that is antithetical to the short-term profit maximizing often found in the corporate private sector.

One of the most basic issues with privatization is with the actual process itself. It is difficult to manage the privatization process and there is frequently the potential for corrupt deals where inside information is leaked, giving particular private interests unfair advantage in bidding for public property. Although government officials are usually bound by strong ethical standards, bid rigging is always a potential form of corruption when government contracts out and there may be powerful local business interests who may be able to apply effective political pressure to achieve their economic goals in this way.

Although the profit motive appears desirable and valuable to proponents of privatization, it may lower performance by adding an extra expense. Public entities do not need to make a profit and can give out services at or below cost, while private entities must raise prices to add profit. This may lead to cuts in essential services as the private entity tries to add profit into the cost mix, possibly increasing problems like poverty in the process as fewer funds make it to the target group. It may also lead to job loss and downsizing for similar reasons. A public entity can afford to keep more people on the payroll or may desire to do so for policy reasons, as during a recession when there is insufficient demand in the economy.

Finally, care must be taken in any privatization as it is possible that a natural monopoly or the production of public goods may be transferred inappropriately to the private sector. However, no true competition will exist and the theoretical benefits of market competition will not be realized.

4. 5　Issues

Service provision is generally judged by residents according to five criteria: is the service provision efficient? is the service provision equitable, or fair? is the service provision effective? is the service responsiveness to the needs and demands of citizens and residents? is the service provided under a system of democratic control through central administration? The first criterion has to do with what residents believe is a reasonable cost for providing a particular level of service. In other words, are they getting fair value in exchange for their taxes? Efficiency is generally a comparison between the quality or quantity of a service and its cost. The higher the quality or quantity per unit cost, the higher the efficiency of service provision.

When prices for services go up, residents often consider whether the cost of the service is generally a fair cost. For example, if the cost of riding the bus goes up by 1 cent, some members of the bus-riding public may consider this increase to be an indication of inefficient service provision. Since public services are generally judged by input factors (how much is spent on the service rather than how much people pay per ride), it can be difficult to determine whether the price of a bus ride is a fair price. After all, there are no other bus services to compare prices with, so there is no effective pricing mechanism for determining a reasonable cost. This can make the claim of "inefficient service provision" a difficult claim to refute. A city government can do much to provide information to the public about why a cost increase might be necessary.

The second criterion addresses the question of overall fairness. Since service provision in cities is decided through political means, there are often problems that arise around the distribution of resources. For example, if a city decides to spend its revenues on building new infrastructure in new neighborhoods to generate growth, this means there is less revenue to spend on existing neighborhoods. In the eyes of residents who cannot afford to move into the new neighborhoods, this kind of policy decision may be viewed as unfair, or inequitable. This approach to service provision can be termed redistributive, since the city takes tax dollars from all its residents and redistributes them to only a very particular kind of resident. Redistributive approaches to service provision can also be highly contentious, since the practice takes resources from a large group (taxpayers) and concentrates them on a smaller group (business or certain group).

The third criterion is effectiveness. How well is a city solving its problems, and how good is the service provision? These are questions raised through the effectiveness criterion. If a city government spends a great deal of money on an event that is meant to increase tourism and revenue for the city, the effectiveness of this policy decision will be watched closely. If no one comes to the event, or if attendance is much lower than anticipated, the city government's efforts will be judged to be ineffective. This can cause a great deal of difficulty for the city's officials, since perceptions of effectiveness are often tied to perceptions of city leaders and their abilities to maintain a certain level of service provision.

The fourth is responsiveness. How does the service provision respond to citizen needs? In other words, this criterion is related to the degree of citizen satisfaction. Even though services may be delivered efficiently, and they may be effective at addressing the problem or need, citizens may still be dissatisfied with the service.

The fifth is the question of internal control. This is the issue of how the individual workers within the service organization are related to, and under the supervision of central management. The real service provider spends most of their time in the field far away from the eyes of supervisors, creating the possibility of undesirable, corrupt, counter-productive, and wasteful effort. A typical example is police service, where officers on patrol and in response to dispatch calls are not directly observable by their supervisors.

Questions

1. Why should the government intervene in local markets to provide urban services?
2. Why do governments fail?
3. Which is more important, efficiency or equity, in the provision of local public services?
4. What are the pros and cons of privatization or contracting out?
5. What are criteria for judging service provision?
6. Why do you agree or disagree with the free school lunch policy?

Key Terms

amenity services

basic services

coproduction

externalities

free riding

government failure

log rolling

mandatory services

utility

voting parado

market failure

moral hazard

network facility

point-pattern facility

pork barrel

principal-agent problem

tyranny of the majority

References

［1］ Peters, B. Guy (2001). *The Politics of Bureaucracy*, 5*thed*. New York: Routledge.

［2］ Weimer, David and Vining, Aidan (2005). *Policy Analysis: Concepts and Practice.* 4th ed. Upper Saddle River, NJ: Pearson/Prentice-Hall: 54 – 191.

第5章 府际管理

5.1 概念及内涵

城市在空间上是有限的，边界是一个城市政府的权力的终止，同时也是另一个城市政府的管辖权的开始。如果政府共享资源，如劳动力或基础设施，有时也会带来一定的问题。如果城市争夺这些资源，竞争有时可能会对所有人产生不利影响，在这种情况下，考虑如何共同管理联合提供服务或共享资源至关重要。

府际管理即地方政府间行政管理，是对地方政府之间共享的资源和服务的管理。由于地方政府对居住在境内的居民负责，因此实现与其他司法管辖区合作而非竞争可能并不容易，所以了解什么样的条件可以促使人们认识到地方政府间合作管理的必要性就显得尤为重要。

5.2 府际管理的必要性

推动府际管理的需求有三大类：资源共享、效率和服务共享，每一项都需要一套不同的行政工具，所有这些都对理解地方政府为满足这些需求可能作出的安排很重要。

资源共享

地方政府有时会分享某种资源：自然资源如水源，或人力资源如劳动力。共享需要管理，以防止过度使用或浪费资源。例如，可能有居住在大城市以外小城市的居民，通勤到大城市上班，这些居民为大城市提供资源（劳动力），但在大城市边界内也使用资源（基础设施），如果资源（劳动力）通过小城市征收的税收来支付基础设施费用，那么大城市可能会为在其边界内为那些不作为居民纳税的人提供基础设施方面承担不成比例的财政负担（Gainsborough，2001），这可能导致城市衰落，因为一个中心城市每天都在努力承担为它带来劳动力的基础设施的维护成本。

当共享资源是一种自然资源时，这两个城市的居民可能面临一个共同的问题。埃莉诺·奥斯特罗姆就这一问题写了大量文章，并认为管理共享资源的最佳方式是制订规则，提供共享资源各方追求的激励措施，并对使用资源过多的一方实施制裁。显然，要使这种制度发挥作用，使用资源的政府之间必须相互承认，它们需要共同负责维护资源的完整性，各方都需要对过度使用或滥用资源负责。

这两种资源之间的关键相似之处在于，都需要一个超越每个地方政府管辖范围的共同管理体系，换言之，地方政府必须找到一种方法，以公平和实用的方式共同管理资源。这可能会给地方政府带来独特的挑战，因为他们往往将对方视为竞争者，而不是合作者，毕竟每个政府都对其境内的居民（选民）负责。

效率

推动府际管理的最常见需求之一是提高效率。当地方政府认为，通过合并其管辖区或合并其政府，可以创造规模经济，减少冗余和重叠。正如迈克尔·詹森（Michael Jensen，2010）所说：新的合并政府希望提高其运营效率，解决未合并前单一地方政府未能有效解决的一系列社会、政治、金融、服务提供和基础设施带来的相关挑战。

合并政府意味着合并某些职能，并创建一个新的、更大的政府，将原有城市纳入合并后的结构内。然而，即使对效率的需求很高，也经常有人反对合并政府，政客们往往不愿意放弃自己的立场，或者担心会失去影响力或权力，政府工作人员和地方公务员往往担心一旦合并，就会失去其职位，因为新的联合政府旨在比单独的政府更有效地运作。通常情况下，合并的决定是由感知到的危机驱动的，当地官员认为没有更好的办法来改善现有的状况，例如财政危机（Johnson and Feiock，2001）。

服务共享

推动府际管理的最后一个重要需求是提供共享服务。共享服务的范围可以从公共交通、街道维护到医疗服务提供，地方政府可用于提供此类服务的安排可以从政府之间的正式合同到成立联合工作组委员会，再到关于谁负责提供哪部分服务的非正式协议。在某些情况下，可能会创建一种全新的政府形式来提供服务（Kent and Sowards，2005）。

服务类型通常是多个城市或地区的居民所需的服务类型，需要协调以确保各辖区服务质量的统一水平（如交通等），基本服务不重复（如医疗保健等），提供适当服务水平的专业知识。最后一类在美国更为常见，各州在州宪法中规定了市级和县级政府之间的职责授权。

当相邻城市的居民需要某项服务时，而两个城市又都没有足够的资源来提供该项服务，通常会联合提供，这也是一个集体行动问题，因为在第一类需要中，个体行为者可能没有意识到合作的必要，将其他城市视为竞争对手而不是合作者，在这种情况下，可能需要采取类似的方法来促进联合行动。

5.3 府际管理的形式

当需要以正式方式进行府际管理时，通常有三种常见形式（Kent and Sowards，2005）：区域合作、功能整合和全面整合。这些形式从最常见到最不常见，但每种形式都需要一定程度的重组，这意味着它们超越了本章前面提到的非正式的合作形式。这三种形式大不相同，但当职责和职能重组成功时，它们有三个共同特征（Kent and Sowards，2005）。

第一个是民主管理。居民知道谁是他们的代表，并清楚地知道如何让代表对其管理表现负责，这对于赋予居民对联合管理的控制感和责任感很重要。

第二个是共同授权。这意味着联合政府无论是哪种形式，都有权解决其管辖范围内出现的所有问题，这对于解决政府共同努力后仍可能出现的意外情况非常重要。如果新合并的政府形式无法应对与创建新形式相关的问题，那么居民将对其失去信心，政府将无法获得成功提供服务或管理资源所需的支持。

第三个是充足的独立资源。这意味着新合并的权力机构拥有自己的资源，这些资源足以执行所需的联合任务，保持了地方政府的独立性，这在美国等联邦制国家中通常是非常重要的，在韩国等中央集权制国家中也可能很重要。充足的资金确保地方政府的联合任务能够按计划进行，而无须中央政府的额外监督。

5.3.1　区域合作

区域合作是最常见的也是最少破坏性的府际管理形式。在这种形式下，所有地方政府签订了正式协议，共同提供必要的服务但各自保持完整和独立性。通过维持现有的政府形式，来自政府官员和公众的阻力都较小。因此，其被认为是改变服务提供和管理性质的一种更为渐进的方式，地方政府可能经常先去尝试这种形式的府际管理，然后再进行更实质性的政府整合。

通过签订合作协议，地方政府可以利用邻居地方政府的资源和专业知识，而不牺牲其管辖权或民主代表权，通常被认为是这种形式的跨地区管理的优势之一。然而，保持这种独立性也可能会带来推卸责任，因为对不合格服务的制裁通常很弱，所以政府通常不会阻止协议的终止。持反对意见者还会抱怨，允许地方政府在附加条件相对较少的情况下签订此类协议，可能会导致建立太多的联合管辖区，从而造成更多的混乱和分裂，而不是更好的合作。

5.3.2　职能合并

当两个或两个以上的地方政府决定合并某一个特定的服务提供领域时就需要进行职能整合。根据肯特和索瓦兹（Kent and Sowards，2005）的观点，某些服务提供领域在功能整合时运行得更好，实现规模经济带来的效率——公共工程，如道路、污水系统、饮用水供应、固体废物处理都是很好的公共服务的例子，这些公共服务会更加高效和有效。这种职能合并也使政府能够思考和规划由于共享管辖区不同部分的增加或减少可能产生的问题，以及这些变化如何影响职能合并的其他区域。

财务的职能整合是可以帮助提高效率的另一领域，特别是通过设立统一的税务机关，这是因为经济学家称之为"无谓损失"的条件。在市场经济中，当需求和供给之间达到平衡或均衡时，即达到愿意以特定价格购买或出售商品的最大买家和卖家数量，效率就会产生。然而，当政府对商品或服务征税时，会自动增加想要购买商品或服务的消费者的商品或服务成本，这意味着更少的买家能够以他们喜欢的价格购买商品或服务，更少的供应商能够为他们生产的商品或服务获得他们想要的价格。由于这种安排的效率低于自由市场，许多自由市场经济学家反对征税的想法，尤其是在更高层级政府。

然而，许多主流经济学家在原则上支持征税的想法，尤其是在需要提供公共物品或市场失灵的情况下。同时，他们认为，在这种情况下，税收是必要的，以产生足够的资金来提供所讨论的商品，或通过对某些种类的商品或服务施加更高的成本来改变人们的行为（例如，对香烟或酒精征税以减少对其的消费和改善健康）。经济学家认为，应尽可能广泛地分配征收的税款，以使税率相对较低，这可以最大限度地减少税收造成的市场扭曲，从而在政府服务提供和私人行为之间创造了一种可接受的平衡。

因此，建立一个统一的税务机关是经济学家认为最有效和高效的征税方式，它允许税收负担尽可能分散到一个大的管辖区，从而降低居民的单位税收价格。这是在不牺牲各个司法管辖区优势的情况下，在某个功能领域创造效率的好方法。

经济发展是另一个受益于功能整合的政策领域。寻求在城市设立分支机构或分公司的大企业通常寻求集中服务，因为这简化了他们必须通过的监管流程。因此，共同追求经济发展的城市对企业更具吸引力，因为当城市共同而非单独推行此类政策时，通常会实现更高的效率。

公共卫生在功能整合下也表现良好，在居民居住在一个城市而在另一个城市工作的情况下尤其如此。当人口流动时，协调卫生保健供应以支持公众的一般健康的能力非常重要。如果各城市正在协调努力遏制一种特别致命的传染病的传播，那么这样做比作为单独管辖区更有可能取得成功。

城市规划是最后一个常见的功能整合领域。城市规划通常被称为城市和区域规划，因为增长模式并不总是承认政治界限，区域规划通常需要考察未来增长和下降的需求和预测，这些需求和预测会产生超出一个城市边缘的影响，并影响周边地区或该地区的其他城市，尤其在考虑土地、水或海岸线等自然资源的使用时，这一点尤其重要。

5.3.3 全面合并

跨越地方政府边界的政府管理的最终形式是全面合并，也称为归并。在这种形式下，以前的各个政府单位被合并成一个集中统一的单一政府结构，以前由较小的、独立的政府单位履行的职能合并为一个系统。这种合并的优势在于创建一个单一实体来取代多个实体：跨地区的标准化程序，集中信息存储和检索，创造能够产生传播效应和提升购买力的规模经济，更统一的服务交付和质量。这通常是在一个国家之内的县和主要城市之间进行的，管辖范围内较小的城市将其部分或全部服务提供给新成立的政府。

全面合并的原因通常是基于财政方面的考量。例如，在美国，宪法要求各县提供某些服务，如穷人的医疗保健、通过治安官办公室履行的治安职责，以及司法机构，如审理其管辖范围内所有案件的县法院。各县可以征收财产税，但通常用于提供公共教育。

另外，城市可以与周边的县分享财产税收入，但不需要其提供相同的服务，许多较大的城市都是这样做的。城市还可以通过额外的税收和服务费来产生其他形式的收入，这意味着，在美国许多地区，城市相对富裕，而周围的县可能比较穷。如果一个城市失去了主要的收入来源或就业机会（如一家大公司或企业），情况可能会发生变化，但通常城市在提供便利设施的能力、人口密度、高等教育水平、熟练劳动力和规模经济方面是县所不及的。

因此，合并是许多地方政府难以接受的建议，收益最大的政府可能不是协议中最有力的合作伙伴，对于有优势的政府来说，放弃短期收益换取长期收益可能很困难。这意味着全面合并形式是最不可能实现的府际合作管理形式。下一节将探讨一些围绕府际管理的问题，既包括它能解决的问题，也包括带来的问题。

5.4　府际管理的讨论

当对服务或公共物品的需求超出满足该需求的地方政府的权力、权限或管辖范围时，就会讨论跨地区管理。一般来说，当地方政府从其区域或中央政府那里获得一定程度的财政和自治权时，就更需要讨论这个问题。

固体废弃物处置和垃圾填埋空间问题是一个不承认行政边界的问题。例如，在韩国仁川市、首尔市和京畿道共用 Sudokwon 垃圾填埋场，严格来讲，它位于仁川市，但该市对垃圾填埋场没有行政管辖权。这是地球上最大的垃圾填埋场之一，从太空中可以看到，目前其承载能力还剩下大约 32 年的可用空间（Lee et al.，2010）。然而，尽管有三个独立的司法管辖区在此进行垃圾填埋，但没有一个管辖区有权独立控制垃圾填埋场的运营。如果出现与垃圾填埋有关的问题，则很难解决，因为没有人对填埋的操作负有直接责任。

目前，三方成立了一个联合工作组，以解决居住在 Sudokwon 垃圾填埋场两公里范围内的居民面临的问题。2011 年夏天，暴雨连绵，气温飙升，垃圾填埋场的气味和进出工地的卡车扬起的灰尘给附近高端住宅区的居民带来了恶劣的环境。测试表明，该地区有毒气体和粉尘的含量是建议限值的四倍，随着夏季的到来，居民的投诉也在增加。一些居民已经无法忍受这样的生活条件，并成立了联合工作队进行抗议，这是对仁川市垃圾填埋活动缺乏权威的直接回应。

由于政府重组、职能合并或归并而产生的问题通常与规模经济相关的权衡有关。虽然在单位服务提供中可以实现效率，但当全面合并发生时，总体支出和收入需求通常也会增加，对于那些不喜欢由一个强大的政府监管其日常生活的居民来说，这可能会遭受居民的质疑并可能降低居民对当地政府的信任。此外，当服务是在整个地区而不是在当地提供时，在一些地区可能会牺牲服务质量，以在整个地区提供统一的服务，合并前服务质量较高的地区会对合并后服务质量水平的降低提出抗议。

府际管理的必要性说明了集权和分权之间有时需要权衡。当中央政府下放权力和权威时，这通常意味着中央政府将某些类型的服务提供的权力和资金交给地方政府，这些政府需要对服务提供的质量和对地方的需求负责。即便如此，地方政府仍然缺乏中央政府所拥有的财政权力和规模，因此，在分权体制下，地方政府可能根据居民居住的地方提供他们所需的服务，但这样的体制也可能存在在服务可用性、质量和提供水平方面因地区而异。另外，集权体制可以使得各地区的服务提供标准化，并更好地保证最低质量，但一些地区可能因此而获得他们不希望或不需要的服务。在高度集权的体制中，如韩国，或在更分散的体制中（如美国），都可能需要地方政府间行政管理，但在提议府际管理的形式之前，应考虑地方政府体制的特点。

导致成功或失败的因素

当地方政府决定尝试改变其合作形式以实现共同目标时，有许多因素可能导致成功或失败。尽管这些因素因地方政府的特点而有很大差异，但仍有一些因素对这一进程非常重要。这些因素大致分为三类：政治因素、程序/结构因素或社会因素。根据地方一级的特点，成功或失败取决于每个类别内的因素组合。

政治因素

决定成败的政治因素有两个维度：政治意愿以及冲突的范围（Schattschneider，1960）。其中每一项都很重要，但各因素的正确组合对于政府是否能够实现最终目标至关重要。

政治意愿是指当选官员的共同意愿，即将跨地区行政作为有关管辖区的优先事项。当只有少数管辖区想要向前迈进时，即使这些管辖区的权力或影响力不如其邻区，缺乏支持也会导致后面的麻烦。政治意愿意味着政治家们将以实质性的方式支持地方政府间安排：投入人力或资金等资源来解决共同的问题。这可能是因为政治家们相信这些安排最终对他们自己的选区有利。此外，这一信念将推动彼此的支持，使多个管辖区的政治家愿意成为相互行动后果的承担者，并向广大公众说明采取这种行动的理由。

冲突的范围直接来源于沙特施奈德关于推动政治变革的因素的观点。冲突的范围是指发生政治分歧或战争的舞台的规模，如果冲突的范围很广，那么就有大量的人和利益集团讨论眼前的问题；如果冲突的范围很窄，那么讨论就会得到控制，只有少数人或利益集团才会讨论这个问题。一般来说，如果有一个主要利益方希望控制对该问题的讨论，那么最好将冲突控制在小范围内。很多情况下都可能如此：如果行动受到时间限制，例如，在危机中，为了保证讨论和辩论的重点，可能会倾向于缩小冲突范围。此外，当政治领导人讨论可能对其选民产生重大影响的政策时，这也可能是存在的。

冲突的范围取决于围绕所辩论的问题的三个前提条件：竞争力、可见性以及权力和资源的规模（Schattschneider，1960）。竞争力是指政治竞争中的失败者是否能够返场并在下次比赛中获胜。政治制度的竞争性越强，冲突的范围就越可能扩大。一个政治体系的竞争力越低，一个政党或候选人越有可能垄断权力，冲突的范围就会缩小，改变的可能性也就越小。可见性是指冲突是否对可能未直接参与辩论或争论的其他人可见。如果冲突非常明显，并且许多人了解争论的内容和争论的对象，那么外部观察者很可能会加入辩论，这也许会改变权力平衡，进而改变最终结果。最后，权力和资源的规模是指冲突发生的舞台。如果没有足够的权力或资源来保护那些失败者免受报复，那么人们进入竞技场参加辩论的意愿就会降低，政府保护那些可能与多数意见不同的人的能力是衡量其权力和资源规模的标准。

程序/结构性因素

当试图弥合地方政府之间的分歧时，可能会出现许多问题，其中一些问题可能会嵌入系统的结构中。府际关系学者提到的结构特征可能会限制合作的尝试，或在地方政府层面上设置合作障碍（Walker，2000；Rich，2003），结构性约束是设计出来的，被认为是控制地方政府活动的正式手段。例如，在美国，《权利法案》（前十项修正案）规定了宪法约束。美国地方政府最重要的修正案之一是第十修正案，有时也称为"州权利"修正案。在这方面，宪法赋予州政府广泛的权力，规定地方政府可以做什么和不能做什么，包括决定选举什么职位以及国家承认哪些政府。

这些因素决定了政府的架构——谁将成为主导力量，以及如何分享权力。这可以包括地方政府进行什么样的选举，无论他们是全部的（所有居民都投票给几个候选人，而这并不取决于这个人住在哪里）还是区级的（候选人投票给将代表其社区的人）。事实已经证明，这种结构对地方政府采取的行动具有重要影响（Clingermayer and Feiock，2001；Rosenthal and Tao，2007），这些因素被称为"结构性"因素。应该回答的问题是：是否存在结构性限制因素阻碍了合并的努力？

程序性因素与地方政府作出决策或完成工作的过程有关。例如，如果一个地方政府想提高税收，为与另一个政府的联合项目提供资金，政府可能会要求公民投票决定是否同意增加税收，这是一个确保公民在纳税时有代表权的程序，但这一程序可能会使地方政府难以及时推进项目。因此，在试图预测联合行动的潜在成功或失败时，也应考虑程序因素（Treisman，2007）。

程序因素的一个次要组成部分可能是官僚阻力。在拥有大量公务员的地方政府中，公共官僚可以成为变革的有益盟友，也可以成为强大的竞争对手。如前所述，并不是所有的合并都能为地方政府工作人员带来光明的未来，因此考虑他们对潜在变化的态度至关重要。

社会因素

在许多关于社会资本的文献和研究中，共享价值观和信任被认为是创造有利于集体行动的环境的关键（Putnam，2000），对于府际管理问题，两者都很重要。如果两个城市政府的官员彼此信任度较低，那么他们很难通过联合获得任何好处，即使这种合作可能会让他们的选民受益。建立信任需要某种持续的积极互动，研究表明，政府间信任水平最低的地方政府是那些接触最不频繁的政府（Carr，Leroux and Shrestha，2009）。信任需要在建立良好关系的情况下定期互动，在试图改变政府管理形式之前，必须进行这项工作。

共同价值观是指地方官员对某些政策活动的态度。例如，一些地方官员可能非常重视保护环境，而他们的邻居可能非常重视经济发展，为了让他们看到合作的好处，需要找到一些彼此共同感兴趣的领域。譬如，在这个例子中，两个地方政府的官员可能会决定，绿色技术可以成为他们通过某种合作努力促进各自管辖区利益的一种方式。

【思考题】

1. 你能给出北京市周边地区的跨地区行政管理的例子吗？
2. 请给出一个可能受益于府际管理的地区的例子。
3. 我国存在哪些府际管理的障碍？

【关键术语】

合并	程序因素
规模经济	区域合作
提供联合服务	冲突的范围
司法权	社会资本
政治意愿	结构约束

参考文献

［1］ Carr, Jered, Leroux, Kelly and Shrestha, Manoj (2009). "Institutional Ties, Transaction Costs and External Service Production." *Urban Affairs Review*, 44（3）：403-427.

［2］ Clingermayer, James and Feiock, Richard C. (2001). *Institutional Constraints and Policy Choice：An Exploration of Local Governance.* Albany, NY：SUNY Press.

［3］ Cox, Wendell (2009). "Local Government Consolidation in Indiana：Separating Rhetoricfrom Reality." Report prepared for the Indiana Township Association. February. Demographia.

［4］ Frederickson, H. George and Nalbandian, John (2002). *The Future of Local Government Administration.* Washington, D. C.：The International City/County Management Association.

［5］ Gainsborough, Juliet (2001). *Fenced Off：The Suburbanization of American Politics.* Washington, D. C.：Georgetown University Press.

［6］ Jensen, Michael D. (2010). "Local Government Consolidation：A Framework for Effective Decision Making". American Planning Association.

［7］ Johnson, Linda, and Feiock, Richard C. (2001). *City-County Consolidation：A Qualitative Comparative Analysis Approach.* Tallahassee：Florida State University.

［8］ Kent, Calvin and Sowards, Kent (2005). "Local Government Consolidation：Lessons for West Virgina, Final Report". February. Center for Business and Economic Research, Marshall University, Huntington, West Virginia.

［9］ Rich, Michael J. (2003). "The Intergovernmental Environment" in *Cities，Politic，and Policy：A Comparative Analysis.* Washington, D. C.：CQ Press：35 – 67.

［10］ Rosenthal, Cindy S. and Tao, Jill L. (2007). "What's a Small-Town Mayor to Do When Things Fall Apart? Normative Limits in Modern Urban Theory". *Public Administration Quarterly*, 31（3）：249 – 283.

［11］ Treisman, David (2007). *The Architecture of Government：Rethinking Political Decentralization.* Cambridge University Press.

［12］ Walker, David B. 2000. *The Rebirth of Federalism.* 2nd ed. New York, NY：Chatham House.

Chapter 5　Local Intergovernmental Administration

5. 1　Definition

Cities have limits in terms of space. There are boundaries where an urban government's power end and another government's jurisdiction begins. This can sometimes lead to difficulties if the governments share resources, such as labor or infrastructure. If cities compete over these resources, the competition may sometimes have detrimental effects for all. In such cases, considering how to administer joint provision of services or sharing of resources is crucial.

Intergovernmental administration is the governing of resources and services that are shared between governments. Intergovernmental administration is the governing of resources and services that are shared between local governments. Since local governments answer to voters and citizens who live within their borders, the recognition of a need to cooperate rather than compete with other jurisdictions may not come quickly. Therefore, it is essential to understand what kinds of conditions may drive the recognition of the need for local intergovernmental administration.

5. 2　The Need for Intergovernmental Administration

There are three general categories of needs that drive intergovernmental administration: shared resources, efficiency, and shared services. Each requires a different set of administrative tools, but all are important to understanding the arrangements local governments may make to address these needs.

Shared Resources

Occasionally local governments will share resources of some kind: a natural resource, such as a source of water, or a human resource, such as labor. The sharing requires management to prevent overuse, or depletion, of the resource. For example, there may be residents who live in small cities outside of a large city, who commute into the large city to work. These residents provide a resource to the large city (labor) but they also use resources when inside the boundaries of the large city (infrastructure). If the resource (labor) is paying for infrastructure through taxes levied in the smaller city, then the larger city may bear a disproportionate fiscal burden in providing infrastructure within its borders for those who do not pay taxes as residents (Gainsborough, 2001). This can lead to urban decline as a central city struggles to bear the cost of maintenance for the infrastructure that brings its labor force in to work each day.

When the shared resource is a natural resource, the problem that can face residents of both cities is a common problem. Elinor Ostrom has written extensively on this issue and has argued that the best way to manage a shared resource is to construct rules that offer incentives that all parties who share the resource will pursue, and to enforce sanctions against parties who use more of the resource than they should. Clearly, for such a system to work, there must be mutual recognition between the governments using the resource that they share responsibility for maintaining the integrity of the resource, and that each party can be held accountable for overuse or abuse.

The fundamental similarity between these two kinds of resources is that both conditions demonstrate the need for a standard management system that goes beyond the jurisdictions of each local government. In other words, the local governments must find a means to manage the resource together in a fashion that is both fair and practical. This can present unique challenges to local governments who often see themselves as competitors rather than collaborators. Each government answers to the residents within its borders (constituents).

Efficiency

One of the most common needs driving the pursuit of intergovernmental administration is a need for higher levels of efficiency. This is most often the case when local governments believe that by combining their jurisdictions, or consolidating their governments, they can create economies of scale and reduce redundancies and overlap. As Michael Jensen (2010: 1) states, new consolidated governments hope to improve their operating efficiencies and solve a wide range of social, political, financial, service delivery, and infrastructure-related challenges that were not being addressed effectively by the previous local government structure.

Consolidating governments means combining certain functions and created a new, larger government that incorporates the original cities within the combined structure. There is often opposition to consolidating governments, however, even if the need for efficiency is high. Politicians are often unwilling to give up their positions or fear that they will lose influence or power should they agree to consolidate. Additionally, government workers and local civil servants are often fearful of losing their positions should consolidation occur, since the new combined government is intended to run more efficiently than the individual, separate governments did. Often, the decision to consolidate is driven by a perceived crisis, usually fiscal, where local officials see no alternative way to improve conditions (Johnson and Feiock, 2001).

Shared Services

The last major need that drives intergovernmental administration is the provision of shared services. Shared services can range from public transportation to street repair to health care provision, and the arrangements that local governments can use to provide such services can range from formal contracts between the governments to the creation of joint task force committees to informal agreements as to who will be responsible for which part of service provision. In some instances, a completely new form of government may be created to provide the service (Kent and Sowards, 2005).

The types of services are generally those that are needed by residents of multiple urban areas, but require coordination to ensure uniform levels of service quality across jurisdictions (e. g. transportation), no duplication of basic services (e. g. health care provision), and appropriate expertise for the appropriate level of service provision. This last category is more common in the United States where each state outlines the delegation of duties between city and county governments in the state constitution.

Joint provision of services can often occur when residents of neighboring cities want a service, but neither city has the resources necessary to provide the service at an operable level. This is also a collective action problem, since as in the first category of need, the individual actors may not perceive a need for cooperation, and may view the other cities as a competitor rather than a collaborator. In this case, similar approaches to promoting joint action may be required.

5. 3　Forms

There are three general forms that can occur when intergovernmental administration is needed in a formal way (Kent and Sowards, 2005): regional cooperation; functional consolidation; and full consolidation. These forms range from the most common to the most unusual, but each requires some degree of reorganization. This means that they go beyond the more informal forms of cooperation mentioned earlier in this chapter. The three forms differ substantially, but they share three characteristics when the reorganization of duties and functions is successful (Kent and Sowards, 2005).

The first is democratic control. Residents know who represents them and have clear ideas about how to hold political representatives accountable for administrative performance. This is important for giving residents a sense of control and responsibility for the combined administration.

The second is general purpose authority. This means that the combined government form, no matter what kind it is, has the authority to address all problems that arise within its jurisdiction. This is important for addressing unexpected circumstances that may arise after the governments combine efforts. If the newly combined government form is unable to react to problems related to the creation of the new form, then residents will lose confidence in the new form, and it will be unable to garner the support necessary to successfully provide services or manage resources.

The third is sufficient independent resources. This means that the newly combined authority has its own resources and those resources are sufficient to carry out the joint tasks required. This preserves the independence of the local governments, which is often quite important in federalist systems such as the US, but it can also be important in a centralized system such as Korea. Sufficient funds ensure that the joint tasks of the local governments can be carried out as planned without additional oversight from the central government.

5. 3. 1　Regional Cooperation

Regional cooperation is the most common and least disruptive kind of interlocal administration. In this form, all the local government entities remain intact and independent, but they enter a formal agreement to jointly provide a necessary service. By maintaining existing forms of government, there is less resistance from both public officials and the public. This is therefore considered a more incremental way to change the nature of service provision and administration. Local governments may often try this form of interlocal administration before moving on to a more substantial form of government consolidation.

By entering into a joint cooperative agreement, a local government can draw on the resources and expertise of their local government neighbors without sacrificing jurisdictional powers or democratic representation. This is often perceived to be one of the strengths of this form of interlocal administration. However, leaving this independence intact can lead to shirking, where one government does not hold up its end of the agreement since the sanctions for substandard service provision are usually weak. Critics also complain that allowing local governments to enter into such agreements with relatively few strings attached can lead to the creation of too many joint jurisdictions, thus creating more confusion and fragmentation rather than more cooperation.

5. 3. 2　Functional Consolidation

Functional consolidation occurs when two or more local governments decide to merge a specific area of service provision. According to Kent and Soward (2005), certain areas of service provision work better when functionally consolidated, providing the efficiencies attendant to economies of scale: public works, such as roads, sewage systems, drinking water provision, and solid waste disposal are all examples of public services that work more efficiently and effectively. Such consolidation also allows governments to think about and plan for problems that may arise from growth or decline in different parts of the shared jurisdictions, and how these changes might affect other members of the functionally consolidated form.

Finance is another area where functional consolidation can help improve efficiency, especially through the creation of a single taxing authority. This is because of a condition economists refer to as "deadweight loss". In a market economy, efficiencies occur when there is a balance, or equilibrium, struck between demand and supply, such that the maximum number of buyers and sellers who are willing to buy or sell a good for a particular price is reached. However, when a tax is levied on a good or service by the government, this automatically increases the cost of that good or service for the consumer who wishes to buy the good or service. This means that fewer buyers will be able to purchase the good or service at the price that they prefer, and fewer suppliers will be able to get the price that they wanted for the good or service they produced. Since this is a less efficient arrangement than that provided by the free market, many free market economists oppose the idea of taxation, especially at high levels.

However, many mainstream economists do support the idea of taxation in principle, especially when there is a public good that needs to be provided or in cases of market failure. Under these circumstances, taxation is necessary to generate sufficient funding to provide the good in question or to create a change in behavior by imposing a higher cost on certain kinds of goods or services (such as taxing cigarettes or alcohol to reduce consumption and improve health). However, under such circumstances, these economists argue that the taxes levied should be as broadly distributed as possible, so that the rate of taxation is relatively low. This minimizes the market distortion caused by the tax, thus creating an acceptable tradeoff between government service provision and private behavior.

Thus, creating a consolidated tax authority does what economists argue is the most effective and efficient way to tax – it allows the tax burden to be spread over as large a jurisdiction as possible, thus reducing the per unit price of the tax for residents. This can be an excellent way to create efficiencies in one functional area without sacrificing the advantages of individual jurisdictions.

Economic development is another policy area that benefits from functional consolidation. Big businesses that are looking to locate to a new city often look for centralized service provision, since this simplifies the regulatory process that they must go through to set up a new branch or store. Cities that jointly pursue economic development are more attractive to businesses for this reason, and because there are generally higher efficiencies realized when this kind of policy is pursued jointly by cities rather than separately.

Public health also does well under functional consolidation. This is especially true in instances where residents live in one city and work in another. The ability to coordinate health care provision to support the general health of the public is essential when populations are mobile. If cities are coordinating their efforts to contain the spread of a particularly virulent type of contagious disease, they are far more likely to be successful than if they are attempting to do this as individual jurisdictions.

Urban planning is the last area of functional consolidation that is common. Therefore, urban planning is often referred to as urban and regional planning, since growth patterns do not always recognize political boundaries. Regional planning often examines the needs and projections for future growth and decline that will have impacts that go beyond the edge of one city and affect a surrounding region or other cities in the area. This is especially important when considering the use of natural resources, such as land, water or shoreline.

5. 3. 3 Full Consolidation

The final form of government administration across local government boundaries is full consolidation, also known as a merger. In this form, the previous individual units of government are merged to form one, centralized, unitary government structure. All the functions previously performed by the smaller, individual units of government come together into one system. The advantages of such a merger are those typical of creating a single entity to replace many: standardized procedures across a district; centralized information storage and retrieval; the benefits of creating an economy of scale that can generate spread effects and promote purchasing power; and more uniform service delivery and quality. This is most commonly done between a county and a major city within the county, where smaller cities within the jurisdiction cede some or all their service provision to the newly created government.

The reasons given for full consolidation are often fiscal. In the United States, for example, counties are required to provide certain services through the state constitution, such as health care for the poor, policing duties through the office of the sheriff, and justice institutions, such as the county court which hears all cases within its jurisdiction. Counties can levy property taxes, but these are generally used to provide public education. Cities, on the other hand, can share the property revenues with the surrounding county, but are not required to provide the same services, although many of the larger cities do. Cities can also generate other forms of revenue through additional taxes and fees for services. This means that in many parts of the US, cities are relatively wealthy while the surrounding county can be quite poor. These positions may shift if a city loses a major source of revenue or job generation, such as a large company or business, but generally, cities offer amenities that counties do not have in population density, higher education levels, skilled labor force, and economies of scale.

Consolidation is therefore a difficult proposal for many local governments to accept. The government that gains the most may not be the strongest partner in the bargain, and it can be difficult for the government that has an advantage to give up short term gains for long term benefits. This means that the full consolidation form is the least likely kind of interlocal administrative form to be found. The following section examines some of the issues surrounding intergovernmental administration, both in terms of the problems it is meant to solve and the issues it is seen to create.

5. 4   Issues

Intergovernmental administration is discussed whenever a need for a service or public good goes beyond the powers, authority or jurisdiction of the local government being asked to meet that need. In general, it is discussed more readily when local governments have a certain degree of fiscal and political autonomy from their regional or national governments.

The problem of solid waste disposal and landfill space is one issue that does not recognize administrative boundaries. For example, the City of Incheon, Seoul, and Gyeong-gi Province in the Republic of Korea currently share the Sudokwon landfill. Technically, it is located within the City of Incheon, but the city does not have administrative jurisdiction over the landfill. It is one of the largest landfill on the planet, visible from space, and currently has approximately thirty-two more years of usable space left in its carrying capacity (Lee *et al.*, 2010). However, even though three separate jurisdictions contribute to the landfill, none has control over its operations. Therefore, if a problem arises related to the landfill, it is difficult to resolve since no one has direct responsibility for its operation.

Currently, a joint task force has been created to address a particular problem that has arisen for residents who live within two kilometers of the landfill site in the Chongna district. In the summer of 2011, when there was very heavy rainfall combined with soaring temperatures, smells from the landfill and dust from trucks traveling in and out of the site created unpalatable conditions for residents of nearby, high-end apartments. Testing indicated that levels of noxious gases and dust were four times the recommended limits within the district, and complaints from the residents were increasing as the summer progressed. By August, conditions were unbearable for some residents, and the creation of the joint task force was in direct response to the lack of authority over landfill activities from the City of Incheon.

The issues that arise because of the reorganizing, consolidation of functions, or merging of governments are generally related to the trade-offs associated with economies of scale. While efficiencies can be realized in per unit provision of services, the overall expenditures and need for revenue generally rise when a full merger occurs. For residents who do not like the idea of a powerful government overseeing several aspects of daily life, such an increase may be viewed with suspicion, and can reduce the trust of residents in their local governments. Additionally, when services are provided on an area-wide basis rather than locally, there may be some sacrifice of service quality in some regions to provide uniform service in all regions. Those areas with superior service quality prior to the merger may object to the reduced quality levels after the reorganization.

The need for intergovernmental administration illustrates the tradeoffs sometimes necessary between centralization and decentralization. When a national government decentralizes power and authority, this generally means that the central government cedes some sort of authority and funding for certain kinds of service provision to local governments, and that those governments then become responsible for the quality of service provision, and for responsiveness to local needs. Even so, a local government will always lack the fiscal power and size that the central government has. Therefore, a decentralized system may have local governments that can give residents what is needed according to where they live, but such a system may also see great differences from region to region in service availability, quality and level of provision. A centralized system, on the other hand, can standardize service provision across regions, and better guarantee a minimum level of quality, but some regions may receive services they do not wish for or need as a result. The need for intergovernmental administration can arise in both a highly centralized system, as in the Republic of Korea, or in a more decentralized system, such as the US, but the characteristics of the local government system should be considered before changes to form are proposed.

Factors Leading to Success or Failure

When local governments do decide to try and change their form to accomplish common goal, there are many factors that can lead to either success or failure. Although these factors vary substantially according to the characteristics of the local government system, there are some factors that have been identified as being very important to the process. Most of these factors fall into one of three categories: political, procedural/structural, or social. Success or failure depends on a combination of factors within each category, according to the characteristics present at the local level.

Political Factors

There are two dimensions that can determine success and failure in the political category: political will; and the scope of conflict (Schattschneider, 1960). Each of these is important in its right, but the correct combination of factors is crucial to whether the ultimate goals are achieved by the governments in question.

Political will refers to a shared willingness by elected officials to make interlocal administration a priority for the jurisdictions in question. When only a minority of jurisdictions want to move forward, even if these are jurisdictions that are less powerful or influential than their neighbors, the lack of support will lead to troubles later. Political will means that politicians support the interlocal arrangements in substantive ways: they will commit resources such as personnel or money to resolving shared problems and issues. This may be because the politicians believe the arrangements are ultimately beneficial for their own constituencies. In addition, this conviction is something that will drive support so that politicians in multiple jurisdictions are willing to be the standard-bearers for mutual action, and will make the case for such action to the public at large.

The scope of conflict is drawn directly from E. E. Schattschneider's ideas about what drives political change. The scope of conflict refers to the scale of the arena in which a political disagreement or battle takes place. If the scope of conflict is broad, then there are a large number of people and interests debating the issue at hand. If the scope of conflict is narrow, then the debate is contained and the issue is only be discussed by a small number of people or interests. Generally, a narrow scope of conflict is preferred if there is one dominant interest who wishes to control the discussion of the issue. This can be true under a variety of conditions: for example, if there are severe time constraints on action, as in a crisis, a narrow scope of conflict may be preferred to keep discussion and debate focused. It can be true when political leaders are discussing policies that may have substantial consequences for their constituencies, and they wish to have thoughtful discussions to flesh out ideas before making those discussions more public. It can also be true when a political party in power wishes to minimize the possibility of redistribution of that power.

The scope of conflict is determined by three conditions surrounding the issue being debated: competitiveness, visibility, and the amplitude of power and resources (Schattschneider, 1960: 16 – 18). Competitiveness refers to whether the loser of a political race can come back and win the next time around. The more competitive a political system is, the more likely that the scope of conflict will expand. The less competitive a political system is, the more likely that one political party or candidate will monopolize power, and the scope of conflict will narrow and change will be less likely. Visibility refers to whether the conflict is visible to others who may not be participating directly in the debate or argument. If the conflict is highly visible, and many people know what is being argued and by whom, then there is a stronger likelihood that external observers will join the debate, perhaps shifting the balance of power, and therefore the eventual outcome. Finally, the amplitude of power and resources refers to the arena in which the conflict takes place. If the arena does not have enough power or resources to protect those who lose from retaliation, then the likelihood that people will be willing to enter the arena and join the debate is reduced. The ability of a government to protect those who may disagree with the majority is the measure of the amplitude of its power and resources.

Structural/Procedural Factors

There can be many points when attempts to bridge differences between local governments can go awry, and some of these may be built into the structure of the system. Scholars of intergovernmental relations refer to structural characteristics that can constrain attempts to cooperate, or establish barriers to cooperation at local levels of government (Walker, 2000; Rich, 2003). *Structural constraints* are there by design and are considered formal means for controlling local government activities. In the United States, for example, there are constitutional constraints, laid out in the Bill of Rights (the first Ten Amendments). One of the more important amendments for local governments in the U S is the 10th Amendment, sometimes referred to as the "states' rights" amendment. Here, the constitution gives broad powers to state governments to regulate what local governments can and cannot do. This may include things such as deciding what offices are elected and which governments are recognized by the state.

These factors decide what the architecture of government will be; who will be the dominant power, and how power will be shared. This can include what kind of elections a local government has; whether they are at-large (where all residents vote for several candidates that do not depend on where one lives) or district-level (where candidates vote for someone who will represent their neighborhood). It has been demonstrated that these kinds of structures have significant consequences for the types of actions local governments take (Clingermayer and Feiock, 2001; Rosenthal and Tao, 2007). Therefore, these factors are referred to as "structural." The question that should be answered is "Are there structural constraints that will prohibit merger attempts from moving forward?"

Procedural factors have to do with the processes local governments go through to make decisions or get things done. For example, if a local government wants to raise taxes to fund a joint project with another government, the government may be required that citizens vote on whether they approve of such a tax increase. This is a procedure that guarantees the right of citizens to have representation when they are taxed. Still, it can be a process that makes it difficult for a local government to move forward with a project in a timely fashion. Therefore, procedural factors should be taken into consideration as well when trying to predict the potential success or failure of joint action (Treisman, 2007).

A sub-component of procedural factors may be bureaucratic resistance. In local governments with large cadres of civil servants, public bureaucrats can be a helpful ally for change or a formidable opponent. As mentioned previously, not all consolidations offer promising futures for local government workers, so taking into consideration their attitudes towards a potential change is crucial.

Social Factors

In much of the literature and research on social capital, shared values and trust are considered key to creating an environment conducive to collective action (Putnam, 2000). For the question of intergovernmental administration, both are important. If two city governments have officials with low levels of trust in each other, they are doubtful to see anything to be gained by joining forces, even if such cooperation could benefit their constituencies. Unfortunately, building trust requires some sort of continuous positive interaction, and research has shown that local governments with the lowest levels of intergovernmental trust are those who have the most infrequent contact (Carr, Leroux and Shrestha, 2009). Building trust requires interaction on a regular basis under circumstances that are likely to build good relationships. This is work that must precede attempts to change the forms of government administration.

Shared values refer to the kinds of attitudes held by local officials towards certain kinds of policy activities. For example, some local officials may feel very strongly about protecting the environment while their neighbors may feel strongly about economic development. For them to see benefits in cooperation, these neighbors need to be able to see some area of shared interest. In this example, the two sets of local officials may decide that green technology could be a way for them to further the interests of their individual jurisdictions through some sort of collaborative effort.

Questions

1. Can you give some examples of intergovernmental administration in the areas surrounding Beijing City?

2. Can you think of an area that might benefit from intergovernmental administration?

3. What kinds of barriers to intergovernmental administration exist in China?

Key Terms

consolidation   *scope of conflict*

economies of scale   *social capital*

joint service provision   *structural constraints*

procedural factors   *jurisdiction*

regional cooperation   *political will*

References

[1] Carr, Jered, Leroux, Kelly and Shrestha, Manoj (2009). "Institutional Ties, Transaction Costs and External Service Production." *Urban Affairs Review*, 44 (3): 403-427.

[2] Clingermayer, James and Feiock, Richard C. (2001). *Institutional Constraints and Policy Choice: An Exploration of Local Governance.* Albany, NY: SUNY Press.

[3] Cox, Wendell (2009). "Local Government Consolidation in Indiana: Separating Rhetoricfrom Reality." Report prepared for the Indiana Township Association. February. Demographia.

[4] Frederickson, H. George and Nalbandian, John (2002). *The Future of Local Government Administration.* Washington, D. C. : The International City/County Management Association.

[5] Gainsborough, Juliet (2001). *Fenced Off: The Suburbanization of American Politics.* Washington, D. C. : Georgetown University Press.

[6] Jensen, Michael D. (2010). "Local Government Consolidation: A Framework for Effective Decision Making". American Planning Association.

[7] Johnson, Linda, and Feiock, Richard C. (2001). *City-County Consolidation: A Qualitative Comparative Analysis Approach.* Tallahassee: Florida State University.

[8] Kent, Calvin and Sowards, Kent (2005). "Local Government Consolidation: Lessons for West Virgina, Final Report". February. Center for Business and Economic Research, Marshall University, Huntington, West Virginia.

[9] Rich, Michael J. (2003). "The Intergovernmental Environment" in *Cities, Politic, and Policy: A Comparative Analysis.* Washington, D. C. : CQ Press: 35 – 67.

[10] Rosenthal, Cindy S. and Tao, Jill L. (2007). "What's a Small-Town Mayor to Do When Things Fall Apart? Normative Limits in Modern Urban Theory". *Public Administration Quarterly*, 31 (3): 249 – 283.

[11] Treisman, David (2007). *The Architecture of Government: Rethinking Political Decentralization.* Cambridge University Press.

[12] Walker, David B. 2000. *The Rebirth of Federalism.* 2nd ed. New York, NY: Chatham House.

第6章 城市财政

6.1 概念及内涵

城市财政是使用分析、技术和管理工具控制和分配稀缺资源的过程，基于资源有限的假设，以地方政府和地方经济的发展为背景，政府在提高收入和控制资源方面有多种选择（Mikesell，2007），这项工作大部分是通过预算完成的。预算是如何确定地方政府服务以及如何为其提供资金，是关于预期支出和结果的规划。城市政府通常没有足够的资金来满足公民的所有需求，因此，预算在帮助城市判断需求和筹集满足这些需求所需的资金方面发挥着重要作用。

严格说来，预算有三个作用。第一，它是一项经济计划，城市预算反映了稀缺资源在各种备选方案之间的分配。第二，它是一份政治文件，城市预算记录了谁得到了（多少）地方政府的支出。第三，它代表了一个决策过程，城市预算的重点是将复杂性降低到可管理的程度。

预算程序的高度常规性及其形式和期限不应埋没该程序在地方政府内部分配资源方面所起的关键作用。公共管理人员认为，这一过程对城市、市民和居民以及他们所依赖的地方政府部门的福利至关重要，这一点也不足为奇。

6.2 预算编制的功能和类型

6.2.1 预算编制的功能

预算编制和财务管理共同为公共管理人员提供了三项重要职能：控制、管理和规划（Aronson，2004）。控制职能的目的是确保资金仅用于授权用途并防止超支，重点是遵守法律要求；管理职能努力避免浪费，提高服务提供的效率；规划职能更广泛地着眼于让组织内的资源分配合理化。问题在于组织应提供的商品和服务应进行适当组合，同时根据组织目标，保证这种组合的有效性。计划决定了应该添加、扩展、结束或缩减的程序。

需要不同类型的预算信息来满足这三项职能中每一项的要求。控制需要获得有关预算项目的目标及其用途的详细信息，管理职能部门受益于绩效预算，绩效预算表明服务或活动的目标水平以及在该水平上提供服务的预期成本，从而可以在整个财政年度对效率和生产率进行判断和评估。最后，规划需要并行的和比较的信息，有助于管理者在项目之间进行权衡（Aronson，2004）。

6.2.2　预算策略类型

预算增量

大多数城市政府预算都基于预算增量文件，预算增量可以定义为根据上一财政期间的总额逐步增加或减少预算的预算提案。实际上，当城市发展和繁荣时，预算增加反映了增长的水平；相反，在城市经济萎靡的地方，预算则能反映需求的下降。预算增量倾向于以一种全面的方式工作，大多数个别预算项目甚至反映了基于前一年预算要求的相同增量。

通常认为地方政府通过预算增量来应对预算饥渴（即无休止地对更多资金的需求，以及在缺乏抵消压力的情况下出现的官僚主义的增长），各国政府和机构通过关注每年可用资源的变化程度，极大简化了预算任务。假设预算基本上是固定的，将该过程转化为调整特定项目的更具技术性的过程，从而将预算冲突的范围缩小到可控范围内。这意味着不需要每年都重新进行基本的分配战，单一预算的采用使得当年的拨款决定合法化，并且更容易处理因收入环境变化而出现的变化。渐进模型的一个重要暗示是，预算每年都不会发生重大变化，这意味着预算不需要作出重大的政策选择，这些政策选择被转移到预算领域之外（Aronson，2004）。

预算增量程度在实际操作中有很大差异。大多数市镇的总体业务预算逐年递增，在部门一级也是如此。当在各个部门中进行预算审查时，会发现资金通常每年都会从一个项目或计划转移到另一个项目。随着项目的完成和新项目的启动，像公共工程部门这样按照项目路线构建的部门，特别可能会看到从一个预算到下一个预算的重大转变。当一个项目是优先级时，该项目将位于队列的顶部，当特定项目完成时，也会出现新的项目。

零基预算

零基预算是增量预算的一个相对较新的替代方案。这种方法假设任何特定活动的适当支出水平的选择都是从零开始，任何大于零的支出都应当得到支持。卡特总统在 20 世纪 70 年代担任乔治亚州州长时采用了这一方法，然后在 1976 年当选总统时将其提交给华盛顿和联邦政府。每年都必须重新考虑每一项预算的每一个要素，并对其进行全面论证。预算采用了典型的分项格式，但他们必须编制决策包，说明政府在每个支出水平上将为公众提供什么，这些决策包括有助于证明或比较选择的运营数据。除了在一些地方和州，特别是在维护方案要素以提高灵活性和绩效时需要作出艰难的预算决策的地方，该方案没有被采纳（Mikesell，2007）。

6.3 财政压力与风险管理

6.3.1 财政压力

从 20 世纪 90 年代初开始，诸如裁员和精简管理等新的发展被政府列为重中之重。从 20 世纪 60 年代末和 70 年代开始，美国和其他西方国家更早发生了这种变化，效率、金融稳定、公平和责任等管理原则反映了这一点。这一管理趋势对中国地方政府的管理产生了重大影响——增长不再是最终目标，且受到了严厉的批评，紧缩和平衡成为理想的管理目标。评估和重组政府组织成为地方公共部门普遍采用的实现行政效率的手段，这一趋势一直持续到 21 世纪。随着社会变得更加复杂和不确定，社会需求迅速增加，政府支出也迅速增加，然而，政府收入却并没有以同样的速度增长，因此这一趋势将地方财政置于地方乃至国家政策议程的首位（Aronson，2004）。

预算编制和财务管理的一项主要任务是寻找控制不断增加的支出的压力的方法。当收入增加时，这项任务相对容易，然而，当不断变化的经济、人口和政治因素限制收入增长时，控制预算变得愈加困难，财政压力可能会导致地方居民的需求与地方收入之间的差距扩大，政策选择不受欢迎，政府很难直接应对这些压力。政府可能会削减商品和服务的供应，也可能会增加收入，这些选择在政治上都不受欢迎，而不幸的是，许多城市不是直接应对财政压力，而是采取财政手段来隐藏、掩饰、拖延或最小化财政压力的直接影响，以避免负面的政治后果。

衡量财政压力可以采用几种不同的方法。一些学者如理查德·内森和查尔斯·亚当斯强调人口和经济指标，如失业、依赖和贫困。林恩·伯尼尔和理查德·宾厄姆则强调财政指标，如收支平衡。还有一些人将这两组指标结合起来。

金融趋势监测系统（FTMS）由国际城市管理协会开发，作为衡量财政压力的一种手段，FTMS 根据城市财务报表中的信息制定一系列城市总体财政状况指标。普遍接受的会计原则使财务报表易于理解，技术知识或财务背景较弱的人也能够进行财务分析。FTMS 用于为公共管理人员提供机会去分析城市财务报表中的财政压力（Aronson，2004）。图 6.1 所示为政府财政状况分析框架。

财务分析的关键是分析政府到期时履行其财务义务可能的状况（Berne and Schramm，1997）。政府的财政状况取决于收入和支出，收入包括可用资源（内部和外部资源），此处的支出包括当前支出压力和来自过去的压力。更多的资源会带来更健康的财务状况，而更多的支出压力则会导致更弱的财务状况。

收入分析试图找出经济基础并从中提取出潜在资源和实际收入。城市政府通过对构成当地经济的企业、房地产和消费模式的研究，决定对哪些经济活动征税，以尽量减少负面经济干预，同时实现收入最大化，然后，预测实际收入并收集实际收入。另外，支出分析试图衡量实际支出和支出压力。消费压力多种多样且很大，每个人和群体都有自己的偏好，希望在不同的领域花更多的钱。增加支出的最大压力来自城市面临问题的解

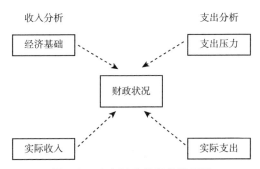

图 6.1　政府财政状况分析框架

决，如污染、犯罪、交通拥堵以及需要增加服务的人口老龄化等。

　　地方政府如何应对财政压力？哈罗德·沃尔曼和芭芭拉·戴维斯确定了政府部门在应对财政压力时所采用的一系列策略，从最受欢迎的到最不受欢迎的。最初，政府采取推迟策略来争取时间，希望问题只是暂时的。如果这些措施不能解决问题，政府接下来会尝试增加收入。就收入而言，地方政府通常首先通过请求上级政府提供帮助来获得政府间收入。如果政府间援助请求失败，他们将考虑增加不太受欢迎的征税方式。只有在政府无法增加额外收入又不得不作出艰难选择的情况下，才会考虑商品和服务的实际减少以及超出次要水平的裁员，当确实需要削减开支时，首先要削减对所提供的服务水平或雇员地位影响最小的领域，政府还可能通过提高效率和生产率来寻求在不削减服务的情况下削减开支。

Table 6.1	Major Determinants of Financial Condition
Determinants	Probable Effect on Financial Condition *
Community Needs：	
- Percent of population below poverty level	–
- Percent of population over 65	–
- Unemployment rate	–
Production & Service Conditions：	
- Population density	+ / –
- Population size	+ / –
- Population growth rate	+
Community Resources：	
- Percent of employment in mining and manufacturing	+
- Retail sales per capita	+
Central Government Policies：	
- Intergovernmental transfers	+
Local Government Financial Policies and Practices：	
- Debt and debt burden measures	–
- Tax burden measures	–

　　* "＋" indicates that an increase in this factor probably improves financial condition；"－" indicates that an increase probably worsens financial condition；"＋/－" indicates that the effect is uncertain, either because of the way variable is defined or because the factor has both positive and negative effects.

削减支出通常发生在完全由当地资金支持的领域，而且是不得不发生的，否则政府间支出一般不会削减。当财政危机严重且紧急时，政府通常会作出全面削减的回应，这通常被认为是公平的，因为共患难有助于政府渡过危机，毕竟每个部门或机构都承担有自己的责任。当削减幅度不是覆盖所有领域时，一般行政部门通常会这样做，外围和非核心服务业（包括娱乐、公园、图书馆和文化活动）面临的削减幅度最大，公共工程也可能大幅减少，公共服务、消防和警务服务往往最不容易遭受削减。公共安全服务受到保护，因为它对公众的重要性具有明显的可见性，人力资源和社会服务之所以得到保护，主要是因为他们可以通过政府间转移获得大量资金。

6.3.2 风险管理

无论是潜在的还是当前的或紧迫的，城市政府领域充满了财政风险，这些可能会影响政府运营的财政风险使得城市政府对支出的控制变得复杂，特别是针对城市政府预算的法律诉讼或其他财务索赔，商业保险成本的快速增长也迫使地方政府关注新兴的风险管理领域。

风险管理包括风险识别、风险频率评估、潜在严重程度，以及决定如何应对风险并监控结果的决策。越来越多的城市政府制定了风险管理政策，并至少设有一个全职风险管理职位，这些职位中的许多人都有保险产业的经验。在缺乏资源支持设置风险管理职位的小型政府或政府单位中，此类职能可由财务总监、助理城市经理或其他指定官员负责。

自我保险和政府间风险分担是为减少风险机制考虑的一些替代战略。随着时间的推移，这些产品已越来越普遍。自我保险仅仅意味着保险只是要准备好面对可能的后果，自我保险的热门领域包括共同责任险、汽车险和工伤赔偿险。政府间风险分担资金池是公共机构另一种流行的风险融资工具。风险分担资金池是一种合作方式，类似于信用合作社，不同于实体间的共享资源，风险分担资金池为自己的风险应对提供资金。参与的政府单位（风险分担资金池成员）向风险分担资金池支付缴款（保费），接受保险并提出索赔。这实际上与保险的概念非常相似，只是在被保险人之间协商和组织安排，而不是由外部机构提供服务。许多基金都有一名全职专业经理，协助风险分担资金池成员实施全面风险管理计划。

公共风险管理不仅仅是城市政府的一个新的且不断扩大的领域，也是一个节省大量资金的路径。鉴于目前政府的成本限制，城市管理者必须确保风险管理流程以用于识别、评估、控制整个城市政府运营范围内的风险。

6.4 使用者付费

近年来，城市政府的问题需要新的收入来源以满足日益增长的支出需求，而传统的收入来源并不能完全满足这些需求，传统的资金来源，如财产税，在应对需求变化方面往往不够灵活，财产税的增加往往受到法律的严格限制，也会受到政治反对派的阻挠。使用者付费已成为城市政府产生更多收入和满足资金需求的一个非常重要的资源，以配合不断增长的支出成本。使用者付费的优点是可以直接抵消特定公共产品或服务的成本，尽管它们通常不能收回全部成本。相反，他们的成本通常基于平均成本的计算，并且往往忽略特定用户、特定地点以及一天的使用时间之间的成本差异（Mikesell，2007），这使得其效率低于私营企业采用的基于市场的定价。

定义

使用者付费是指选择使用服务或设施的个人支付的费用，是一种伪装成价格的税，是对使用公共产品或服务的收费，是一种利用准市场机制对公共产品进行成本核算和融资的手段。除上述使用者付费外，高速公路通行费、城市停车费、公园和博物馆门票以及垃圾回收也是使用者付费的一些典型例子。政府生产和供应一些公共产品，如教育、图书馆、公园和交通系统，这些商品的"价格"也是使用者付费。

广义上的定义

使用者付费是公共部门中类似市场的交易，此类交易将特定付款和特定利益联系在一起。广义定义下的使用者收费可能包括费用及收费、租金和特许权使用费、指定消费税、许可证和执照、政府财产销售收入、政府贷款利息、为任何特殊保险收取的保费、政府创造的财产权收入以及政府退休人员或健康计划的保险费或年金。

狭义上的定义

使用者付费是指自愿购买的、与纯公共物品密切相关的公共服务的收费，即使这些服务是由个人消费的。该定义不包括当地政府公共事业（包括水、污水、电力和天然气等）的收入，因为公共事业费是公共产品的公共价格，这些产品实际上是私人产品。根据这一定义，许可证和许可证费用也不包括在内，因为它们与政府授予的特权相关且不是自愿的（Mikesell，2007）。

这一定义与本章中使用的使用者付费最接近，即专注于不强迫个人作出贡献的明显的公共部门活动。使用者付费是对自愿购买政府提供的服务的付款，这些服务有利于特定的个人，但具有公益性质或与有益品（具有公共物品特征或与公共物品密切相关的物品通常称为有益品）密切相关。

当个人不愿意为某件商品付款，并且与该商品相关的利益可以明确地与个人或消费者群体联系在一起时，可能会被排除在有益品消费之外。受益人费用一词描述了非税收入来源，更广泛的定义通常包括使用者付费，如公用事业收入、特殊评估、许可证费用以及上述费用（Pascal，1984）。

6.5　关于城市财政的讨论

城市财政是由城市经济决定的，同时又反作用于城市经济，城市经济规模及经济效益决定城市财政的规模，制约城市财政发展速度，是城市财政的基础。城市财政属于地方财政，是国家财政的重要组成部分，是城市政府凭借国家给予的权限，利用价值形式参与国民收入分配和再分配的工具，是实现城市政府职能的经济基础和财力保证。

基于支出压力，一些城市的总支出和人均支出水平和增长速度更快，城市支出会影响城市债务水平，而债务能力是债务分析中需要考虑的关键因素。城市的债务能力不同，有几种债务能力指标，如收入来源、收入准备金检查和支出压力，另一个组成部分是实际债务，评估城市债务的一种方法是将现有债务与税收能力进行比较。城市债务可以显示为人均债务，以便在不同地区之间具有可比性。随着支出和支出压力的增加，大多数城市的未偿债务总额和人均债务会随着时间的推移而增加。

【思考题】

1. 预算在城市管理中发挥什么作用？
2. 城市预算的三大功能是什么？
3. 预算周期是什么？
4. 使用 FTMS 方法分析某个城市的财务状况。
5. 某个特定城市（比如你生活的城市或选择的城市）的收入趋势是什么？其支出趋势如何？
6. 简述某一城市的物业税趋势。

【关键术语】

拨款制度	财务趋势监控系统
大宗拨款	财政压力
资本预算	横向税收权益
分类财政补助	增量预算
缩减管理	项目预算
债务能力	收入弹性
支出压力	风险分担
财务状况	使用者付费
零基预算	纵向税收权益

参考文献

［1］Aronson, J. Richard（ed）（2004）. *Management Policies in Local Government*. Washington, D. C：International City Management Association.

［2］Bierhanzl, Edward J. and Downing, Paul B.（2004）. "User Charges and Special Districts," pp. 315 – 348 in Aronson, J. Richard（ed）*Management Policies in Local Government*. Washington, D. C：International City Management Association.

［3］Mikesell, John L.（2007）*Fiscal Administration：Analysis and Applications in the Public Sector*,

7th ed. Belmont, CA: Thomson-Wadsworth.

[4] Raphaelson, Arnold H. (2004). "The Property Tax," pp. 257 – 287 in Aronson, J. Richard (ed) *Management Policies in Local Government*. Washington, D. C: International City Management Association.

[5] Rubin, Irene (1988). *New Directions in Budget Theory*. Albany, NY: State University of New York Press.

[6] Young, Peter C. and Lee, Claire (2004). "Risk Management," in Aronson, J. Richard (ed) *Management Policies in Local Government*. Washington, D. C: International City Management Association: 455 – 489.

Chapter 6　Urban Finance

6. 1　Definition

Urban financial management is the process of using analytical, technical, and managerial tools to control and allocate scarce resources. It assumes limited resources, and it takes place in the context of the local government and local economy, where the government has several options in terms of raising revenue and controlling resources (Mikesell, 2007). Much of this work is done through the budgetary process. The budget is how local government services are determined and how they are financed. A budget is a plan of expected expenditures and outcomes. Urban governments never have enough money to meet all the needs and wants of their citizens. The budget, therefore, plays an important role in helping the city judge its needs and in planning to raise the funds necessary to meet these needs and wants.

More technically, the budget serves three roles. First, it serves as an economic plan. The urban budget reflects the allocation of scarce resources among various alternative uses. Second, it is a political document. The urban budget records who gets to spend what the local government unit has to spend. Third, it represents a decision-making process. The urban budget focuses on the reduction of complexities to manageable proportions.

The highly routine nature of the budget process, with its forms and deadlines, should not obscure the critical role that the process plays in allocating resources within local government. It is not surprising that the process is regarded by public managers as totally crucial to the welfare of the city, its citizens and residents, and the local government departments on which they depend.

6. 2　Functions and Types of Budget

6. 2. 1　Functions of Budget

Budgeting and financial management together provide three important functions for public managers. These are the control, management, and planning functions (Aronson, 2004).

The purpose of the control function is to make sure that funds are only disbursed and spent on authorized purposes as well as to prevent overspending. The major point is to comply with legal requirements. The management function tries to eliminate waste and improve productivity in the delivery of services. The planning function looks more broadly at rationalizing resource allocation within the organization. The concern is with the proper mix of goods and services that should be provided by the organization. A further point is the effectiveness of this mix in light of organizational objectives. Planning determines the programs that should be added, expanded, ended, or cut back.

Different types of budget information are needed to meet the requirements of each of these three functions. Control requires detailed information concerning the objects and purposes of budget items acquired. The management function benefits from a performance budget that indicates the target level of service or activity and the expected cost of providing services at that level so that efficiency and productivity can be judged and evaluated throughout the fiscal year. Finally, planning demands parallel and comparative information that will help managers make tradeoffs among programs (Aronson, 2004).

6. 2. 2   Types of Budget Strategy

Incrementalism

Most urban government budgets are incremental documents. Incrementalism can be defined as a budget proposal that incrementally increases or decreases the budget based on the total from the previous fiscal period. In practice, when the city is growing and prosperous, the budget shows an increase reflecting the level of growth. Conversely, where the urban economy is shrinking, the budget may reflect this condition with declining requests. Incrementalism tends to work in a blanket way, with most individual budget items even reflecting identical increments based on the previous year's budgetary requests.

The standard argument has been that local governments deal with budgetary hunger, the never-ending demands for more funding and bureaucratic growth that occurs in the absence of countervailing pressures, by adopting incrementalist budgeting. Governments and agencies considerably simplify their budgetary tasks by focusing attention on the level of changes in resources available from year to year. This assumes the budget is essentially fixed, transforming the process into a more technical process of adjusting specific line items and thus reducing the scope of budget conflict to the incremental percentage increase or decrease. This means that basic allocation battles do not need to be refought every year. The adoption of a single budget legitimizes the allocation decisions for that year and makes it easier to work on changes opened or forced by changes in the revenue environment. An important implication of incrementalism is that no major changes in budgets are made from year to year, meaning that the budget does not require or make significant policy choices which are transferred outside of the budget realm (Aronson, 2004).

The extent to which real budgets are incremental varies a great deal in real practice. The overall operating budget changes incrementally from year to year in most municipalities. The same is true at the departmental level. There are often major shifts in funds from one project or program to another on a yearly basis when the budget is viewed within various departments. Departments, like public works, that are structured along project lines are especially likely to see significant shifts from one budget to the next as projects are completed and new ones initiated. When one is the priority, that project goes to the top of the queue, with new ones appearing when a particular project is completed.

Zero-base Budgeting

Zero-base budgeting is a relatively recent alternative to incrementalism. Under this approach, it is assumed that the choice for an appropriate level of expenditure for any given activity starts at zero and any expenditure greater than that must be supported. Former President Carter, as governor of Georgia, employed the method in the 1970s, then brought it to Washington and the Federal Government when he became president of the US in 1976. Every element of every budget had to be reconsidered and justified in its entirety every year. The budget employed a typical line-item format but they had to prepare decision packages showing what the government would provide for the public at each spending level. These decision packages were expected to include operating data that would help justify or compare choices. The system has not survived, except in some localities and states, particularly where elements of the system have been maintained to improve flexibility and performance in making difficult budget decisions (Mikesell, 2007).

6. 3　Fiscal Stress and Risk Management

6. 3. 1　Fiscal Stress

New developments like cutback and retrenchment management took a high priority from the early 1990s. This change occurred earlier in the United States and other Western countries starting from the late 1960s and 1970s. Administrative principles such as efficiency, financial stability, equity, and responsibility reflect this. This administrative trend has had a major impact on the management of local governments in China. Growth changed from being the ultimate goal and came under severe criticism. Retrenchment and balance became desirable administrative goals. Consequently, evaluation and restructuring of government organizations become popular in the local public sector as a means of attaining administrative efficiency. This trend has continued into the 21st Century. As society has become more complex and uncertain societal demands have increased rapidly, accompanied by rapid increase in governmental expenditures. Governmental revenue, however, has not increased at the same rate. This trend, as a result, brought local finances to the top of the local and even, in cases, national policy agenda (Aronson, 2004).

A major task of budgeting and financial management is to finding ways to contain constant pressures to increase expenditures. This task is relatively easy when revenues are expanding. However, when changing economic, demographic, and political factors limit the growth of revenues, containment of the budget becomes much more difficult, and fiscal stress may result as a gap widens between what the local electorate demands and what the local revenue stream will support. It is difficult to deal with these pressures directly due to the unpopularity of the policy options. The government may cut back provision of goods and services or it may raise revenues. None of these choices are politically popular so, unfortunately, instead of dealing with fiscal stress forthrightly, many cities resort to financial trickery to hide, disguise, delay, or minimize the immediate impacts of fiscal stress to avoid negative political consequences.

Several different approaches are used in measuring fiscal stress. Some scholars, such as Richard Nathan and Charles Adams, stress demographic and economic indicators, such as unemployment, dependency, and poverty. Others, like Lynne Bernier and Richard Bingham, emphasize fiscal indicators, such as the balance between revenues and expenditures. Still others prefer an approach that combines both sets of indicators.

The Financial Trend Monitoring System (FTMS) was developed as a means by the International City Management Association to measure fiscal stress. The FTMS uses information from city financial statements to develop a series of indicators of a city's overall fiscal condition. Generally-accepted accounting principles have made financial statements easily understandable, allowing people with a minimal level of technical knowledge or a financial background to do fiscal analysis. The FTMS is used to give public administrators the opportunity to analyze the financial statements cities for fiscal stress (Aronson, 2004). Figure 6.1 shows framework for the analysis of goverment financial condition.

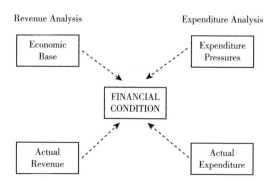

Figure 6.1   Framework for the Analysis of Government Financial Condition

The key to financial analysis is to analyze the financial condition under which it is likely that a government will be able to meet its financial obligations as they come due (Berne and

Schramm, 1997: 68). The financial condition of a government depends upon revenues and expenditures. Revenue includes available resources, including both internal and external resources. Expenditures here include current expenditure pressures and pressures from past commitments. More resources lead to a healthier financial condition, whereas more expenditure pressures lead to a weaker financial condition.

Revenue analysis tries to determine the economic base, potential sources drawn from that base, and the actual revenues. The urban government will look at the businesses, properties, and consumption patterns that make up the local economy and then decide what economic activities can be taxed to minimize negative economic interventions while maximizing revenue. After that, the actual revenue streams are forecast and actual revenue is collected. On the other hand, expenditure analysis tries to measure actual expenditures and expenditure pressures. Pressures for spending are diverse and great, with each individual and group having their own preferences for more money to be spent in different areas. The collective pressures that place the greatest pressure for increasing expenditures are addressing urban issues like pollution, crime, congestion, and an aging population that requires increased services. Figure 6. 1 shows the framework for the analysis of government financial condition.

How do local governments cope with fiscal stress? Harold Wolman and Barbara Davis identified a hierarchy of strategies that governmental units resort to when responding to fiscal pressures, ranging from most to least preferred. Initially, governments respond with postponing strategies to buy time in the hope that the problem is only temporary. Governments next try revenue increases if these measures fail to solve the problem. In terms of revenues, it is perhaps not surprising that local governments usually try first to obtain intergovernmental revenues by making appeals to higher levels of government for help. They will then consider less popular tax or fee increases if the appeal for intergovernmental assistance fails. Actual reductions in goods and services and layoffs of personnel beyond a minor level are only considered and occur only when governments are prevented from raising additional revenue and must start making hard choices. When expenditures do need to be reduced, the first cuts are made in areas that have a minimum impact on the level of services delivered or on the status of employees. They also may seek to cut expenditures without cutting services through efficiency and productivity gains. Table 6. 1 shows major determinants of financial cordition.

Table 6. 1   **Major Determinants of Financial Condition**

Determinants	Probable Effect on Financial Condition*
Community Needs:	
- Percent of population below poverty level	−
- Percent of population over 65	−
- Unemployment rate	−

Continued

Determinants	Probable Effect on Financial Condition *
Production & Service Conditions:	
- Population density	+ / −
- Population size	+ / −
- Population growth rate	+
Community Resources:	
- Percent of employment in mining and manufacturing	+
- Retail sales per capita	+
Central Government Policies:	
- Intergovernmental transfers	+
Local Government Financial Policies and Practices:	
- Debt and debt burden measures	−
- Tax burden measures	−

* " + " indicates that an increase in this factor probably improves financial condition; " − " indicates that an increase probably worsens financial condition; " + / − " indicates that the effect is uncertain, either because of the way variable is defined or because the factor has both positive and negative effects.

Expenditure reductions usually take place in areas that are completely funded locally when they must occur. Intergovernmental expenditures are not generally cut. Governments typically will respond with an across-the-board cut when a fiscal crisis is severe and acute. This is often cast as being fair, with shared sacrifice helping the government through the crisis. Every department or division bears its share of the burden. Peripheral and non-core services face the deepest cuts when the reductions are not across the board. These include areas like recreation, parks, libraries, and cultural activities. Public works may also experience severe reductions, as general administration typically does. Human services and fire and police protection tend to be the least vulnerable to cuts. Public safety services are protected because of the apparent importance and visibility to the public. Human and social services are protected largely because they are heavily funded through intergovernmental transfers.

6.3.2   Risk Management

The urban government realm is fraught with financial risks, whether potential or current and pressing. Control of city government spending is complicated by these financial risks that may impact government operations. Essential here are legal suits or other financial claims against city government budgets. A rapid increase in the cost of commercial insurance has forced local governments to look at the emerging field of risk management.

Risk management consists of identifying risks, evaluating their frequency, potential severity, and in deciding how to deal with risk exposure. It then monitors the results of those decisions. An increasing number of municipal governments have written risk management policies and have at least one full-time risk position. It is not surprising that many in these positions have experience in the insurance industry. In smaller governments or governmental units that lack the resources to support a risk management position, such functions may be taken care of by finance directors, assistant city managers, or other designated officials.

Self-insurance and intergovernmental risk pooling are some alternative strategies for financing risk-reduction mechanisms. These have become more popular over time. Self-insurance simply means going without insurance and being prepared to face the consequences. Popular areas for self-insurance include general liability, automobile liability, and workers' compensation. Intergovernmental risk-sharing pools are another popular risk-financing tool for public agencies. A pool is a cooperative arrangement, similar to a credit union where different entities share resources to finance their own risk response. Participating governmental units (members of the pool) pay a contribution (premium) to the pool, receive coverage, and make claims. This is actually very similar to the concept of insurance, except that the insured negotiate and organize the arrangements among themselves instead of going to an outside party for the service. Many pools have a full-time professional manager who also assists member governments with overall risk-management programs. The most common areas for risk pooling are general liability and workers' compensation.

Public risk management is not simply a new and expanding field of municipal government. It also represents an opportunity for major financial savings. Given the cost constraints on government today, urban managers must ensure that the risk management process is used to identify, evaluate, control, and finance risk across the entire range of city government operations.

6.4 User Charges

The problems of urban governments in recent years have required new sources of revenue to meet rising demands for increased expenditures, which have not been met completely by traditional revenue sources. Traditional sources of funding, such as the property tax, have often not been flexible in responding to changes in need. Increases in the property tax are often strictly limited by law as well as stymied by political opposition. User charges have become a very important resource for city governments to generate more revenue and meet the demands for funds to match the cost of rising expenditures. User charges have the advantage of directly offsetting the cost of a particular public good or service, thought they do not usually recover the full cost. Instead, their cost is usually based on a calculation of the average costs and tends to ignore cost differences between particular users, particular locations, and time of day or day of use (Mikesell, 2007). This makes it less efficient than the market-based pricing employed by private businesses.

Definition

A user charge is defined as a sum of money paid by an individual who chooses to use a service or access a facility. A user charge is a tax disguised as a price. It is a charge for the use of a publicly-provided good. It is a means of employing a quasi-market mechanism for costing and financing public goods. In addition to the examples of user fees noted above, highway tolls, municipal parking, park and museum entrance fees, and garbage bags are some typical examples of user charges. Government produces and supplies several near-public goods, like education, libraries, parks, and transportation systems. The "prices" for these goods are user charges.

Broad Definition

User charges are market-like transactions in the public sector. Such transactions link a particular payment and a particular benefit. User charges under this definition may include fees and charges, rents and royalties, earmarked excise taxes, permits and licenses, revenues from the sale of government property, interest on government loans, premiums collected for any special insurance, revenues raised from government-created property rights, and premiums or annuity payments for government retirement or health programs.

Narrow Definition

User charges are prices charged for voluntarily-purchased, publicly-provided services that are closely associated with pure public goods, even though they are consumed by individuals. This definition excludes revenues raised by local government utilities, including water, sewage, electric, and gas utilities because utility charges are public prices for publicly-provided products that are truly private goods in nature. License and permit fees are also excluded according to this definition because they are associated with privileges granted by government, not publicly-provided goods and special assessments because they are not voluntary (Mikesell, 2007).

This definition is the closest definition for user charges and fees in this chapter, focusing on distinctly public-sector activities that do not force individuals to contribute. User charges and fees are payments for voluntarily-purchased, publicly-provided services that benefit specific individuals, but have public-good characteristics or are closely associated with public goods. Goods that have public-good characteristics or are closely associated with public goods are often called merit goods.

Individuals may be excluded from consuming a merit good when they are not willing to pay for the good and when the benefits associated with the good can be clearly linked to individuals or group of consumers. The term beneficiary charges describe nontax-revenue sources that broader definitions often include under the heading user charges and fees such as utility revenue, special assessments, and license and permit fees, as well as user charges and fees as defined above (Pascal, 1984).

6. 5 Issues

Urban finance is determined by the urban economy, and at the same time, it acts on urban economy. The scale of urban economy and its economic benefits determine the scale of urban finance and restrict the development speed of urban finance, which is the basis of urban finance. Urban finance belongs to local finance and is an important part of national finance. It is a tool for the city government to participate in the distribution of national income in the form of value by virtue of the authority granted by the state. It is the economic basis and financial guarantee for realizing the functions of the city government.

The level and growth of total and per capita expenditures increase more rapidly in some cities based on expenditure pressures. City expenditures naturally have an impact on the level of city debt. Debt capacity is a key component to be considered in debt analysis as cities have different debt capacities. There are several debt capacity measures, such as sources of revenue, examination of revenue reserves, and expenditure pressures. Another component is actual debt. One method for evaluating the indebtedness of a city is to compare the existing debt to a measure of revenue capacity. City debt can be shown as per capita debt to have a measure that is comparable between different areas. Both the total and per capita debt outstanding have increased over time in most cities, in line with increasing expenditures and expenditure pressures.

Questions

1. What roles do budgets play in urban administration?

2. What are three major functions of urban budgeting?

3. What is the budget cycle?

4. Analyze a city's financial condition using the FTMS method.

5. What is the revenue trend in a particular city (the city you live or any cities you choose)? What is the expenditure trend in the city?

6. Describe the property tax trend in a particular city.

Key Terms

allotment system	fiscal stress
block grants	horizontal tax equity
capital budget	incrementalism
categorical grants	program budget
cutback management	revenue elasticity
debt capacity	risk pooling
expenditure pressures	user charge
financial condition	vertical tax equity
financial trend monitoring system	zero-based budgeting

References

［1］ Aronson, J. Richard (ed) (2004). *Management Policies in Local Government.* Washington, D. C: International City Management Association.

［2］ Bierhanzl, Edward J. and Downing, Paul B. (2004). "User Charges and Special Districts," pp. 315 – 348 in Aronson, J. Richard (ed) *Management Policies in Local Government.* Washington, D. C: International City Management Association.

［3］ Mikesell, John L. (2007) *Fiscal Administration: Analysis and Applications in the Public Sector,* 7th ed. Belmont, CA: Thomson-Wadsworth.

［4］ Raphaelson, Arnold H. (2004). "The Property Tax," pp. 257 – 287 in Aronson, J. Richard (ed) *Management Policies in Local Government.* Washington, D. C: International City Management Association.

［5］ Rubin, Irene (1988). *New Directions in Budget Theory.* Albany, NY: State University of New York Press.

［6］ Young, Peter C. and Lee, Claire (2004). "Risk Management," in Aronson, J. Richard (ed) *Management Policies in Local Government.* Washington, D. C: International City Management Association: 455 – 489.

第 7 章　城市规划

7.1　概念及内涵

城市规划试图规范土地和其他物质资源的使用，以符合公共利益，规划可以显著改善城市居民的生活质量和福利。城市规划的一个非常广泛的定义，它是一个明确城市目标的过程，确定哪些城市行动者应采取什么行动，何时采取，用什么样的方法，以及以何种成本实现预期的目标。

规划可以按功能或项目进行。当规划为特定领域内的决策者制订适当的行动方案时，规划就发挥了作用，项目规划比功能规划更广泛。例如，规划城市更新项目的所有程序都是基于一系列广泛的目标，而不仅仅是在某一个领域内。项目规划者必须在基本标准基础之上处理工程学、社会学、经济和政治目标。因此，项目规划非常复杂，需要跨学科的努力。功能性规划和具体项目的规划可广泛应用于城市管理的任何方面，商业、工业以及政府都会雇用专业规划师，城市政府内的许多不同行政机构经常进行规划，利用规划师开展广泛的公共活动。

规划物理空间使用的目的是什么？规划师倾向于从物理角度考虑环境，但在考虑物理空间使用标准时，必须考虑社区的政治、经济和社会目标。有关土地使用强度、不同价格范围内的住房存量、社区设施的需求和选址、各种土地使用之间的适当关系以及交通模式的问题都是基于并源于社区的社会经济价值。此外，城市规划与许多其他政府职能有着明显的关系。

城市规划通常只在城市市政边界内的地理区域内进行，因此，它可能无法解决跨越这些边界的一些重大问题。除非有更广泛的区域范围内的社区间协调机制，否则无法使规划与邻近社区的规划同步。如今，美国的大多数大城市都包含多个郊区开发节点，这些节点通常以大型购物区为中心，位于高速公路交汇处，这些节点有时被称为城市村庄、外围城市或边缘城市，是吸引办公综合体、更多商业开发和住宅建设的强大磁石。

规划类型

规划分为几种类型，针对特定情况具有不同的特征，包括：结构计划、总体规划、地方土地利用计划、战略规划和非正式规划。我国城市规划通常分为总体规划和详细规划。其中，详细规划根据规划的深度和管理的需要，又分为控制性详细规划和修建性详细规划。城市总体规划是对一定时期内城市性质、发展目标、发展规模、土地利用、空间布局以及各项建设的综合部署和实施措施。从规划的层面来看，我国的城市规划可以分为战略层面和操作层面，总体规划被视为战略层面，修建性详细规划属于操作层面，控制性详细规划是两个层面的衔接，同时也是我国城市规划管理的重要依据。

7.2　城市规划流程

在对现实情况进行分析之后，班菲尔德制定了一个由五个步骤组成的合理规划模型，这五个步骤分别是：减少和细化目标、设计行动方案、对结果进行比较评估、选择备选方案和选定备选方案的实施。这并不是规划流程的唯一可能方式，例如，五个步骤后来被简单地描述为 5D：欲望、设计、演绎、决策和行动。

减少和细化目标

一旦对情况进行了分析，并且产生了所有可能实现目标或目的的选项，就有必要对目标进行缩小和细化。班菲尔德将目标描述为行动所指向的未来状态的图像，最终目标的最初表述可能（而且往往）过于模糊或分散，这是目标需要被细化和缩小的阶段，以便规划者能够陈述目标并清楚地解释其含义。如果要素不完全一致，规划者必须按优先顺序对其进行排序，以便目标中最重要的要素是最后一个被放弃的要素，并且不会被无意写进一个满足更多目标却失去关键目标的规划中。

设计行动方案

这是作为规划一部分的行动计划，细节上可能或多或少有些过于笼统，最一般的行动方针将包括作为计划一部分展开的关键行动。在这一点上，更具体的行动应限于那些不会因不同的总体规划而有所改变或排除的行动。这一步的重点不是确定任何具体的行动方案，而是生成几个不同的选项，可以对这些选项进行评估，然后可以在下一步骤中进行选择。虽然最好有更多的选择，因为创造性的选择可能会开辟新的领域，但出于经济的考虑，不要过于详细地制定任何选项，因为随着最终选项的选择和潜在行动方案的被拒绝，大部分工作会是无用的。

对结果进行比较评估

这一规划过程的要点是要理性。如果这个过程是真正理性的，那么需要对所有的结果进行评估。人们很容易关注并强调规划者所期望的结果，但其实也需要对不期望的结果加以权衡。班菲尔德认为，良好规划的特点是积极寻找环境中包含的成功实现目标可能产生的所有意外后果。评估必须采取对每个潜在行动方案相关的净值进行比较的形式，这样做的典型程序是成本效益分析（CBA）。如果无形资产是公式的一部分，则必须尽可能将其转换为现金价值或其他等价物，以便与其他要素进行比较。

选择备选方案

在实际操作过程中，最终实施方案的选择必须基于使用最初的评估标准去分析。成本效益分析或其他分析方法（视情况而定）需要结合现有的可利用的证据，最终选择应以这些证据为依据。

选定备选方案的实施

一旦选定了备选方案，就可以开始实施，但这并不是与早期进程之间的联系的结束，仍然需要根据得出的结论重新对数据进行评估，以寻找新出现的不可预见的问题。早期规划是规划成功实施的关键因素，如果其他步骤已被正确执行，那么这项工作应在实际执行阶段就可以产生足够的资源。

这些步骤被频繁复制用以描述复杂的人类规划的问题解决框架，该模式由于对资源和专业知识的复杂需求而无法实现。班菲尔德也认识到了其复杂性，包括为公众利益服务的目标难以实现，以及科学分析的政治阻力等。理性规划模型甚至一开始提出来就遭到了批判，而且自那以后，一直受到来自许多方面的严肃而持续的批评。尽管如此，班菲尔德模型仍然是获得最广泛支持的规划理论，它的逻辑仍然存在于大多数规划的导言中给出的理由和大纲，也是许多规划课程的主要支柱和基础。该模型负责创建和推广城市规划者在方法论写作和讨论中使用的主要语言。此外，细化和扩展模型的理论和方法工作一直持续到现在，包括努力比较用于汇总个人偏好的替代规则，检查风险和不确定性的影响，考虑新的更快的计算机对确定公众偏好、收集信息、生成更多替代方案和进行必要计算的能力的影响。

7.3 城市规划的思想流派

7.3.1 现代规划理论的诞生

现代规划的理论基础和规划的理论化过程可以追溯到规划师们职业生涯的第一天。然而，最早且仍然有影响力的理论并非始于美国建国时期，而是始于美国的新政时期。罗斯福总统身边有一群顾问，被称为"智囊团"，其中包括波多黎各前总督雷克斯福德塔·格韦尔，他大力倡导规划，甚至将其宣传为所谓的"第四种力量"或政府部门的一个分支。以新兴凯恩斯主义经济原则为指导的新政规划实验包括国家资源规划委员会、移民安置管理局和田纳西河谷管理局，其规模很大，而且是全国性的，建立了现代城市规划的模式。这些计划倡导一种基于数据收集和检验、备选行动方案评估以及实施系统的建设规划，他们将规划的定义扩展为一种设计活动，并将科学技术纳入其中。不过，更具体地说，城市管理部门感兴趣的是新政的示范城市规划，这可能是对城市规划专业最有影响力的新政计划，因为它在城市层面展示了这种新的社会科学模式。

在美国人忙于这些规划实践的同时，流亡在美国的德国社会学家卡尔·曼海姆正在准备一份极具影响力的理论和规范性声明来解释为什么规划对于自由和开放的社会是必要的。曼海姆在《重建时代的人与社会》一书中区分了四种可能的社会结构——独裁、无政府状态、失范和民主计划，这四种结构是由参与和集权的差异导致的。其中，独裁是基于低水平的参与和高水平的集权而形成的；无政府状态是高度参与和低度集权的结果；失范是一个同时具有低参与度和集权的系统的结果。曼海姆最喜欢的选择是民主计划社会，这是高度参与和中央集权的结果。

曼海姆（Mannheim）相信，规划是技术发展与人口增长相结合的必然结果。一旦人们认为必须进行规划，摆在桌面上的主要问题是由谁负责进行规划，与此形成鲜明对比的是，规划是由法西斯独裁势力完成，还是通过民主进程和参与性机构完成。曼海姆告诫规划者不要过分依赖功能理性，这意味着过分关注手段，而不是将重点放在最终目标上。取而代之的是，曼海姆坚持规划者在谨慎地定义正确的目标和最终状态时要注重实体理性。

曼海姆的书并非毫无争议，它标志着大辩论的开始。这些辩论涉及学术和政治斗争，其影响既是理论上的，也是实践上的。一方面，规划倡导者支持提高政府组织水平和在经济中的影响力；另一方面，自由主义倡导者，如弗雷德里克·哈耶克，认为政府是笨拙而低效的，并且害怕一个更强大的政府的力量。1941 年，美国国会也以非常公开的方式拒绝重新授权国家资源规划委员会。大辩论的一个重要见解是区分"免于……的自由"和"享有……的自由"的概念。芭芭拉·伍顿（Barbara Wooten, 1945）认为，只关注不受政府胁迫的自由是愚蠢的，同时，她还进一步主张，政府必须允许人们自由地做一些事情——如果没有政府和社会组织和机构组织参与，通过政府来确定和实现这些目标，人民将无法做到这些事情。

7.3.2 理性规划

继罗斯福新政和第二次世界大战后的成功规划之后，塔格韦尔（Tugwell）加入了芝加哥大学战后创建的教育和规划研究项目，他在芝加哥大学的同事包括著名的规划倡导者哈维·佩洛夫、爱德华·班菲尔德和朱利叶斯·马戈利斯（Harvey Perloff, Edward Banfield and Julius Margolis）。这个项目只持续了九年，但在制定规划理论方向方面仍然具有极为重要的影响。凯恩斯主义经济学家珀洛夫推动教职员工定义并系统化规划中的核心知识领域，这些领域被认为是将规划付诸实践的关键，这种对产业核心的探索导致了资本主义民主中理性规划的一般模式的发展，并将不同社会科学学科的思想纳入其中，包括经济学、公共行政和政治科学。班菲尔德（Banfield's 1955, 1959）的新理性规划模型，作为公共领域解决问题的一种方法，成为该产业及其他领域的标准指南。马戈利斯后来通过提供指导原则将该模型引入公共政策分析这一新兴领域。

理性规划借鉴了凯恩斯主义经济学和政治学中的政策研究，将众多社会科学概念纳入规划研究，它强调了规划在纠正与一系列市场失灵方面相关问题的作用，这些问题包括外部性、公共产品、不公平、交易成本、市场失灵或缺失。他们的规划理由包括通过宜居性改善公民和居民的生活质量，减少滋扰和拥堵，改善环境质量，通过保护资源、减少税收和公共成本促进稳定的商业环境。

规划采用成本效益分析和运筹学的工具和语言，包括决策标准、多目标、约束、影子定价法、支付意愿、优化和最小化（Weimer and Vinning, 1992；Klosterman, 1994）。

理性规划的一个主要考虑是个体理性与集体理性之间关联性的缺乏。微观经济学考虑个人和企业的合理性，但在考虑复杂的公共实体时，很难采用这一概念，因为这些公共实体可能存在巨大规模，让个体和企业相形见绌。个人和企业可能知道他们想要什么，但城市和地区如何决定？他们的愿望是什么？他们的偏好是什么？托马斯·谢林断言，在某些情况下，个人偏好聚合到社会层面会产生不合逻辑或不理想的结果，这可能包括由于路人放慢速度去目不转睛地盯着因为摩托车驾驶员不戴头盔造成的事故和公路延误。在这种情况下，如果小组作为一个整体作出决定，这将与成员的个别决定之和大不相同。在市场经济中进行规划的原因与这一对比密切相关，即如何使规划在提供市场无法实现的合理结果方面发挥作用。

对理性规划的批判与拓展

政治学家查尔斯·林德布卢姆（Charles Lindblom）对理性规划进行了渐进式批评，这种批评在 20 世纪 60 年代早期广泛传播。他表示全面规划是不可能实现的，与政治现实脱节。政治领导人不能像理性模型所要求的那样提前就目标达成一致，他们更喜欢同时选择政策和目标。他认为，理性模型专注于比较所有可能的备选方案，并对所有绩效指标进行全面评估，这超出了人类的能力，并认为科学与政策选择之间的关系充其量是间接的。林德布卢姆的渐进决策理论要求同时选择目标和政策，考虑与现状略有不同的备选方案，对备选方案进行简化比较，以及优先考虑社会实践结果而不是理论作为分析基础。林德布鲁姆的批评很有力且广受欢迎，并影响了许多规划者，阿米泰·埃齐奥尼的中距理论是一种旨在协调理性规划与渐进决策理论的努力。战略规划运动在很大程度上借鉴了林德布鲁姆的思想，主张关注组织生存而非社会利益。

林德布鲁姆在 20 世纪 70 年代辩称，他的观点被误解了，他的渐进决策理论实际上有三层含义：战略分析、不连贯的渐进主义和简单的渐进主义，规划者们设法模糊了这三层含义。战略分析代表了任何简化复杂政策问题以使其更清晰、更容易理解的尝试。不连贯的渐进主义意味着在没有首先确定目标的情况下进行分析，考虑的备选方案很少，使用的数据复杂度有限。简单的渐进主义是指所考虑的备选方案与现状仅略有不同。规划包含了第三种含义即简单的渐进主义，而林德布卢姆声称他一直在为支离破碎的渐进决策理论辩护。

艾伦·阿特舒勒（Alan Altshuler）研究了明尼阿波利斯－圣保罗的土地和交通规划，他发现，规划者通常无法实现他们合理的科学目标，他们的主张实际并没有实现——决策者往往无视规划者的建议，而是听从政治上重要利益攸关方的意愿，参与规划的公众倡导者抱怨说，规划往往毫无意义。马克思主义对规划的批评认为，规划者有效地竞标了发展利益，并没有真正解决有意义的政策选择（Kravitz，1970；Goodman，1971）。保罗·戴维多夫（Paul Davidoff，1965 年）的文章《规划中的倡导与多元化》是20 世纪 60 年代以来对规划最重要的批评。大卫杜夫回应了规划者的沮丧，他们觉得无法应对当时挑战美国城市的重大社会和经济问题，呼吁通过倡导规划者将规划服务分配到低收入和少数族裔社区，因为他们在附近居住或工作，并在城市规划中代表居民的利益。

戴维多夫的想法是，规划者之间的讨论将以公共利益为出发点，这样，城市的更广泛需求将超越狭隘的社区利益。美国联邦政府建立了与戴维多夫的提议相近的机构，许多最贫困地区开设了店面规划服务，非营利倡导计划公司和合作社兴起，并与大学和社会福利组织合作，城市规划者的许多假设都得到了讨论和辩论，许多贫困居民获得了进入城市政治的权利。但批评者指出，倡导性规划者与他们服务的居民截然不同，规划的宣传可能带来了这些社区无法满足的不切实际的期望，这可能会给人留下城市会照顾他们的印象，从而阻止居民在政治上为自己发声。倡导性规划运动使规划者摆脱了代表全面公共利益的立场，并迅速蔓延到了市中心以外，也开始为环保团体服务，甚至代表产业协会和公司为他们狭隘的利益进行宣传。

新方向

在倡导性规划表明规划可以走一条新的道路之后，规划理论家开始朝着许多方向前进，理性规划模型逐渐失去了支持。斯蒂芬·格雷博和艾伦·赫斯金批评理性规划框架无法满足穷人的需求，呼吁进行系统性变革，包括权力下放、生态关注、自发性和实验。激进的批评虽没有提出一个明确的解决方案，但确实鼓励了渐进式的规划运动，该运动寻求渐进式的变革，随着时间的推移，导致了结构变革，从而提高合法性、平等性和参与性。一些进步人士还组织了社区自助活动，认为增长机器主导了美国各地的市议会和规划委员会，并推动了促进增长的议程。这种增长机制使得环境或其他反对团体难以赢得决策权，由增长机器的支持者组成的董事会和委员会甚至无法理解人们为何反对增长。

随着激进批评的发展，新的理论即社会学习理论随之发展起来，它强调规划者在几个关键领域的作用，包括将受规划影响的有关各方聚集在一起，收集和分享信息，以及帮助社会组织和机构从经验中学习。约翰·弗里德曼发展了互动式规划，强调公民和城市领导人而不是规划者必须成为规划实施的核心。克里斯·阿格里斯和唐纳德·肖恩提出了一种行动理论，在这个理论中，规划者起到了催化剂的作用，将跨越边界的人们聚集在一起，创建从经验中学习的结构。

重回同一阵地

规划者将科学/理性的规划概念视为将他们与参与制定关键规划决策的政治行为者区分开。德国批判理论家尤尔根·哈贝马斯（Jurgen Habermas）对社会科学提出质疑，他在有意将社会学习和进步计划结合起来的规划者中产生了影响。弗雷斯特提出了沟通规划理论（Forester，1989），主张数据和对公共决策的理解将赋予社会弱势和城市少数群体和穷人以权利，规划者应使用现代沟通策略向公民传达问题，告知他们现状，并通过在建立共识的过程中鼓励社区规划。拉里·苏斯金德和其他人支持这种建立共识的发展方向，因为技术和分析技能与调解人的传统方向是并行的，因此，规划者能够在复杂问题和参与规划的众多利益攸关方之间进行调解。苏斯金德认为，规划者应该通过学习调解人的人际交往技能来承担这一角色，并努力确定潜在利益，制订备选方案，并确定公平的决策标准。这项工作得到了经验性文献的支持，这些文献遵循了规划者的实际工作，并提出了切实可行的建议。

7.3.3　后现代的挑战与回应

随着移民问题的兴起，人们对性别、种族、族裔和区域差异的认识以及从 20 世纪 80 年代开始在北美和西欧以及其他地方出现的全球化的世界经济，有了多样性和对同时存在的多个观点的认识，规划者的部分回应是着眼于后现代思想，即个人和群体理解社会和政治问题的方式具有普遍的多样性，强调在各行各业中一个群体对另一个群体的支配。尽管后现代哲学对人类解决这些趋势的能力非常悲观，但后现代规划理论家们正在寻找克服这种悲观主义的方法。后现代规划者尊重并呼吁承认和尊重多样性，同时承认群体之间的差异，并努力让社区尽早参与规划过程。后现代的一个积极发展是为规划者寻找更好的方式，在不同的政治和多元文化环境中推进他们的想法。规划的技术和定量基础不适合说服典型的行政和政治决策者，他们常常被关于人的故事和他们可以理解的人类隐喻所感动，因此，讲故事被提议作为一种规划方法，以完成统计分析无法完成的任务。在一个不同但相关的方向上，批判性实用主义理论家认为公共决策者的解决问题取向与统计规划方法所要求的演绎推理不兼容，他们呼吁规划者使用归纳推理和演绎推理。社会资本理论强调社会网络和社区领导的复杂性和有效性，以推动社区应对新的挑战。

女权主义规划理论与后现代规划批评相关，通常来自后现代规划理论，它呼吁规划者更多地考虑家庭生活和社区再生产，而不是传统的以经济发展为重点，女性主义规划者也试图解释男性和女性使用空间的方式不同。在规划分析中使用的经济效益措施没有重视家庭儿童保育、社区老年人保育或公民和社区组织的志愿工作。当女性（和男性）进行许多不属于日常从家到工作场所的出行时，交通在强调通勤方面也被认为存在缺陷。

彼得·卡尔索普和安德烈斯·杜安尼提出的新城市主义吸引了许多政府官员的注意，并将规划从主要的程序性问题转向了实质性问题。新城市主义对规划的纯粹物理方面的关注有助于提升公民生活和社会资本。可持续发展运动在国际上得到大规模的发展，其重点是可再生资源、保护和保存，同时，它也关注贫富之间的关系。该运动提出了基于全球合作和促进公平的新决策标准和模式。

7.3.4　设计的概念和路径

物理视角

尽管并非所有城市政府所做的规划都基于这样的方向，但地方政府的规划主要关注物理空间的使用。规划专业在决定如何使用城市空间时非常重视物理标准，对于不同用途的土地（如住房、商业和工业）的位置和空间要求，通常有严格的标准并基于不同的设计理念。许多早期的规划者都有工程或建筑学背景，自然地保持和推进了物理偏见。规划确实涉及社会经济研究，但直到最近，规划者才开始注意如何利用这些研究来制定土地使用标准。

设计

设计是解决城市问题的方法，也是规划的主要方法。设计解决方案是一个创造性和艺术性的过程，在这个过程中，物理设计概念被调整以适应具体情况的要求，解决方案很少基于社会科学研究，而是基于精心设计的规划标准。物理环境是城市问题的基础这一观点形成了早期规划实践中的关注重点。因此，人们推测物质环境的改善将改善城市地区的社会和经济问题。

社会行为的视角

尽管仍存在强烈的物理偏见，但规划最近已朝着更广阔的方向发展。社会科学研究正被用于制定城市空间设计和规划的使用。斯图亚特·查宾将社会过程和行为作为影响土地使用的特征之一，这些因素可能包括经济变量，例如，财产价值、就业机会和交通成本、当地政治制度的规范和实践以及土地的物理特征。他强调，制定基于当地价值观和当地文化的规划目标非常重要，建议规划者在目标确定后，根据目标对社会、经济和物质因素进行详细研究，应利用这些因素为不同的土地用途制定合适的空间标准，这些标准是反映社区目标的规划基础。

数学模型

近年来社会科学和经济数据相结合并开始建立数学模型以模拟和预测城市发展。经济学家、社会科学家和规划者一直在研究地理位置与不同社会经济变量之间的关系，特别是在土地使用问题上。他们提供了关于地理位置、经济活动和经济健康之间关系的新信息。通过这些努力，进一步了解土地使用的决定因素，模拟各种备选城市规划（如交通规划）的模型已经在多个案例中使用，并且比实施规划所涉及的实际实验成本低得多。

规划理论重视城市发展所涉及的关系的复杂性，模拟和数学模型的设计和构建有助于更好地理解复杂性。一些规划者和理论家利用游戏模拟来了解城市发展的复杂性，该方法中的个人在规划过程中扮演了不同的角色，并根据其在模拟环境中的角色作出决策，然后他们会看到他们的决定如何对一个假定的社区带来影响，这一技术也生动地说明了不同的变量是如何影响城市发展的。

选择和倡导性路径

给传统强调物理空间的质疑带来了对规划分析中一些被忽视的因素的考虑，与其将规划划分为物理的、经济的和社会的因素，不如将不同类型的规划结合在一起的系统方法更吸引人。例如，规划师的角色是设计有意义的备选方案，然后为在这些备选方案中进行选择建立系统的基础。

戴维多夫和雷纳提出了一种规划理论，其基础是规划过程应包含一系列选择。这种选择理论认为，必须在备选目标和实现这些目标的方法之间作出选择，他们建议有必要为作出规划选择制定广泛的标准。戴维多夫认为，应该有代表每个社区的不同价值观的不同规划，代表涵盖广泛范围的政策声明，其理念是不同的规划者充当社区中不同群体价值观的倡导者，政府的规划活动需要解决社区中存在的经济、社会和物质价值。他们还发现，规划是地方政府的一项职能，应该关注与决定未来行动方向相关的所有政府政策的制定。

从历史上看，规划过程并没有为公民参与提供多少机会，私人房地产开发商没有太多理由邀请公民参与他们的规划。公民的参与不受重视，因为考虑到意见和利益的多样性，公民往往会很挑剔。此外，公民的意见通常可以归结为否决权。公共规划者、规划人员和规划机构对公民群体也有类似的负面看法，认为他们是无知的，是规划的障碍。城市计划通常会要求公民参与规划，但通常在规划起草后才邀请公民参与，因此公民参与可能仅仅是在规划宣传会议上了解规划的具体实施，其结果可能是，面对大型项目给他们的社区带来的重大变化，公民往往会感到被疏远和无助。

戴维多夫的宣传规划是在公民参与下解决这些问题的一项重大努力。他认为，规划机构与当地其他机构有联系，但忽视了穷人和少数群体成员的合法需求。大卫杜夫建议公民团体雇用专业规划师来制定自己的规划，然后提交给公共规划机构考虑。这样，公民就可以积极参与并提出合理的建议，而不是仅仅通过抗议和消极行动来阻止正在进行的规划。

行动路径

亨利·费金还提倡规划应解决更广泛的问题，认为规划是一项以行动为导向的活动，它包括研究、制定目标、制定规划、协调、一般援助和咨询。这些基本的规划活动分散在政府内部的各种机构中。费金建议，不同的职能，如编制实体规划、预算计划和政府活动的总体协调，应在一个单一的政府机构内结合起来，从而形成一个广泛的政策规划，该政策规划提倡将政府的所有规划活动纳入单一的规划机构加以考量。

7.4　城市规划的标准规范

公共利益经常被用作确定公共目标的标准，无论是使用警察权力、征用权还是征税权。在土地使用规划中，通常与公众利益相关的九个因素是健康、安全、便利、效率、节能、环境质量、社会公平、社会选择、舒适度。这九个公共目的中的每一个都有更广泛的含义，在界定城市规划中的公共利益方面都很重要。

美国公共卫生协会制定了一份舒适环境所需的标准清单，包括事故预防、疲劳、传染病、过度噪声、污染和道德风险，还包括保持清洁、充足的日光、通风、隐私、正常家庭和社区生活的机会以及满足对美丽和迷人的便利环境的审美需求的机会。就公共利益的构成而言，便利往往被视为次要考虑因素。尽管如此，它与公共利益密切相关，应是政府行动的主要基础。健康与安全可能对生活至关重要，而便利则为城市系统注入了活力，因为公民自然会寻求便利，并避开缺乏便利的空间。

接下来的主要因素都与效率有关。效率与公共成本相关，公共成本可以是市政支出或城市居民的成本。效率是从整个社区的角度来看土地开发，而不是从企业家或个人的集体行动的角度来看，最根本的问题是什么样的土地使用对市政当局和公民来说成本最低。节能是对昂贵和稀缺能源的高效利用，可以通过土地使用和建筑规划来解决。

环境问题被认为是健康的一部分。气候变化和全球变暖、油价上涨、对接近或已达到石油峰值（最大石油产量）的担忧、污染和生活质量问题日益突出，这些事态发展以及对经济和人口增长压力的相关公众讨论有助于提高对环境问题的认识，也让人们对规划环境问题的解决方案产生了更多的紧迫感。

社会公平和选择涉及城市中的人权问题，两者都关注城市社会的多元化和多样性，出于公共利益的考虑，社会公平和选择涉及公共部门和私营部门中不同群体利益的平等对待权。社会公平是获得工作、住房、教育和医疗的平等机会。社会选择与参与、范围以及选择和机会的定义有关，这些选择和机会涉及最直接影响城市地区不同群体利益的问题。

最后一个要素涉及城市地区的美观、舒适和享受，最常与一个或多个其他元素结合使用。近年来，人们对舒适性及其在规划中的作用有了更新的看法，随着城市模式从生产模式转变为消费模式，构成城市生活的娱乐设施和其他设施变得更加重要，这些非市场舒适因素在推动城市发展方面发挥着重要作用。人们搬到一个城市是因为学校、公园、医院、剧院、交通系统，毕竟工作以外的时间他们都要待在那里。来访者和游客也是如此，他们访问一个城市是为了体验各种景点（设施）或整体氛围或体验（场景），这些无形的非市场因素的发展在城市空间的设计中变得更加重要。

7.5 关于城市规划的讨论

关于规划的争议

赞同

约翰·弗里德曼（John Friedmann，1987）是一位规划倡导者，他看到了规划解放人的潜力并看到市场的局限性，认为市场在提供人类福利方面具有内在的局限性——市场允许拥有充足资源的人采取行动，是在受到指导和监管以控制过度行为的情况下附带的福利。市场是专制的，不考虑需求，只考虑货币资源方面的需求。规划让社区更有效地利用资源，通过民主进程满足居民的需要和目标。

反对

反对政府规划的是弗雷德里克·哈耶克（Hayek，1944）等古典自由主义者，他们关注个人在社会生活中的角色，认为社会的最高美德是个人追求快乐或自身利益的实现程度。个人最有资格了解自己的需求和愿望，社会应该围绕降低界限以实现个人追求快乐或自我利益的能力，无限制的市场是鼓励和发展个人自治的最有效的手段。政府可能是一个障碍，政府规划可能会导致规划失败，无法实现预期目标。实现个人自治或享乐和追求利益的社会的最有效方式是政府实行极简主义或自由放任。

公民参与

规划中的一个大问题是公民是否以及如何参与这一过程。早期发展阶段，规划通常是按照政治家和政策精英的意愿执行的，而没有公众的大量参与，其假设是这一过程中技术官僚是价值中立的。如上所述，戴维多夫打破了这一观念，并强烈呼吁在这一进程中增加更多的少数群体代表。与此同时，民主和社区活动家也呼吁在这一进程中倾听更多的社区声音。即使在民主进程普遍存在的地方，当地社区（少数群体）也完全有可能因为一个没有充分考虑当地居民需求的民主进程而输给全市的利益（多数群体）。

非预期后果

规划并不容易，完全理性地预测每一个潜在的问题是不可能的，除了眼界和认知的局限性，规划者在进入项目时还会有自己的观点和偏见，这会导致他们对问题的看法有局限，此外，关注熟悉事物的倾向也可能会进一步扭曲问题。同时，群体凝聚力（没有受到不同观点、信息、想法和经验的外来者挑战）倾向于群体思维，同质群体更倾向于强化证实群体偏见的证据，除非受到挑战，否则会有组织地忽略与其想法相矛盾的信息。最后，寻求手头第一个解决方案的渐进主义倾向意味着更完善的解决方案可能被忽略。总之，所有这些都意味着，即使在最完美的情况下，也会有不可预见的和意料之外的结果发生，甚至可能会严重偏离规划者的目标。

【思考题】

1. 我国的城市规划过程是怎样的？
2. 什么是理性规划？对此有何批评？
3. 规划的标准是什么？
4. 倡导规划的主要特征是什么？
5. 为什么有规划比没有规划好？

【关键术语】

倡导性规划	同心圆地带论
便利设施	成本效益分析
竞价曲线	女性主义规划理论
规划的选择理论	渐进主义
集体理性	个人理性
沟通式规划理论	总体规划

多核心理论	重组（改制）计划
职位租金	社会价值论
公共利益	执行性计划
理性规划	都市政体（市政体制）

参考文献

［1］Friedmann，John（1987）. *Planning in the Public Domain.* Princeton，NJ：Princeton University Press.

［2］Hayek，Frederich A.（1944）. *The Road to Serfdom.* Chicago：University of Chicago Press.

Chapter 7   Urban Planning

7. 1   Definition

Urban planning tries to regulate the use of land and other physical resources in the public interest. In doing so, planning can significantly improve the quality of life and welfare of people living in cities. One comprehensive definition of urban planning is that it is a process of clarifying urban objectives and then determining what action shall be taken by what urban actors, when, how methods, and at what costs to achieve the desired goals.

Planning can be oriented either by function or by project. Planning is functional when it develops an appropriate course of action for decision—makers within a particular field. Project planning is broader than functional planning. Planning all the procedures for an urban renewal project, for example, is based on a broad set of objectives and not just within a single field. A project planner must deal with engineering, sociological, economic, and political objectives on top of the basic criteria. Project planning is therefore very complicated and requires interdisciplinary effort. Both functional and project-oriented planning may be applied broadly to practically any aspect of urban administration. Professional planners are hired by business and industry, as well as by governments. Planning is frequently done by many different administrative agencies within municipal government. City governments use planners for a wide range of public activities. Because of this broad area, this chapter will necessarily focus on public planning for the use of physical space.

What is the purpose of planning the use of physical space? Planners tend to think of the environment in physical terms but they must consider the political, economic, and social goals of the community when they consider standards for the use of physical space. Physical questions concerning intensity of land use, housing stock in different price ranges, the need for and siting of community facilities, the appropriate relationship between various land uses, and transportation patterns are based on and stemming from the social and economic values of the community. Moreover, physical planning bears a distinct relationship to many other governmental functions.

Urban planning normally takes place only within the geographic areas contained inside of a city's municipal boundaries. As a result, it may not address even significant problems that cross over those boundaries. Unless there is some broader area-wide mechanism for inter-community coordination, it cannot synchronize plans with those of neighboring communities. Most large metropolises in the U. S. today contain several suburban development nodes that are usually centered on large shopping areas and are located at freeway interchanges. Sometimes called urban villages, periphery cities, or edge cities, these nodes are powerful magnets that attract office building complexes, more commercial development, and residential construction.

Types of Planning

Plannings are divided into several types that have different unique features for addressing particular situations. These include structure plans, master plans, local land use plans, strategic plans, and informal plans. Urban planning in China is usually divided into master plan and detailed plan. Detailed plan can be divided into regulatory detailed plan and residential district detailed plan according to the depth of plan and the needs of management. The urban master plan is a comprehensive deployment and implementation measure for the urban nature, development goals, development scale, land use, spatial layout and various constructions in a certain period. From the perspective of planning, China's urban planning can be divided into strategic level and operational level. The master plan is regarded as the strategic level, the constructive detailed planning belongs to the operational level, and the residential district detailed plan is the connection of the two levels, and an important basis for China's urban planning management.

7. 2   The Planning Process

Banfield developed a rational planning model consisting of five steps. Following an analysis of the situation, these five steps are ends reduction and elaboration, design of course of action, comparative evaluation of consequences, choice among alternatives, and implementation of the chosen alternative and they are described below. This is not the only possible way to cast the planning process as, for example, the five steps were later simply described as the 5Ds: desires, design, deduction, decision, and deeds.

Ends Reduction and Elaboration

Once the situation has been analysed, and all the options that may be able to address the goals, or ends, have been generated, it is necessary to reduce and elaborate the goals. Banfield described an end as an image of a future state of affairs towards which action is oriented. The initial formulation of the end goal may have (and often is) too vague or diffuse, this is the stage where the goal is clarified and reduced so that the planner may be able to state the end and clearly explain its meaning. Where the elements are not fully consistent the planner must rank them in order of preference so that the most essential elements of the goal will be the last to be surrendered and will not inadvertently be written out of a plan that meets more goals but loses key ones.

Design of Courses of Action

This is the planning for the actions to be taken as part of the plan. These may be more or less general in terms of details. The most general courses of action would entail the key actions that would unfold as part of a plan. The more specific actions should be limited at this point to ones that would not be changed or precluded by a different choice of general plans. Remember that the point of this step is not to fix on any specific course of action, but to generate several different options that can be evaluated and then a choice can be made at later. While it is better to have more options to choose from, and creative choices may open up new venues, it is economic not to develop any options in too great detail at this point as most of the work will be lost as final options are selected and potential courses of action rejected.

Comparative Evaluation of Consequences

The point of this planning process is to be rational. If this process is to be truly rational, then all consequences need to be assessed. There is the temptation to focus on and highlight the consequences desired by the planner, but it is essential that the undesirable is weighed as well. Banfield asserts that the hallmark of good planning is the search for and inclusion of unintended consequences that may flow from successfully achieving active and contextual ends. The evaluation must take the form of comparing the net value associated with each potential course of action. The typical procedure for doing this is the cost-benefit analysis (CBA). Where intangibles are part of the formula, they must be converted, however realistically as possible, into a cash value or other equivalent, to compare like with like.

Choosing among Alternatives

The choice of the final alternative for implementation as an actual course must be based on the initial evaluative criteria used in assembling the ends and analysing the situation. The cost-benefit analysis, or other method of analysis, as appropriate, needs to have incorporated the best available evidence, the final selection should rest on that evidence.

Implementation of the Chosen Alternative

Once the alternative has been selected, implementation begins, but that does not end the connection to the early process and conclusions must continue to be drawn and data reevaluated as necessary to search for the emergence of unforeseen problems. Early planning is a key element in successful implementation. Assuming that the other steps have been followed correctly, this work should have generated ample resources to rely on in the actual implementation stage.

Frequently reproduced since, these steps describe a problem-solving framework for complex human enterprises. The model is unachievable due to its complex demands on resources and expertise. Banfield recognized the complexities, including the elusiveness of the aim of serving the public interest and political resistance to scientific analysis. The rational planning model had critics even before publication. The model has continued to suffer serious and sustained criticism from numerous quarters since. Even so, Banfield's model has remained the most widely-subscribed planning theory. Its logic is still found in the justifications and methodological outlines given in the introductions to most plans. It remains a major mainstay of and basis for any planning school curriculum. The model is responsible for creating and popularizing the principal language that urban planners use in their methodological writings and discussions. Moreover, the theoretical and methodological work of detailing and extending the model continues to the present. This includes efforts to compare alternative rules for aggregating individual preferences, examination of the implications of risk and uncertainty, and consideration of the impact of new and faster computers on the ability to determine public preferences, gather information, generate more alternatives, and do the necessary calculations.

7.3 Schools of Thought

7.3.1 The Birth of Modem Planning Theory

The theoretical basis for planning and the process of theorizing about planning go straight back to the first days of the profession. However, the earliest theories still influential do not date from the founding, but come from the New Deal Era in the United States. President Roosevelt was surrounded by a group of advisors, famously known as his "Brain Trust. " This group included Rexford Tugwell, the former Governor of Puerto Rico, who was strong advocate for planning. He went so far as to promote it is as a so-called "Fourth Power" or branch of government. New Deal experiments with planning, guided by emerging Keynesian economic principles, included the National Resources Planning Board, the Resettlement Administration, and the Tennessee Valley Authority. Though large and national in scope, they helped set the pattern for modern urban planning as well as these programs championed a kind of planning rooted in the collection and examination of data and the evaluation of alternative courses of action along with the creation of systems for implementation. They expanded planning's definition as a design activity and incorporated scientific techniques. More specifically of interest to urban administration, though, was the New Deal's Demonstration Cities program, which was perhaps the most influential New Deal program for the urban planning profession, because it illustrated this new social science model at the urban level.

At the same time as Americans were busy with these planning experiments, German sociologist Karl Mannheim, an exile living in the US, was preparing what would become a highly influential theoretical and normative statement of why planning was necessary for free and open societies. Mannheim's *Man and Society in an Age of Reconstruction* distinguishes four possible social structures from differences in participation and centralization. These are dictatorship, anarchy, anomie, and democratic planning. Dictatorship is formed based on low levels of participation and high levels of centralization. Anarchy is the result of high levels of participation and low levels of centralization. Anomie represents the outcome of a system featuring low levels of participation and centralization at the same time. Mannheim's favorite option, the democratically-planned society, would result from both high participation and centralization.

Mannheim clearly believed that planning was the inevitable outcome of technological developments coupled with population growth. Once it was supposed that planning must happen, the major issue left on the table was who would be responsible for doing the planning. The stark contrast was whether planning would be done by fascist forces of dictatorship or through a democratic process and through participatory institutions. Mannheim cautioned planners against over-reliance on functional rationality, meaning paying excess attention to means, as opposed to keeping the focus squarely on the ultimate ends. In its place, Mannheim insisted that planners focus on substantial rationality in the careful definition of the correct goals and end states.

Mannheim's book was not uncontroversial and marked the beginning of the Great Debates. These debates involved both scholarly and political fights that were at once theoretical and practical in their impact. On the one side, planning advocates favored increased levels of government organization and influence in the economy. On the other side were laissez-faire advocates such as Frederick Hayek. Hayek saw government as clumsy and inefficient at best, and feared the power of a stronger government. The US Congress also weighed in by refusing to reauthorize the National Resources Planning Board in a very public manner in 1941. One important insight from the Great Debates was the distinguishing of the concepts of *freedom from* and *freedom to*. Barbara Wooten (1945) argued that it was folly to focus only on freedom from government coercion. At the same time, she further argued for the need for a government that allows the freedom to do things that the people would be unable to do without government and social organizations and institutions to organize participation to determine and achieve these purposes through government.

7. 3. 2 Rational Planning

Following the planning successes of the New Deal and plannings after World War II, Tugwell joined the University of Chicago's newly-created Program in Education and Research in Planning after the war. His colleagues at the University of Chicago included famous planning advocates Harvey Perloff, Edward Banfield and Julius Margolis. This program only lasted nine years, but was still extremely influential in setting the direction of planning theory. Perloff, a

Keynesian economist pushed the faculty to define and systematize core areas of knowledge in planning that were perceived essential to putting planning into practice. This search for the core of the profession led to the development of a generic model for rational planning in capitalist democracy and to the incorporation of ideas from different social science disciplines, including economics, public administration, and political science. Banfield's (1955, 1959) new rational planning model, became the standard guide in the profession and beyond as an approach to problem-solving in the public sphere. Margolis later carried the model into the emergent profession of public policy analysis by providing guiding principles.

The rational planning incorporated numerous social science concepts into planning offices, drawing on Keynesian economics and policy studies in political science. It highlighted the role of planning in correcting market failure related to a host of issues that included externalities, public goods, inequity, transaction costs, market power, and nonfunctioning or absent markets. Their rationales for planning included improving citizen and resident quality of life through livability, the reduction of nuisance and congestion, improvement of environmental quality, and promotion of a stable business environment through protection of resources, reduction of taxes and public costs.

Planning employs the tools and language of cost-benefit analysis and operations research. This includes decision criteria, multiple objectives, constraints, shadow pricing, willingness-to-pay, optimization, and minimization (Weimer and Vining, 1992; Klosterman, 1994). A major planning consideration of rational planning is the lack of connection between individual rationality and collective rationality. Microeconomics considers rationality for individuals and firms but it is more difficult to employ the concept when looking at complicated public entities that may exist on an enormous scale that dwarfs individual firms. Individuals and firms may know what they want, but how do cities and regions decide? What are their desires and what are their preferences? Thomas Schelling asserted that, in certain situations, individual preferences aggregated to a societal level produce illogical or undesirable outcomes. These may include delays on highways due to passersby slowing down to gawk at accidents or where motorcycle riders do not want to wear helmets. In such situations, if the group made a decision as a whole, it would be far different from the sum of the individual decisions of the members. The reason for planning in a market economy is closely connected to this contrast, giving planning a role in providing rational outcomes that would not be made by the market.

Criticisms and Extensions of Rational Planning

Political scientist Charles Lindblom gave the incrementalist critique of rational planning, which spread widely by the early 1960s. he indicated that comprehensive planning was unachievable and out of step with political realities. He stated that political leaders cannot agree on goals in advance, as the rational model requires. They prefer to choose policies and goals at the same time. He considered that the rational model's preoccupation with the comparison of all possible alternatives and their comprehensive assessment on all measures of performance would exceed human abilities. He saw the relationship between science and policy choice to be indirect at best. Lindblom's incrementalism calls for the simultaneous selection of goals and policies, and a consideration of alternatives that are only marginally different from the status quo, examination of simplified comparisons among the alternatives, and a preference for the results of social experimentation over theory as the basis of analysis. Lindblom's critique was powerful, widely received, and influenced many planners. Amitai Etzioni's middle-range bridge was an effort to reconcile rational planning with incrementalism. The strategic planning movement drew heavily from Lindblom's ideas, arguing for a focus on organizational survival rather than societal benefit.

Lindblom later argued in the 1970s that he had been misunderstood. His idea of incrementalism really had three meanings that planners had managed to blur. These were strategic analysis, disjointed incrementalism, and simple incrementalism. Strategic analysis represented any attempt to simplify complex policy problems to make them clearer and easier to understand. Disjointed incrementalism meant analysis carried out without determining goals first, considered few alternatives, and employed data of limited complexity. Simple incrementalism was where the alternatives considered would be only marginally different from the status quo. Planning had embraced the third meaning, simple incrementalism, while Lindblom claimed he had been arguing for disjointed incrementalism.

Alan Altshuler examined land and transportation planning in Minneapolis-St. Paul. He found that planners could not usually achieve their rational scientific goals and their claims were not achieved in real situations. Decision—makers often ignored the recommendations of planners and instead followed the wishes of politically-important stakeholders. Advocates of public participation in planning complained it was often meaningless. Marxian critiques of planning argued that planners effectively did the bidding of development interests and did not really address meaningful policy choices (Kravitz, 1970; Goodman, 1971). Paul Davidoff's (1965) article, "Advocacy and Pluralism in Planning", was the most significant critique of planning from the 1960s. Davidoff echoed the frustration of planners who felt unable to deal with the major social and economic issues challenging American cities at the time. Davidoff called for the distribution of planning services into low-income and minority neighborhoods through advocate planners. They would live or work in the neighborhood and would represent the interests of its residents in urban planning.

Davidoff's idea was that the discussion among planners would take place in the public interest so that the broader needs of the city would be advanced over narrower neighborhood interests. The US federal government created structures close to Davidoff's proposals. Storefront planning services opened in many of the poorest districts. Nonprofit advocacy planning firms and cooperatives sprang up independently, and in partnership with universities, and social welfare organizations. Many of the assumptions of city planners were discussed and debated. Many poor residents were empowered and entered city politics. Critics pointed out that advocate planners were quite different from the residents they served. Advocacy planning may have raised unrealistic expectations that could not be met in those communities. It may have discouraged residents from working for themselves politically by creating the impression that the city would care for them. The advocacy planning movement freed planners from representing comprehensive public interest positions and quickly spread well beyond the inner city. Advocate planners also started serving environmental groups, but even went on to represent trade associations and corporations in advocating for their narrower interests.

New Directions

After advocacy planning showed that planning could take a new path, planning theorists began moving in many directions. The rational planning model lost favor. Stephen Grabow and Alan Heskin's criticized the inability of the rational planning framework to respond to the needs of the poor, calling instead for a systemic change including decentralization, ecological attentiveness, spontaneity, and experimentation. The radical critique did not propose a clear solution, but did encourage the progressive planning movement that sought incremental changes that would result in structural changes over time that would advance legitimacy, equality, and participation. Some progressives also organized community self-help initiatives argued that a growth machine dominated city councils and planning boards across America and advanced a pro-growth agenda. This growth machine made it difficult for environmental or other opposition groups to win decisions. Boards and commissions staffed by partisans of the growth machine would not even understand how people could oppose growth.

Following the development of the radical critique new theories, called social learning theories, were developed. These emphasized the planners' role in several key areas, including bringing interested parties affected by the plan together, gathering and sharing information, and helping social structures and institutions learn from experience. John Friedmann developed transactive planning, which stressed that citizens and city leaders, not planners, had to be at the core of planning for plans to be implemented. Chris Argyris and Donald Schon came up with a theory of action where the planner acts as a catalyst and brings people together across boundaries to create structures that learn from experience.

Reunifying the Field

The scientific/rational notions of planning had come to be seen by planners as having divided them from political actors involved in making the key planning decisions. Jurgen Habermas, a German critical theorist who questioned social science, came to be influential among planners interested in bringing together social learning and progressive planning. Forester advanced communicative planning theory (Forester, 1989), asserting that data and understanding of public decision making would empower the socially weak and underprivileged urban minorities and poor. Planners would use modern communication strategies to communicate issues to citizens, inform them about the status of their technical work, and encourage community planning through consensus-building processes. Larry Susskind and others supported this consensus-building orientation on the basis that the technical and analytical skills were parallel to the traditional orientation of mediators and that, therefore, planners were well-positioned to mediate among the complex issues and numerous stakeholders involved in planning. Susskind argued that planners should embrace this role by learning the interpersonal skills of mediators and work to determine underlying interests, to forge alternatives, and determining fair decision-making criteria. This work was supported by empirical literature that followed the actual work of planners and made practical recommendations.

7. 3. 3　The Post-modern Challenge and Response

Diversity and the awareness of simultaneous multiple points of view came with the rise of issues of immigration, awareness of gender and racial and ethnic and regional differences, and a globalizing world economy starting from the 1980s in North America and Western Europe and emerging elsewhere. Planners responded in part by looking to post-modern ideas that saw universal diversity in how individuals and groups understood social and political issues and highlighted domination of one group over another in myriad walks of life. Although post-modern philosophy was very pessimistic about the ability to address these tendencies, post-modern planning theorists look for ways to overcome this pessimism. Post-modern planners respect and call for others to acknowledge and respect diversity, while recognizing differences among groups, and try to involve communities early in the planning process. One positive development of the post-modern focus has been to search for better ways for planners to advance their ideas in diverse political and multicultural situations. The technical and quantitative foundation of planning is not well-suited to persuading typical administrative and political decision makers who are often moved by stories about people and metaphors they can understand in human terms. Storytelling is therefore proposed as a planning method to accomplish what statistical analysis cannot. In a different but related direction, the problem-solving orientation of public decision—makers has come to be seen by theorists of critical pragmatism as incompatible with the deductive reasoning called for by statistical planning methods. They call on planners to use both inductive and deductive reasoning. Theories of social capital emphasize the complexity and effectiveness of social networks and community leadership in moving the community toward responses to new challenges.

Related to, and often coming from within the post-modern critique of planning, feminist planning theory calls on planners to take more into account family life and reproduction of community in place of the traditional economic emphasis. Feminist planners also try to account for the different ways men and women use space. Economic efficiency measures used in planning analysis have not attached value to home child care, to community elder care, or to volunteer work for civic and community organizations. Transportation is also seen as flawed in emphasizing commuting when women (and men) make many trips that are not part of a daily trip from home to the workplace.

The new urbanism introduced by Peter Calthorpe and Andres Duany captured the attention of many public officials and moved planning away from largely procedural concerns in the direction of substantial concerns. The new urbanism's focus on purely physical aspects of planning serves to enhance civic life and social capital. The sustainability movement has grown to enormous proportions internationally focusing on renewable resources, conservation, and preservation. At the same time, it has a concern for the relationship between rich and poor. The movement proposes new decision criteria and models based on global cooperation and advancement of equity.

7. 3. 4　Design Concepts and Approaches

Physical Perspectives

Urban planning tends to focus on the use of physical space, though not all the planning done by city governments has such an orientation. Local government planning is mostly concerned with the use of physical space. The planning profession places a great emphasis on physical criteria when deciding how to use urban space. There are usually rigid standards for the location and space requirements of different uses of land such as housing, commerce, and industry and based on different design concepts. Many of the early planners had engineering or architectural backgrounds and naturally maintained and advanced the physical bias. Planning did involve socio-economic research, but planners paid very little attention until recently to how such studies were to be used in formulating land use standards.

Design

Design was the solution to urban problems and was the predominant method of planning. Design solutions were part of a creative and artistic process where physical design concepts were adapted to the requirements of specific situations. Solutions were rarely based on social science research, but on engineered planning criteria. The view that the physical environment was the foundation of urban problems formed the physical emphasis in early planning practice. As a result, it was presumed that improvements in the physical environment would improve the social and economic problems in urban areas.

Social Behavior Perspectives

Planning has recently moved in the direction of taking a broader perspective, even though there is still a strong physical bias. Social science research is being used to contribute to formulating plans for the design and use of urban spaces. F. Stuart Chapin cites social processes and behavior as among the features that affect land use. These may include things like economic variables such as property value, employment opportunity, and transportation costs as well as the norms and practices of local political systems in addition to the physical characteristics of the land. Chapin stressed that it was important to generate planning goals that were based on local values and local culture. Chapin suggested the planner should do a detailed study of social, economic, and physical factors in light of the goals after they have been decided. These factors should then be used to develop local location and space standards for different land uses. These standards are the foundation for planning that reflects community goals.

Mathematical Models

The recent work incorporating social science and economic data has resulted in the creation of mathematical models for the purposes of simulating and projecting urban development. Economists, social scientists, and planners have been looking into the relationships between the location and different socio-economic variables, particularly with respect to land use questions. They have produced new information about the relationship between location, economic activity, and economic health. An understanding of the determinants of the location of land use has also come out of these efforts. Models that can simulate the impact of various alternative urban plans, such as for transportation plans have been used in several cases and are much less costly than the actual experimentation involved in implementing a plan.

Theories of planning now emphasize the complexity of the relationships involved in urban development. The design and construction of simulations and mathematical models has contributed to a better understanding of the complexity. Some planners and theorists have used gaming simulations to learn more about the complexities of urban development. Individuals in this method play the roles of different actors in the planning process and make decisions based on their roles in a simulated environment. They then see how their decisions impact a hypothetical community. This technique dramatically illustrates how different variables influence urban development.

Choice and Advocacy Approach

The questioning of the traditional emphasis on physical space has led to a consideration of some of the neglected aspects of planning analysis. Instead of dividing planning into physical, economic, and social factors, there is more interest in systematic approaches that allow different kinds of planning to be combined together. One example is the idea that the planner's role is to devise meaningful alternative plans and then develop a systematic basis for choosing among these alternatives.

Davidoff and Reiner advocated a theory of planning based on the idea that the planning process should involve a series of choices. This choice theory says that choices must be made among alternative goals and means of achieving these goals. They suggest the need to develop broad criteria for making planning choices. Davidoff says there should be different plans representing diverse values for each community, representing statements of policy that cover a broad range. The idea is that different planners act as advocates of the values of diverse groups in the community. Planning activity in government needs to address the economic, social, and physical values that exist in the community. They find planning to be a function of local government that should be concerned with the development of all government policies related to deciding future courses of action.

The planning process has historically not provided much opportunity for citizen input. Private real estate developers do not have much reason to invite citizen participation in their planning. Citizen input is not valued because citizens may always disagree with features of projects and, given the diversity of opinion and interests, citizens often do find fault. Further, citizen input generally comes down to a veto. Public planners, planning staff, and planning agencies have a similar negative view of citizen groups, viewing them as uninformed at best and obstacles to planning at worst. Urban programs frequently require citizen participation in planning but the participation is usually invited after a plan is drafted so citizen participation may come down to citizens learning about the specifics of projects that are slated for implementation at a meeting to publicize the plan. The result may often be citizen alienation and helplessness in the face of major changes to their neighborhood caused by big projects.

Davidoff's advocacy planning was a major effort to address these issues with citizen participation. Davidoff argued that the planning bureaucracies are connected to local establishments and neglect the legitimate needs of the poor and members of minority groups. Davidoff proposed that citizens' groups hire professional planners to prepare their own plans to submit to public planning agencies for consideration. Citizens would then be able participate affirmatively with positive proposals instead of just through protest and negative actions to block plans in progress.

Action Approach

Henry Fagin also advocated planning to address a broad range of issues. He conceives of planning as an action-oriented activity. It involves research, the formulation of goals, the development of plans, coordination, general assistance, and advice. These essential planning activities are spread out among a variety of agencies within government. Fagin suggested that different functions like responsibility for preparing the physical plan, the budget plan, and general coordination of government activity should be combined within a single government agency that would create a broad policy plan. This policy plan would bring all planning activities of the government into a single planning agency.

7. 4   Criteria for Urban Planning

The public interest is frequently used as the standard for determining a public purpose, whether for the use of police power, the power of eminent domain, or the power of taxation. Nine factors usually identified with the public interest in land use planning are health, safety, convenience, efficiency, energy conservation, environmental quality, social equity, social choice, and amenity. Each of the nine public purposes has a broader meaning and is important in defining the public interest in planning urban areas.

The American Public Health Association generated a list of criteria necessary for an adequate environment. These included protections against accidents, fatigue, contagion, excessive noise, pollution, and moral hazards. They also included provisions for the maintenance of cleanliness, the protection of adequate daylight, sunshine, ventilation, privacy, opportunities for normal family and community life, and the opportunity to satisfy esthetic needs for beauty and attractive and convenient surroundings. Convenience is often viewed as a lesser consideration in terms of what constitutes the public interest. Nonetheless it is closely associated with the public interest and is a major foundation for governmental action. Even though health and safety may be essential for life whereas convenience is not, it breathes life into any urban system as citizens naturally seek convenience and avoid spaces that lack it.

The next major elements both concern efficiency. Efficiency is associated with public costs that may take the form of municipal expenditures or costs to the residents of an urban area. Efficiency is looking at land development from the view of the whole community instead of the entrepreneur or of collective actions of individuals. The fundamental concern is what land use is the least costly to the municipality and to the citizens. Energy conservation is efficiency in use of expensive and scarce energy resources and can be addressed through land use and planning for building requirements.

Some environmental concerns are recognized as a part of health. The salience of climate change and global warming, rising oil prices, concerns about approaching or having reached peak oil (maximum oil production), pollution, and quality of life issues. These developments and related public discussions of the pressures of economic and population growth have contributed to greater awareness of environmental problems. This has created more of a sense of urgency about planning solutions to environmental problems.

Both concerns involve human rights on the urban scene. Both give attention to pluralism and diversity in urban society. Considering the public interest, social equity and choice concern the right to equal treatment of different group interests in both the public and private sectors. Social equity is equal opportunity to access work, shelter, education, and medical care. Social choice relates to the participation, range, and definition of choices and opportunities concerning issues most directly affecting different groups in an urban area.

This last element concerns the esthetic appearance and comfort and enjoyment in urban areas. Amenity is most frequently used in combination with one or more of the other elements.

A more recent view of amenity and its role in planning has emerged in recent years. Entertainment and other amenities that make up life in a city are more important as the urban paradigm has shifted from a production to a consumption paradigm. These nonmarket amenity factors have a major role to play in driving development. People move to a city because of the schools, parks, hospitals, theaters, transportation system where they will spend all the time outside of their working hours. The same is true for visitors and tourists, who visit a city to experience various attractions (amenities) or an overall atmosphere or experience (scene). The development of these intangible non-market factors has become much more important in the designing of urban spaces.

7. 5 Issues

Planning Controversies

Pro-planning

John Friedmann (1987) is a planning advocate who sees the potential for planning to liberate and free people. He is one of the people who sees the limits of the market and views the market as inherently limited in providing for human welfare. The market allows people with adequate resources to act but is only seen as incidentally providing for well-being unless it is directed and regulated to moderate its excesses. The market is authoritarian and does not consider need, only looking at demand in terms of monetary resources. Planning in this model would allow the community to use resources efficiently to meet the needs and goals desired by the people through democratic processes.

Anti-planning

Against government planning are classical liberals like Frederick Hayek (1944), who focus on the role of individuals in social life. The highest virtue of society is the degree to which individuals can pursue pleasure or their self-interest. Individuals are the most qualified at understanding their needs and wants. Society should be structured around lowering boundaries to realizing individual's ability to seek pleasure or self-interest. The unrestrained market is the most efficient means of encouraging and developing individual autonomy. Government may only be an obstacle and government planning may only lead to planning failure and the inability to achieve the desired ends. The most effective way to achieve individual autonomy or a pleasure and interest-seeking society is for the government to be minimalist, or laissez faire.

Resident Participation

One of the big issues in planning is whether and how citizens participate in the process. In its early stages it was common for plans to be carried out based on the desires of various political and policy elites without much input from the public. The assumption was that the process was technocratic and value-neutral. As noted above, Davidoff shattered that notion and made strident calls for more minority representation in the process. At the same time, there were democratic and community activists making calls for more community voice to be exerted in the process. Even where a democratic process prevails, it is entirely possible for the local community (the minority) to lose out to the city-wide interests (the majority) through an entirely democratic process that does not consider the needs of local residents.

Unintended Consequences

Planning is not easy. It is impossible to be purely rational and anticipate every potential problem and issue. Apart from the limits of foresight, planners enter a project with their own perspectives and biases that will lead them to have a limited view of a problem. Further, the tendency to focus on what is familiar may further skew the issue. At the same time, cohesive groups that are not challenged by outsiders with different perspectives, information, ideas, and experience have a tendency towards groupthink, where homogeneous groups tend to reinforce evidence that confirms the group's biases and systematically ignore information that contradicts their ideas unless challenged. Finally, incrementalist tendencies to seek the first solution at hand mean that more complete solutions may be ignored. Together, all of this means that, even under the best of situations, there will be unforeseen and unexpected consequences that may seriously skew the outcomes of a project away from the intent of the planner.

Questions

1. What is the process of urban planning in China?
2. What is rational planning? What are the criticisms of it?
3. What are the criteria for planning?
4. What are the main features of advocacy planning?
5. Why is planning better than no planning?

Key Terms

advocacy planning

amenity

bid-price curve

choice theory of planning

collective rationality

communicative planning theory

concentric-zone concept

cost-benefit analysis

feminist planning theory

incrementalism

individual rationality

master plan

multi-nuclei concept　　　　　　　　*restructuring plan*

position rent　　　　　　　　　　　*social value theory*

public interest　　　　　　　　　　*transactive planning*

rational planning　　　　　　　　　*urban regime*

References

［1］Friedmann, John (1987). *Planning in the Public Domain.* Princeton, NJ: Princeton University Press.

［2］Hayek, Frederich A. (1944). *The Road to Serfdom.* Chicago: University of Chicago Press.

第8章 城市设计

8.1 概念及内涵

设计是一个学科

尽管城市设计一直在城市形成发展中发挥着重要作用，但仍是一个相对较新的专业，无论是谁作出城市设计决策，在不同的时间和地点对城市功能的定义的不同，都会对城市产生影响。"城市设计"一词在1957年美国建筑学会首次使用，20世纪60年代，随着凯文·林奇和简·雅各布斯（Kevin Lynch and Jane Jacobs）以及克里斯托弗·亚历山大和莱昂、罗伯·克里尔和罗伯特·文图里（Christopher Alexander and Leon and Rob Krier and Robert Venturi）的作品逐渐传播开。

城市设计师往往难以界定自己的领域，他们希望对城市设计下一个明确而简短的定义，但这是不现实的。仅出于管理目的对城市设计进行精确定义是必要的，最好遵循关于城市设计的特征、动机、方法和角色的相关指导方针，但是对于设计者来说则不是必要的。城市设计过程试图以整体和有机的方式，以技术和多元化的方式，创造积极的城市空间，满足传统和现代的关注，新的城市研究路径为城市地区的不同行为者提供了这样的世界观。

城市设计主要涉及公共空间的设计和管理，以及如何使用和体验这些空间。公共空间包括公众自由使用的所有空间，包括街道、广场、购物中心、公共基础设施和公园等公共设施。建筑物的外部和私人拥有的私人景观也有助于对公共空间的感知和体验，因此，它们也被视为城市设计的一部分。城市设计关注城市公共空间的塑造和使用，包括城市区域的布局、外观和功能等因素。传统意义上，城市设计被视为城市规划、景观建筑或建筑学科的一部分，近年来，城市设计与城市景观等新学科联系在一起。从广义上讲，即使是房地产开发和城市经济等不同领域也可以理解为有助于城市设计，因此熟悉这些领域对设计师来说是有益的。

城市设计涉及城市和城镇及其要素的安排和设计，如建筑、公共空间、交通系统、服务和设施，是定义和赋予建筑物、社区和整个城市的形状、特征和体验的过程。设计采用各种元素并使其成为一个街道、广场和街区构成的连贯网络。城市设计充分利用建筑、景观建筑和城市规划的特点，使城镇既美观又实用。好的设计应该通过从不同学科中提取的各种方法将人和空间结合在一起，从而创造出人们向往的地方。它与规划学、建筑学、发展经济学、工程学和景观学相关。设计创造了所有这些不同的元素，并为社区、地区或城市创造了愿景，设计者必须汇集所需的资源和技能去实现这些愿景。

很明显，除了规划学和建筑学，其他学科在创建和研究城市地区方面也发挥着重要作用。景观建筑、工程学（土木、通信和交通）、社会学、经济学、心理学，甚至艺术和人文塑造了城市环境。城市设计有潜力将所有与城市环境有关的专业联系起来，城市设计的作用有助于他们在相互合作中充分发挥各自的潜力。图8.1所示为城市设计是一门交叉学科。

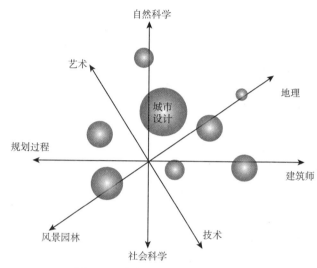

图 8.1　城市设计是一门交叉学科

8.2　城市设计的历史发展

詹姆斯·奥格索普在佐治亚州萨凡纳的规划试图促进该殖民地的良好治理和功能性，为通过周围环境改造罪犯提供了一个乌托邦式的愿景。在现代城市设计作为专业出现之前，城市设计是由雕塑家、建筑师、景观设计师、工程师、测量师、天文学家甚至军事工程师完成的，18～19世纪，城市设计主要是由测量师和建筑师完成的。随着城市人口的增加和许多与城市化相关的现代问题如传染病的传播等，促进了英国的市政工程建设，例如，规定了最低的街道宽度，以提供照明和通风并促进公共卫生。

现代城市设计是更广泛的城市规划学的一部分，城市规划最初是一场与所谓的城市设计有关的运动。20世纪，汽车对城市设计的发展产生了很大的影响，城市设计运动开始的部分原因是应对汽车和汽车带来的负面影响。1956年，哈佛大学举办了一系列城市设计的会议，城市设计首次作为一个专业术语出现。

8.3　城市设计原则

城市设计注重改善公共空间的物理环境方面。公共空间的设计、建造和管理是一个复杂的问题，涉及与多个不同利益方的谈判和商议，因为管理责任的交叉，以及附近业主的利益，更不用说不同用户的不同且往往相互冲突的需求。与其他设计学科（如建筑）相比，需要更少的艺术调度。跨学科咨询也是必要的，工程、生态、地方历史和交通规划等多个领域都有发言权。

城市设计通常与城市规划相重叠，可能包括设计指南、监管框架的准备，甚至包括宣传和广告，还可以参与制定管理这一进程的立法。它可能与建筑、景观建筑、公路工程和工业设计重叠，因为它可能与特定空间的特定布局相关。城市设计可以为城市公共空间的使用和维护提供指导和帮助，甚至可以帮助维护更广泛的城市区域。尽管一些城市设计师经过专门培训并被认定为城市设计师，但许多城市设计工作却是由建筑师、景观设计师和城市规划师完成的。城市设计被纳入许多建筑、景观建筑和规划项目，甚至有大学专门提供城市设计学位，特别是研究生学位。

8.3.1　考虑因素

在城市设计中有几个主要考虑因素：结构、类型学、可达性、易识别、富有生命力、功能、混合用途的互补、特征和内涵、秩序和冲突、连续性和变化，以及公民社会。城市结构代表了一个地方的组织，以及各个部分之间的相互配合和关联。城市类型学解释了将城市空间定义为与使用强度、资源消耗和社区维护相关的空间类型。可达性是指在到达城市空间和在城市空间周围移动时可以提供方便和安全的选择。易识别意味着人们能够找到自己的路，了解一个地方是如何运作的。富有生命力是一种能刺激活跃的公众活动的设计。功能是对设计与用途相匹配的场所的考虑。互补的混合使用是基于不同的活动定位，以实现协同作用和建设性互动。特征和内涵是对地方特殊性和独特性的重视。秩序和冲突代表了城市环境中的一致性和多样性之间的平衡，因此人们可以同时利用和欣赏这两种特征。连续性和变化带给城市居民和游客一种历史感，以及与过去不同的联系和变迁。最后，公民社会是考虑鼓励人们通过民间组织形成和活动的空间进行建设性互动来实现社会资本。

8.3.2　环境

城市设计允许规划方法考虑到环境，并充分考虑与一个地区的经济、环境、社会状况和工程要求的最佳匹配，这也适用于高速公路和公共交通网络。环境设计要求简单性、功能性、一致性和物有所值。

最好的设计往往是最简单的，有一些为城市规划提供了一个优雅的解决方案。而复杂性通常是由于设计质量差、条块分割、过于仓促或考虑不周造成的，且复杂设计的建造和维护也可能很昂贵。从长远来看，简单的解决方案往往会更有效。

功能是下一个环境设计特性。除了看起来有吸引力和感染力，城市设计必须提供良好的基础设施和空间。良好的设计需要满足诸如安全和工程标准、对当地社区建设及其标准作出贡献、保护自然和建筑环境等要求，但最重要的是它必须具有功能性。例如，需要高维护的天然的便利设施，美观但未充分利用的设施，有吸引力的、僻静的公园却不安全，都不是好的设计。好的城市设计解决方案应考虑安全、维护、耐用性、维修和更换以及美观等因素，才能发挥其功能并得到更好的使用。

对设计一致性的关注。城市设计的一致性表明，所有不同的元素都应该是相互关联的，例如，简单性应该用功能来表示，功能性应该提供良好的可用性，从而带来更好的价值和效率。

城市设计不应使用过多的公共资金，但应在与城市的其他方面必须应对的成本效益高、成本控制的环境中运作，否则不仅会削弱政治支持，而且会与设计的基本原理背道而驰，因为设计是为了让事情真正变得更好，而不仅仅是看起来更好。为了确保资金支配合理，所有的成本和收益都需要确定、说明和证明。最佳的城市设计成果需要考虑可承受性和效率，因此，应根据常规的分析原则，避免产生非显著效益的成本。与对任何成本和收益的比较的考量一样，重要的是要考虑所有包括经济、社会和环境方面的成本和收益。

8.4 新城市主义

8.4.1 定义

新城市主义是一场改革建成环境设计的国际运动，特别是一场旨在发展具有共同特点的充满活力的混合型社区的运动，该运动促进以多样化、紧凑的和"适合步行的"的综合方式构建的完整的社区，与通过更传统的城市发展获得的增量和无计划性结果形成对比。社区的设计和建造不仅让居民拥有住房，同时拥有工作场所、商店、娱乐场所、学校、公园和居民日常生活所必需的市政设施，这些设施均设计在步行距离范围内。新城市主义通过增加火车和轻轨而不是公路和高速公路的使用，并用公共交通取代更多的私家汽车。

新城市主义旨在创造一个更美好、更宜居的城市未来，通过努力创造更好的生活场所来提高生活质量和生活水平。新城市主义力图创建依据现有社区的成功设计，将城市环境重组更为完善的城市、城镇、村庄和社区，这既包括修复城市，也包括创建紧凑的新城镇和村庄。

新城市主义是一种城市设计运动，旨在促进混合居住和就业的可步行社区的发展，它始于 20 世纪 80 年代初的美国，并逐渐开始创新城市发展、规划和土地使用。这一运动受到了20世纪中叶汽车主导城市规划之前的城市设计标准的强烈影响，新城市主义也符合地方分权、环保主义和智能增长的理念。

新都市主义的倡导者支持就业和住房的平衡发展、开放空间的区域规划以及与环境相匹配的规划和建筑的发展策略，这些策略旨在减少交通拥堵和郊区扩张，增加经济适用房的供应。新城市主义宪章于1993年随着新城市主义大会的成立而创立，该宪章涉及安全街道、绿色建筑、历史保护和城市棕地空间的再开发。

8.4.2 新城市主义原则

新城市主义原则可以在任何规模上得到应用——从单体建筑到整个社区。这些原则包括适合步行的、连通性、混合使用和多样性、优质建筑和城市设计、传统街区结构、增加密度、智能交通、可持续性和生活质量。

适合步行的意味着一种对行人友好的街道设计，工作地点和大多数生活必需品都在步行十分钟内可达。行人必须有没有汽车的专用路，甚至是限制或禁止汽车通行的街道。

连通性是指一个相互连接的街道网络用以分散交通并帮助行人。街道应该按照狭窄街道、林荫大道和小巷的层次结构来完成上述任务。一个高质量的步行网络应该让步行变得愉快，而一个无障碍的公共领域应该通过让步行变得有意义和重要目的地的可达性来鼓励步行。

混合使用和多样性要求房屋、公寓、商店和办公室在同一空间内。这意味着在同一社区、同一街区，甚至在同一建筑物内混合使用。多样性指能让所有年龄、收入水平、文化和种族的人都能在附近生活、工作和购物。混合住宅是一个相关的概念，因为不同类型、不同的面积和不同的价格范围的住房比邻而立有助于确保居民和社区成员的多样性。

优质建筑和城市设计强调美感和美学，同时也要求舒适和便利，以及塑造地方感。居民建筑、社交聚会和场所应位于社区内，以便于进入并营造基于当地的城市公民意识，与壮观的摩天大楼和无尽的公寓建筑群相比，建筑应该基于人的规模，保持与自然和谐相处的自然和怡人的环境，通过保持社区与自然的亲近来滋养精神。

传统街区结构是关于在人类历史演变过程中起作用的基本原则的回归，因为人们在城市地区共同生活，城市区域应具有可识别的中心和边界，公共空间应该是周边任何地方可平等出入的中心。应认识到优质公共领域的重要性，并将其纳入城市设计中，包括将开放式公共空间设计为体现社区美德和价值的公民艺术。传统街区在任何一个点的短距离内都有一系列的用途和密度，因此，步行10分钟即可到达各种地方。采用断面规划时，应在市中心及其附近呈现最高密度，城市边缘密度应逐渐降低。

增加密度实际上是另一个行人友好原则。这一原则要求将更多的建筑、住宅、商店和公共服务紧密地连在一起，以使步行更容易。密度有助于更有效地利用公共服务和资源，也让居住变得更加便捷和愉悦。最后，从小城镇到密集的城市中心，这些原则以及所有新城市主义原则适用于各种规模和密度的城市地区。

智能交通需要高质量的列车将社区、城镇和城市连接在一个高效的网络中。在始发站和终点站之间，行人友好的设计鼓励人们步行，但也鼓励更多地使用自行车、轮滑、滑板车和其他人力交通工具进行定期通勤。

可持续性是一个以环境为导向的术语，意味着发展和正常运作对环境的影响最小，这样发达地区就有能力实现可持续发展。实际上，它意味着环保技术、尊重当地和全球生态以及重视自然系统。用于这些目的的方法包括提高能源效率，减少不可再生燃料和资源的使用，增加当地资源的产量，增加步行和尽量少开车。

生活质量不仅是新城市主义的一个原则，也可以说是整个新城市主义运动的最终目标之一，因为通过所有其他原则的共同努力，为我们提供了高质量的生活，并且减少了许多困扰城市生活的问题，对生活质量的关注创造了丰富、提升和激励人类精神的场所。

8.4.3　新城市主义的好处

新城市主义的迅速传播和扩展，并在以灵活的方式提供广泛利益基础之上的可持续发展，这些方式可以应用于许多不同的环境中，受益于新城市主义所追求的方法的群体包括居民、企业、开发商和城市政府。

对居民的好处

居民是直接受到新都市主义设计影响，也是最明确和最明显的受益者，居民可以获得更好的生活质量、更美的居住环境、更高的房产价值、更少的交通拥堵和更少的驾驶、更健康的生活方式、更多的步行和更少的压力，紧邻主要街道的零售和服务业、自行车道、公园和自然环境。新都市主义设计创造的行人友好型社区提供了更多的机会，让人们认识自己的邻居和镇上的其他人，与更多的人建立更有意义的关系，从而形成一个更友好、更邻里的社区。学生可以步行或骑自行车去自己所在社区的学校，减少居民和学校的公交车费用以节省开支。居民可以利用多样化的小型特有的商店和服务，这些商店和服务由当地业主经营，他们参与并满足社区需求。居民可以通过减少开车以此节省大量开支，从而减少了交通拥堵，减少了汽车尾气排放，进而改善空气质量。更独特的建筑为居民提供了更好的地方归属感和社区认同感，同时有更多的受到保护的开放空间。最后，税收的使用效率更高，用于广泛分布的设施或用于城市服务所需的公用设施和道路的资金更少。

对企业的好处

当地商业社区也获得了一些好处，比如由于步行流量增加带来的销售额增加，居民在当地消费更多，而在汽车和汽油上的花费更少。由于在广告和大型标牌上的支出减少，企业有机会获得更多利润。商人自己可以拥有更好的生活方式，比如住在店铺楼上，从而避免通勤压力和昂贵的通勤费用。由于与其他当地企业的紧密联系和合作，当地企业将能够在营销中充分利用规模经济。此外，较小的空间可以促进当地小型企业的孵化和增长，企业支付较低的租金，因为所需空间较小。停车场较小，因为汽车较少，行人较多。作为个人，商人可能会受益于更健康的生活方式，因为更多的步行和靠近更健康的本地餐厅，他们的生活质量受益于更多的社区参与，成为社区的一部分，了解居民，从而使他们的业务更具竞争力，更好地满足社区的需求。

对开发商的好处

如果失去对开发商的吸引力，任何城市运动都不会有稳固的基础，因为开发商经常推动、组织和资助这一进程。开发商从更高密度的混合使用项目中获得更多的潜在收入，并因更大的可销售和可租赁面积而产生更多的利润，更高的潜在房地产价值也会带来更多的利润和回报。采用新城市主义原则的开发商可以在实行智能增长原则的社区或任何需要对环境和其他影响进行评估的情况下获得更快的准入，从而节省时间和成本。此外，混合使用的停车设施可进一步节约成本，因为全天候共享可用空间，从而减少停车场的重建和浪费，步行街区也需要较少的停车设施。由于设计紧凑，公用设施成本较低，开发商还将受益于更大的政治氛围，即公众的接受程度，以及对 NIMBY 抗议的抵制程度。最后，开发商也可能因为消费者更容易接受大量的产品而从快速销售中受益，从而获得更大的市场份额。

对城市政府的好处

城市政府也可能从实施的新城市主义原则中获益。第一个好处是税基的稳定和增值。由于紧凑和高密度的发展，与典型的郊区发展相比，新城市的人均基础设施和公用事业支出需要减少。税收基础的增加是因为更多的建筑被挤进了一个较小的区域，由于可步行，交通拥堵较少，由于有更多的人可以昼夜不间断地对所在区域进行治安监管，犯罪率往往会降低，治安支出也会减少。社区往往有更好的形象和更强的地方感。为了避免城市蔓延，新都市主义社区在紧凑而有吸引力的城市核心区内扩张的趋势和压力都较小。公共交通比以汽车为主的社区更容易发展和运营。最后，社区的阻力较小，参与程度较高，而公民参与程度越高，治理效果会越好。

8.5 精明增长

8.5.1 定义

精明增长代表了一种城市规划理念，即让城市空间更加紧凑，以避免或抵消城市蔓延风险。与新城市主义在某些方面类似，这一概念是关于通过混合使用分区和土地利用，充分利用步行能力、自行车通行、公共交通便利、紧邻就业的密集住房。该理念强调规划、可持续发展和长期规划目标而不是短期目标。精明增长往往是由环境问题和有效利用基础设施的需求驱动的，通常通过在社区内建造学校等设施来实现，欧洲人经常用"紧凑城市"这个词来指代这一理念。

精明增长已成为一种流行的方式，意味着负责任或平衡的增长，但很少有人非常精确地对其加以定义或使用。它起源于富裕郊区的中心，那里的居民开始担心郊区生活的好处正在受到损害。精明增长是一个将其倡导者与反增长环保主义者区分开来的术语，精明增长倡导者包括保守派支持者，他们通常对环保主义者怀有敌意，但他们也相信发展需要规划和指导。

大都市地区政府的分散助长了城市的蔓延，各市政府利用限制性分区来保持低基数和高房产价值，同时争夺商场、商业和高档住宅。郊区居民被吸引在郊区之间迁移，以寻找优质的学校、更低的税收和更好的分区。精明增长是一种限制城市发展的战略，因为富裕的孤岛与其他城镇隔绝开了。

精明增长的倡导者认为，通过规划可以降低基础设施成本。此外，精明增长有望改善郊区的物理环境，为中心城市和周边城市带来共同的城市繁荣。研究表明，计划外增长所需的基础设施投资比计划增长时要多，因为更大的空间、更少的密度意味着需要更多的设施。相比之下，高密度规划开发的许多类型的基础设施（如公路、道路、下水道、水厂和公用事业）的成本要比低密度扩张低得多。因为旧有投资无法完全收回，空心化的过程推高了整体基础设施成本。因此，需要进行全面规划，以控制旧基础设施的废弃和浪费，并限制不必要的投资。

8.5.2　精明增长的必要性

蔓延和不可控以及无计划的发展问题是推动精明增长理念的主要动力。蔓延对环境造成了额外的负担，因为它加速消耗稀缺的资源和开放的空间，除了适应无计划的汽车友好型增长之外，几乎没有什么影响。因此，精明增长的部分原因是基于对环境的关注，对长途通勤和其他面向汽车的发展问题的关注，还有就是与计划外增长相关的低效率和浪费。精明增长取代了对无计划的短期目标的关注，转而强调可持续性的长期区域规划。

取代单调的汽车文化，精明增长的目标包括实现独特的社区和地方感，同时扩大交通、就业和住房选择的范围，公平分担开发成本和收益，保护自然资源，加强文化遗产保护，促进公共健康。这一理念试图将增长集中在紧凑和可步行的城市中心，以避免扩张。为此，它提倡紧凑、交通导向、步行和自行车友好的土地利用，包括完整街道、社区学校以及提供多种住房选择的混合使用开发。

精明增长的倡导者认为，人口过剩、交通拥堵、学校过度拥挤以及新的细分市场的不断开发等问题可以通过精明增长加以控制。这些措施包括在城市地区周围划定绿化带，建立风景区，以及拒绝提供公共基础设施或计划增长地区以外的改善设施。智能增长以推进最小化增长影响的最佳实践而闻名，包括支持现有社区、重视社区和邻里、重新开发未充分利用的地区、提供更多交通选择、发展所谓的宜居性、提供公平的负担得起的住房、重新定义住房负担能力、使住房政策透明，促进可持续增长的愿景，鼓励和加强综合规划和投资，调整并协调政府政策，充分利用更高级别的政府援助的杠杆作用。

8.5.3 精明增长的目标和原则

精明增长有几个目标。首先，提高社区的商业竞争力和吸引新企业，为居民日常活动提供可选择的空间和场所，如购物、工作和玩耍以提高生活质量。其次，精明增长努力创造更好和更独特的地方感。经济目标包括提供就业机会、增加房地产的价值和扩大税基。最后，还有更为普遍的目标即保护开放空间，提高安全性和控制增长。

精明增长原则旨在发展可持续社区。这些社区应该是宜居，既有利于做生意，有利于工作和养家糊口。为了居民的利益，精明增长旨在增加家庭收入和财富，改善获得优质教育的机会，鼓励宜居、安全和健康。社区通过刺激经济活动而受益，同时开发、保护和投资不同的物质、自然和文化资源。

公认的精明增长的原则包括混合土地使用、紧凑的建筑设计、一系列住房选择、可步行街区、多种交通选择、保护开放空间、保护农田、保护自然美景、社区和利益相关者在发展决策中的合作。这一切都是为了加强和引导现有社区的发展，使得发展决策具有可预测性、公平性和成本效益，以鼓励具有强烈地方感的有吸引力和特色的社区建设。

8.5.4 精明增长的关键要素

精明增长的五个要素是其实现承诺的关键：负责任的均衡增长、有计划的城市发展、有规律的增长、强调新发展的美学理念和绿化带建设。负责任的均衡增长意味着允许和促进增长，但不能不惜一切代价地实现增长。相反，增长要与可持续性、宜居性和环境友好等观点相一致。有规划的城市发展意味着对城市空间的设计可以预见问题的存在，而不是让地方政府以更高的成本去解决问题。绿化带可以让居民能够随时接触自然，并将自然和城市的利益紧密结合在一起。

8.6 关于城市设计的讨论

为提高生活质量而设计

城市设计必须致力于在不断变化和转型的条件下构建城市环境。没有规划和设计，临时使用会以一种不连贯和随意的方式发展，这种状态与总体规划相反，短期解决方案来自当前环境和条件，而不是遥远的目标，临时使用利用已经存在的东西，而不是创造一切，小空间、过短的周期和不同时间点的变化条件才是其重点。设计可以利用这一现状来解决各种问题，如蔓延、交通、人口规模规划、社区和负担能力等。

城市蔓延和土地利用效率低下导致了许多问题，从缺乏负担得起的住房到交通问题，即使在没有总体规划的情况下，设计也可以帮助解决和改善这些问题。设计可以通过改造空间，使其更适合步行、骑自行车的人的活动，而不是汽车，从而为日益增加的汽车和拥堵的交通提供可替代方案，设计更多是依据人口规模而不是为汽车和商业的发展。设计可以激励社区创造愉快的生活环境，增加社区的认同感和凝聚力。大部分设施的使用便捷性增加了社区的活力，并发展了当地需求，从而形成了强大的本地经济。汽车模式导致了孤立、与邻居不熟悉、邻里经济疲软、更多的出行次数。通过环境敏感（响应性）的设计可以节约能源和水，进而保护资源。

城市设计的机会

城市设计过程意味着一个城市的经济、社会和政治结构的变化，它对城市环境中的许多环境和社会变化负有责任，其影响与变化问题有关。快捷的城市设计使其提供能源、教育、医疗保健、交通、卫生和安全等服务的能力受到限制。大规模的城市蔓延、严重的环境问题和普遍贫困的问题，部分原因是政府用于城市基本维护和服务提供的收入减少。对这些系统的设计可以更好地节约资源和满足城市居民的需求。

【思考题】

1. 城市设计作为一门学科的特点是什么？
2. 新城市主义的原则是什么？
3. 新城市主义的好处是什么？
4. 精明增长提出的理由是什么？
5. 精明增长的目标是什么？
6. 精明增长的关键要素是什么？

【关键术语】

连通性	新城市主义
一致性	公共空间
环境、背景	精明增长
文化经济学	可持续性
差异性/多样性	城市设计
绿化带	可步行性

参考文献

［1］Carmona，Matthewand Tiesdell，Steve（2007）．*Urban Design Reader.* Boston，MA：Elsevier Press.

［2］Gosling，David and Maitland，Barry（1984）．*Concepts of Urban Design.* St. Paul，MN：University of Minnesota Press.

［3］Hardinghaus，Matthias（2006）．"Learning Outcomes and Assessment Criteria in Urban Design：A Problematisation of Spatial Thinking"，*Cebe Transaction*，*The Online Journal of the Centre for Education in the Built Environment.*

［4］ Hillier B. and Hanson J.（1984）. *The Social Logic of Space.* Oxford：Cambridge University Press.

［5］ Larice，Michael and MacDonald，Elizabeth（2007）. *The Urban Design Reader.* New York：Routledge.

［6］ Lewis，Rebecca，Knaap，Gerrit-Jan and Sohn，Jungyul（2009）"Managing Growth with Priority Funding Areas：A Good Idea Whose Time Has Yet to Come，" *Journal of the American Planning Association.*

［7］ Mindali，O.，Raveh，A. and Salomon，I.（2004）. Urban density and energy consumption：a new look at old statistics. Transportation Research Part A：Policy and Practice.

［8］ Randall J. Pozdena，（2002）. Smart Growth and its Effects on Housing Markets：The New Segregation，National Center for Public Policy Research.

［9］ "Smart Growth." Wikipedia online at：http：//en. wikipedia. org/wiki/Smart_growth Retrieved 5/10/2022.

Chapter 8   Urban Design

8. 1   Definition

Design as a Discipline

Urban design is a relatively new occupation even though it has always historically played a major role in forming cities. Whoever has controlled urban design decisions, regardless of different definitions of the function in different times and places, have made the impact on cities. The term urban design was only first used in 1957, by the American Institute of Architecture. It gradually spread through the work of people Kevin Lynch and Jane Jacobs in the 1960s, as well as Christopher Alexander and Leon and Rob Krier and Robert Venturi in the 1970s and 1980s.

Urban designers often have trouble defining their field. They desire a clear and short definition, but this is not practical. A precise definition of urban design is necessary only for administrative purposes, while it is not necessary for the designer. It is much better to follow guidelines about the substance, motives, methods, and roles of urban design. The urban design process tries to provide positive urban space in both a holistic and organic way, and in a technological and pluralistic way, meeting both traditional and modern concerns. New urban approaches provide such a worldview for the different actors in urban areas.

Urban design deals primarily with the design and management of public spaces and how those spaces are used and experienced. Public space includes all spaces used freely by the public. This includes streets, squares, plazas, public infrastructure, and public amenities like parks. The exterior of buildings and private landscaping are privately-owned spaces that also contribute to the perception and experience of public space. They are therefore also considered part of urban design.

Urban design is concerned with the concerns of the shaping and uses of urban public space, including such factors as arrangement, appearance, and functionality of urban areas. Urban design has traditionally been regarded as part of the disciplines of urban planning, landscape architecture, or architecture. More recently, urban design has been linked to new disciplines such as urban landscape. In the broad sense, even fields as diverse as real estate development and urban economics can be understood as contributing to urban design and thus familiarity with them is useful for designers. Urban design involves the arrangement and design of cities and towns and their elements, such as buildings, public spaces, transport systems, services, and amenities. Urban design is the process of defining and giving shape and character and an experience to buildings, neighborhoods, and entire cities. Design takes elements and makes them into a coherent network of streets, squares, and blocks. Urban design uses features of architecture, landscape architecture, and city planning to make cities and towns esthetically attractive but also functional and convenient. Good design should bring people and places together through a variety of methods drawn from different disciplines that create places that people want to use. It is related to and has developed from planning, architecture, development economics, engineering, and landscape. Design makes all these various elements and creates a vision for the neighborhood, district, or city. Designers must then bring together the resources and skills needed to bring these visions into being.

It is clear that, apart from planning and architecture, other disciplines play important roles in making and studying urban areas. Landscape architecture, engineering (civil, communications, and transportation), sociology, economics, psychology, even arts and humanities shape the urban environment. Urban design has the potential to connect all these specialties that deal with the urban environment Urban design should serve to manage and transform the interactions of the different parts of urban life into a physical form. The role of urban design helps them realize their full potential in league with each other. Figure 8. 1 shows urban design is an interdisciplinary subject.

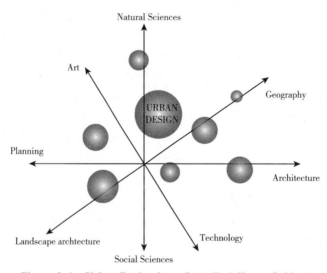

Figure 8. 1 Urban Design is an Interdisciplinary Subject

8. 2 History

James Oglethorpe's plan for Savannah, Georgia, tried to promote good governance and functionality for this colony for prisoners, providing a utopian vision of reforming convicts through their surroundings. Prior to the modern urban professions, urban design was done by sculptors, architects, landscapers, engineers, surveyors, astronomers, and even military engineers. Urban design was particularly done by surveyors and architects in the 18th and 19th centuries. The increase in urban population and many of the modern problems associated with urbanization, such as the spread of infectious diseases, encouraged municipal engineering in Great Britain. Here minimum street widths were mandated, for example, to provide light and ventilation for promoting public health.

Modern urban design is part of the broader discipline of urban planning. Urban planning started as a movement concerned with matters of what are now called urban design. Automobiles had the most significant influence on the development of urban design in the 20th Century. The urban design movement started in part as a reaction to the negative features of the impact of cars and car-orientated design. Urban design was first used as a distinctive term when Harvard University hosted a series of Urban Design Conferences starting in 1956.

8. 3　Principles

Urban design focuses on improving the physical environmental aspects of public spaces. Designing and building, and then managing public spaces is a complicated matter that involves negotiating and consulting with multiple different interests due to overlapping management responsibilities as well as the interests of nearby property owners, not to mention different, often conflicting, demands of different users. This results in less artistic control than may be the case in other in design disciplines such as architecture. Interdisciplinary consultation is also necessary, with multiple fields such as engineering, ecology, local history, and transportation planning all having some voice.

Urban design often overlaps with urban planning in that it may include the preparation of design guidelines, regulatory frameworks, and even promotion and advertising. It may also participation in the creation of legislation to govern the process. It may overlap with architecture, landscape architecture, highway engineering, and industrial design in that it may be concerned with the particular arrangement of specific spaces. Urban design may offer guidelines for and assist in the use and maintenance of urban public spaces, even to the extent of helping out in the maintenance of broader urban areas. Although some urban designers are trained and identified specifically as urban designers, a lot of urban design work is done by architects, landscape architects, and urban planners. Urban design is incorporated into many architecture, landscape architecture, and planning programs and there are even university programs that offer degrees specifically in urban design, especially at the graduate level.

8. 3. 1　Considerations

There are several major considerations in urban design. These include structure, typology, accessibility, legibility, animation, function, complementary mixed use, character and meaning, order and incident, continuity and change, and civil society. Urban structure represents the organization of a place as well as how the parts fit and are related to each other. Urban typology accounts for the spatial types that define urban spaces as related to intensity of use, resource consumption, and maintenance of community. Accessibility is about providing for convenient and safe options when getting to and moving around urban spaces. Legibility means the ability of people to find their way and to understand how a place works. Animation is design that stimulates lively and animated public activity. Function is the consideration about designing places to match the use. Complementary mixed use is locating different activities to allow for synergy and constructive interaction. Character and meaning is the consideration of valuing places for their particularity and uniqueness. Order and incident represents the balance between consistency and variety in the urban environment so that people can take advantage of and appreciate both features at the same time. Continuity and change give urban residents and visitors a sense of history and of the connections to and movement away from different points in the past. Finally, civil society is the consideration of building social capital through encouraging the constructive interaction of people through the civil organizations and the spaces that encourage their formation and activities.

8. 3. 2　Context

Urban design allows for approaches to planning that accounts for the context and most fully considers the best match for the economy, environment, social situation, and engineering requirements of an area. This also goes for highways and public transportation networks. The context includes simplicity, functionality, consistency, and value for money.

The best designs are often the simplest. These are the ones that provide an elegant solution to an urban planning issue. Complexity usually results from designs that are poor quality and compartmentalized or are rushed and poorly-considered. Complex designs can also be expensive to build and maintain. The simple solution will often prove more efficient in the long run.

Functionality is the next contextual design feature. Urban design must provide infrastructure and space that works well in addition to looking attractive and appealing. Good design needs to meet such requirements as fulfilling safety and engineering standards as well as contributing to the local community and its standards and protecting the natural and built-up environment, but above all it must be functional. For example, natural amenities that require high maintenance are not well-designed, beautiful but underused features are not good design, while attractive and secluded parks are not well-designed if they are seen as unsafe. To be functional and well-used, good urban design solutions consider safety, and maintenance, durability, repair and replacement, and esthetics.

After that is the concern for consistency in design. Consistency in urban design suggests that all the different elements should be related to each other. For example, simplicity should be expressed in terms of functionality. Functionality should provide good usability so that it brings good value and efficiency as well.

Urban design should not use excessive public funds but should function in the same cost-effective, cost-containment environment that the rest of the urban order must contend with. To do otherwise will not only undermine political support but will counter a basic rationale for doing design in that it is about making things work better not just look better. To help make sure that money is spent well, all costs and benefits need to be identified, accounted for, and justi-fied. The best urban design outcomes require considering affordability and efficiency so costs that do not deliver significant benefits should be avoided as per the usual principles of analy-sis. As with any comparative accounting of costs and benefits, it is important to consider all costs and benefits, including economic, social, and environmental ones that will affect the project over its entire life, not just in the shortterm.

8. 4   The New Urbanism

8. 4. 1   Definition

New urbanism is an international movement to reform the design of the built environment. It is a movement to develop vibrant mixed-use communities that share particular features. In parti-cular, the movement promotes diverse, compact, and "walkable" communities structured in an integrated manner to form complete communities in contrast to the incremental and haphazard results often obtained through more conventional urban development. These communities are de-signed and built so that they do not just have housing, but already have the workplaces, shops, entertainment, schools, parks, and civic facilities essential in the daily lives of the residents available. These amenities are all designed to be within easy walking distance of each other. New urbanism promotes mass transit in the place of more automobiles by increasing the use of trains and light rail, instead of highways and roads.

New urbanism is about creating a better and more livable urban future. It strives to raise quality of life and standard of living by creating better places to live. New urbanism tries to re-order and reorganize the urban environment into complete cities, towns, villages, and neigh-borhoods by striving to create communities that are designed and organized and constructed along the lines of successful existing communities. The movement involves both fixing cities and creating compact new towns and villages.

New urbanism is an urban design movement that promotes walkable neighborhoods with a mixed variety of housing and employment. It started in the United States in the early 1980s, and gradually started to reform urban development, planning, and land-use. The movement has been strongly influenced by the urban design standards from before the dominance of the automobile in planning cities from the middle of the 20th Century. These include principles such as traditional neighborhood design and development oriented towards mass transit. New urbanism is also consistent with the values of regionalism, environmentalism, and the concept of smart growth.

Advocates support balanced development of jobs and housing, regional planning for open space, and planning and architecture designed to match the context. These strategies are supposed to reduce traffic congestion and suburban sprawl, and increase the supply of affordable housing. The Charter of the New Urbanism, created in 1993 with the founding of the Congress for the New Urbanism, also addresses safe streets, green buildings, historical preservation, and redeveloping of brownfield space.

8. 4. 2 The Principles of the New Urbanism

The new urbanism principles can be applied at any scale from a single building to an entire community. These principles include walkability, connectivity, mixed use and diversity, quality architecture and urban design, traditional neighborhood structure, increased density, smart transportation, sustainability, and quality of life.

Walkability means a street design that is friendly to pedestrians and where most necessities are within ten minutes of home and work by foot. Pedestrians must have special walkways free of cars and even streets where automobile traffic is restricted or prohibited.

Connectivity refers to an interconnected network of streets that disperses traffic and assists pedestrians. Streets should be structured in a hierarchy of narrow streets, boulevards, and alleys to accomplish the above tasks. A high-quality pedestrian network should make walking pleasurable and an accessible public realm should encourage walking by making it meaningful with important destinations easy to reach.

Mixed use and diversity call for houses, apartments, shops, and offices together in the same space. This means mixed use in the same neighborhood, in the same block, and even in buildings. Diversity includes people so that people of all ages, income levels, cultures, and races live and work and shop in close proximity. Mixed housing is a related concept, as a range of types of housing, different sizes, and different price ranges in close proximity will help guarantee the diversity of residents and community members.

Quality architecture and urban design stresses an emphasis on beauty and esthetics, but it also calls for comfort and convenience, and for molding a sense of place. Civic buildings, functions, and sites should be located within the community for easy access and for creating a shared sense of locally-based urban citizenship. In contrast to massive skyscrapers and endless apartment complexes, architecture should be on a human scale. Natural and beautiful surroundings working with nature should be maintained to nourish the spirit by keeping the community close to nature.

Traditional neighborhood structure is about returning to the basic principles of what has worked throughout the evolution of human history as people have lived together in urban areas. An urban area should have an identifiable center and boundaries. Public spaces should be at the center for equality of access from anywhere on the periphery. The importance of a quality public realm should be recognized and incorporated into designs, including having open public spaces designed as civic art celebrating the virtues and values of the community. The traditional neighborhood contains a range of uses and densities within a short range of any single point so that ten minutes on foot will access a urban variety. Transect planning should be employed with the highest densities appearing at and near the town center, with progressively less density towards the edge of the urban area.

Increased density is actually another pedestrian-friendly principle. This principle calls for more buildings, residences, shops, and services packed in closer together in order to make walking easier. Density helps make more efficient use of services and resources. Density makes a more convenient and enjoyable place to live. Finally, these principles, along with all new urbanism principles are applied to urban areas of all sizes and densities, from small towns to dense city centers.

Smart transportation calls for high-quality trains connecting neighborhoods, towns, and cities together in an efficient network. Between the local stop and final destination, a pedestrian-friendly design encourages walking, but also a greater use of bicycles, rollerblades, scooters, and other human-powered modes of transportation for regular commuting.

Sustainability is an environmentally-oriented term that means minimal environmental impact of development and regular operations so that a developed area has the capacity to endure and continue. In a practical sense, it means eco-friendly technologies, respect for the local and global ecology, and valuing natural systems. Methods used to these ends include energy efficiency, and less use of non-renewable fuels and resources, increased production from local sources, and more walking and less driving.

Quality of life is not just a principle of the new urbanism, but it may be said to be one of the ultimate goals of the entire movement as all the other principles work together to deliver a high quality of life and is free from many of the problems that despoil and plague city life. A focus on quality of life creates places that enrich, uplift, and inspire the human spirit.

8.4.3   Benefits of the New Urbanism

The new urbanism spread and expanded rapidly and has endured based on delivering broad benefits in flexible ways that can be applied in many different contexts. The groups that have benefitted from the approaches pursued by the new urbanism include residents, businesses, developers, and municipalities.

Benefits to Residents

The people most directly affected by new urbanism designs are the clearest and most obvious beneficiaries. Their benefits include a higher quality of life, better places to live, higher property values, less traffic congestion and less driving, a healthier lifestyle with more walking and less stress. Close proximity to main street retail and services, to bike trails, to parks, and to nature are further benefits. The pedestrian-friendly communities created by new urbanism designs offer more opportunities to meet and get to know neighbors and others in the neighborhood and town. This results in more meaningful relationships with more people and thus a friendlier and more neighborly community. Residents and school boards enjoy savings with reduced busing costs as school children can walk or bike to schools in their own neighborhood. Residents have access to a greater diversity of smaller unique shops and services run by local owners who are involved in the community and respond to its needs. Residents enjoy big savings through driving less and owning and operating fewer cars, leading to less ugly and congested sprawl to deal with and better air quality from less car exhaust. More unique architecture delivers a better sense of place and community for residents to identify with while there is more open space and open space is protected. Finally, there is more efficient use of tax money with less money spent on amenities widely distributed or on the utilities and roads needed to accommodate urban services.

Benefits to Business

The local business community also receives benefits such as more sales due to increased foot traffic and residents able to spend more locally with people spending less on cars and gas. Businesses have an opportunity for more profits due to having less spending on advertising and large signs. Businesspeople themselves can take advantage of a better lifestyle by living above their small shops, saving themselves from a stressful and costly commute. Local businesses will be able to take advantage of economies of scale in marketing due to close proximity and cooperation with other local businesses. Further, the smaller spaces will promote local small business incubation and growth. Businesses will pay lower rents due to smaller space requirements and smaller parking lots needed due to less automobile and more foot traffic. As individuals, businesspeople may benefit from a healthier lifestyle due to more walking and being near healthier local-oriented restaurants. Their quality of life will benefit from more community involvement from being part of the community and knowing the residents, which will, in turn, allow their business to be more competitive by better meeting the needs of the community.

Benefits to Developers

No urban movement would be on a firm footing without an appeal to the developers who often drive, organize, and fund the process. Developers benefit from more potential income from the higher density of mixed-use projects, generating more profit due to more salable and leasable area. Higher potential property values also promise more profits and greater returns. Developers who have adopted new urbanism principles can expect faster approvals in communities that have adopted smart growth principles or in any case where environmental or other impacts must be assessed, resulting in time and cost savings in either case. In addition, further cost savings can be found in parking facilities in mixed-use properties where there is a sharing of available spaces all around the clock, resulting in less duplication and waste in parking provided with fewer parking facilities also necessary on account of walkable neighborhoods. Utilities are less costly due to compact and dense design. Developers will also benefit from a greater political climate of acceptance from the public with less resistance from NIMBY protests. Finally, developers may also benefit from faster sales due to greater consumer acceptance with a wider product range that results in wider market share.

Benefits to Municipalities

Cities and other municipalities may also reap benefits from the implementation of new urbanism principles. The first benefit would be a stable and appreciating tax base. New urban municipalities need to spend less on infrastructure and utilities on a per capita basis than in typical suburban developments due to the compact and high-density developments. The tax base increases due to more buildings packed into a smaller area. There is less traffic congestion due to walkability. There tends to be less crime and less spent on policing due to the presence of more people observing spaces around the clock. The community tends to have a better image and a more developed sense of place. Designed to avoid sprawl, new urbanism communities have less tendency and fewer pressures to sprawl with a compact and attractive urban core. Mass transit is easier to develop and run than in car-dominated communities. Finally, there is less resistance and more participation by the community with the greater civic involvement leading to better governance.

8. 5   Smart Growth

8. 5. 1   Definition

Smart growth represents an urban planning concept about making urban areas more compact to avoid or counteract urban sprawl. Similar to new urbanism in some ways, the concept is about using walkability, bicycle access, mass transit convenience, dense housing in close proximity to employment through mixed—use zoning and land usage. The concept emphasizes planning, sustainable growth, and long-term planning goals over short-term ones. Smart growth is often driven by environmental concerns and the desire for efficient use of infrastructure. Compactness is often emphasized through building amenities like schools in neighborhoods. Europeans often use the term compact city to refer to the concept.

Smart growth has become a popular that means responsible or balanced growth, and is rarely defined or used very precisely. It grew from the centers of wealthier suburbs where residents began to worry that the benefits of suburban living were being compromised. Smart growth was a term to differentiate its advocates from anti-growth environmentalists. Smart growth advocates have includes conservative constituencies usually hostile to environmentalists but who have come to believe that development needs to be planned and directed.

The fragmentation of governments in metropolitan areas has encouraged urban sprawl and municipalities have used restrictive zoning to keep their bases low and property values high while competing over shopping malls, businesses, and upscale residential housing. Suburban residents are lured to move between suburbs in search of quality schools, lower taxes, and better zoning. Smart growth is a strategy to limit municipalities from developing as isolated islands of affluence set off from other towns and cities.

Smart growth advocates claim that planning lowers the cost of infrastructure. In addition, smart growth is supposed to improve the physical environment of suburbs and bring joint urban prosperity to the central city and surrounding urban areas. Studies have shown that unplanned growth demands more infrastructure investment than is needed when growth is planned as greater space less density require more facilities on a per resident basis. In contrast, costs for many types of infrastructure like highways, roads, sewer, waterworks, and utilities are much lower with high-density planned development than for low-density sprawl. The process of hollowing out drives up overall infrastructure costs as old investments are not fully recouped before being duplicated further out. Comprehensive planning was thus seen as needed to control abandonment and waste of old infrastructure as well as to limit unnecessary investments.

8.5.2　The Need for Smart Growth

Sprawl and the problems of uncontrollable, unplanned development are main motivators driving the concept of smart growth. Sprawl places an extra burden on the environment by using up a scarce resource, open space, at an accelerated rate for little effect other than accommodating unplanned automobile-friendly growth. Therefore, smart growth is driven in part by concern for the environment, in part by concern for long commutes and other problems of automobile-oriented development, and in part by the inefficiencies and waste associated with unplanned growth. Smart growth replaces the unplanned focus on short-term goals with an emphasis on long-range regional considerations of sustainability.

In place of a monochromatic car culture, the goals of smart growth include achieving a unique sense of community and place while expand the range of transportation and employment and housing choices, fairly sharing development costs and benefits, preserving natural resources, enhancing cultural heritage, and promoting public health. The concept tries to concentrate growth in compact and walkable urban centers to avoid sprawl. To do so, it advocates compact, transit-oriented, walkable, and bicycle-friendly land use. This includes things like complete streets, neighborhood schools, as well as mixed-use development that provides a variety of housing choices.

Smart growth advocates often argue that problems such as overpopulation, traffic congestion, overcrowded schools, and nonstop development of new subdivisions can be controlled through smart growth methods. These include designating greenbelts around urban areas, establishing scenic areas, and refusing to supply public infrastructure or improvements outside of areas planned for growth. Smart growth is known for advancing best practices of minimizing growth impact that include ideas such as supporting existing communities, placing a value on communities and neighborhoods, redeveloping underused areas, providing more transportation choices, developing so-called livability, providing fair affordable housing, redefining housing affordability, making housing policy transparent, promoting a vision of sustainable growth, encouraging and enhancing integrated planning and investment, aligning and coordinating government policies, and leveraging higher-level government assistance.

8.5.3   Goals and Principles of Smart Growth

There are several objectives to smart growth. The goals of smart growth include making the community more competitive for business and attracting new businesses. It also includes providing alternative spaces and places for regular daily activities like shopping, working, and playing to improve quality of life. Smart growth strives to create a better and unique sense of place. Economic goals include providing jobs, increasing property values, and expanding the tax base. Finally, there are the more general goals of preserving open space, improving safety, and controlling growth.

Smart Growth principles are designed for developing sustainable communities. These communities should be good places to live, good for doing business, good for work, and good for raising families. For the benefit of residents, smart growth aims to increase family income and wealth, to improve access to quality education, to encourage livable and safe and healthy places. Communities benefit through stimulating economic activity while developing, preserving, and investing in different physical, natural, and cultural resources.

The accepted principles of smart growth include mixed land use, compact building design, a range of housing options, walkable neighborhoods, a variety of transportation choices, preservation of open space, preservation of farmland, protection of natural beauty and critical environmental areas, community and stakeholder collaboration in development decisions. All of this is done to strengthen and direct development towards existing communities, making development decisions predictable, fair, and cost-effective to encourage attractive and distinctive communities with a strong sense of place.

8.5.4   Key Elements of Smart Growth

There are five elements of smart growth that are key to helping it realize its promise. These are responsible balanced growth, planned urban development, regulated growth, an emphasis on the esthetics of new development, and greenbelts. Responsible balanced growth means allowing and promoting growth but not growth at all costs. Instead, growth is pursued in concert with other concerns such as sustainability, livability, and the environment. Planned urban development means designing spaces where problems are anticipated and dealt with upfront instead of having problems being addressed by local government at greater cost later. Greenbelts preserve nature, give residents ready access to nature, and bring the benefits of nature and city close together.

8.6　Issues

Design for Better Quality of Life

Urban design must work to construct an urban environment under conditions of continual change and transition. Without planning and design, temporary use evolves in an incoherent and haphazard way. This state is the opposite of the master plan. Short-term solutions come out of the current context and the current conditions, not from a distant goal. Temporary usage takes advantage of what already exists rather than inventing everything. Small spaces and brief periods and changing conditions at various points in time are the focus. Design can take advantage of this state of affairs to address various issues like sprawl, transportation, human-scale planning, community, and affordability.

Urban sprawl and inefficient use of land causes numerous problems, from lack of affordable housing to transportation issues. Design can help smooth over and ameliorate many of these issues, even in the absence of a master plan. Design can provide for alternatives to the ever-present automobile and congested traffic where development does not support public transportation by reworking spaces to be friendly for walking and cycling and movement on a human scale instead of friendly for cars. This means design specifically for human scale development instead of for cars and commerce. Design can inspire community and create a pleasant living environment. This can add to community and neighborhood identity and community cohesiveness. Easy access to most facilities within the local area adds to community and develops local demand that forges a strong local economy. The car model results in isolation, lack of familiarity with neighbors, a weak neighborhood economy with more trips out of the neighborhood. Energy and water can be conserved through environmentally-sensitive design and conservation may be promoted.

Opportunities for Urban Design

The urban design process means changes in the economic, social and political structures of a municipality. It is responsible for many environmental and social changes in the urban environment and its effects are related to change issues. The rapid design of cities strains their capacity to provide services such as energy, education, health care, transportation, sanitation, and safety. Cities have become areas of massive sprawl, serious environmental problems, and widespread poverty in part because governments have less revenue to spend on the basic upkeep of cities and the provision of services. These systems may be better designed to save resources and provide for the needs of city residents.

Questions

1. What are the characteristics of urban design as a discipline?
2. What are the principles of the new urbanism?
3. What are the benefits of the new urbanism?
4. What is the argument for smart growth?
5. What are the goals of smart growth?
6. What are the key elements of smart growth?

Key Terms

connectivity	*new urbanism*
consistency	*public space*
context	*smart growth*
cultureconomics	*sustainability*
diversity	*urban design*
greenbelt	*walkability*

References

[1] Carmona, Matthewand Tiesdell, Steve (2007). *Urban Design Reader.* Boston, MA: Elsevier Press.

[2] Gosling, David and Maitland, Barry (1984). *Concepts of Urban Design.* St. Paul, MN: University of Minnesota Press.

[3] Hardinghaus, Matthias (2006). "Learning Outcomes and Assessment Criteria in Urban Design: A Problematisation of Spatial Thinking", *Cebe Transaction*, *The Online Journal of the Centre for Education in the Built Environment.*

[4] Hillier B. and Hanson J. (1984). *The Social Logic of Space.* Oxford: Cambridge University Press.

[5] Larice, Michael and MacDonald, Elizabeth (2007). *The Urban Design Reader.* New York: Routledge.

[6] Lewis, Rebecca, Knaap, Gerrit-Jan and Sohn, Jungyul (2009) "Managing Growth with Priority Funding Areas: A Good Idea Whose Time Has Yet to Come," *Journal of the American Planning Association.*

[7] Mindali, O., Raveh, A. and Salomon, I. (2004). Urban density and energy consumption: a new look at old statistics. Transportation Research Part A: Policy and Practice.

[8] Randall J. Pozdena, (2002). Smart Growth and its Effects on Housing Markets: The New Segregation, National Center for Public Policy Research.

[9] "Smart Growth." Wikipedia online at: http://en. wikipedia. org/wiki/Smart_growth Retrieved 5/10/2022.

第9章　城市经济发展

9.1　概念及内涵

第 1 章指出，城市管理是一个跨学科的研究领域，经济视角是看待城市管理的一种方式，城市经济学是经济学的一个分支，涵盖城市地区的经济学研究。经济学的观点认为，城市是一个大市场，是生产和消费的场所，在更广泛的经济领域提供专门研究。城市可以被看作是独立的，也可以是作为更大经济体系的一部分。本章将对城市经济发展进行深入探讨。

城市经济学研究城市经济的性质及其经济结构，以及市场经济在城市发展中的作用，经济发展是城市经济的重要组成部分。经济发展是城市经济学的一个方向，促进增长学派取得压倒性的关注。这一流派关注的问题包括城市在工业化进程中的作用，以及导致规模经济产生的集群效应和聚集效应。城市经济学的另一个观点与流动性有关，着眼于城市行为者如何在城市区域内和区域之间作出地段决策，研究家庭和企业作出的搬迁决定的原因和影响（Bluestone et al.，2008）。

占主导地位的促增长学派受到了相当大的批评，被指责只为促进人为需求，而没有解决公平问题，助长了商业周期的波动，耗费更多有限的资源。增长模式的倡导者尤其受到那些认为在有限的星球上不可能实现无限增长的人的批评。

城市发展是一个广义术语，最初指的是将城市向自然区域的扩展。布莱克利将地方经济发展视为刺激商业活动和就业的过程。布莱尔将城市经济增长与城市经济发展进行了对比，因为经济增长通常（但并非普遍）被视为经济发展的基本要素，经济规模和居民福利的增加是有区别的，增加了经济规模，但可能无法改善居民的经济状况。例如，增长可能带来污染，破坏历史遗迹，可能带来拥堵，不一定改善生活质量。快速增长增加了整体财富，但主要是在高收入群体中，可能不会像更广泛分享的增长那样促进发展。

城市更新是指在中、高度密集的市区进行土地重建，与以商业为导向的住房重建项目有着复杂的联系，而这些项目一直是争议的根源，因为衰败的街区已被新的发展取代。城市复兴是对一个地区的社会、经济和环境福祉的改进，是一个相对近年来越来越普遍的城市更新具有更中性或积极联系的术语。再发展则是一个更一般的术语，涵盖在已经开发的区域内发生的任何开发形式。

未解决的增长问题可能与城市经济萎缩的城市衰退问题有关，也可能是由于过度增长导致的，这种增长不会改善居民福利。工业日益集中导致空气质量差或人口大量集中导致犯罪率较高的情况下，这可能是正确的。无论是哪种情况，城市经济的增长最终都会破坏城市经济的发展，促使居民迁往其他地区。

可持续发展的概念可以追溯到 20 世纪末，与早期的资源管理和环境管理思想有关，这一概念在很大程度上是由于资源枯竭和环境破坏而产生的。可持续发展是可以延续到未来的发展，并不会损害后代利益且满足其需求和享受高质量生活的能力（Rees，1998）。依赖碳基燃料和闲置土地等不可再生资源的发展是不可持续的，同样，需要在有限空间内不断增长的发展也是不可持续的。因此，对于如何发展当地经济存在的分歧，意见的范围从完全依赖增长，到基本上将发展等同于增长，到拒绝增长，再到强调增长的可持续性。

9.2　促增长学派

如上所述，发展的一个主要路径是将发展与增长同等对待，或至少强调增长在推动发展中的作用，即使不是关键因素，增长也被认为是发展的必要因素。因此，本节的论点提出了扩大经济以造福所有居民的必要性。其论点是通过扩大经济规模，可以将更多的利益分配给最需要的人，而不必直接从一个群体重新分配到另一个群体。相反，福利的增加可以源于新经济增长带来的共同利益，也可能会避免再分配和社会结构重组等存在分歧的问题。发展、工业化和现代化与非发展中国家通常所说的西化是一样的，城市发展进程在某种程度上与第 2 章提到的城市化进程相似同城市化一样，工业化涉及城市中更多的人、更多的产业和新的社会组织形式。

然而，这并不是促进增长的发展模式唯一考虑的因素，事实上，有许多重要的机制有助于城市的增长效应，其中包括城市地区的规模经济（包括消费市场的规模）、贸易和运输成本的降低、集聚效应、获取顶级信息和技术发展（Bluestone et al.，2008）。本节将考察工业化和其他有助于城市经济增长并最终促进城市经济发展的概念。

9.2.1　工业化

在历史早期，对于城市是如何形成的存在着一些争论。布卢斯通等（Bluestone et al.，2008）指出，许多人认为，城市是基于农村剩余的存在，换言之，城市发展得到了来自农村的支持，并引用了雅各布斯（Jacobs，1969）的观点，即城市通过创新提高生产力来支持农村。到了工业化时代，城市化、工业化和城市增长之间存在着明显的关联（赫希，1984）。

城市的位置由向心力和离心力驱动，向心力推动城市居民和企业向城市中心靠近，离心力则使人们离开城市中心（Bluestone et al.，2008：62）。在工业化的历史背景下，向心力最初占主导地位，交通枢纽周围的空间需求旺盛，港口、海滨和码头是早期工业城市的经济中心。水上运输由风力和后来的蒸汽驱动，成为最有效的运输方式，城市是农产品运输的枢纽，由于农产品的易腐性，大部分贸易发生在海滨或其附近，街道从海滨向外延伸。这些城市既紧凑又密集，行人很容易通过。富人和他们的制造业和商业企业集中在港口附近的主要街道上，而穷人则被安置在后巷。

水力发电和水车的发展，为厂商创造了利用新能源的需求，这意味着水车是一种离心力，它将许多经济活动从港口拉向河流、溪流和人工运河，引导稳定的水流为磨坊提供动力，结果，许多城镇沿着河流发展起来。一旦厂商选定了厂址，向心力会吸引工人在附近建房，也会吸引为工厂和工人服务的企业。

蒸汽动力以更有效的资源开采的形式，进一步分散了城市经济活动，通过铁路快速运送到劳动力充足的城市中心，这导致城市生活更加集中。具有讽刺意味的是，这种集中迫使中心城区土地价格上涨，促使许多企业在土地更便宜的城市郊区建厂，带来了更多的住宅开发，并进一步向外推进。一个相反的趋势是百货公司的发展，它在一个地点提供了高效购物和前所未有的商品种类，这将购物集中在市中心地区，以及靠近密集住宅区，在那里建造大型百货公司以满足购物需求是有效的。

电力的发展以及铁路、有轨电车和其他大众交通工具的扩张也产生了类似的复杂影响，同时通过促进城市中心的交通发展，将发展拉向城市中心，商业和制造业越来越轻松实现远距离分离。向心压力要求在紧凑的空间内建造更多更高的建筑，尤其是不需要重型制造设备的零售和商业建筑。离心力意味着制造业可以与市场距离很远，因为快速的运输和电信可以解决指挥和控制问题。到20世纪初，这已经形成了一种模式——娱乐、购物、商业和政府均集中在中央商业区。

总之，工业化进程使城市快速集聚，同时又将城市分散到更广大的地区。与此同时，它以前所未有的规模带来了人类城市成倍的增长并创造了前所未有的巨大财富，将人类生产力提升到了一个新水平，文明不再依赖于榨取微薄的剩余价值来生存，而是能够自由地为所有人创造足够的财富。然而，这并不意味着每个人都可以获得足够的财富，也不意味着这些新创造出来的财富被平均分配。阶级分化在加深和加固，产业工人往往挤在最不理想的地方，仍然过着相当边缘的生活，而富人则靠惊人的财富生活。

9.2.2 规模经济和其他因素

推动城市经济增长有几个重要因素：规模经济、运输成本、集聚经济、消费市场和技术进步。这些因素中的每一个都适用于许多不同情况，但它们的相对权重会因城市和时间而异。

规模经济

规模经济是指生产大量产品的效率更高。换言之，当生产规模扩大时，提供商品或服务的平均成本会下降，规模经济很大程度上源于城市集聚效应。当人口和工业均匀分布时，正如自然资源的自然分布所预期的那样，不可能有足够大的规模生产并从规模经济中受益。

因此，规模经济是推动城市经济发展的一个主要向心力，将工业引向更大的劳动力供应和资本及其他自然和人工资源更加便利集中的地方。企业则将工厂搬迁到可以进行大规模生产、效率更高、生产率更高的地区。这些因素使企业和地方政府能够提供更多种类的当地商品和服务。在很大程度上，城市生活给人的印象是更有趣、更令人兴奋，并且提供了更多吸引人们来到城市的事物，这都归功于规模经济。此外，规模经济与运输成本、集聚经济和消费市场具有强大的互动效应。

运输成本

长期以来，原材料和货物的运输一直是一个麻烦和危险的产业，随着技术的进步，这一产业取得了根本性的进步。当运输由人和动物进行时，它是痛苦的、缓慢、昂贵且危险的。技术发展的每一个阶段，从人力到风力，到蒸汽，再到内燃机，都提高了速度和效率，同时降低了成本，并降低了运输过程的危险和困难。

更快速且高效的交通运输意味着可以以更低的成本获得更多种类资源的投入，并且可以集中在生产点，然后再分散到遥远的市场，这与规模经济相一致，并产生了强大的影响。当大多数商品必须在当地生产，主要用于当地消费时，规模经济几乎没有机会，因为几乎所有的生产都必须在每个地方重复。

从集中到分散到不同的地点进行分散生产带来两个较大的影响：分工和专业化。正如亚当·斯密在《国富论》中描述的那样，分工是将一项任务分解为几个简单程序的过程，这意味着生产一种商品需要雇用多人，这导致了专业化，工人不仅会专门生产特定产品，而且可以是专注于生产产品的特定组成部分或阶段。专业化提高了技能、效率和生产力，从而可以生产更多的高质量商品，以换取其他商品。因此，需求和愿望可以通过交易来满足，而不仅仅是通过生产来满足，从而为所有各方带来更多种类和更高质量的商品。

即使降低了运输成本，仍然存在与运输相关的成本和损失，因此，聚集在密集的城市里仍然是明智的选择。这一趋势与新型高效交通的结合促进了城市的进一步集聚，使得周边地区的人们可以乘坐有轨电车和轻轨前往市中心。同时，它允许城市增加并划分专业部门，这种影响与其他趋势协同作用，交通便利化并推动其他趋势的发展。

集聚经济

分工专业化的兴起以及规模经济有利于集聚经济的发展，这是一种经济密度形式，来自同一产业或部门的许多公司都集中在一个小的物理区域。一家企业将靠近其他能够支持它发展的产业，由于邻近而提高效率，吸引更多的公司来提高竞争力，或者仅仅是在成熟的环境中创业。通过这种方式，通过更高效的方法进一步带来更高的密度。

就规模经济而言，集聚经济是城市化自我延续的一种模式。对于单个公司来说，投入和产出的购买和销售可能会带来大幅波动，但集聚可以提供更多的可预测性，并产生更大的集体需求，从而使整个地区能够更有效地运作，更好地实现就业。供应链更具可预测性，随着支持企业承担起向整个集聚区域提供投入的角色，企业能够更多地专注于自己擅长的领域。更多的供应商会吸引更多的买家，进一步提高可预测性（Mills and Hamilton，1984）。

集聚还允许劳动力和产品供应实现互补，一个地区一个产业的某个特征满足另一个产业的需求时就会发生这种情况。例如，生产单一商品的企业聚集可能会吸引那些包装或进一步加工该商品的企业。某个特定产业的大量熟练劳动力能够满足另一个具有相关技能的产业的需求，那对熟练劳动力的需求可能会吸引能为当地产业开发熟练劳动力的职业学校或学院。技能劳动力的过度生产和过剩可能会为其他相关产业而不是最初吸引教育机构的产业提供服务。

一种更普遍的集聚现象是，集中本身会带来意想不到的创造性联系，从而带来发展（Jane Jacobs，1969）。这在单一产业集中的情况下是显而易见的，在这个产业中，很多人都在思考同样的问题，他们可能会想出许多解决方案，这些解决方案可以在竞争中得到快速检验，并提出最佳解决方案。然而，即使不相关的公司、混合使用住宅、商业和产业都很近的地方，也有创造力和创新。事实上，正是基于此，雅各布斯才主张城市在经济发展方面的优势。有一种观点认为，不同人群的大量聚集将带来一个领域对另一个领域的问题产生意想不到的组合和见解，也正是这种联系使城市得以发展，并成为经济发展中最具创造性和进步的力量。

消费市场

城市是人、企业和政府的大集合，它们共同构成了对商品和服务的巨大需求的大市场。城市和城市地区通常从两个方面受益于消费市场的规模：第一，不同来源的需求融合将城市变成了需要各种服务的巨大市场，最合理有效的商品和服务来源往往是城市本身。这是一个良性循环，每一个创造就业的新机构都会累加经济，同时机构及其员工需要支撑，又增加了城市的需求，进而产生了新的商业活动并刺激了新的发展。第二，产业集中在一个地区，随着对该产业需求的增加，也会带来快速增长，该地区对产品的需求强度决定了该地区的增长速度。当市场增长时，供应该市场的城市也会迅速增长。目前，由于对高科技产品的持续需求，美国硅谷持续繁荣。然而，产业集中是一把双刃剑，因为需要应对产业需求的下降，否则会带来城市的衰落。

技术进步

地方发展的最终决定因素是技术和技术进步。技术投入和新技术不仅可以加速发展，而且还可以塑造发展采用的形式。风力发电决定了将生产地点选在靠近风车的地点附近，因为水车需要安装在溪流上。大型综合工厂造就了工业小镇，新技术在城市中不断出现。如上所述，雅各布的观点表明，城市本身就是新技术和创新的发电机，这些都为城市的财富创造提供了基础，然后再将其输出，新技术可以提高生产力，并转化为发展与增长。

未来，新技术将决定城市经济的新范式。分散的可选择的新能源如太阳能，将需要进行新的部署，如智能电网，它可以从多种来源收集并储存能量，然后集中在需求最大的地方和时间使用。这是一种与城市附近的大型发电厂截然不同的部署，这些发电厂在相对较短的距离内从一个集中点向分散的消费者网络发电和输送电力。个人家庭和企业可能会通过分散的发电网络系统在发电中发挥作用，然后为分散的消费者网络供电。

9.3　资本和劳动力的流动

9.3.1　城市增长地理学

在研究流动参与者在城市增长中的作用之前，有必要回顾与城市地理有关的一些因素，已经有一些规划城市地理的模型。麦肯齐（Mckenzie，1925）根据城市所扮演的经济角色，确定了四种不同类型的城市，从采掘业、商业、制造业到其他（政治、军事、娱乐、教育等）。

赫德（Hurd，1903）认为，城市的总体结构是以中心区域周围的增长为基础的，中心区域由多条轴线分割而成。例如，中央商业区（CBD）围绕十字路口发展，而增长沿着道路（轴线）推进，轴线之间的间隙随着径向增长而被缓慢填充。

伯吉斯（Burgess）试图创建一个城市无计划增长模式的认知地图，推进了同心圆模式，CBD 位于一系列辐射式区域的中心，向商业区和轻工业区（包括贫民窟）、工人阶级区和住宅区移动。虽然这一模型在研究城市增长模式方面仍有影响力（它很好地解释了城市中心的空心化/绅士化现象以及郊区化），但并非每个城市都遵循这一模式，区域间往往没有明确界定，而是逐渐划分，城市不一定以交通网络为中心。

霍伊特（Hoyt，1939）发现，许多区域看起来更像披萨切片或被切片平分的同心区域，时尚住宅区往往从中心向外围移动，并且随着相互矛盾的区域相邻而变得更加分散。霍伊特还将美学和地理因素添加到了伯吉斯模型的观光领域的经济因素中，因为一些时尚区位于"高地"或迷人的海滨。同样，随着财产值和审美因素的下降，许多地区被让给了低声望群体。

哈里斯和厄尔曼（Harris and Ullman）提出了更详细的多核理论。他们认为历史、文化和经济因素决定了区位。现代城市可能会有一个中央商务区，但其他部门将基于与该部门所需资源的有效接近度进行布局。当房地产价格较低时，重工业可能会在 CBD 附近起步，但随着城市发展和中央区域房地产价格上涨，新的产业可能会被迫在其他地方开辟新的区域。这一理论可以解释中产阶级化的原因，因为靠近中心区域的房产价值下降可能会使其附近的房地产有再开发和新开发的吸引力。这一理论也很好地解释了许多分区法的力度变化，倾向于将反美学的活动划分为不同的区域。它还反映了 CBD 的一些微妙特征，在这里，一些企业被吸引，但其他企业会被吸引到其他地方，甚至会有企业因资金出逃而消失。在他们看来，这座城市严格来讲是不可预测的，因为许多不可预测的因素存在。

最近，了解城市发展地理的尝试包括因子生态学、社会区域分析或社会地理学，这些都是根据区域居民的社会特征将城市景观分成若干部分（Read，2002）。部分研究根据早期区域理论的几何学方法对城市街区进行细分。按种族地位、家庭地位、经济地位对城市进行细分，这些因素叠加在物理空间上，构成了有形不动产。

新近的研究以洛杉矶为中心，并将其与第三世界的发展中国家的城市进行比较，认为城市正在蔓延且无法控制。中央商务区被视为一个壮观的消费场所，通常是一个拥有企业大本营的全球指挥中心，贫民区化的内城被隔离得零星分散，边缘地区被由工业飞地、门控社区、边缘城市、大型购物中心、主题公园和高科技产业组成的多元化郊区占据（Dear，2002）。

阿隆索

阿隆索关注城市地区的租金或土地价格，他用了一个简单的模型，以一个单一的城市中心为起点描述了土地价格与城市区位之间的关系。该模型假设城市遵循同心圆模式，中央商务区是最理想的位置，所有土地使用者都需要前往该中心。当控制所有其他因素时，运输成本会在离中心更近的位置降到最低。因此，土地价格将趋向于在靠近中央商务区的地方上涨，并在中心达到最高点。另外，随着运输成本的增加，远离市中心的土地价格会下降。对于单一土地使用，所得租金曲线是一条与 x 轴相交的直线，并向下倾斜，直到与 y 轴相交。大都市区的曲线是城市区域内所有土地使用的所有曲线的合集。

如果市中心的地价更高，那么贫民窟和其他城市居民区的贫困居民住在市中心附近，而更富裕的居民住在离市中心更远的地方怎么可能？阿隆索解释了这个明显的悖论，他指出，低收入者通常租住价格较低的房子，相对于远离城市中心的收入，他们的低住房成本不会随着交通成本的上升而下降，而更富裕的中产阶级可以支付更高的交通成本，可以支付更高远离城市中心的地价，而那里的住房也不那么拥挤。

蒂布特

"地址、地址、地址"是房地产的口号，也是资本和劳动力自由迁移的世界中的一个关键考虑因素。正如特定地点更具吸引力一样，资本和劳动力也因偏好而被吸引到城市。城市参与稀缺企业和投资的竞争，试图创造有利于企业发展的环境，吸引雇主来提供就业机会。与此同时，还是一场吸引居民和培养人才的竞争。

蒂布特（Tiebout，1956）认为，人们可以通过"用脚投票"在不同的城市之间自由选择，并通过搬到最能表达自己偏好的城市来改变他们的生活方式，而这种方式在国家层面上是无法做到的，因为在国家层面，其中对于更高服务水平的争论相当于表示愿意为实现期望的水平而比其他人付出更多。他断言，人们可以在当地一级通过迁往提供他们想要的服务的城市来表达他们对特定服务的偏好，最重视为孩子提供高质量教育的父母会选择拥有最好的社区学校和图书馆的城市地区，退休人员可能会寻求更好的长者服务，关心环境和娱乐的人会寻找在公园和娱乐方面投入更多资金以及拥有更多绿化带的地区。

同样，个人不仅试图迁移到其所需服务的地区，还试图迁移到具有其所需水平的服务组合的地区，这意味着人们寻求期望中的税收和支出水平。他们不仅在提供个人公共产品和产品组合方面寻求相对优惠，而且在支持其所需产品的总体支出水平以及他们愿意为其所需公共产品支付的税收方面也寻求优惠。这就产生了一种推挽式的紧张关系，即最终的期望水平可能低于理想的公共服务水平，但自掏腰包的税收成本又高于理想的税收水平，因此最优水平应介于两者之间。这些影响对企业和个人可能都有效，除了推动竞争优势的促增长因素外，城市政府还制定政策来增强竞争优势。

9.3.2 资本的流动

竞争力不仅在地方、区域甚至国家层面发挥作用，而是在全球层面发挥作用。国际贸易和外国投资以及所谓的自由贸易协定（FTA）带来了商业全球化。运输成本的下降起到了一定作用，更高效的海上运输（超级油轮和集装箱船）、快速铁路和航空运输（大型喷气式飞机和快速航空服务）的兴起使得生产与市场分离。计算机、互联网、移动电话等通信技术以及广泛接入的电信卫星连接也在领导和管理的指挥和控制职能与市场和生产分离方面发挥了作用（Bluestone et al.，2008）。

由此改变的阿隆索租金曲线降低了运输和通信成本，改变了商业等式，曾经的土地成本因素不再是他们主要考虑的因素。相反，新的等式将劳动力作为主要投入，增加了商业竞争以降低劳动力成本，包括跨国甚至国际贸易都在寻找廉价劳动力（Cowie，1999）。大型跨国公司现在可以利用廉价劳动力将生产转移到世界任何地方。他们可以将总部设在母国公司，也可以将总部迁至税收和法律法规符合公司需要的任何地方，通过先进的通信技术实现对生产和分销链进行远程控制，这意味着世界现在是"平的"，企业现在几乎可以位于任何地方（Friedman，2005）。这带来了一种新的活力，城市现在在真正的全球层面上为企业及其创造的就业机会进行竞争。

这种全球化的竞争导致城市政府通过利用绝对、比较和竞争优势来吸引资本。绝对优势是一个人、一家公司、一个国家或一个城市地区能够提供比其他人/地区更好的商品或服务。在该地区拥有天然产品的城市，或拥有与特定工艺或产业相关的传统，该地区可能具有绝对优势。城市地区可以专注于他们擅长的领域，以最大限度地发挥绝对优势（Bluestone et al.，2008）。

比较优势有点不同。一个城市地区没有必要更好地生产特定的商品或服务，它只需要有能力以比竞争对手更低的成本生产商品或服务以获得相对或竞争优势。竞争优势意味着，即使一个城市地区可以生产大量的商品和服务，它也应该把重点放在以较低的机会成本生产产品方面具有优势的领域。这意味着它应该进口本地生产成本更高的产品，并比其竞争对手更有效率地出口其生产的产品。这一理论只适用于考虑多种商品和服务时，不同的领域可以专门研究不同的商品和服务。当每一个地区发展并专注于其比较优势领域时，这种贸易会在理论上带来所有人获益（Bluestone et al.，2008）。

竞争优势是在特定的商品和服务市场中的优势。这不是基于更好产品的绝对优势，也不是基于最小化机会成本的比较优势。相反，它由公司或地区在某一商品或服务市场中获得的优势组成。这是通过降低生产成本来降低价格，以压低竞争对手的价格来实现的。或者，可以通过产品差异化实现竞争优势，以与竞争对手相同的价格销售更具吸引力和独特的产品（Bluestone，2008）。

这些不同类型的优势为城市地区发展当地产业提出了各种战略。第一，一个地区可以推广独特的当地农产品和海洋产品，这些产品是可取的，并且具有或可能被开发以提供绝对优势，历史或传统工艺和产业也可以做到这一点。第二，一个城市可以利用比较优势，从生产相对昂贵、进口相对便宜的产业转向生产相对便宜、进口相对昂贵的商品和服务。第三，一个地区可能会试图通过生产比竞争对手的产品更有吸引力的独特的产品或通过降低成本来发展竞争优势。在每一种情况下，地方政府都试图帮助企业，要么孵化企业，要么吸引企业，作为创造就业机会的竞争战略的一部分，通常采取特定诱因的形式，如减税或向目标企业提供低息贷款。

9.3.3 劳动力的流动

劳动力不像资本那样流动，也不像具有更大的迁移灵活性的资本那样灵活地寻找城市，尤其是在全球化时代。另外，在选择地点方面，劳动力远比资本有限。对于大多数劳动者来说，要在真正全球化的环境中工作是很困难的，劳动者在许多方面受到限制，而公司和投资却没有。与资本不同，劳动力只由人组成，且人具有局限性。受国籍、语言和文化的限制，他们只能在有限的国家工作。劳动者希望与家人和朋友住在一起，住在让他们感到舒适的地方。他们通常不喜欢经常搬家，更喜欢作为社区的一部分参与社会活动。他们至少希望在就业方面有一定的工作保障和稳定性，因此受就业限制，只能在通勤范围内生活。从功能上说，所有这些意味着，对大多数劳动者来说，搬迁是一种不常见的选择，在很大程度上仅限于选择城市地区内的特定社区或特定大都市地区内的市镇。虽然他们可能会搬家，但不会经常搬家，除非生活发生重大变化，而且居住地点之间的主要选择并不是很自由，而是局限于大都市不同地区之间的增量选择。

对于城市来说，这带来了许多发展途径。城市可能会试图通过创造一个吸引人的环境来吸引人们移居城市或阻止他们离开，从而实现增长。这一过程的一部分可能涉及提供就业机会，并需要类似于发展和吸引资本的战略，可能还包括建设一个人们愿意定居和养家的地方。另一种方法可能涉及人力资本开发，要么通过教育和其他投入提供直接支持，要么通过发展社会资本环境，从而实现人力资本开发。

简·雅各布斯强调，城市是创新的独特源泉。她认为，城市密集的多样性是创新和经济活力的关键（Jacbos，1969），城市的创新源于不同人群的密集聚集，促进增长的创新来自不同的人，他们有不同的想法，这些想法可以以新的方式结合在一起，从而使城市中形成关系带来发展（Jacbos，1993，Florida，2002）。格莱泽证明，随着知识溢出、工人共享信息以及人力和社会资本的增加，多样化产业集中促进了增长。下面考虑两种可能通过劳动力流动实现这一目标的方法。

直到最近，大多数人几乎没有自由选择住在哪里，他们需要住在离工作很近的地方。现代交通和由许多中心甚至许多城市组成的分散的都市区给了人们更多的选择。人们选择住在有文化氛围又舒适的社区，父母选择有好学校的社区，选择生活在对他们重要的地方。正是由于这一趋势，一项新的城市发展战略应运而生，城市规划者可以开发人们愿意住的城市。

创意阶层

理查德·佛罗里达（Richard Florida，2000，2002，2007）确定了城市间竞争的三个关键要素，他把这些元素称为三 T 原则：人才、技术和包容。技术不是劳动因素，但人才和包容是。佛罗里达确定了现代劳动力中的关键"人才"是创造性的专业知识工作者，他们构成了他所称的"创意阶层"。这一群体由科学家、工程师、设计师、艺术家、作家、音乐家、建筑师以及其他从事类似创造性工作的人组成，他们创造了推动文化和经济新发展的创新。佛罗里达关于发展城市经济需要什么的想法已经朝着为发展城市培养人才的方向发展，他关于高度期望的创造性知识工作者的创造性的想法包括投资于发展本地人力资本，并通过创造有利于鼓励创造性活动和吸引创意阶层的环境来吸引创意阶层。

佛罗里达表示，人们现在更认同自己的职业或专业，而不是公司。越来越多的不同层次的人可以通过其生活方式或休闲活动加以识别。创意工作者自然对他们生活的创造性和开放的社会氛围感兴趣，这是包容的来源。佛罗里达发现创意阶层会被包容的社会氛围吸引。以创造性和包容氛围著称的城市地区鼓励有创造力的人和工人，他们不会迁离包容地区，除非迁往其他更包容的地区。通过这种方式，佛罗里达发现，城市更需要人文氛围，而不是商业氛围，这意味着要全面支持创造力。例如，佛罗里达（2002）发现种族多样性与高科技产业和人口增长呈正相关，人力资本和创造性资本与创新和增长相关。开发这些功能会吸引创意工作者，而备受期待的高科技公司、电子商务和新的创业者也将紧随其后。城市政府可以通过努力鼓励创造力，创造一个包容多元文化和多重身份的城市内所有群体均能被理解和包容的城市环境，这有助于建立创造性的人才队伍，吸引高科技企业，并吸引构成创意阶层的人才，将人才、技术和包容融为一体。

城市消费

与传统的强调生产的发展相反，克拉克（Clark，2004）发现消费的重要性在与日俱增，人们通过选择来定义自己，这可以通过有意识地选择认同特定的群体身份或通过个人消费选择来实现，人是他们的风格和个人品味的产物。就像佛罗里达的方法一样，克拉克建议城市利用文化激励来促进经济发展和社会进步，过去以生产为导向的经济转向现在以消费为导向的文化经济。传统的城市发展理念以自上而下的过程为中心，精英们设定目标，人民通过民主进程接受或否决这些目标，城市发展涉及在一个地区开发或吸引产业。最近，市场也被用于同样的过程，采取市场激励的形式，如减税、商业津贴和商业补贴。人们发现，这些激励措施非常昂贵又不是特别有效（区域内除外）。

便利设施（舒适物）是城市居民和产业所渴望的各种城市非市场特征。城市可以将城市的特色与产业的需求相匹配，以此作为吸引商业竞争的一种方式，这是一个积极的战略，但主要解决基础设施业务需求，包括交通网络、通信网络、电网和辅助商业服务等。一种更人性化且有效的方法是将城市的特征与创意阶层的需求相匹配（或与任何被企业视为员工的公民群体所重视的设施相匹配）。这样，城市变得更加宜居，同时也吸引了企业为该地区发展提供经济基础。

虽然单个的便利设施本身很有吸引力，但人们并不仅仅使用单一的便利设施，一个社区的氛围或特征来自赋予它这种特征的一组便利设施。西尔弗等（2006）提到了一组便利设施，这些设施赋予社区作为场景的特征。不同的场景营造出不同的氛围。这些可能从传统的家庭友好到沉湎酒色。场景会吸引不同类型的居民，可以满足非常具体的业务、劳动力和居民需求。克拉克还提出了将便利设施打包成场景的想法，以吸引各类游客。

9.4　关于城市经济发展的讨论

9.4.1　批评

城市发展的概念本身并非没有争议，有人对发展的一般概念、增长学派的观点和流动性的一般概念以及典型的发展工具提出批评。

对增长的批评。增长的概念本身受到来自两个方面的攻击，一是环境和资源约束与现实，二是基于增长的公平性和谁受益的问题。

增长的有限性。资源有限。越来越多的人需要更多的资源，但无论有没有更多的人，根据当前的技术和发展模式，越来越多的发展需要大幅增加煤炭、石油和贵重矿物等不可再生资源的消耗。污染和全球变暖等主要环境问题因当前增长模式下的发展而严重恶化，增长的逻辑与地球有限的人类照顾能力背道而驰。

权力与平等。尽管对增长的讨论通常是以价值中立的方式进行的，但真正的问题是谁受益，发展的真正目的是什么。罗根和莫洛奇（Logan and Molotch，2007）提出了城市作为一个资本导向型增长机器的问题，并在推动发展和再发展的共同问题上达成了共识。莫伦科普夫看到了一个"有争议的城市"，这是政治斗争的场所，让商业精英与城市政党的政治精英共同对抗更广泛的公民利益。城市贫困的基础是对城市问题采取非阶级方法，以牺牲城市穷人的利益为代价，让中产阶级和上层阶级受益。

流动性发展问题。以吸引新的居民和企业为基础的发展路径的主要弱点在于蒂布特模式的问题，"用脚投票"即从一个不受欢迎的城市搬到一个出于任何原因（蒂布特解释中的税收和支出水平）而喜欢的城市。尽管弗罗里达的3T原则中提到包容，但对包容到底有多重要还是存在一些疑问。克拉克（2004）认为，佛罗里达的一些研究可以在包容的重要性似乎减弱或消失的情况下进行更详细的研究。此外，佛罗里达的观点在西欧和北美等许多西方社会中具有更直观的意义，但似乎被东亚充满活力的经济发展所抵消。真正的问题是，包容是否一项普遍要求，在不同的文化中可能会有不同的表达，到底是西方社会特有的因素，甚或根本不是一个因素？

9.4.2　去工业化

去工业化和向信息导向及服务型后工业城市的转型往往伴随着制造业的大量失业。

这是一个问题，因为制造业工作为低收入且较少接受高等教育的城市居民提供了广阔的就业基础，工资和福利都很好，为他们提供了进入中产阶级的途径。去工业化给城市带来了一个挑战，即用大量其他高质量工作岗位取代了高质量的制造业工作。

服务性工作通常被分为两类，一类是报酬低、福利少，也可能是临时的，另一类是通常需要专业且受过高等教育的服务性工作，信息技术工作遵循类似的模式，无论哪种情况，地方政府的任务都是设计某种新的制度以保障公民的福祉。第一种可能是，城市政府通过为低收入人群提供更广泛的服务，以弥补工资和福利水平的下降，从而寻找弥补机会减少的路径。第二种可能是，城市可以在不断减少的符合旧工业模式的就业岗位中争取更大份额。第三种可能是，可以利用市政资源创造新的符合那些失业的人的特点的就业机会。第四种可能是，城市可以尝试提升其教育和人力资本发展水平，为工人提供更高质量的新经济岗位。

【思考题】

1. 城市增长、城市发展和可持续城市发展之间有什么区别？
2. 什么因素带来城市经济的发展？
3. 为什么家庭和企业选择搬迁？
4. 你认为吸引创意阶层会带来城市的发展吗？
5. 城市发展的主要学派存在哪些问题？

【关键术语】

聚集经济　　　　　　　　　流动性
中央商务区（CBD）　　　　促进增长学派
离心力　　　　　　　　　　公共企业家精神
比较优势　　　　　　　　　专业化
创意阶层　　　　　　　　　税收减免
去工业化　　　　　　　　　蒂布特假说
劳动分工　　　　　　　　　城市更新
规模经济

参考文献

［1］Bluestone, Barry, Stevenson, Mary Huff, Williams, Russell（2008）. *The Urban Experience：Economics, Society, and Public Policy*. New York：Oxford University Press.

［2］Clark, Terry N. （ed）（2004）. *The City as an Entertainment Machine*. Amsterdam：Elsevier.

［3］Dear, Michael（2002）. *From Chicago to L. A. ：Making Sense of Urban Theory*. Thousand Oaks, CA：Sage.

［4］Eisinger, Peter（2000）. "The Politics of Bread and Circuses：Building the City for the Visitor

Class." *Urban Affairs Review.* 35 （3）：316－333.

［5］ Florida, R. （2000）. "Competing in an Age of Talent：Quality of Place and the New Economy. " Report prepared for the R. K. Mellon Foundation, Heinz Endowments, and Sustainable Pittsburgh.

［6］ Florida, R. （2002）. *The Rise of the Creative Class.* New York：Basic Books/Perseus.

［7］ Florida, R. （2007）. *The Flight of the Creative Class.* New York：Harper Collins.

［8］ Florida, R. , Gates, G. （2004）. "Technology and Tolerance：The Importance of Diversity to High-Technology Growth. " in Clark, T. N. （ed） *The City as an Entertainment Machine.* Amsterdam：Elsevier.

［9］ Friedman, Thomas （2005）. *The World is Flat：A Brief History of the Twenty-First Century.* New York：Ferrar, Strauss, and Giroux.

［10］ Glaeser, E. , Kolko, J. , Saiz, A. （2004）. "Consumers and Cities. " in Clark, T. N. （ed） *The City as an Entertainment Machine.* Amsterdam：Elsevier.

［11］ Jacobs, Jane （1969）. *The Economy of Cities.* Random House, New York.

［12］ Jacobs, Jane （1993）. *The Death and Life of Great American Cities.* Random House, New York.

［13］ Logan, John, and Molotch, Harvey （2007）. *Urban Fortunes：The Political Economy of Place.* Los Angeles：University of California Press.

［14］ Reed, Richard （2002）. "The Importance of Demography in the Analysis of Residential Housing Markets" Paper presented at AsRES/AREUA Joint International Conference Seoul July 4, 2002.

［15］ Silver, D. , Clark, T. N. , Rothfield, L. （2006）. "A Theory of Scenes. " online at：http：// sites. google. com/site/tncresearch/atheoryofscenes Retrieved2/12/2012.

［16］ Stiglitz, Joseph E. （2007）. *Making Globalization Work.* New York：Norton.

Chapter 9   Urban Economic Development

9. 1   Definition

In Chapter 1, it is noted that urban administration is an interdisciplinary field of study and that the economic perspective was one means of viewing urban administration. Urban economics is a field of economics that covers the study of economics within urban areas. The economic viewpoint sees the city as a large market, a site of production and consumption, and as providing specialized functions within the broader economy. Cities may be seen both as independent and as part of a larger economic system. This chapter takes a closer look at urban economic development.

Urban economics investigates the nature of the urban economy with its economic structures, and the working of market economies in cities. Economic development is an important element in urban economics. Economic development is the overwhelming concern of the first school of urban economics, the pro-growth school. This school is concerned with issues like the city's role in industrialization, and the clustering and concentration effects that result in the creation of economies of scale. A second view stemming from urban economics is related to mobility. This approach looks at how urban actors make location decisions within and between urban areas. It researches the causes and effects of decisions where to move made by households and businesses (Bluestone et al., 2008).

The predominant pro-growth school has attracted considerable criticism. It is criticized as promoting artificial wants, not addressing questions of equity, contributing to the fluctuations of the business cycle, and depleting finite resources. The advocates of the growth model particularly receive criticism from those who point out that infinite growth is not possible on a finite planet.

Urban development is a broad term that originally referred to the expansion of cities into natural areas. Blakely refers to local economic development as the process of stimulating business activity and employment. Blair contrasts urban economic growth and urban economic development in that economic growth is often (but not universally) considered an essential element for economic development. The distinction is made between the increase in the size of the economy and increase in the welfare of residents. Growth increases the size of the economy but may fail to improve the economic situation of residents. For example, growth may bring pollution, may destroy historic sites, and may bring congestion without necessarily improving the quality of life. Rapid growth that increases overall wealth, but mostly among upper income groups may not increase development as much as growth that is more broadly shared.

Urban renewal means land redevelopment in moderately to highly dense urban areas. Urban renewal has complicated associations with business-oriented housing redevelopment projects that have been the source of controversy as decaying neighborhoods have been displaced by new development. Urban regeneration is the promotion of the social, economic, an environmental well-being of an area and is a term with more neutral or positive associations than urban renewal that has become more common in recent years. Redevelopment is a more general term that covers any development that occurs over an area that has already been developed.

The unaddressed problems of growth may be related to issues of urban decline, where the urban economy shrinks. This may be caused by excessive growth that does not improve resident welfare. This may be true in situations where increasing concentrations of industry lead to poor air quality or where large concentrations of people have higher rates of crime. In either case, the very growth that may or may not have developed the urban economy ultimately undermines it, encouraging residents to leave for other areas.

A more recent concept that dates from the late 20th Century, but is related to earlier ideas of resource management and environmental stewardship is the concept of sustainable development, which has arisen in large part due to resource depletion and environmental destruction. Sustainable development is development that can continue into the future and that does not compromise the ability of future generations to meet their needs and enjoy a quality life (Rees, 1998). Development that depends on non-renewable resources such as carbon-based fuels and undeveloped land is unsustainable. Likewise, development that requires endless growth in finite space is also unsustainable. Therefore, there is a split over how to go about developing the local economy. Opinion ranges from depending almost solely on growth in a way that basically equates development with growth to opinions rejecting growth, emphasizing sustainability in growth.

9. 2   Pro-growth School

As noted in the definition above, one major approach to development is to equate development closely to growth, or at least to emphasize the role of growth in driving development. Growth is assumed to be a necessary ingredient, if not the key ingredient, to development. As a result, arguments from this quarter address the need for expanding the economy for the welfare of all residents. The argument is that by expanding the economy, more benefits can be targeted to those most in need without redistribution directly from one group to another. Rather, increases in welfare can stem from shared benefits coming from new economic growth, possibly sidestepping divisive questions of redistribution and restructuring the structure of society. Development is the same as industrialization, modernization or, as it is often known in non-Western developing nations, Westernization. The urban development process is similar in some respects to the urbanization process noted in the second chapter. Just like urbanization, industrialization involves more people in larger cities, more industry, and new forms of social organization.

However, this is not the only consideration of the pro-growth model of development. In point of fact, there are a number of important mechanisms that contribute to the growth effect in cities. These include the greater economies of scale found in urban areas (including the size of the consumer market), decreased trade and transportation costs, the effects of agglomeration, access top information, and technological development (Bluestone *et al.*, 2008). This section will consider both industrialization and other concepts that contribute to urban economic growth and, ultimately, to urban economic development.

9. 2. 1   Industrialization

Early in history there is some debate as to how cities came into being. Bluestone *et al* (2008) note that many assumed that cities are based on the existence of rural surplus. In other words, they are supported by the countryside. They also cite Jacobs (1969), however, that cities support the countryside with productivity gains from innovation. By the time of industrialization, there was a clear connection between urbanization and industrialization and urban growth (Hirsch, 1984).

The location of cities is driven by both centripetal forces that push urban residents and businesses to move close to the center, as well as centrifugal forces that pull people away from the center (Bluestone *et al.*, 2008: 62). Under historical industrialization, centripetal forces dominated at first. Initially, the space around transportations hubs was in peak demand, with ports, waterfronts, and the docks the economic focus of early industrial cities. Water transportation, powered by wind, and later steam, was the most efficient mode of transportation. The city was a hub for the transportation of raw agricultural goods. Due to the perishable nature of agricultural products, much of the trade took place on or close to the waterfront, with streets radiating away from the waterfront. The cities were compact and dense, and could easily be negotiated by pedestrians. The wealthy and their manufacturing and commercial businesses were concentrated on main streets near the port, while the poor were relegated to back alleys.

The development of waterpower, with water mills, created a demand for manufacturers that could take advantage of the new source of energy. This meant that the waterwheel was a centrifugal force that pulled much economic activity away from harbors and towards rivers, streams, and manmade canals that channeled a steady flow of water to power the mills. As a result, many towns grew up along rivers. Once the manufacturers were established, centripetal forces drew in workers who built houses close by, as well as businesses to serve the mills and the workers.

Steam power allowed further dispersal of economic activity, usually in the form of more efficient resource extraction that could then be rapidly transported via rail to the centers of existing cities where plentiful labor was available. This led to further increased concentration of city life. Ironically, this concentration forced central prices up and drove many businesses to open up on the outskirts of cities where land was cheaper, bringing more residential development, and further pushing outward. A counter-trend was the development of the department store, which provided access to efficient shopping and an unprecedented variety of goods in a single location. This anchored shopping around the central downtown area, as well as near dense residential areas where it was efficient to build a large department store to meet shopping demand.

The development of electricity and the expansion of railroads and street cars and other means of mass transportation had a similarly complicated effect, simultaneously pulling development to the center of the city by facilitating movement there and allowing for development to be widely dispersed. The centripetal pressures called for more and taller buildings in compact space, particularly with retail and commercial buildings that did not require heavy manufacturing equipment. The centrifugal forces meant that manufacturing could be separated from the market by great distances, with speedy transportation and telecommunications taking care of command and control issues. By the early twentieth century, this had created a pattern whereby entertainment and shopping and commerce and government would be concentrated in the central business district.

In sum, the process of industrialization concentrated cities and dispersed them across a greater area at the same time. At the same time, it multiplied human cities on an unprecedented scale, and allowed for fabulous wealth never seen before, lifting human productivity to levels whereby civilization no longer depended on the extraction of meager surplus for survival, but could reliably produce enough for all. This does not mean that everyone had enough or that this new wealth was equally divided, however. Class divides deepened and hardened, with the industrial working class often crowded into the least desirable spaces and still living a fairly marginal existence, while the wealthy lived on fabulous wealth.

9. 2. 2 Economies of Scale and Other Factors

There are several important factors involved in driving urban economic growth. These include economies of scale, transportation costs, agglomeration economies, consumer markets, and technological progress. Each of these factors is applied in many circumstances, but their relative weight varies from city to city and time to time.

Economies of Scale

An economy of scale is where it is more efficient to produce something in greater quantities. In other words, the average cost of providing a good or service falls per unit produced when production increases. Economies of scale are responsible in large part for the concentration of cities. When population and industry is evenly distributed, as would be expected with the naturally-occurring distribution of natural resources, it is impossible to produce on a large-enough scale to benefit from scale economies.

This is therefore a major centripetal force that drives urban economic development, drawing industry towards larger supplies of labor and convenient concentrations of capital and other natural and manmade resources. Businesses relocate sites to areas where larger-scale production is possible, more efficient, and increases productivity. These factors allow firms and local governments to provide a greater variety of local goods and services. In no small part, the impression of city life as more interesting, more exciting, and as providing more that pull people to the city is attributable to this factor. Furthermore, economy of scale has powerful interactive effects with transportation cost, agglomeration economies, and consumer markets.

Transportation Costs

The moving of raw materials and goods has long been a difficult and dangerous business that has advanced radically with technological progress. When transportation was by man and animal, it was painfully slow, expensive, demanding, and dangerous. Each stage of technological development, from muscle power to wind to steam to internal combustion, produced a multiplier that increased speed and efficiency, while it reduced costs and the danger and difficulty of the process.

More efficient and rapid transportation means a greater variety of inputs are available at a lower cost and may be concentrated at the point of production and then dispersed to far-off markets. This has a powerful impact in concert with economies of scale. When most goods had to be produced locally and mostly for local consumption, there was little opportunity for scale economies as almost all production had to be replicated in every locality.

Concentration at and dispersal to different locations allowed for dispersal of production. This had two powerful effects: division of labor and specialization. Division of labor, as famously described by Adam Smith in *Wealth of Nations* as the ultimate source of wealth, is the process of breaking down a task into several simpler procedures. This means that multiple people are employed in producing a single good. This leads to specialization, whereby workers will not only specialize on producing a particular good, but will focus on making a particular part or stage of a product. This enhances skill and efficiency and productivity, allowing to produce a greater number of higher-quality goods to be shipped out of the locality in exchange for other goods. Needs and desires can thus be met through trade instead of solely through manufacture, allowing for a much greater variety and higher quality in overall goods to the benefit of all parties.

Even with reduced costs to transportation, there are still costs and losses associated with transportation. Therefore, it is still sensible for people to cluster together in dense cities. This trend, plus the combination of new efficient transportation facilitated further cluster in cities, allowing people on the periphery to travel by street car and light rail to the city center. At the same time, it allowed cities to expand and divide into specialized sectors. The effect is synergistic with the other trends, with transportation facilitating and driving other trends.

Agglomeration Economies

The rise of specialization from the division of labor along with economies of scale favors the development of what are known as agglomeration economies. These are a form of economic density where many firms from the same industry or sector are concentrated in a small physical area. One business would be located close to other specialists that would support it, increasing efficiency due to proximity, drawing in further firms to be more competitive or just to start business in a fertile environment. In this way, density leads further to greater density through the path of greater efficiency.

In connection with economies of scale, agglomeration economies are one way in which urbanization becomes self-perpetuating. Purchases and sales of inputs and outputs may fluctuate greatly for single firms, but an agglomeration can afford greater predictability and exercise greater collective demand, allowing for the entire area to operate more efficiently and closer to full employment. The supply chain is much more predictable and large inventories become less necessary as support firms take on the role of supplying inputs to the entire agglomeration, allowing firms to concentrate more on what they do best. The greater number of suppliers will attract a greater number of buyers, further contributing to predictability (Mills and Hamilton, 1984).

Agglomeration also allows for complementariness in labor and product supply. This happens where one feature of an industry in an area meets the needs of another industry. For example, an agglomeration of firms producing a single good may attract firms that package or further process that good. A large supply of labor skilled for a particular industry may be able to meet the needs of another industry with related skills. The demand for skilled labor may attract vocational schools or colleges that develop skilled labor for the local industry. Overproduction and overabundance of skilled labor may supply other related industries instead of those that initially attracted the educational institution.

Returning to Jane Jacobs (1969), a more general sort of agglomeration is that concentration itself brings about unexpected and creative connections that lead to development. This is obvious in the case of a single concentrated industry where a lot of people thinking about the same problems are likely to come up with many solutions that can be rapidly tested with competition pushing the best solutions to the fore. Even where unrelated firms and mixed housing and commercial and industrial are in close proximity, however, there is creativity and innovation. In fact, it is particularly under these conditions that Jacobs argues for the advantages of the city in terms of economic development. The argument goes that large concentrations of different people in close proximity will lead to unexpected combinations and unanticipated insights from one area into the problems of another. It is precisely this sort of connection that leads the city to develop as well as to be the most creative and progressive force in the economy.

Consumer Markets

Cities are large collections of people and firms and governments, which collectively make them into large markets that offer a large demand for goods and services. Cities and urban areas generally benefit from the size of consumer markets in two ways. First, the amalgamation of demand from different sources turns cities into huge markets that need to be served. The most logical and efficient source of goods and services is often the city itself. This is virtuous cycle where each new institution that creates employment adds to the economy and then the institution and its employees require support and adds to the demand in the city. This generates new business activity and spurs new development. Secondly, concentration of industry in a single area brings rapid growth with increases in demand for the industry. The strength of demand for the area's products determines the growth of an area. When a market increases, the cities supplying that market grow rapidly in response. Currently, Silicon Valley in the United States has continued to prosper due to the continued demand for high-tech products. This concentrated industry is a double-edged sword, however, as the decline of demand in the industry needs to be countered, or the city will decline as well.

Technological Progress

A final determinant of local development is technology and technological progress. Not only can technological inputs and new technologies speed development, they also shape the forms that development takes. Wind power determined that production be sited near good sites for windmills. Waterwheels needed to be sited on streams. Large-scale integrated factories generated factory towns. New technologies arise in cities. Jacob's argument, noted above, suggests that cities are themselves the generators of new technology and innovation. These provide the basis for the wealth of cities, which are then exported. New technologies allow for increases in productivity that are translated into increases in development.

In the future, new technologies will determine new paradigms of urban economics. New sources of dispersed alternative energy, such as solar, will require new arrangements, like a smart electrical grid that can gather energy from many sources, store it, and then concentrate at the places and times when demand is greatest. This suggests a very different arrangement from the large power plants located near cities that generate and deliver power over relatively short distances from one concentrated point to a dispersed network of consumers. Individual homes and businesses may come to play a role in power generation through dispersed power generation network systems that then supply dispersed consumer networks.

9.3　Capital and Labor Mobility

9.3.1　Geography of Urban Growth

Before looking at the role of mobile actors in urban growth, it is necessary to review some factors involved in the geography of urban. There have been a few models that have mapped out the geography of the city. McKenzie (1925) determined four different types of cities, depending on the economic role they played, from extractive, to commercial, to manufacturing, to other (political, military, recreational, educational).

The general structure of the city was identified by Hurd (1903) as being based on growth around a central area bisected by various axes. For example, the central business district (CBD) would develop around a crossroads and growth would advance along the roads (axes) with the gaps between the axes being filled in more slowly with the radial growth.

Burgess tried to create a cognitive map of the unplanned growth patterns of the city, advancing the concentric zone model, with the CBD at the center of a radiating succession of zones, moving to a zone in transition businesses and light industry along with ghettoes, a working-class zone, and the residential zone. While this model is still influential in looking at the pattern of urban growth (it does a good job of accounting for the hollowing out/gentrification phenomenon of the city center, as well of suburbanization), not every city follows this pattern, zones are often not clearly defined but gradually delineated, and cities do not necessarily center on transportation webs.

Hoyt (1939) found that many of the sectors tended to look more like slices of pizza or concentric zones bisected by slices, finding that fashionable residential areas tended to move out from the center towards the periphery and to become more dispersed as contradictory sectors were adjacent. Hoyt also added esthetic and geographical factors to the economic factors of the Burgess model in sighting sectors, as some fashionable areas are located on "high ground" or along attractive waterfronts. Likewise, many areas are handed over to lower-prestige groups as property values and esthetic factors decline.

Harris and Ullman advanced the more detailed general theory of multiple nuclei. They determined that a mixture of historical, cultural, and economic factors determined locations. Modern cities would likely have a CBD, but other sectors would be placed based on efficient proximity to the resources needed by the sector. Heavy industry might start close to the CBD when property values are low, but new industry may be forced to open up new districts elsewhere as the city develops and central property values rise. This theory could also account for gentrification as declining property values near the center may make property attractive for redevelopment and new development close to the center. This theory accounts well for many of the dynamics of zoning laws that tend to keep antithetical activities separated into different districts. It also addresses the nuanced nature of the CBD, where some businesses are drawn, but others would be drawn to other locations, or even disappear due to capital flight. The city, in their view, is not strictly predictable, depending on numerous unpredictable factors.

More recent attempts to understand the geography of urban development have included factorial ecology, social area analysis, or social geography, all including attempts to break down the urban landscape according to the social characteristics of the people living there (Reed, 2002). Some of these studies have been able to break down urban neighborhoods according to the geometry of earlier sectoral theories. Murdie (cited in Reed, 2002) broke down the city by ethnic status, family status, economic status, as layers that are superimposed on the physical spaces to make up the visible real estate.

More recent work centered on Los Angeles and drawing parallels with developing cities in the Third World sees the city as sprawling and out of control. The CBD is seen as a spectacular site of consumption and often a global command center with corporate citadels, the ghettoized inner city is broken up by pockets of gentrification, the edge is dominated by sprawling diverse suburbs made up of industrial enclaves, gated communities, edge cities, large shopping centers, theme parks, and high-tech industry (Dear, 2002).

Alonso

Alonso was concerned about rent, or land prices, in urban areas. He used a simple model with a single urban center and started with a single land use to describe the relationship between land price and location in the city. The model assumes that the city follows a concentric model where the CBD is the most desirable location and all land users need to travel to the center. When all other factors are held steady, transportation costs fall closer to the center. Therefore, land prices will tend to rise closer to the CBD, reaching the maximum at the center. On the other hand, land prices will fall moving away from the center as transportation costs increase. With a single land use, the resulting rent curve is a straight line intersecting the x-axis and sloping down until it intersects with the y-axis. The curve for a metropolitan area is the amalgamation of all the curves for all land uses within the urban area.

How is it possible for poor residents in slums and other urban settlement to be living near the city center while more affluent residents live further away from the center if land prices are higher at the center? Alonso explains the apparent paradox by pointing out that the poor generally rent and live in less-expensive housing. Their low housing costs do not decline in cost relative to income moving away from the center as fast as their transportation costs rise moving from the center, while the more-affluent middle classes can afford the higher transportation costs and can afford more land further away from the center where housing is also less crowded.

Tiebout

"Location, location, location" is the watchword of real estate and it is also a key development consideration in a world where capital and labor have the freedom to relocate. Just as particular locations are more attractive, capital and labor are drawn to locate cities due to preferences. Cities participate in a competition for scarce businesses and investment, trying to create a business-friendly environment that will attract employers to provide jobs. At the same time, there is a competition to attract residents and to develop a talented labor force.

Tiebout (1956) argued that people may choose freely among different municipalities by "voting with their feet" and changing where they live by moving to the municipality that most closely expresses their preferences in a way they cannot do at the national level where an argument for a higher level of services amounts to an expression of willingness to pay more than others for the desired level to be realized. He asserted that people could express their preference at a local level for specific services by moving to cities that provided the services they desire. Parents who place the greatest value on high-quality education for their children would seek out the urban area with the best neighborhood schools and best libraries. Retirees might seek out better senior services. Those concerned about the environment and recreation would look for areas with more invested in parks and recreation and lands set aside as green belts.

Likewise, individuals seek not only to move to areas with their desired services but also to those with their desired mix and level of services. This means that people seek out a desired level of taxes and expenditures. Not only do they seek out preferences as to the provision of individual public goods and the relative mix of goods but also to the overall level of expenditures that will support their desired goods and the taxes that they are willing to pay in return for their desired public goods. This creates a push-pull tension where the eventual desired level is presumably less than the ideal level of public services but out-of-pocket tax costs are higher than the preferred level of taxation so that the optimal level falls somewhere in-between. These forces may work both for businesses and individuals. In addition to the pro-growth factors driving competitive advantage, urban governments enact policies to enhance competitive advantage.

9. 3. 2 Capital Mobility

Competitiveness no longer plays out on a local, regional, or even on a national level, but on a global level. International trade and foreign investment, along with so-called free-trade agreements (FTAs), have brought about the globalization of commerce. Declining transportation costs have played a role, with the rise of more efficient maritime transportation (super tankers and container ships), fast rail, and air transportation (jumbo jets and express air service) allowing for production to be separated far from markets. Telecommunications technologies such as computers, the internet, mobile phones, and widespread access to telecommunications satellite connections have also played a role in allowing for the command and control functions of leadership and management to be separated from both market and production (Bluestone *et al.*, 2008: 143).

The resulting altered Alonso rent curves have lowered transportation and communications costs, changing the equation for business, with land costs no longer necessarily the major consideration they once were. Instead, the new equation has left labor as a major input, increasing business competition to reduce labor costs, including a transnational and even international search for cheap labor (Cowie, 1999). The large multinational corporations can now relocate production virtually anywhere in the world, taking advantage of cheap labor. They can leave the headquarters in the home company or relocate it to anywhere the taxes and legal regulations suit the company's needs communicating remotely with the production and distribution chain via advanced telecommunications. This means that the world is now "flat" and businesses may now be located virtually anywhere (Friedman, 2005). This has ushered in a new dynamic where cities now compete on a truly global level for businesses and the jobs they create.

This globalized competition has led urban governments to respond by trying to attract capital by taking advantage of absolute, comparative, and competitive advantages. An absolute advantage is where an individual, a firm, a country, or an urban area can produce a good or a service better than others. Cities that have natural products in the area, or have a tradition related to a particular craft or industry, may have an absolute advantage in that area. Urban areas can specialize in what they are good at to maximize absolute advantage (Bluestone *et al.*, 2008: 174).

　　A comparative advantage is a little different. It is not necessary that an urban area be better at producing a particular good or service, it just needs to have the ability to produce a good or a service at a lower cost than competitors to have a relative, or competitive advantage. A competitive advantage means that, even when one urban area can produce numerous goods and services, it makes economic sense for it to focus on the areas where it has an edge over others to produce at a lower opportunity cost. This means that it should import what costs more to produce locally and export what it produces more efficiently than competitors can. This theory is only employed when considering multiple goods and services, with different areas able to specialize on different ones. This trade leads to the theoretical benefit of all when each area develops and focuses on its fields of comparative advantage (Bluestone *et al.* , 2008: 175 – 77).

　　Competitive advantage is an advantage within a particular market for goods and services. This is not an absolute advantage based on better products or a comparative advantage based on minimizing opportunity cost. Instead it consists of advantages obtained by firms or areas in a single good or service market. This is done through lowering the cost of production to lower prices to underprice competitors. Alternately, competitive advantage may be achieved through product differentiation to sell more attractive and unique products at the same price as competitors (Bluestone *et al.* , 2008: 179 – 181).

　　These different kinds of advantage suggest various strategies for developing local industry in an urban area. First, an area may promote unique local agricultural and marine products that are desirable and have or may be developed to provide an absolute advantage. The same can be done with historic or traditional crafts and industries. Secondly, a city may take advantage of comparative advantage by shifting away from industries that are relatively expensive to produce and cheap to import towards goods and services that are relatively cheap to produce and expensive to import. Finally, an area may try to develop competitive advantage with unique products that are more attractive than competitor's products or through lowering costs. In each case, the local government tries to help business, either to incubate or to attract businesses as part of a competitive strategy to create jobs. This often takes the form of specific inducements such as tax abatements or low interest loans to targeted businesses.

9. 3. 3　Labor Mobility

　　Labor is not as mobile as capital and does not have the flexibility to seek out cities in the way that capital can. Capital has more flexibility to relocate, particularly in the global era. Labor, on the other hand, is far more limited than capital in the choice of location. It is difficult for most workers to operate on a truly global scene. Workers are limited in several ways that corporations and investments are not. Unlike capital, labor consists solely of people and has human limitations. Workers are limited by their nationality, language, and culture to a limited range of countries. Workers want to live close to family and friends and in areas where they feel comfortable. Workers do not generally prefer to move frequently and prefer to participate in society as a part of their community. Workers prefer at least some job security and stability in employment and are therefore constrained by their employment to living within a commuting range. Functionally, what all of this means is that, for most workers, relocation is an uncommon choice largely restricted to the choice of a particular neighborhood within an urban area or of a municipality within a specific metropolitan area. That means that, while workers may move, they do not move often except for a major life change and the major choice between places to live is not very free, but is limited to an incremental choice between different parts of a metropolitan area.

For cities, this leaves number of development approaches. A city may try to grow by creating an attractive environment to draw people to move to the city or to keep them from moving away. Part of this process may involve providing jobs and would entail strategies similar to developing and attracting capital. This may also involve creating a place where people would like to settle and raise their families. Another approach may involve human capital development, either through providing direct support through education and other inputs or through an environment that develops social capital, leading to human capital development.

Jane Jacobs stressed the city as a unique generator of innovation. She saw the close-packed diversity of the city as the key to innovation and economic dynamism (Jacobs 1969). The innovation of the city comes from the tightly-packed concentrations of diverse people. Growth-promoting innovations come from exposure to different people with different ideas that may be combined in new ways so that the relationships formed in cities lead to development (Jacobs, 1993: 180 – 181, Florida, 2002). Glaeser demonstrated that the concentration of diverse industries promotes growth as knowledge spills over and workers share information and human and social capital increase. Two means that this may be accomplished through labor mobility are considered below.

Until recent years, most people have had little choice of where to live. They needed to live close to work. Modern transportation and decentralized metropolitan areas consisting of many centers and even many cities give people more choices. People choose to live in neighborhoods that are culturally comfortable. Parents choose neighborhoods with good schools. People choose to live close to the things that are important to them. A new urban development strategy has emerged as a result of this trend. City planners can develop the city so that people want to live there.

Creative Class

Richard Florida (2000, 2002, 2007) has identified three elements as key to the competition among cities. He calls these elements the three Ts. They stand for talent, technology, and tolerance. Technology is not a labor factor, but talent and tolerance are. Florida has identified the critical "talent" in the modern workforce to be the creative professional knowledge workers who make up what he calls the "creative class". This group is made up of people like scientists, engineers, designers, artists, writers, musicians, architects, and others who do similar creative work that generates innovations that drive new developments in the culture and the economy. Florida's idea of what it takes to develop the urban economy has moved very far in the direction of developing people for developing cities. His ideas about the creative class of highly-desired creative knowledge workers include both investing in developing human capital locally and attracting the creative class by creating an environment conducive to encouraging creative activities and attractive to the creative class.

Florida says that workers now identify more with their occupation or profession than with a company. Increasingly workers at all levels identify with a lifestyle or with leisure activity. Creative workers are naturally interested in and appreciate a creative and open-minded social atmosphere where they live. This is where tolerance comes in. Florida finds the creative class is attracted to a social atmosphere of tolerance. Creative people and workers are encouraged by urban areas known for their creative and tolerant atmosphere, do not relocate away from tolerant areas except to other tolerant areas. In this way, Florida finds that cities need a people climate more than they need a business climate and that this means supporting creativity across the board. For example, Florida (2002) found that ethnic diversity is positively associated with high tech industry and population growth. Human capital and creative capital were associated with innovation and growth. Developing those features will attract the creative workers, and the highly desired high-technology firms, e-businesses, and new entrepreneurs will follow. Urban governments may respond by trying to encourage creativity and by making an urban environment that embraces understanding and tolerance of all groups within a city that embraces multiculturalism and multiple identities. This may both help build the creative workforce that will draw high-tech business and attract the talent that constitutes the creative class, bringing talent, technology, and tolerance together.

Urban Consumption

In contrast to the traditional development emphasis on production, Clark (2004) has found the increasing importance of consumption. People define themselves through choices. This is done either through the conscious choice of identifying with a particular group identity or through personal consumption choices. People are the product of their styles and individual tastes. Much like the Florida approach, Clark suggests cities use cultural incentives for the purposes of economic development and social improvement. What used to be done economically with a production orientation is now done culturally with a consumption orientation. The traditional idea of urban development was centered on top-down processes. Elites set the goals and the people either accepted or vetoed them through the democratic process. Urban development involved building or attracting industry to an area. More recently, the market has been harnessed for the same process. This has taken the form of market incentives such as tax breaks, business perks, and business subsidies. These incentives have been found to be very expensive, not particularly effective (except within a region).

Amenities are the various non-market urban features that residents and industry desire in their city. The city can match the features of the city to the features industry desires as one way of competitively attracting business. This is a positive strategy, but mostly addresses the infrastructure business needs. This includes the transportation network, the communications network, the power grid, and ancillary business services. A more human approach, but one that is also effective is to match the features of the city to the features the creative class wants (or to the amenities valued by any group of citizens valued as employees by business). This way the city becomes more livable at the same time it attracts businesses to provide the economic foundation for the area.

While individual amenities are attractive in their own right, people do not use a single amenity. A neighborhood receives its atmosphere or character from the group of amenities that give it that character. Silver *et al.* (2006) referred to a group of amenities that give a neighborhood its character as scenes. Different scenes construct very different atmospheres. These may range from traditional and family-friendly to anything-goes drunken debauchery. Naturally scenes attract types of residents and can be for particular specific business, workforce, and resident needs. Clark also raised the idea of packaging amenities into scenes to attract types of tourists as well.

9. 4   Issues

9. 4. 1   Critics

The very concept of urban development is not without controversy. There are critics of general concepts of development, of the growth school and the concepts of mobility in general, and of typical development tools.

Critics of Growth. The concept of growth itself has been attacked from two directions. The first is the basis of environmental and resource limitations and reality. The second is based on the equitability of growth and the question of who benefits.

Limits to Growth. Resources are limited. More people require more resources but with or without more people, more development according to current technologies and current development models requires major increases in consumption of non-renewable resources like coal and oil and precious minerals. Major environmental problems like pollution and global warming are significantly aggravated by development under current models of growth. The logic of growth is contrary to the finite capacity of the planet to care for people.

Power and Equality. Although discussions of growth are often framed in neutral terms, there is a real question who benefits and what is the real purpose of development. Logan and Molotch (2007) raised the issue of the city as a capital-oriented growth machine that coalesces on shared questions of driving development and redevelopment. Mollenkopf sees a "contested city" that is the site for political struggle for control, pitting business elites in concert with political elites in urban parties against broader citizen interests. Urban poverty is based on non-class approaches to urban issues that benefit middle and upper classes at the expense of the urban poor.

Issues with Mobility Development. The major weakness with approaches to development that are based on attracting new residents and new businesses are based on issues with the Tiebout model of "voting with your feet" by moving away from an undesirable municipality to one they prefer for whatever reason (levels of taxation and expenditures in the explanation of Tiebout). Although Florida argues for his three Ts of talent, technology, and tolerance, there is some question as to how important tolerance is really. Clark (2004) has argued that some of Florida's research can be examined in greater detail in ways where the importance of tolerance seems to lessen or disappear. There is a real question whether tolerance is a universal requirement that may be expressed differently in different cultures.

9. 4. 2   Deindustrialization

Deindustrialization and the shift to information-oriented and service-oriented post-industrial cities have often come with major job losses in manufacturing. This has been problematic because manufacturing jobs have provided a broad base of jobs with good wages and benefits that have provided a path into the middle class for lower-income urban residents with less opportunity for higher education. This presents a challenge to cities to replace quality manufacturing jobs with sizable numbers of other quality jobs.

Service jobs are often segregated between a very large number that have low pay and few benefits and may be contingent and a much smaller number of service jobs that are often professional and require advanced education. Information technology jobs follow a similar pattern. In either case, the task for local government is negotiating some sort of new system that provides for citizen well-being. One possibility is that the urban government looks for ways to compensate for declining opportunity by providing broader services for those who fall into low-income categories to compensate for declining wages and benefits. Another is that the city can scramble for a greater share of the declining number of jobs that fit the old industrial model. A third approach may be to use municipal resources to create new jobs that match the characteristics of some of those that have been lost. A final possibility is that a city can upgrade its education and human capital development efforts to prepare workers for the higher-quality new economy jobs.

Questions

1. What are the differences between urban growth, urban development, and sustainable urban development?

2. What factors lead to the economic develop of cities?

3. Why do households and businesses choose to relocate?

4. Do you think attracting the creative class develops cities?

5. What are some problems with the main schools of urban development?

Key Terms

agglomeration economies	*mobility*
central business district (*CBD*)	*pro-growth school*
centrifugal forces	*public entrepreneurialism*
comparative advantage	*specialization*
creative class	*tax abatements*
deindustrialization	*tiebout's hypothesis*
division of labor	*urban regeneration*
economy of scale	

References

[1] Bluestone, Barry, Stevenson, Mary Huff, Williams, Russell (2008). *The Urban Experience: Economics, Society, and Public Policy.* New York: Oxford University Press.

[2] Clark, Terry N. (ed) (2004). *The City as an Entertainment Machine.* Amsterdam: Elsevier.

[3] Dear, Michael (2002). *From Chicago to L. A.: Making Sense of Urban Theory.* Thousand Oaks, CA: Sage.

[4] Eisinger, Peter (2000). "The Politics of Bread and Circuses: Building the City for the Visitor Class." *Urban Affairs Review*, 35 (3): 316 – 333.

[5] Florida, R. (2000). "Competing in an Age of Talent: Quality of Place and the New Economy." Report prepared for the R. K. Mellon Foundation, Heinz Endowments, and Sustainable Pittsburgh.

[6] Florida, R. (2002). *The Rise of the Creative Class.* New York: Basic Books/Perseus.

[7] Florida, R. (2007). *The Flight of the Creative Class.* New York: Harper Collins.

[8] Florida, R., Gates, G. (2004). "Technology and Tolerance: The Importance of Diversity to High-Technology Growth." in Clark, T. N. (ed) *The City as an Entertainment Machine.* Amsterdam: Elsevier.

[9] Friedman, Thomas (2005). *The World is Flat: A Brief History of the Twenty-First Century.* New York: Ferrar, Strauss, and Giroux.

[10] Glaeser, E., Kolko, J., Saiz, A. (2004). "Consumers and Cities." in Clark, T. N. (ed) *The City as an Entertainment Machine.* Amsterdam: Elsevier.

[11] Jacobs, Jane (1969). *The Economy of Cities.* Random House, New York.

[12] Jacobs, Jane (1993). *The Death and Life of Great American Cities.* Random House, New York.

[13] Logan, John, and Molotch, Harvey (2007). *Urban Fortunes: The Political Economy of Place.* Los Angeles: University of California Press.

[14] Reed, Richard (2002). "The Importance of Demography in the Analysis of Residential Housing Markets" Paper presented at AsRES/AREUA Joint International Conference Seoul July 4, 2002.

[15] Silver, D., Clark, T. N., Rothfield, L. (2006). "A Theory of Scenes." online at: http: // sites. google. com/site/tncresearch/atheoryofscenes Retrieved2/12/2012.

[16] Stiglitz, Joseph E. (2007). *Making Globalization Work.* New York: Norton.

第10章　城市经营

10.1　概念及内涵

经营是一个来自商业的概念，是商品和服务的设计或呈现方式，用以满足消费者的需求，城市经营是应用于城市的相同过程的一个版本。城市经营建议通过选择规划和组织城市的方式以满足对城市发展感兴趣的不同群体的需求。当公民和工商业（以及任何其他相关群体或目标群体）对城市的社会经济环境感到满意，同时也满足游客和投资者的期望时，城市经营就达到了其最终目标（Kotler, Hamlin, Rein and Haider, 2002）。城市经营已成为城市经济发展战略的重要组成部分，经济发展需要制定长期的经营战略，以保护和发展当地社区的潜力。城市经营是城市地区之间竞争加剧的市场竞争过程的一部分，这种竞争是为了吸引投资和人力资本，作为城市经营持续背景的竞争以频繁的经济、政治和社会变化为特征。

城市经营也用于实现其他几个目标：创造积极的社区形象，吸引新的和搬迁企业及其他机构，吸引游客和熟练的劳动力。除此之外，积极的形象还可以帮助该地区的出口产品找到市场，并为该地区创造独特的城市品牌（Kotler and Gertner, 2002）。持续不断的快速变化意味着城市地区的传统方式不再像过去那样有效，城市地区需要从经营角度补充地方发展战略。因此，城市要提供居民、当地经营者和投资者以及潜在的国内和国际游客所需的商品和服务。

城市经营在美国尤其受欢迎，在全球范围内，其城市商品和服务的推广规模达数十亿美元。城市地区利用城市经营来创造积极的新形象或克服消极的旧形象，城市地区同私营企业一样利用营销手段进行促销。营销适应了城市地区的需求，通过基于该地区的特性创建独特的城市品牌来促进发展。城市经营利用城市品牌在目标市场细分中进行区域推广，这需要通过创造、改进和塑造城市形象来实现，有助于实现理想的城市发展模式。城市经营是旨在吸引目标市场的活动，希望为地区提供潜在利益。城市经营的主要目标是在公共政策和消费者需求之间建立强有力的关系以提高城市系统的运作效率。

10.2　城市经营的思想体系

近几十年来，城市经营的发展基于公共关系和广告学的发展以及公民对政府的态度认知。20 世纪 70 年代，在美国和英国，政府官僚机构回应公民不及时的现状迅速升温，在这两个国家，官僚机构往往被视为以更专业的客户关系而非公民—公务员关系来主导他们所服务的人。这种观点带来了 20 世纪 80 年代三种看待官僚机构与公民之间关系的方式：扩大市场、扩大民主和新管理主义。

经营方法采用了自由协议的市场原则，提供了将退出选择作为一种赋权战略并将接受官僚机构服务的人视为消费者，被服务者可以选择不参与市场交易。民主方法通过发言权赋予人们权利，将他们视为对项目运行有发言权的公民，赋权公民可以投诉，并有权期望政府会听取他们的意见（Hirschman，1970）。新管理主义则提供了自我完善的路径——公民与官僚机构打交道时他们之间的关系就像客户向企业寻求服务一样。这三种观点被引入被认为回应不及时的官僚作风的观点中，存在四种可能的关系：客户、消费者、公民或顾客（Hambleton and Hoggett，1998）。

管理主义有三个主要特征，强调分配国家盈余，而不是吸引私人投资。与传统的自由主义模式相反，尽管这是一种远离专业客户关系的做法，官僚机构仍然是服务的主要提供者。管理主义还以社会福利意识形态为特征，远离竞争的市场价值或财富创造。

古典自由主义专注于个人在社会和经济发展中的作用，社会的最高美德是个人追求幸福或自身利益的程度，个人最了解自己的需求和愿望。社会应该围绕降低界限来构建，以实现个人追求快乐或自我利益的能力。不干预的市场是鼓励和发展个人自治的最高效且有效的手段，同时追求个人幸福也不会陷入混乱或道德败坏。国家的作用应该是有限的和不干预，实现个人自治或幸福和追求利益的社会的最有效方式是政府实行极简主义或自由放任。

平等自由主义的核心仍然是自治，但自治生活需要自由和享有基本福利的权利，个人必须保证基本的商品消费水平（公共住房、食品券和基本的收入再分配），才能享有自由和自主权，政府不仅应保护自由，还应提供基本的福利权利。这一观点很普遍，但哈耶克和弗里德曼等古典自由主义者认为平等自由主义根本不是自由主义，因为它背离了其所主张的自由主义的核心：对市场的关注以及在市场中自由追求幸福的机会（Hackworth，2007）。

虽然这两种自由主义都允许政府基于市场失灵采取行动，但古典自由主义者很少看到市场失灵，只会将"失灵"视为市场的最佳运作。另外，平等自由主义者则对市场失灵提出了一种更为广泛的观点，其中包括市场不是自我监管的，市场可能会产生不完美的竞争，如果不受政府监管，最终会造成破坏性甚至自我破坏。凯恩斯主义的平等自由主义者主张政府维持有效需求以保持经济运行，同时也为重新分配提供理由，以允许个人参与社会并行使自由的权利。在城市和全国范围内，平等主义者将促进最低限度可接受的社区标准作为干预的理由。市场不仅在失灵时会发生变化，而且在未能产生预期结果（如良好的住房、工作环境和高质量的医疗保健）时也会发生变化。在城市一级，所采取的各种法规和干预措施包括欧几里得式区划、财产税、建筑法规和国家计划在地方的实施（Hackworth，2007）。

新自由主义者拒绝平等自由主义的方法并呼吁重新回归古典自由主义。虽然哈耶克和弗里德曼等认为，国家限制地方的自由会给个人自由带来潜在的灾难，但大多数新自由主义者都满足于缩减国家在监管市场方面的作用，新自由主义植根于对个人、自由市场和非干涉主义国家的忠诚。政府失灵包括效率低下、不公平和腐败等观念，即使政府能够发挥某种作用，它也会通过其低效、不公平和腐败行为来约束市场，造成更多的损失而不是益处。这一观点认为，政府发挥的任何作用都会被其通过限制资本和劳动力流动而阻碍竞争力的作用所抵消。在地方一级，政府失败被视为一种减少政府干预的观念形态，以帮助政府摆脱困境与企业合作或像其一样运作（Hackworth，2007）。

这有助于从新管理主义转向新的企业家精神（Harvey，1989a）。在国家计划的背景下，地方政府不再负责城市区域的管理，相反，城市政府现在作为企业家或企业家的支持者的角色在市场上取得成功。管理主义削弱了经营者的竞争力，相反，地方一级的经济政策应着眼于刺激经济发展，城市的繁荣取决于就业、投资和产业提供就业的有效竞争（Cochrane，2007）。个人的积极性是解决城市社会和经济问题的答案，国家是实现这一积极性的体制障碍，应尽量减少国家的干预，除非有助于促进和发展个人的积极性，社会福利只能通过经济成功来实现，因此，城市政策的作用是创造财富，重点放在城市地区市场的再创造上。

哈维（1989b）提供了城市企业主义的四种基本选择。第一，城市可能试图通过生产获得竞争优势，这可以通过投资新的生产技术和社会或物质基础设施来实现。第二，城市可能会争夺消费性支出，并通过在城市地区创建高档购物、娱乐和文化中心来实现这一目标，也可以通过鼓励绅士化来吸引富裕的居民。第三，城市可能会争夺重要的金融和政府中心。例如，可以建造机场或支持服务体系以增加集聚经济效应。第四，城市可以尝试争取对国家基金和国际基金的竞争。

城市企业主义是随着国家在福利支出和社会消费方面的支出不断扩大而发展起来的社会民主福利体制。代表着新自由主义对平等自由主义国家的排斥，以及通过制定社会提供的最低标准使平等参与成为可能。在城市领域，这种企业主义是为了应对财政压力和削减支出管理的财政压力而出现的，企业主义是在管理主义终结之后基于新经济增长源的渴求出现的。

10.3　城市经营过程

10.3.1　实施城市经营

实施城市经营计划需要几个条件。第一个条件是认同城市内部社区力量在城市经营过程中的作用。城市需要采用新的战略方法和规划来保持或加强竞争优势。城市经营是帮助城市实现其发展目标的战略工具。第二个条件是建立战略愿景，这意味着要对居民和商业人士希望如何评估社区这一重要问题制定答案，确定愿景也是确定发展目标的第一步。第三个条件是建立地方城市政府、居民和商业社区之间的伙伴关系，需要在追求共同利益的过程中推进和实现这种伙伴关系。城市的任何合作经营发展都必须吸引所有当地参与者的注意，无论他们代表谁的利益，必须维持不同部门之间的合作关系以实施面向市场的战略。

一个专门的作为城市经营的象征或宣传城市的中心公共机构可能会非常有帮助，该机构需要以市场友好的类似于私人环境的方式运行，同时该机构必须是公开的，因为城市经营过程由市政府来运行，在许多情况下，这是一项困难的活动。城市政府必须发挥核心作用，因为即使城市营销行为与私营部门的产业和技术有关，而且城市经营包括城市形象和身份，所以城市政府必须保证将该机构的活动与政治隔离开，以有效提升形象，毕竟存在着政治利益凌驾于更广泛公共利益之上的危险。

此外，还有必要在地方预算中分配由城市形象宣传和上述经营结构的运营成本决定的公共支出。对于城市来说，保持有效维持和提升城市形象的体制和财政能力非常重要，所以重要的是在当地社区一级采用基于项目的多年预算，并通过预算、目标和成本对管理活动进行协调以适应管理和财务工具。该项活动的财政资源应来源于在城市开展的经济活动所征收的税款，前面提到，公共和私营部门之间的伙伴关系是确保城市经营效率的最重要因素之一。

城市形象的创建和管理是城市经营的关键要素。城市形象是公民与地方政府关系的决定性因素，是界定城市环境的因素相互作用的产物。城市形象的战略管理意味着分析哪些因素决定了城市形象，城市形象如何量化，城市形象的形成过程，城市形象是如何传达的，以及如何纠正负面形象。

进行市场分析很重要也很必要，因为可以收集和评估有关城市发展演变的相关数据，评估目标市场的潜力和需求，并与其他城市进行交流，最大限度地利用发展机会，与国际组织建立有效的伙伴关系，并对竞争对手进行评估。接下来是内部环境分析，需要根据公民、经济主体、游客、非政府组织和公共组织的利益来设想城市，还需要确定相关目标市场的处境，分析公民与政府之间的关系，并对公私伙伴关系进行评估。

发现并确认市场细分体系是一个涉及内部和外部市场的重要过程，利用特定的细分标准来对内部目标市场进行细分以确定内部市场及其最佳定位。尽管城市产品和服务的营销方式可能不同，并且对不同的细分市场的吸引力也不同，但可以同时提供给不同的目标人群，这些人群因收入水平、态度和消费模式的不同而不同。外部市场细分使用为内部市场制定的标准，细分一旦确定，对于城市营销专家来说，有助于确定和瞄准外部机构和组织，以提供适当的信息，并与当地发展机构和公共机构建立联系，以建立潜在的伙伴关系。城市需要通过考虑互动和伙伴关系对城市地区及其环境的正面或负面影响来评估潜在的目标市场。

城市必须根据城市地区的独有特质制定一套宣传方案，包括愿景、战略、宣传技巧和时间框架，在考虑并选择了最合适的宣传城市形象的方法后，便可组合宣传包。这一过程考虑并突出了城市形象的独特属性，这些属性被城市经营专家用来在目标市场中创造具有吸引力和竞争力的形象，接下来的促销方案包括将在目标市场中最佳定位该形象的具体行动和实施计划、对计划的具体行动的说明、建立灵活的备选方案和适应性强的行动规划。城市经营专家根据特定城市环境的独特优势和劣势制订灵活的行动计划，强调优势，淡化劣势。

建立城市经营政策对城市发展影响的反馈、控制和评估程序的阶段非常重要，因为它提供了城市营销政策结果的清晰形象。该规划各部分的结果将根据其对经济发展和城市竞争力的影响进行评估，同时，也会凸显限制城市发展努力的障碍和壁垒，因为可能有多种因素制约了营销计划的有效性。地方行政机构可能很薄弱，没有足够的权力，不能在没有足够资源的情况下有效地承担责任。内部市场可能已经形成，其价格不能反映实际的社会和环境成本。动机可能是不成熟或不充分的，进展和成功只以短期经济增长而不是长期生活质量来衡量。

信息技术的空前发展和技术创新带来的变化也深刻影响了居民的生活方式、城市的运作方式以及公民和居民对城市的认同。地方化和全球化的双重影响意味着城市需要最大限度地利用当地城市经济参与与全球经济和全球发展相联系的发展。城市可以利用前所未有的知识和新技术，推进创新这一进程。通过创新，城市可以提高其竞争力，发展成为更有吸引力的地方，同时最大限度地利用其为居民、本地和全球市场提供服务。

10.3.2 过程总结

城市经营分析需要维系利益相关者、消费者和市场之间的关系，城市通过内部城市经营发展利益相关者之间的互惠关系，同时试图通过外部经营与城市地区以外的主体建立关系。无论哪种情况，其目标都是通过利用城市的独有特征，识别出最渴望这些特征的人，并以最具吸引力的方式向各个感兴趣的细分市场展示这些特征，从而提高社区的价值和吸引力。

城市经营已成为城市经济发展战略的重要组成部分。这是一个以市场为导向的过程，包括将城市包装成商品，并将其作为产品进行营销。为了城市及其居民的利益，这一过程涉及制定一项长期营销战略，以保护和发展当地城市地区的自然、经济和开发潜力。在快速变化的市场环境下，旧的促进地方发展的战略不再有效，城市需要从市场营销的角度制定地方发展战略，才能更具竞争力。由于社区同产品一样被商品化和营销，营销工具被应用于社区的问题以提升其发展潜力，从而创建一个基于独特身份的独特形象支持的品牌。

在当前全球化的国际竞争环境中，城市面临的条件与在不确定的竞争环境中运作的私营企业面临同样的境遇，这意味着城市具备了维持城市经营的初始条件，并将其作为地方发展和提高城市竞争力的有效工具，经营随后成为整个城市战略规划过程的一部分。

10.4　城市经营策略

城市经营有助于城市的总体战略愿景的实现，因此成为城市经济发展的必要组成部分。城市经营还可以帮助城市实现许多目标，如吸引新公司、巩固工业基础设施、发展旅游业和改善交通，因此有必要保持一定的营销水平，否则可能不得不削减公共开支。城市经营面临的最大挑战是市场和竞争结构的变化，这些变化往往超出了城市面对吸引新投资者的激烈竞争时的应对能力。因此，城市经营已成为一项极其重要的经济活动，在某些情况下，营销已成为当地福利的来源，特别是在吸引访客和游客方面。经营不仅是营销技巧的技术问题，也是一个概念问题，即根据公众的价值观来设想和定义特定地区的城市发展（Stanciulescu，2009）。

有效的城市经济发展意味着一项长期的经营战略，旨在保护和开发城市的潜力。斯坦福研究所建议将不同的因素结合起来，通过城市经营对城市发展做出总体展望，其中包括通过生活质量、正面形象和正面经营、经济发展能力和基础设施这四个社区因素以及技术可获得性、人力资源和资金可用性这三个有吸引力的经济因素用于评估。

10.4.1 经营策略：宣传和广告

与企业相比，城市用于宣传的预算通常很少，但通常会采用非常复杂的方法弥补这一点。城市宣传活动通常由当地规划和经济发展机构以及旅游业官员而不是由国家认可的专业广告机构在当地发起，当地城市官员会通过各种主题来创造独特的地方感。

经营策略中用来强调城市独特性的策略数量有限，一种常见的方法是强调信息传递过程中的变化，地方推广的一个非常常见的主题是运动，特别是向上和向前的运动，这意味着走向更美好的未来。"更美好的明天""塑造未来""向前迈进"是典型的主题，"更新"和"复兴"是同一主题的另外表达。这一信息可以与强调历史或传统文化的主题相结合，或与文化和历史相关，通常强调地理位置的优势，主要是商业优势。城市地区可以突出其作为通往重要区域市场的门户，靠近资源或与交通网络相连。此外，城市地区也可以突出其作为一个地区的中心、"国家的中心"、国际中心或枢纽的战略地位。

10.4.2 基于事件的策略：节日和城市景观

城市和城市地区经常举办特别的活动，这些节日和盛会可能会持续很长时间，规模也很大，作为城市宣传的一种方式，这些大型的景观和活动备受追捧，包括奥运会和世界杯等大型体育赛事，这些赛事每隔几年定期举办一次，持续几周，还有可能持续数月的世界博览会和展览，可能会产生永久性的设施。也包括在区域、国家或国际舞台上宣传主办城市重要象征和文化资源的影响的壮观场面及仪式，这类城市节日的传播现在也包括许多不同类型的活动。

节日的形式

节日可以按照不同的维度进行分类。一个维度是大众参与节日创作。节日可以是当地传统和习俗的自然产物，当地居民只是邀请外来游客作为客人，也可能是外部团体创设的某一事件，由该团体决定事件的形态和形式。另一个维度是，事件是周期性的或者一次性的，周期性事件和单一事件涉及考虑的因素有很大区别，单一事件只需要一次成功，而周期性事件可能会随时间而发生变化，但有更多的时间完善活动并接收持续的反馈。历史事件是另一个维度，即一个景观是长期的历史发展过程中形成的还是新近才出现的。世界杯代表着一个特定城市的一次赛事，但一旦成功举办，"夺冠公式"会被很好地确立和默认，另外，在城市中新创设的本地活动可能需要一段时间才能产生成功的影响。区分节日的下一个维度是它是面向普通大众还是特定群体，一个小的、有责任感且热情的团体可以通过无私的奉献和热情来支持一个节日，无论是资金方面还是通过作为志愿者的努力。针对大众的活动可能需要更多的外部支持，尤其是在其创设期间。最后，问题强调的重点。节日是社区庆祝活动、社区表达，节日的焦点是否落在更具工具性的目标，包括吸引游客或获得更高级别的政府支持以改善基础设施？

从这些特殊事件的特点出发，舒斯特将其分为六种不同的一般类型。第一类是奇观。奥运会和大型博览会就是最好的例子，这些都是大规模的活动，代表了阶段性成果。第二类是仪式。塞维利亚的圣周游行就是一个例子，该仪式是一个周期性事件，有着悠久的历史传统，不是由表演者或参与者创造的，而是由过去事件的模式决定的。第三类是艺术节目。这是一个基于媒体或表演艺术的活动，苏格兰的爱丁堡音乐节就是这样一个例子。无论是在节目中单独活动的数量还是出席人数上，艺术活动的规模可能都很大。然而，艺术节目通常不具有壮观场景中的戏剧性的中心事件特征，游客和当地参与者的社交范围有限。第四类是商展。如夏纳、上海国际电影节以及法兰克福书展等文化活动。第五类是大众的活动，有风筝、气球和棋盘游戏等参与性的活动。第六类是受欢迎的市民节日。这些受欢迎的节日主要是作为发展公民社会和促进社会凝聚力的一种方式，如游行和街头表演，社区中的任何人都可以自由参加。

举办任何节日都可能带来高风险，大型景观费用高昂，尤其是需要大型新的物质基础设施时，如体育场馆、展览空间、会议空间和新的交通线路的建设。与节日相关的风险不仅与引人注目的场面有关，风险不仅是财务方面的，更可能是面临失败的风险——投入在演出上的资源可能无法产生预期的效果。也可能是经济回报，但同样重要或甚至更重要的可能是活动的总体出席率、观众人数、媒体形象的提升或社区参与度。

10.4.3　景观策略：城市设计与场所经营

城市设计和场所经营涉及全新城市景观的创造，可能涉及对世界各地公认的独特的高知名度建筑的昂贵投资，世界著名的超级巨星建筑师会被招募来实现这一目标。他们出于文化用途来设计建筑，如博物馆、美术馆和歌剧院，作为高级娱乐和消费中心。现在的重点是调整城市以适应在金融、保险和房地产等高端服务产业工作的高收入人员的生活方式的偏好。此外，独特的设计和场所营销还包括机场、桥梁、通信塔以及高层办公楼的建设，尤其是争夺世界最高建筑称号的超高层建筑，它们是通过先进设计创造的独特的地标，也是全球城市的标志，由塞萨尔·佩利设计的吉隆坡双子塔（2004 年以前世界上最高的建筑）就是一个很好的例子。尽管它作为世界上最高的建筑的时间注定是短暂的——只有七年之久——但它仍是独特而著名的。

这一过程不仅需要局限于特定的建筑物和遗迹，还可以扩展到特定社区和地区的定义标签新包装。国际上，这也可能包括从唐人街（如纽约或世界其他许多主要城市）到洛杉矶珠宝区或士绅化的城中村。北京有几个有趣的街区，比如 798 艺术区的艺术文化区、王府井街的高档购物和娱乐场所，等等。这是一个城市景观主题化的过程，这个现代主题也包括 24 小时的不夜城。

10.4.4　经营取得成功的因素

城市经营的成功因素可以解释一些城市政府如何利用专业化的营销工具成功实施经济发展战略，城市政府通过城市经营实践识别问题并解决问题的能力，有八个成功因素决定了城市经营过程的结果。

规划团队

规划团队是负责规划和执行城市政府内特定城市经营流程的小组或机构，在不同的国家和地区有所不同。在美国，该团体由公共和私营部门的代表组成，而欧洲则是具有地方和地区权威的公共机构的代表。规划团队可由外部顾问和/或当地经济服务机构的代表以及提供支持的当地企业和行业代表组成。

愿景和战略分析

城市经营过程中的愿景是对城市未来在市场中所处位置的预测，战略分析需要详细考量相关战略要素的信息。与私营公司相比，为社区实施市场战略规划更为困难。如果社区没有将不同的利益群体纳入共同的城市经营愿景和战略，战略规划就不会成功。

城市形象与特征

城市的形象和特征是有助于城市品牌塑造的重要要素。如果不建立战略层面的城市形象，就不可能成功塑造城市形象。城市特征是通过其形象和特色投射出来的希望被感知的方式，是城市选择出来的代表其基本元素的一组独特的关系，城市形象是区别于其他城市的特征的总和。特征和形象是城市经营过程中规划的结果。城市特征是由城市系统的每一个要素相互作用产生的，特征被视为所有要素合体呈现出来的单一形象。

公私合作

公私合作意味着两个部门的代表之间的合作进程，经常被认为是城市面临的新变化需要决定的必要性。比较美国和欧洲的城市经营实践，这种合作关系的历史和经验在美国要漫长和丰富得多，欧洲的做法通常不让当地商业行为主体参与城市一级的规划过程。然而，未来的城市经营实践应努力让这些伙伴关系在城市领导层不同要素之间的关系中更有效率。

政治共识

政治共识是城市公共事务管理中政治行为体之间达成的协议，这一成功因素表明了政治作为城市营销因素的重要性。市政一级的利益冲突可能会限制城市经营，从而限制城市发展所做的努力。当这些利益达成一致时，战略规划过程会更加顺利。单一的决策体系也是促成政治共识的一个重要因素，城市经营决策过程不应划分为过多部分以达成共识。

全球化和本土化

地方发展需要将地方市场与全球市场结合在一起加以考虑，城市发展的两个方面本土化和全球化密切相关。作为一个术语，全球化意味着城市必须参与国际竞争，以吸引人才、获取资源并进入市场。另外，本土化发展表明，地方城市管理部门必须重视地方城市发展，使其成为全球市场的有力竞争者。

偶然事件

偶然或幸运的事件可能在城市营销过程中发挥积极作用因而同样值得关注。这些事件不会频繁发生，但会影响市政绩效，有时会影响投资决策。关键是，当随机或其他类型的偶然事件发生时，城市营销规划体系需要准备好利用事件带来的机会，许多决策并不总是根据精心构建的营销战略来决定的，而是根据城市无法控制而只能回应的因素所形成的感知来决定的。

领导力

城市经营领导力代表了城市或城市地区协调城市营销复杂过程、制定战略、组织和动员的总体能力。市政当局应在必要时通过领导层的干预，帮助所有利益攸关方参与进来，以便听取和理解每个人的意见。只有这样，才能实现意见发表和可能影响决策的参与的机会（克拉克，2002）。

10.5　关于城市经营的讨论

地方经营并非没有争议，尤其是人们对它的意识形态效应、社会倒退和投机性持批评态度。地方经营的意识形态效应包括对意义和感知的操纵以及选择性关系的建立，即意义是为特定目的而确定的，任何文化斗争都涉及赢家和输家（Parenti，2006）。社会倒退包括通过复杂的社会过程将资源从城市的实际社会和经济问题上转移开。因为缺乏对确保备受瞩目的发展所需的公共支出的真实水平和定位的准确了解，地方经营的投机性成为一个关键性的指控。通过这些批判的观点，政府愿意补贴私人投资而不是其他公共目的这一点受到了或含蓄或明确的批评。

【思考题】

1. 哈维列出的城市经营的四个基本选择是什么？
2. 城市经营思想的背景是什么？
3. 古典自由主义和平等主义自由主义的相似之处和不同之处。

【关键术语】

古典自由主义	新企业家精神
民主方法	新管理主义
景观策略	场所/空间经营
市场路径	促销套餐
市场细分	促销策略

参考文献

［1］ Clark, G. (2002). *Emerging Local Economic Development Lessons from Cities in the Developed World, and their Applicability to Cities in Developing and Transitioning Countries.* World Bank Urban Forum.

［2］ Cochrane, Allan (2007). *Understanding Urban Policy: A Critical approach.* Oxford: Blackwell.

［3］ Hackworth, J. (2007). *The Neoliberal City: Governance, Ideology and Development in American Urbanism.* Ithaca NY: Cornell University Press.

［4］ Hambleton, R. and Hoggett, P. (1998). "Consumers, Customers and Citizens-The Accountability Agenda in the Modernization of Public Services." Paper to the British-German workshop on 'Public sector modernization in the UK and Germany,' Berlin.

［5］ Harvey, David (1989a). "From Managerialism to Entrepreneurialism: The Transformation of Governance in Late Capitalism." *Geografiska Annaler*, 71B, 3 – 17.

［6］ Harvey, David (1989b). *The Urban Experience.* Oxford: Basil Blackwell.

［7］ Hirschman, Albert O. (1970). *Exit, Voice, and Loyalty: Responses to Decline in Firms, Organizations, and States.* Cambridge, MA: Harvard University Press.

［8］ Kotler, P. and Gertner, D. (2002). "Leveraging Export Brands through a Tourism Destination Brand." *Journal of Brand Management*, 9 (4 – 5): 249 – 261.

［9］ Kotler, P., Hamlin, M. A., Rein, I. and Haider, D. H. (2002). *Marketing Asian Places.* Hoboken, NJ: John Wiley & Sons.

［10］ Parenti, Michael (2006). *The Culture Struggle.* New York: Seven Stories Press.

［11］ Stanciulescu, Gabriela Cecilia (2009). "The Role of Urban Marketing in the Local Economic Development." *Theoretical Researches in Urban Management*, 1 (10): 114 – 135.

Chapter 10　Urban Marketing

10. 1　Definition

Marketing is a concept that comes from the world of business. It is how goods and services are designed or presented to correspond to the needs or desires of consumers. Urban marketing is a version of the same process applied to cities. As such it suggests choosing ways of projecting and organizing cities to meet the requirements of different concerned groups interested in urban development. Urban marketing has met its ultimate goal when citizens and the business community (and any other concerned groups or target segments) are satisfied with the socio-economic environment in the city and when the expectations of visitors and investors are achieved (Kotler, Hamlin, Rein and Haider, 2002). Urban marketing has become a major part of local economic development strategy. Economic development requires creating a long-term marketing strategy to preserve and develop the potential of the local community. Urban marketing is part of a competitive market process of increasing competition among urban areas. This competition is fought over attracting investment and human capital. This competition that serves as the constant backdrop to urban marketing is marked by frequent economic, political, and social changes.

Urban marketing is also used to accomplish several additional objectives. These include creating a positive image for the community, attracting new and relocating businesses and other institutions, and attracting tourists and a skilled work force. On top of that, the positive image needs to help find markets for the area's exports and to create a unique urban brand for the area (Kotler and Gertner, 2002). Ongoing rapid change at an unrelenting pace means that traditional ways of promoting urban communities no longer work as well as in the past. Urban areas need to complement local development strategies with a marketing perspective. As a result, cities produce goods and services desired by residents, local employers and investors, and by potential national and international visitors.

Urban marketing is especially popular in the USA, amounts to an industry of several billion dollars worldwide, with urban goods and services promoted in an aggressive way. Urban areas use urban marketing to create a positive new image or to overcome a negative old one. Urban communities use marketing for promotion in the same ways that private businesses do. Marketing is adapted to the needs of urban communities to promote development by creating a unique urban brand based on the identity of the area. Urban marketing then uses this urban brand to promote the area among targeted market segments. This is done through the creation and promotion and shaping of an urban image for the city that contributes to the desired forms of urban development. Urban marketing represents activities aimed at attracting target markets with the hope of providing potential benefits for the community. The main objective of urban marketing is creating a strong relation between public policies and consumer requirements to make the functioning of urban systems more efficient.

10. 2　Ideology

Urban marketing developed over decades based on developments in PR and advertising and in how government is viewed by citizens. The view of government bureaucracies as not responsive to citizens picked up speed in the 1970s in the US and the UK where bureaucracies were often seen as dominating the people they served in a more of a professional-client relationship than a citizen-civil service one. This view led to three ways of looking at the relationship between the bureaucracy and citizens. These three ways of looking at the bureaucracy that appeared in the 1980s were extending markets, extending democracy, and the new managerialism.

The market approach used the market principle of free agreements and offered the choice of exit as an empowerment strategy and saw those served by the bureaucracy more as consumers. Those served would be able to choose not to participate in a market transaction. The democratic approach empowered people through voice by treating them as citizens with a say in how programs are run. Empowered citizens would be able to complain and would have the right to expect that government would listen to them (Hirschman, 1970). The new managerialism offered self-improvement, where the relationship between citizens and the bureaucracy would be like that of customer seeking a service when dealing with a bureaucratic organization. These three views are added to the view of bureaucracy as unresponsive, with four possible relationships: client, consumer, citizen, or customer (Hambleton and Hoggett, 1998).

Managerialism had three main traits. It emphasized allocation of state surpluses instead of attracting of private investment. In contrast to the classical liberal model the bureaucracy was still the main provider of services even though it was a move away from a professional-client relationship. Managerialism also featured a social welfare ideology that was not close to the market values of competition or wealth creation.

Classical liberals focused intently on the role of individuals in social and economic thought. The highest virtue of society is the degree to which individuals can pursue pleasure or their self-interest. Individuals are the most qualified at understanding their needs and wants. Society should be structured around lowering boundaries to realizing individual's ability to seek pleasure or self-interest. The unrestrained market is the most efficient and effective means of encouraging and developing individual autonomy. The simultaneous pursuit of individual pleasure would not devolve into chaos or debauchery. The role of the state should be limited and non-interventionist. The most effective way to achieve individual autonomy or a pleasure and interest-seeking society is for the government to be minimalist, or laissez faire.

The core of egalitarian liberalism continued to be autonomy but the autonomous life required both freedom and the right to a basic level of welfare, with individuals guaranteed a basic level of goods (public housing, food stamps, and basic income redistribution) in order to enjoy their freedom and autonomy. Government should protect not only freedoms, but also provide for a basic level of welfare rights. This view was widespread, but classical liberals such as Hayek and Friedman rejected egalitarian liberalism as not being liberal at all because it departed from what they saw as the progressive core of liberalism: the focus on markets and the opportunities for free pursuit of pleasure within them (Hackworth, 2007).

While both liberalisms would allow for government action based on market failure, the classical liberals rarely saw markets failing and would simply view "failure" as the optimal working of the market. Egalitarian liberals, on the other hand crafted a much more expansive view of market failure that included the idea that markets were not self-regulating, that markets could produce imperfect competition that would end up being destructive and even self-destructive when not regulated by government. The Keynesian egalitarian liberals argued for government maintenance of effective demand to keep the economy moving but also to justify redistribution to allow for individuals to participate in society and exercise their freedoms. In the urban context but also nationally, the egalitarians looked to the promotion of minimally-acceptable community-based standards as a justification for intervention. Not only could markets be altered when they failed, they could also be altered when they failed to produce the desired outcomes such as good housing, good workplace conditions, and quality healthcare. At the city level, the kinds of regulations and interventions pursued included Euclidean zoning, the property tax, building codes, and local implementation of national programs (Hackworth, 2007).

The neoliberals rejected the egalitarian liberal approach and called for a modified return to classical liberalism. While some, like Hayek and Friedman saw the state in limiting freedoms anywhere as leading to potential disasters for personal liberty, most neoliberals have been content to scale back the role of the state in regulating the market. Neoliberalism is rooted in the fidelity to the individual, to the unrestrained market, and to the noninterventionist state. Government failure includes ideas like inefficiencies, inequities, and corruptions. Even where it may be able to serve some role, it will do more damage than good through its inefficient, unfair, and corrupt actions to tie up the market. The idea is that any useful role played by government is more than offset by its effect in retarding competitiveness through limits on capital and labor flows, for example. At the local level, government failure has been used as the ideology of rolling back government intervention in favor of government helping out, collaborating with, or functioning like its corporate partners (Hackworth, 2007).

This has facilitated the move away from the new managerialism to the new entrepreneurialism (Harvey, 1989a). The local government is no longer responsible for the management of the urban area in the context of state planning. Instead the local city government is now an actor that competes as an entrepreneur or as an entrepreneurial supporter to achieve success in the marketplace. Managerialism undermined the competitiveness of employers. Instead, economic policy at the local level should be oriented towards stimulating economic development. The prosperity of cities depends on effective competitiveness for jobs, investment, and the industry that would provide it (Cochrane, 2007). Private initiative is the answer to the city's social and economic problems. The state is an institutional barrier to the realization of this initiative that is to be minimised except where it may help facilitate and assist private initiative. Social welfare may only be delivered through the medium of economic success. The role urban policy is therefore to assist the creation of wealth and emphasis is placed on the recreation of the market in the urban area.

Harvey (1989b) provides four basic urban entrepreneurialism options. First, cities may try to achieve a competitive advantage through production. This may happen through investing in new production technologies or in social or physical infrastructure. Second, the city may compete for consumption expenditures. Urban areas do this through creating zones and districts for upscale shopping, entertainment, and culture. It may also do this through encouraging gentrification to attract affluent residents. Third, cities may compete for important financial and government centers. For example, airports or support services may be constructed that then add to agglomerative economies. Finally, cities can try to compete for state funds. This may include competition for national and international funds.

Urban entrepreneurialism evolved through the end of expanding state expenditures on welfare spending and social consumption that had been known as the social democratic/social welfare order. This represents the neoliberal rejection of the egalitarian liberal state and egalitarian participation made possible through the setting of minimal social standards to be provided for by society. In the urban sphere, this entrepreneurialism emerged specifically in response to fiscal stress and the response to fiscal stress of cutback management. This emergence of entrepreneurialism following the end of managerialism was based on a desire for new sources of economic development.

10.3　The Urban Marketing Process

10.3.1　Implementing Urban Marketing

There are several conditions for implementing an urban marketing plan. The first is accepting the role of community forces internal to the city in the process of urban marketing. Cities have to adopt new strategic methods and plans to maintain or intensify competitive advantages. Urban marketing is a strategic instrument that helps cities to achieve their development goals. A second condition is the establishment of a strategic vision and implies formulating an answer to the important question of how residents and businesspeople want their community evaluated. Identifying a vision is the first step previous establishing development objectives. The next condition is the partnership between local urban public authorities, residents, and the business community. This partnership must be advanced and realized in the pursuit of common interests. Any cooperative marketing development of the city must draw the attention of all local actors, regardless of the interests they represent. A cooperative relationship between different sectors must be sustained to implement the market-oriented strategy.

A special public institution that serves as the symbol of urban marketing or as a focal point for promoting the city can be very helpful. This institution needs to function in a market-friendly way that is similar to the functioning of a private environment. It must be public because the processes of urban marketing are under the municipality's control. This is a complex activity in many cases. The municipality must take the central role since urban marketing consists of the city image and identity even when urban marketing actions are associated with industry and technology in the private sector. The municipality must guarantee to insulate the activity of this institution from politics to promote the image efficiently as there is the danger of political interest prevailing over the broader public interest.

It is also necessary to allocate public expenses determined by the promotion of the city image and the operational costs of the aforementioned marketing structure in the local budget. It is very important for the city to hold the institutional and financial capacity to sustain and promote the city image efficiently. It is important to adopt multiyear budgets based on projects at the most local community level as coordinated with the utilization of management through budgets, objectives, and costs to adapt managerial and financial tools. The financial resources granted to this activity should originate from taxes charged on economic activities carried out in the city. It was previously mentioned that the partnership between the public and private sectors is one of the most important elements for ensuring the efficiency of urban marketing.

The creation and management of the city image is a key element of this process. The image of the city is a determining element of citizen-municipal relations, as it is the product of the interaction of elements that define the urban environment. Strategic management of city image implies the analysis of which factors determine the city image, how the city image can be quantified, the process how the city image is created, how the city image can be conveyed, and how a negative image can be corrected.

It is important to develop a market analysis. It is necessary because it allows for collecting and assessing data concerning the evolution of urban development, assessing the potential and needs of target markets, effecting exchanges with other cities, bringing about the best utilization of development opportunities, realizing an efficient partnership with international organizations, and conducting an assessment of competitors. The internal environment analysis is next. It is necessary because it allows envisioning the city according to the interests of citizens, economic agents, visitors, non- governmental organizations and public authorities. It further permits identifying the position concerning target markets, an analysis of the relationship between citizens and public authorities, and an evaluation of the public-private partnership.

Identifying and determining a system of market segmentation is an important process that involves the internal and the external markets. Segmentation of the internal target market makes use of specific segmentation criteria to identify internal markets and the best positioning regarding them. Although they may be marketed differently and may have different appeal to different segments, urban products and services are offered simultaneously to various target segments that are distinguished by different income levels, different attitudes, and different consumption patterns. Segmentation of external markets uses the criteria established for internal markets. Segmentation, once determined, is useful for urban marketing specialists in identifying and targeting external institutions and organizations for appropriate messaging, and for linking to local development agencies and public institutions for potential partnerships. The city needs to assess potential target markets by taking into account the impact, whether positive or negative, that interaction and partnership will have on the urban area and its environment.

The city must create a promotional package that includes the vision, a strategy, promotional techniques, and a time frame according to the unique characteristics of the urban area. The promotional package is assembled after considering and choosing the most appropriate methods for promoting the city image. This process considers and highlights the distinguishing attributes of the city image. These attributes are used by urban marketing specialists to create an attractive and competitive image in target markets. The promotional package next includes the specific actions and implementation plans that will best position that image in the target market. This involves stating the specific actions that make up the plan, establishing flexible alternatives, and adaptable action plans. Urban marketing specialists create flexible action plans that are based on the unique distinguishing strengths and weaknesses of the specific urban environment, emphasizing the strengths, and playing down the weaknesses.

The phase of establishing feedback, control, and assessment procedures of the impact of urban marketing policies on the development of the city is fundamental because it provides a clear image of the result of urban marketing policies. The results of each part of the plan are evaluated relative to the impact they have on economic development and city competitiveness. At the same time, the obstacles and barriers that limit the efforts for urban development are also highlighted. There may be a variety of factors that limit the effectiveness of a marketing plan. Local administration may be weak and may not have enough authority, effectively having responsibility without adequate resources. Internal markets may have been created that do not have that reflect actual costs, including the social and environment costs. Motives may be immature or incomplete, with progress and success measured solely in terms of short-term economic growth instead of long-term quality of life.

The unprecedented rapid development of informational technology and the changes caused by technological innovation also profoundly affect residents, the way they live, and the way the city functions and how citizens and residents identify themselves with their city. The twin effects of the local and the global mean that cities must maximize the way the local urban economy is involved in development that links to the global economy and global developments. Cities may take advantage of the unprecedented volume of knowledge and new technologies that can help the process of innovation. Through this innovation, cities may improve their competitive attributes and grow into more attractive places while taking best advantage of what they have to offer their residents, and the local and global markets.

10. 3. 2　Summary of the Process

Urban marketing analyzes the stakeholders, the consumers and markets that need to be maintained. Cities develop mutually beneficial relations among stakeholders through internal urban marketing while trying to establish relationships with actors outside of the urban area through external marketing. The goal in either case is increasing the value and attractiveness of the community by making use of the city's distinctive attributes, identifying those who most desire those traits, and presenting the traits in the most attractive way for the various interested market segments.

Urban marketing has become an important component of urban economic development strategy. This is a market-oriented process that involves packaging the city as a commodity and marketing it like a product. For the benefit of the city and its residents, the process involves establishing a long-term marketing strategy oriented towards the preservation and development of the natural, economic, and developed potential of the local urban community. The old strategies of promoting localities are no longer as effective in the context of rapidly-changing markets. Urban communities need to ground local development strategies from the marketing perspective to be competitive. As the community is commodified and marketed like any product, marketing instruments are adapted to the problems of the community to promote their potential for development to create a brand backed by a unique image based on a unique identity.

In the current globalized environment of international competition, the conditions facing urban municipalities are similar to those facing private businesses that are acting in the unstable competitive environment. This means the municipality has the preliminary conditions for sustaining urban marketing as an efficient tool for local development and for an increased urban competitiveness. Marketing then becomes part of the strategic planning process for the whole city.

10. 4　Strategies

Urban marketing contributes to the overall strategic vision for a city and is thus a necessary part of the economic development of the city. It also helps cities achieve many objectives such as attracting new companies, consolidating industrial infrastructure, developing tourism, and improving transportation. It is necessary to maintain a certain level of marketing or face the possibility of having to cut off public expenses. The biggest challenges for urban marketing are changes in market and competitive structure. These changes have often exceeded the ability of cities to respond in the face of harsh competition over attracting new investors. Urban marketing has become an extremely important economic activity as a result. In some cases, marketing has become a source of local welfare, particularly in attracting tourists and other visitors. Marketing is not only a technical problem of marketing technique but also a conceptual problem of envisioning and defining urban development in a particular area in terms of the values of the public (Stanciulescu, 2009).

Effective urban economic development suggests a long-term marketing strategy oriented towards preserving and developing the potential of the city. The Stanford Research Institute recommends combining different factors to produce a general outlook on city development through urban marketing. These include attractiveness as evaluated through the four community factors of quality of life, positive image and positive marketing, economic development capacity, and infrastructure as well as the three economic factors of accessible technology, human resources, and availability of finance capital.

10. 4. 1 Promotional Strategies: Publicity and Advertising

Cities usually have publicity budgets that are quite small compared to corporations but they make up for this by following a very sophisticated approach. Urban publicity campaigns are usually created locally by local planning and economic development agencies and tourism officials rather than by professional advertising agencies that are nationally-recognized. Local urban officials employ a variety of themes to promote a unique sense of place.

Promotional strategies produce a limited number of strategies that cities use to stress their uniqueness. One common method involves an emphasis on change in the message being conveyed. A very common theme of place promotion is movement, particularly movement up and ahead, suggesting movement into a better future. "A better tomorrow", "shaping the future" and "moving forward" would be typical themes. "Renaissance" and "renewal" are other common themes in the same vein. This message may be combined with traditional themes that stress history or traditional culture or references to culture and history. Advantages of location, primarily for business, are often stressed. An urban area may be emphasized as a gateway to important regional markets, as close to resources, or as connected to transportation networks. In addition, the urban area is stressed as the center of a region, "at the center of the nation," or as an international center or hub.

10. 4. 2 Event-Based Strategies: Festivals and Urban Spectacle

Cities and urban areas often host specially-constructed events. These festivals and spectacles may take place over a long time and may be on a grand scale. These large-scale spectacles and events are highly sought-after as a method of publicizing a city. These events range from massive sporting events like the Olympics and the World Cup that are put on regular intervals every few years for a couple of weeks to world fairs and exhibitions that may last for months and may spawn facilities that are permanent. These include spectacles and ritualized ceremonies that convey important symbolism and manipulate cultural resources to advertise and promote the host city on a regional, national, or international stage. The spread of these kinds of urban festivals now includes many different types of events.

Forms of Festivals

Festivals may be classified along different dimensions. The first dimension is the level of popular participation in the creation of the festival. It is possible the festival is a natural outgrowth of local traditions and practices where residents are simply inviting in outside visitors as guests. An alternate possibility is that there is a decision by an outside group to locate the event and that that group also determines its shape and form. Another dimension is whether the event is cyclical or just a one-time occurrence. Cyclical and single events involve very different considerations. The single event needs to be successful one time while cyclical events may vary over time but have more time to establish themselves and receive ongoing feedback. The history of an event is another dimension, that is, whether a spectacle is long-established or only recently established. The World Cup represents a one-time event in a particular city but it is well-established and therefore the formula for success is much better established and understood. On the other hand, a local event that is newly created in a city may take some time before it makes a successful impact. The next dimension that distinguishes a festival is whether it is orientated to a general mass audience or to a selective group. A small, committed and motivated group may support a festival through dedication and enthusiasm, whether monetarily or through volunteer efforts. An event aiming for a mass audience will likely require more outside support, particularly while it is being established. Finally, there is the question of emphasis. Does the event focus on community celebration and community expression or does the focus of the festival fall on more instrumental goals that may include attracting visitors or getting higher-level government support for improving infrastructure?

Starting from these characteristics of special events Schuster has divided events into six different general types. The first is the spectacle. The Olympic Games and large expositions are prime examples. These take place on a large scale and represent staged productions. The second type is the ritual. An example would be the holy week processions in Seville. Rituals are cyclical events that come from long-established traditions. They are not created by the performers or participants, but the elements are dictated by the pattern of past events. The third type is the artistic program. This is an event based on the media or the performing arts. The Edinburgh Festival in Scotland is an example. The artistic event may take place on a large in scale, whether in terms of the number of separate events on the program or in the number of attendees. Artistic programs do not usually have the dramatic central event characteristic of a spectacle, however, and there is a limited social range of visitors and local participants. The fourth type is the trade fair. This includes cultural examples like the Cannes and Shanghai International Film Festivals, as well as the Frankfurt Book Fair. The fifth type is the popular fair with participatory activities such as kite flying, ballooning, and board games. The final type is the popular citizen festival. These popular festivals primarily as a way of developing civil society and promoting social cohesion, such as processions and street performances, where anyone in the community feels free to participate.

Putting on any festival may be associated with high levels of risk. Major spectacles are very costly, especially when they require major new physical infrastructure such as sports stadiums, exhibition spaces, convention spaces, and new transportation connections. The risks associated with festivals are not only related to high-profile spectacles. Further, the risks are not just financial, either, but more likely is the risk of failure. The resources invested in putting on a show may fail to produce the expected result. This may be the financial return, but equally or even more important may be the overall attendance of the event, the number of visitors, enhanced media profile, or community participation.

10. 4. 3　Landscape Strategies: Urban Design and Place Marketing

Urban design and place marketing involve the creation of whole new urban landscapes. This may involve expensive investments in distinctive high-profile buildings that are recognized around the world. World-renowned superstar architects are recruited to achieve this. They design buildings for high culture uses such as for museums, art galleries, and opera houses that serve as high-class centers of pleasure and consumption. An emphasis is now placed on adjusting cities to the lifestyle preferences of higher-income employees who work in high-end "service" industries like finance, insurance, and real estate. In addition, distinctive design and place marketing also includes construction of airports, bridges, and communication towers, as well as high-rise office towers. This is especially the case with the super tall buildings that compete for the title of the tallest building in the world. These are distinctive markers of place created through advanced design and are the hallmarks of the global city. The Petronas Towers of Kuala Lumpur designed by Cesar Pelli, the world's tallest building from 1998 – 2004 is a case in point. It is distinctive and famous, even though its status as world's tallest was destined to be short-lived, at a mere seven years.

This process does not just need to be limited to particular buildings and monuments, but can be extended in role to the labeling and repacking of particular neighborhoods and districts. Internationally, this may include anything from a Chinatown (as in New York, or many other major cities of the world) to jewelry districts or gentrified urban villages. Beijing has several interesting neighborhoods such as the arts and culture district in 798 ArtDist, the upscale shopping and hangouts in Wangfujing Street, among others. This is a process of theming the urban landscape. This modern theme includes the dawn of the 24-hour city that never sleeps.

10. 4. 4   Marketing Success Factors

Urban marketing success factors explain how some municipalities succeed at implementing economic development strategies, using the instrument specific to this marketing specialization. The ability and capacity of a municipality to identify a problem and solve it through the urban marketing practices is based on success factors. There are eight success factors that determine the outcome of processes specific to urban marketing.

The Planning Group

The planning group is the group or structure that is responsible for planning and execution of processes specific to urban marketing within an urban government. This presents some particular distinctions. In the US, this group is formed by representatives of the public and private sector, whereas the members in European municipalities are representatives of public institutions with local and regional authority. The planning group may be supported by an outside consultant and/or representatives of local economic agencies as well as representatives of local businesses and industries.

Vision and Strategic Analysis

Vision in the urban marketing process represents future projections of the position held by the city within the market. Strategic analysis entails a detailed examination of information about strategic elements. It is more difficult to implement a market strategic plan for a community than it is in the case of private companies. Strategic planning will not succeed in the case of communities where different interests have not been brought to the common urban marketing vision and strategy.

City Image and Identity

The city's image and identity are elements that help form the city's brand. It is impossible to create a city image without establishing a strategic-level urban identity. The identity projects the way it wishes to be perceived through its image and identity. This image represents a unique set of relationships between the basic elements the city chooses to represent it. The city image is the sum of the traits that differentiate it from other cities. Identity and image is the result of planning within urban marketing programs. An urban identity results from the interactions of each element of the urban system and the identity is perceived as a single collective representation of all of the elements together as a single image.

Public-Private Partnerships

Public-private partnerships suggest a process of cooperation between representatives of the two sectors. They are often suggested as a necessity determined by new changes that cities face. These kinds of partnerships have a much longer history and experience in the US when American and European urban marketing practices are compared. European practices have less frequent involvement by local business actors in the planning process at an urban level. However, future urban marketing practices should give work to make these partnerships more efficient in the context of the relationships among the different elements of the urban leadership.

Political Consensus

A political consensus represents an agreement among the political actors in the administration of urban public affairs. This success element suggests the importance of politics as a factor in urban marketing. There are conflicts of interest at the municipal level that can limit urban marketing, and thus urban development efforts. The strategic planning process functions much more smoothly when these interests are agreed upon. A single structure for making decisions is also a factor in contributing to political consensus. The urban marketing decision making process should not be divided into many parts to promote consensus.

The World Market and Local Development

Local development needs to be considered together along with and in the context of the global market. The two perspectives of urban development, local and global, are strongly related. The global market, as a term, suggests that cities must participate in an international competition to attract talent, acquire resources, and gain access to new markets. Local development, on the other hand, demonstrates the importance that local urban administration needs to give to local urban development to be a strong competitor in the global market.

Fortuitous Events

Fortuitous, or lucky, events deserve attention because they may play an active part in the urban marketing process. These do not take place at a high frequency, but can affect municipal performance, sometimes influencing investment decisions. The key point is that, when a random or other kind of fortuitous event occurs, the urban marketing planning structure needs to be ready to take advantage of the opportunity presented by the event. Many decisions are not always determined in response to a well-constructed marketing strategy, but in response to perception as shaped by factors that a city cannot control but can only respond to.

Leadership

Leadership in urban marketing represents the general capacity of the city or urban area to coordinate the complex process of urban marketing, to set strategies, and to organize and mobilize power. Municipalities should help involve all stakeholders, through the intervention of leadership if necessary, so that the viewpoint of everyone can be heard and understood. Only then is there an opportunity for meaningful voice and participation that may affect decisions (Clark, 2002).

10. 5　Issues

Place marketing does not occur without controversy. In particular, it is viewed critically for its ideological effects, socially-regressive consequences, and speculative nature. The ideological effects of place marketing include the manipulation of meanings and perceptions and the creation of a selective relationship. Meanings are determined for specific purposes and any cultural struggle involves both winners and losers (Parenti, 2006). Socially-regressive consequences include diverting resources away from the city's real social and economic problems through a complex social process. The speculative nature of place marketing is a critical allegation due to the lack of exact knowledge of the actual level and location of public spending necessary to secure high-profile developments. The readiness of the state to subsidize private investment instead of other public purposes is implicitly or explicitly criticized through these critical perspectives.

Questions

1. What are the four basic options for urban entrepreneurialism listed by Harvey?
2. What is the ideological background of urban marketing?
3. What are the similarities and differences between classical and egalitarian liberalism?

Key Terms

classical liberals　　　　　　　　　　*new entrepreneurialism*

democratic approach　　　　　　　　　*new managerialism*

landscape strategies　　　　　　　　　*place marketing*

market approach　　　　　　　　　　　*promotional package*

market segmentation　　　　　　　　　*promotional strategies*

References

[1] Clark, G. (2002). *Emerging Local Economic Development Lessons from Cities in the Developed World, and their Applicability to Cities in Developing and Transitioning Countries.* World Bank Urban Forum.

[2] Cochrane, Allan (2007). *Understanding Urban Policy: A Critical approach.* Oxford: Blackwell.

[3] Hackworth, J. (2007). *The Neoliberal City: Governance, Ideology and Development in American Urbanism.* Ithaca NY: Cornell University Press.

[4] Hambleton, R. and Hoggett, P. (1998). "Consumers, Customers and Citizens-The Accountability Agenda in the Modernization of Public Services." Paper to the British-German workshop on 'Public sector modernization in the UK and Germany,' Berlin.

[5] Harvey, David (1989a). "From Managerialism to Entrepreneurialism: The Transformation of Governance in Late Capitalism." *Geografiska Annaler*, 71B, 3 – 17.

[6] Harvey, David (1989b). *The Urban Experience.* Oxford: Basil Blackwell.

[7] Hirschman, Albert O. (1970). *Exit, Voice, and Loyalty: Responses to Decline in Firms, Organizations, and States.* Cambridge, MA: Harvard University Press.

[8] Kotler, P. and Gertner, D. (2002). "Leveraging Export Brands through a Tourism Destination Brand." *Journal of Brand Management*, 9 (4 – 5): 249 – 261.

[9] Kotler, P., Hamlin, M. A., Rein, I. and Haider, D. H. (2002). *Marketing Asian Places.* Hoboken, NJ: John Wiley & Sons.

[10] Parenti, Michael (2006). *The Culture Struggle.* New York: Seven Stories Press.

[11] Stanciulescu, Gabriela Cecilia (2009). "The Role of Urban Marketing in the Local Economic Development." *Theoretical Researches in Urban Management*, 1 (10): 114 – 135.

第 11 章　未来城市管理

11.1　未来城市发展展望

　　未来的城市会是什么样子的？这一直是城市学者感兴趣的话题，也是数百年来吸引无数电影制作人、作家和艺术家的一个话题，因为城市过去常常是艺术、文化和习得的中心，因此成为关于未来的故事和想法的背景也就不足为奇。在未来，城市很可能会继续扮演这些角色，但城市的公民从他们的城市中想要和需要得到的是什么呢？随着城市性质的演变，城市服务将发生怎样的变化？

11.1.1　全球化和城市的角色

　　之前许多城市学者和作家写下了他们对未来城市的愿景。19 世纪末，法国巴黎被认为是文化和高水平的中心。20 世纪初，作家、艺术家和学者都来到光明之城巴黎学习，学习成为其"未来愿景"的一部分。亚当·戈普尼克在 2000 年出版的《巴黎到月球》一书中描述了一位巴黎艺术家在世纪之交画的海报，海报上描绘的火车从巴黎出发，在轨道上行驶，直达夜空，最后到达月球。当然，未来的愿景植根于当下的理念，如果有前往月球的交通工具（正如儒勒·凡尔纳 50 年前所写的），那将是最现代、最舒适的交通工具，驶离地球上最现代、便利的地方，因此，从巴黎到月球的火车会很有意义。

　　然而，在 21 世纪初，城市正在以可见和不可见的方式发生变化。巴黎被伦敦、位于大西洋彼岸的纽约和遥远的东京掩盖。当前是一个全球性城市的时代：城市可以影响其自身边界以外的政治，拥有远远超出其所在国家边界的经济影响力，是文化、信息技术和教育的中心（Hales，King and Mendoza Pena，2010），科技也日益加大了富人和穷人之间的鸿沟。值得注意的是，世界上一些大的城市并不是全球性的领导者，如尼日利亚的拉各斯、孟加拉国的达卡和菲律宾的马尼拉都是世界上较大的城市，在过去 20 年中经历了快速增长，但没有带来随着全球城市的增长而带来的生活水平的逐步提高。占据区域而非中心位置的大城市通常不可能成为全球领导者。

　　马塞尔·卡斯特尔斯（1985）就城市历史以及城市和民族国家在历史上代表着政治表达的竞争形式这一观点进行了大量的研究。他在讨论中世纪城市作为一种政治形式时，认为民族国家不是城邦的逻辑演进：

自由城市……不仅仅是迈向民族国家的一步。它们是一种另类的政治形式，另一种走向现代的社会工程，在技术、政治效力甚至军事力量方面并不一定低劣……事实上，城邦和民族国家并不构成必然的历史序列；它们是极为对立的政治形式，国家与公民社会之间的关系存在着深刻的差异（Castells，1985）。

一些学者认为，全球城市可能会在重要性和影响力上取代民族国家（Sassen，2001），尤其是作为国际经济的驱动力，如果这一切发生，那么未来的城市将与今天的城市大不相同。

11.1.2　技术的作用和智能城市

今天的"技术"通常与"高科技"联系在一起，利用电子、计算机和通信硬件和软件，帮助人们提高工作和娱乐活动的效率和质量。但是，技术具有更广泛的含义，在讨论技术在未来城市建设中的作用时，一般意义的技术可能更有用。技术的一般定义是对技能、艺术或工艺的研究或学习，或如《韦氏词典》所提供的："知识的实际应用，尤其是在特定领域"和"知识的实践应用所赋予的能力"。换言之，技术是指利用知识或信息来实现特定目标。

随着技术变得越来越先进并迅速融入个人的日常生活（想象一下一个没有智能手机的世界，虽然这在 20 年前是很正常的事），技术已成为未来愿景的一个组成部分，尤其是对于城市生活而言——交通技术的进步改变了日本等国的生活方式——新干线改变了人们的生活和工作方式；20 世纪 60 年代的农业绿色革命改变了全球粮食生产和分配的方式；通信技术的进步，以及万维网和互联网的诞生，则彻底改变了人们彼此联系的方式，从住在隔壁的邻居到远隔半个世界的朋友。

城市既受益于科技进步，也为科技进步作出了贡献。"智能城市"的概念在过去 20 年中随着通信技术的发展而发展。"智能城市"通常被理解为居民可以通过多种方式与其他人以及更高级版本的城市本身进行交流的城市。智慧城市的重点是为居民创造一种"无缝体验"，以便他们能够以高效且极具成本效益的方式找到工作和娱乐所需的一切。而这项工作通过使用安装在整个城市的通信技术来实现，要求居民拥有或有权使用一种设备来访问该技术，如无线互联网和手机。城市的角色集中于管理可供居民使用的信息，以及维护（和升级）使信息检索成为可能的基础设施。例如，在一个智能城市，一个居民可能希望从一个社区搬到另一个离工作地点更近的社区，然而，她的工作地点被多个街区包围，这些街区的房价不同，公寓提供的设施也不同。智能城市的居民可以在网上比较可用公寓的信息，包括管理费和每个社区可用学校的信息，而不是去每个社区亲自走访每个可用公寓，这些信息可以使用计算机或可以上网的手机进行检索。

在这个例子中，政府的作用取决于市场已经向居民提供了什么，以及仍然缺些什么。在一些智能城市中，私人公司提供了让"虚拟购物"成为可能的所有组件：互联网接入（通过某种网络技术）；通过互联网提供的信息（不同的房地产公司可以发布带有潜在买家可能需要的各种信息的房源清单）；接收技术，如计算机、平板电脑或手机，可能由私营公司提供。但在另外一些城市，这些技术领域中的一个或多个可能没有足够的市场投资，在这种情况下，市政府可能会直接参与提供一种或多种此类技术，以便居民能够更高效地工作，并利用节省下来的时间从事其他可能对城市有帮助的活动。

智能城市"智能"的关键在于它能够将每个居民与适当的信息联系起来。这不是一项简单的任务，因为居民可能需要许多类型的信息，城市的任务是弄清楚如何对信息进行优先排序，以便及时向提出请求的人提供信息。例如，在夏季，更多的居民可能会要求提供最近的游泳池或提供游泳指导的学校的信息，而一旦秋季天气变冷，此类请求的数量可能会下降。如果城市正在提供信息访问，它可能会预期某些网站的流量会更大，并在特定时间发布某些类型的信息。另一个例子是在选举前几周：居民可能会要求提供更多关于竞选候选人的信息、投票地点的位置，甚至如何通过公共交通工具到达投票地点。因此，城市的工作变成了信息管理。

从这个意义上讲，技术在很大程度上是一种人类的创造。几千年来，人们一直在创造工具和技术，让生活变得更轻松、更愉快。但作为人类的创造，技术也可能具有破坏性和危险性，如同工具可以用来建造，也可以用来拆除和摧毁。我们的技术通常反映我们的价值观，因此，它反映了人性当中的光明面和黑暗面，在许多方面，城市及其发展也反映了这些价值观。在这个意义上，未来的城市也不会有什么不同。

11.1.3　安全和犯罪率

随着城市的持续增长和人口密度的增加，要求城市政府改善和推进安全和刑事司法领域的服务提供。由于收集信息是城市政府的一项重要职能，因此利用这些信息来改善居民的安全是一个自然的过程。当今世界上的许多城市都使用闭路电视摄像机来监控从交通流到多个城市地点的个人活动。如何收集、存储和最终使用这些信息一直是全球热议的话题。使用这种技术的社会越民主，争论就越激烈。

未来的城市将如何处理城市安全和犯罪问题？这个问题已经在各种场景中上演，许多场景被小说和电影所捕捉。例如，在 1993 年的电影《越空狂龙》中，一个 2031 年的未来城市——旧金山，一个没有犯罪的社会诞生了。然而，一位来自过去的犯罪策划者逃脱了低温监禁，这座城市发现自己无法应对他的犯罪活动。因此，他们从过去复活了一名警察，以帮助追捕罪犯，恢复城市居民享有的社会秩序。电影强调的一个关键主题是利用信息和技术维持秩序，以及这种技术如何创造和受社会系统的影响。一旦通过技术消除了犯罪，技术就会发生变化，从而不再解决它所解决的问题，因此它被用来教育和激励公民以更"文明"的方式行事。不幸的是，这使得新社会容易受到旧有社会更暴力的倾向和技术的影响，这些倾向和技术来自未来的博物馆。

未来的城市将不仅仅收集视频数据，当今城市的信息数据库已经在跟踪居民的活动：他们去哪里，在哪里工作，吃什么样的食物，经常去什么社区，甚至喜欢什么样的电影，所有这些都基于存储在不同地方的不同数据：身份数据（出生日期、性别、职业），购买数据（购买内容、地点和时间），以及旅行数据（去哪里、多久、出行方式、和谁一起去）。城市必须决定如何处理此类信息，如何利用技术让生活更安全，以及如何保护技术，使其不被滥用。

随着技术日益融入我们的日常生活，犯罪的性质将发生变化。网络犯罪已经是全球城市犯罪增长最快的领域之一。随着犯罪分子贩运信息而非货物本身的利润越来越丰厚，对非法活动的侦查将成为执法的重点。而人口密度高、信息流量大的城市将成为网络犯罪的主要目标。因此，未来的城市可能会在收集、汇编和保护信息方面投入大量资源。

11.1.4 公共卫生

公共卫生一直是城市面对的一个问题。鉴于人口密度高，传染病在城市中的传播速度比在人口稀少的地区快得多。几千年来，城市政府一直使用不同的工具，从检疫到大规模接种来控制传染病，但在未来的城市中，保护只是公共卫生官员知识库的一部分。随着城市的发展和生活方式的改变，公共卫生将需要纳入一些工具，而这些工具在过去几十年中并不一定被视为其使命的核心，公共卫生将远远超越传染病和一般保护的范畴。随着人们寿命的延长以及前往偏远地区旅行变得更方便、成本更低等，解决城市公共卫生问题将不得不考虑远远超出特定城市边界的全球趋势。预防、健康维护以及对延长寿命（或年轻的容貌）的日益关注将成为城市政府日益普遍的领域。

2007年，18万美国公民离开美国出国旅行，寻找医疗服务，从印度的髋关节表面置换到泰国的心脏瓣膜置换（Woodman，2008）。美国肿瘤学家约瑟夫·伍德曼表示，主要原因是发达国家医疗成本的上升，以及发展中国家服务质量的提高的同时保持较低的成本。伍德曼回避的"医疗旅游"一词主要与一些深度的治疗方法有关，比如没有医疗价值的整形手术，尽管目前这是一个蓬勃发展的医疗保健领域，尤其是对韩国和巴西等国而言，但伍德曼认为这不是未来增长潜力最大的领域。在未来，将是内科疾病导致世界各地的人需要接受治疗，而城市会发现自己需要作为全球患者的医疗保健提供者而竞争。移植技术的进步已经开始改变高收入阶层寻求医疗保健的方式，而这只会随着技术进步提高且手术成本下降的同时质量得到提高。因此，随着医疗资源面临更高需求的压力，城市将面临多个问题，而国内居民将希望获得与外界相同的资源。社会内部的资源分配一直是一个政治问题，同时也是一个经济问题，因此，城市政府必须就供应作出决定（谁可以担任医生，在哪些领域？）以及需求（谁可以获得服务，以及什么类型的服务？）。

卫生保健和预防也将变得更加重要。肥胖症过去是一种只有富人才会患的疾病，现在发达国家的肥胖症主要集中在中下层阶级。交通技术的发展、相对于体力劳动的桌面工作激增，以及高热量食品成本的下降，这些因素结合在一起，形成了一种危险的集合体。加工食品和高脂肪食品的成本低于健康、低热量食品，如新鲜蔬菜和水果，人们运动和锻炼也越来越少。因此，公共卫生将侧重于"保健和预防"，需要采取更加积极主动的方式提供服务，而不是在疾病发生后处理疾病。城市公共卫生部门已经开始解决这些问题，在城市规划布局中提供锻炼区域以及公共交通或工作区步行距离内的住宅。在未来的城市中，这种帮助居民过上更健康、更有活力的生活的综合方案将构成公共卫生的关键部分。

最后，随着城市的发展，对环境的压力将增加。我国和印度都证明了城市增长对家庭收入水平不断上升、购买汽车或个人电脑等中产阶级生活标志的能力有所提高的居民意味着什么。随着大量新汽车的引入，印度德里和加尔各答等大城市的空气质量迅速下降。在德里，遏制空气质量下降的努力要求采取严厉措施，如车牌号码轮换限行，居民只能在车牌号码有效的日子使用车辆。这在一定程度上改善了空气质量，但也存在其他问题，尤其是在我国北方，比如在冬季使用煤炭进行家庭取暖，这使得空气质量的改善难以实现。

这突出了公共卫生的另一个领域，它将以某种新的方式获取未来的城市政府官员的关注。城市并不是处于真空环境中。例如，距离北京100多公里的天津是我国北方的一个主要工业中心。当风从西北方向吹来时，天津的空气污染会让北京的污染进一步加剧。然后，没人能改变风向，但却可以选择影响空气质量的政策，这些政策可能会影响（或可能会受到）另一个城市的选择。这些跨越城市边界和距离的关联将在未来的城市公共卫生政策中变得越来越重要。

11.2　城市管理体制变革

正如前面的例子所表明的那样，未来的城市需要在非常具体的领域挑战当前城市管理的技能和工具。曼努埃尔·卡斯特尔斯强调了信息管理和使用将发挥的中心作用，以及社会建设将如何塑造技术，使城市成为未来社会看待自身和现实的表现形式，城市将在其行政系统中反映这些变化。因此，改变和改革当前的城市管理体制将是未来城市发展的必然要求。

从历史上看，城市管理体系的改革是由于城市人口的变化（新移民的涌入或现有人口的老龄化）或城市经济系统的冲击（主要工业的丧失或新工业区的崛起），居民类型和数量的改变需要改变管理的政治制度，改革的影响可能对不同阶层的人口产生重大影响。快速回顾一下美国城市改革政府的历史可以说明这一点。

美国前总统伍德罗·威尔逊被称为"公共行政之父"，是城市改革的有力倡导者。作为20世纪早期进步运动的一员，他主张通过建立招聘人员的奖励制度，让市政府更加专业化。这是为了取代20世纪之交美国大多数大城市实行的"恩庇制"或"分肥制"。威尔逊在1887年发表的文章《行政研究》中重申了自己的立场，他主张通过创建一个可以在不受政治官员"干预"的情况下运作的行政系统，将"政治与行政"分开。这是为了给城市的所有居民提供连续的服务，而不是优先考虑那些支持市长执政的人。在强市长制度中，腐败现象经常很猖獗，而在一个城市中，那些在选举中没有为获胜的政党或市长候选人提供足够支持的选区会发现自己缺乏消防或警察保护等城市服务。

改革的目的是解决与美国大城市的强市长制度相关的具体问题。为了削弱选举的政治机器，许多较小的城市选择了无党派选举，因为政党在选举中无法发挥核心作用。此外，设立了城市经理的职位，以使政治和行政正式分离。城市经理是一名专业管理人员，负责管理所有城市服务和人员。政策事项由市议会和市长决定，但如第 3 章所示，市长的权力并不强大。这种改革政府的目的在于在提供服务方面更加专业，减少政治偏见，目前是美国最常见的地方政府形式，但改革是有代价的。

众所周知，美国地方政府选举的投票率很低。对为什么会出现这种情况，人们有很多猜测，这似乎比强市长政府更严重地困扰着改革后的政府。从统计数据来看，美国改革后政府的投票率低于拥有强市长制度的城市（在改革后的城市中，选民人数减少了约10%），在过去 25 年中，所有大城市的平均投票率约为 27%（Caren，2007）。因此，有证据表明，尽管强市长制度可能存在问题，但低投票率并非其中之一。

11.3　未来城市面临的挑战

11.3.1　世代流动

如今，有许多二十年前不存在的问题：网络战、黑客攻击、博客对人们所知的影响、信息对日常生活的重要性，以及个人和政府相互交流方式。然而，1950 年之前出生的人比 1950 年之后几十年出生的人更不可能意识到或相信这些活动（Safian，2012）。未来学是一个学术领域，它假设"另类未来"可以通过将一些变量投射到未来 20 ~ 50年的方法来实现，其前提是，未来很大程度上取决于我们今天所做的决定，而这些决定往往不是我们认为特别重要的决定。

"世代流动"是一个术语，用于描述当前专注于技术开发、数学建模或人类服务交付的小领域企业家（Safian，2012）。世代流动概念的关键是，组织模式越来越过时，正如数字广告公司 R/GA 的首席执行官鲍勃·格林伯格所说，关于如何使组织成功的旧知识正在被改写（Safian，2012）。格林伯格 2011 年 9 月在他的公司中设置了 200 个新职位，但不得不雇用 500 人来填补这些职位，这是因为他雇用的员工需要非常精通技术，他们或者被其他公司雇用或者创办了自己的企业，所以有 300 名员工流失，正如大多数组织理论教科书所建议的那样，他不认为这是一个问题，因为他认识到，在竞争激烈的市场中，营业额背后的原因是一个技能问题。人们没有离开是因为他的公司提供了令人不满意的工作，人们离开是因为他们对技能的需求非常高，因此他们跳槽能比留在这一岗位上获得更多。

世代流动是指一代工人以前所未有的频率从一个岗位转移到另一个岗位，并具有跨越部门、大洲和文化的可移植性。他们的技能随着全球不同产业的需求而变化，尽管他们可能从某一领域的培训和教育开始，但无法预测他们的职业道路会受到他们选择的学习道路的何种影响。这一代人并没有打算在整个职业生涯中保持同样的职位。据估计，世代流动员工在其工作生涯中将担任 10 ~ 30 个全职专业工作，稳定不是他们所追求的，也不是环境所要求的。

这些想法和情况将如何影响未来的城市？随着信息成本的下降，政府提供和控制信息的能力将变得愈加困难。但规模仍然很重要，商品从世界一个地区转移到另一个地区的技术也同样重要，仍然是商品和信息贸易中心的城市会成为未来的主导城市，但商品和信息的种类将决定这些城市的居民类型。预测未来的城市将是什么或它将提供什么服务，需要预测人类本性的哪些方面将在下个世纪显现出来，正如今天的许多技术所证明的那样，这样的预测很难做出。

11.3.2　未来城市与自然灾害

2007 年，联合国人口基金会研究了城市易受自然灾害影响的脆弱性，特别是普遍贫困持续存在的城市。该报告估计，在 1980 年至 2000 年间，世界总人口的 75% 生活在受自然灾害影响的地区。总体而言，较贫穷国家的城市情况更糟，因为洪水或泥石流等自然灾害造成的问题因基础设施差以及缺乏规划或分区执法而加剧。然而，即使在发达国家，随着全球气候变化，城市也会面临一些问题，城市将在应对变化和应对适应方面发挥作用，或者忽视它们的作用，从而使问题变得更糟。正如世界观察研究所 2007 年指出的那样："特别具有讽刺意味的是，拯救地球上剩余的健康生态系统的战斗不会在受到威胁的热带森林或珊瑚礁中获胜或失败，而是在地球上最不自然的景观街道上。"

随着人类越来越集中在城市中心，自然灾害的规划和应对问题将变得越来越重要。即使是拥有最先进的规划和灾害管理系统的城市，也可能因大规模灾害而措手不及，2011 年日本东海岸海啸就是例证。海啸及其后果造成了巨大的动荡，地震和海啸发生前两天，曾被任命为菅直人首相内阁成员五十岚崇义，负责解决农村地区的衰退问题。他认为，如果一场大地震袭击东京，它将使日本瘫痪，因为首都的"一切都在这里"（Ito, 2011）。政府解决这一损失的能力非常有限，任何复苏都需要更长的时间，从而导致伤亡人数增加，公众信心下降。海啸发生后，将关键应急职能下放的呼吁成为日本中央政府的一项任务。

在传统的城市政府中，自然灾害的规划和应对通常被称为"重点活动"，但通常不被视为核心职能。中央政府是唯一能够筹集足够的资金和人力资源来应对大规模的破坏的。但正如 Igarishi 所指出的那样，如果像东京这样的国家首都资源过度集中，对该城市的打击可能会对整个国家造成毁灭性的影响，这在较老的国家尤其如此，在历史上，城市中心的资源和专业知识积累缓慢，从而确定了民族国家的身份。但在像美国这样的年轻国家，情况并非如此。正如 2001 年 9 月 11 日纽约袭击事件的后果所表明的那样，在美国，多个城市可以在灾难期间和之后提供援助。

未来城市之间的相互联系将决定它们能否在此类事件中幸存下来，还是仅仅被孤立和荒废，这也可能取决于他们将自己的活动视为更大系统的一部分的能力。如果未来的城市仍以今天常见的方式竞争和合作，那么共享信息的规模，或许还有治理，将以今天难以想象的方式增加。无论未来会带来什么，城市将在未来几代人体验生活的方式中发挥核心作用。仅出于这个原因，我们也应该更加密切关注我们城市的管理方式，以及这种管理会如何影响现在和未来的居民。

【思考题】

1. 未来城市的功能与今天的功能有什么不同？
2. 未来城市政府对哪些技能的需求会更高？

【关键术语】

聚焦事件　　　　　　　　　　　　巨型城市
世代流动　　　　　　　　　　　　智慧城市
全球城市　　　　　　　　　　　　技术
全球化　　　　　　　　　　　　　虚拟购物
医疗旅游

参考文献

［1］Caren，Neal（2007）. "Big City，Big Turnout? Electoral Participation in American Cities". *Journal of Urban Affairs*，29（1）：31 - 46.

［2］Castells，Manuel（1985）. *The City and the Grassroots：A Cross-Cultural Theory of Urban Social Movements.* Berkeley，CA：University of California Press.

［3］Gopnik，Adam（2000）.*Paris to the Moon.* New York：Random House.

［4］Hales，Mike，King，Samantha，and Mendoza Pena，Andres（2010）. *The Urban Elite：The A. T. Kearney Global Cities Index* 2010. Chicago，IL：A. T. Kearney，Chicago Council on Global Affairs and *Foreign Policy* Magazine.

［5］Ito，Aki（March 28，2011）. "Kan Told to Decentralize Japan on Tokyo Annihilation Danger". Bloomberg News Services，New York.

［6］Safian，Robert. Jan. 9，2012. "This is Generation Flux：Meet the Pioneers of the New（and Chaotic）Frontier of Business". *Fast Company*. New York：Fast Company.

［7］Sassen，Saskia（2001）. *The Global City：New York，London，Tokyo.* 2nd ed. Princeton，NJ：Princeton University Press.

［8］United Nations Population Fund（UNFPA）（2007）. "Urbanization and Sustainability in the 21st Century". In *State of the World Population* 2007：*Unleashing the Potential of Urban Growth*，Chapter 5. online at：http：//www. unfpa. org/swp/2007/english/chapter_5/poverty. html retrieved 5/6/2022.

［9］United States Federal Bureau of Investigations（2011）. "Cyber Crimes. " online at：http：//www. fbi. gov/aboutus/investigate/cyber/computer-intrusions retrieved 1/11/2021.

［10］Woodman，Josef（2008）.*Patients Beyond Borders：Everybody's Guide to Affordable，World-Class Medical Travel* 2nd ed. Chapel Hill，NC：Healthy Travel.

Chapter 11　Future Urban Administration

11. 1　Prospects for the Urban Environment of the Future

What will cities of the future be like? This has been a topic of interest for urban scholars, but it is also an idea that has also captured the imagination of filmmakers, writers and artists for centuries. Since cities have often served as centers of art, culture and learning in the past, it is not surprising that they would also serve as the settings for stories and ideas about the future. Cities will most likely continue to play these roles in the years to come, but what will their citizens want and need from their cities? How might city services change as the nature of what cities are evolves?

11. 1. 1　Globalization and the Role of Cities

Many urban scholars and writers from previous generations wrote about their visions of cities of the future. At the end of the 19th century, Paris, France was considered a center of culture and sophistication, and in the early 20th century, writers, artists, and scholars all made their way to the City of Light to study, learn and be part of the "vision of the future". In his 2000 book, *Paris to the Moon*, Adam Gopnik describes a poster drawn by a Parisian artist at then turn of the century, depicting a train that departs from Paris and runs on tracks that go up into the night sky and end at the moon. The vision of the future was, of course, rooted in the idea of the present—if there was going to be transportation to the moon (as written about by Jules Verne fifty years earlier), it would be the most modern and comfortable transportation available, and it would leave from the most modern and convenient place on Earth. Hence a train from Paris to the moon made perfect sense.

However, at the beginning of the 21st century, cities are changing in ways that are both visible and invisible. Paris has been overshadowed by its rival to the north, London, a usurper from across the Atlantic, New York and the farthest afield, Tokyo. This is the age of the global city: cities that can influence politics beyond their own borders, wield economic clout that is felt far beyond the boundaries of the nations they occupy, and are centers of culture, information technology, and education (Hales, King and Mendoza Pena, 2010). Technology has also increasingly defined the divide between the haves and the have-nots. What is notable about the global city is that some of the world's largest cities are not global. Lagos Nigeria, Dhaka, Bangladesh, and Manila, the Philippines, are some of the world's largest cities, experiencing rapid growth over the past twenty years, but without experiencing the gradual improvement in standard of living that accompanies such growth in a global city. Mega-cities, which occupy regions rather than a central place, may not always be global leaders.

Marcel Castells has written extensively on the history of cities and the idea that cities and nation-states have historically represented competing forms of political expression (Castells, 1985: 11). In discussing his idea of what the medieval city represented as a political form, he argues that the nation-state was not a logical progression from the city-state:

> The free cities…were not just a step toward the nation state. They were an alternative political form, another social project towards modernity, not necessarily inferior in terms of technology, political effectiveness, or even military power… in fact, the city-state and the nation-state do not constitute an inevitable historical sequence; they are deeply antagonistic political forms in which the relationship between the state and civil society differ profoundly (Castells, 1985: 11).

Some authors have argued that the global city may usurp the nation-state in importance and influence (Sassen, 2001), especially as drivers of the international economy. If this is to happen, then the cities of the future will have to be quite different from the cities of today.

11. 1. 2 The Role of Technology and the Smart City

The term *technology* today is generally associated with "hi-tech" conceptions. The use of electronics, computers, and communications hardware and software developed to help people improve the efficiency and quality of production in both work and recreation activities. But *technology* has a broader meaning that is perhaps more useful when discussing the role of technology in building cities of the future. The general definition of technology is the study or learning of a skill, art or craft, or as the Merriam-Webster dictionary offers: "the practical application of knowledge especially in a particular area" and "a capability given by the practical application of knowledge." In other words, technology is about the use of knowledge, or information, to achieve particular goals.

As technology has become more advanced and has rapidly become more integrated into the daily lives of individuals (imagine a world without cell phones—very common less than twenty years ago), it has become an integral part of the vision of the future, especially for urban life. Advances in transportation technology have transformed the way people live in countries like Japan, with the *shinkansen* changing where people live and work. The green revolution in agriculture during the 1960s transformed the way in which food was produced and distributed across the globe. And advances in communications technology, along with the creation of the World

Wide Web and internet, have revolutionized the way in which people connect with each other, from neighbors who live next door to friends who live halfway across the world.

Cities have both benefitted from and contributed to the advances in technology. The idea of a "smart city" has evolved over the past twenty years as an outgrowth of developments in communications technology. A "smart city" is generally understood to be a city where residents can communicate in several ways with both other residents and, in more advanced versions, with the city itself. The focus of the smart city is on creating a "seamless experience" for residents, so that they might find what they need to work and play in an efficient and very cost-effective way. This is done using communications technology installed throughout the city and requires that residents either own or have access to a device that allows them to access that technology, such as wireless internet and a cell phone. The city's role becomes focused on managing the information that can be made available to residents, and maintaining (and upgrading) the infrastructure that makes information retrieval possible. For example, in a smart city, a resident may wish to move from one neighborhood to another that is closer to her place of work. However, her place of work is surrounded by multiple neighborhoods that have different prices for housing and with apartments that offer different amenities. Instead of going to each neighborhood and viewing each available apartment individually and in person, a resident in a smart city might be able to compare information on available apartments on-line, including information on property tax, association fees, and available schools in each neighborhood. This information could be retrieved using either a computer or a cell phone that has internet access.

In this example, the role of the government may depend on what the market has already made available to residents, and what is still lacking. In some smart cities, private companies provide all the components that would make such "virtual shopping" possible: the internet access (via some kind of network technology); the information provided through the internet (different real estate companies could post listings with a variety of information that potential buyers might want); the receiving technology, e. g. computers, tablets or cell phones might be provided by private companies. But in other cities, there may not be sufficient market investment in one or more of these technology areas. In these cases, the city government may become directly involved in the provision of one or more of these technologies, so that residents might work more efficiently and use the time saved to engage in other activities that may be helpful to the city.

The key to making a smart city "smart" is its ability to connect each resident with appropriate information. This is not a simple task, since there may be many kinds of information needed by residents, and the city's task becomes figuring out how to prioritize the information so that it might be provided in a timely fashion to those who are requesting it. In summertime, for example, more residents may be requesting information on the nearest swimming pool or school where swimming instruction is offered. But such requests may drop in number once colder weather arrives in fall. If the city is providing access to information, it may anticipate higher levels of traffic on certain websites and requests for certain kinds of information at particular times. Another example might be during the weeks prior to an election: residents may be requesting more information on the candidates who are running for office, the location of their polling place, and even how to get to polling places via public transportation. So, the city's job becomes one of information management.

In this sense, technology is very much a human construction. People have been creating tools and techniques to make life easier and more enjoyable for thousands of years. But as a human construction, technology can also be destructive and dangerous. Tools can be created to build, but also to tear down and destroy. Our technology often reflects our values, and as such, it reflects both the light and the dark sides of human nature. In many ways, cities and their development over time reflect these values as well. Cities of the future will be no different in this sense.

11. 1. 3 Safety and Crime

As cities continue to grow and population density increases, city governments will be called upon to improve and advance service delivery in safety and criminal justice. Since collecting information will be a key city government function, using that information to improve the safety of residents will be a natural progression. Many cities today worldwide use closed-circuit television cameras to monitor activities that range from traffic flow to individual activities in multiple urban locations. How this information is collected, stored and eventually used has been a topic of hot debate around the globe. The more democratic the society in which such technology is used, the more contentious the debate.

How will cities of the future approach the urban issue of safety and crime? This issue has been played out in a wide range of scenarios, many captured in novels and in film. In the 1993 film, "Demolition Man", for example, a future city in 2031, San Angeles, a crime-free society has been created. However, a criminal mastermind from the past has escaped his cryogenic incarceration, and the city finds itself unable to deal with his criminal activities. So, they resurrect a police officer from the past to help track down the criminal and restore the social order enjoyed by the city's residents. One of the key themes highlighted by the film is the use of information and technology to maintain order, but also how such technology creates and is affected by social systems. Once crime has been eliminated through technology, technology shifts so that it no longer addresses the problem it has solved. The technology morphs so that it is used to educate and inspire citizens to behave in a more "civilized" fashion. Unfortunately, this leaves the new society vulnerable to the old society's more violent tendencies and technologies, borrowed from a museum of the future.

Cities of the future will collect more than simply video data; information databases in today's cities already track the activities of residents: where they go, where they work, what kinds of food they eat, what neighborhoods they frequent, and even what kinds of movies they like, all based on combining different data available in different places: identification data (birthdate, gender, occupation); purchasing data (what one buys, where and when); and travelling data (where one goes, how often, by what means, and with whom). As public entities, cities will have to decide what to do with this kind of information; how it might be used to make lives safer, but also how it might be protected so that it may not be abused.

The nature of crime will change as technology becomes more integrated into daily life. Already cyber-crime is one of the fastest growing areas of urban crime worldwide. As it becomes increasingly lucrative for criminals to traffic in information rather than goods themselves, detection of illicit activities will become the focus of law enforcement. And cities, with their high density populations and high levels of information traffic, will become prime targets for cyber-criminals. Thus, cities of the future may expect to spend significant resources on the collection, compilation and protection of information.

11. 1. 4　Public Health

Public health has always been an issue for cities. Given the high population density, contagious diseases can spread through a city much more quickly than in more sparsely populated areas. Throughout millennia, city governments have used different tools, ranging from quarantine to mass vaccinations, to control contagion. But in cities of the future, protection will only be one component of the knowledge base for public health officials. As cities evolve and lifestyles change, public health will need to incorporate tools that it has not necessarily considered central to its mission in previous decades. Public health will move well beyond the realm of contagious disease and general protection. As people live longer, endure fewer physical challenges, and live in places where travel to distant locales becomes more convenient and less cost-prohibitive, addressing public health concerns in cities will have to consider global trends that go well beyond a given city's borders. Prevention, health maintenance, and an increasing focus on extending life (or the appearance of youth) will become areas that city governments will find increasingly pervasive.

In 2007, 180000 US citizens left the US to travel abroad and find health care services that ranged from hip resurfacing in India to heart valve replacements in Thailand (Woodman, 2008, pp. 7). The main driver, according to Josef Woodman, a US oncologist, is the rise of costs for medical procedures in developed countries and the increase in quality of services in developing countries while maintaining lower costs. The term "medical tourism", which Woodman avoids, is largely associated with esoteric treatments, such as plastic surgery that has no medical value. Although this is a booming area of health care, especially for countries such as the Republic of Korea and Brazil, this is not the area that Woodman sees as the one with the highest potential for growth in the future. In the future, it will be internal maladies that send people all over the world for treatment, and cities will find themselves competing as health care providers for world-wide patients. Advancements in transplant technology have already begun to change the way people seek health care at the top of the income spectrum. This will only increase as technological advancements improve quality of surgical outcomes while costs per surgery decline.

Thus, cities will face several issues as health care resources are pressured by higher demands, and the population at home will want access to the same resources that are offered to outsiders. The distribution of resources inside society has always been a political question as much as an economic one, so city governments will have to make decisions about supply (who can serve as a physician and in what fields?) and demand (who can access services, and what kinds?).

Health care maintenance and prevention will also become far more important. Obesity, which used to be a malady that only the wealthy suffered, is now found in developed countries as concentrated in the middle and lower classes. Developments in transportation technology, the explosion of desk jobs as opposed to physical labor, and the decline in the cost of high calorie food products have combined to create a dangerous mixture. The cost of processed and fatty foods is lower than healthier, lower calorie foods, such as fresh vegetables and fruit, and people are moving and exercising less. Thus, public health will focus on "maintenance and prevention" which requires a more pro-active approach to service delivery than addressing illness after it has already occurred. Public health officials in cities have already started to address these elements by providing exercise areas within city planning layouts, open spaces close to worksites and residences that are within walking distance of public transport or work districts. In cities of the future, this kind of integrative approach to help residents live healthier, more productive lives will be a crucial part of public health.

Finally, as cities develop, stress on environmental factors will increase. China and India have both demonstrated what urban growth can mean for residents whose level of household income is rising, and whose ability to purchase hallmarks of middle-class existence, such as automobiles or personal computers, has increased. In both countries, air quality in the largest cities, such as Delhi and Calcutta in India, has declined rapidly with the introduction of massive numbers of new automobiles. In Delhi, attempts to curb the decline of air quality have required draconian measures, where license plate numbers are rotated so that residents can only use their vehicles on days when their numbers are valid. This has improved air quality somewhat, but there are additional problems, especially in northern China, such as the use of coal for household heating in winter, that makes improvements in air quality elusive.

This highlights another area of public health that will occupy city officials of the future in somewhat new ways. Cities do not exist in a vacuum. Beijing is only 111 kilometers northwest of Tianjin, a major industrial center in northeastern China. This means that when the wind is blowing out of the northwest, Tianjin's air pollution gets an added boost from Beijing. Thus, Tianjin and Beijing are connected in ways that may be difficult to manage. Neither can do anything about prevailing wind direction, so both have choices to make about policies that affect air quality that may have an impact on (or may be affected by) the choices that the other city makes. These kinds of connections that span city boundaries and distances will become increasingly relevant in public health policies for cities in the future.

11. 2   Reform and Change in Urban Administration Systems

As the previous examples have demonstrated, cities of the future will require skills and tools that will challenge current urban administration in very specific areas. Manuel Castells has highlighted the central role that information management and use will play, and how social constructions will shape technologies in ways that will make cities of the future manifestations of the way society sees itself and the way it really is. As social orders change, for example, as some sectors of society become more powerful and others retreat, cities will reflect these changes in their administrative systems. Thus, change and reform of current urban administrative systems will be a necessary development in the future.

Historically, reform of urban administration systems has resulted because of changes in city populations (influx of new immigrants or the aging of an existing population) or because of shocks to a city's economic system (loss of a major industry or the rise of a new area of industry). Change in the type and number of residents requires a change in the political system that governs them, and the implications of reform can be substantial for different sectors of the population. A quick examination of the history of "reform" governments in cities in the United States illustrates this point.

Woodrow Wilson, the former president of the United States and sometimes referred to as "the Father of Public Administration" was a strong advocate of urban reform. As a member of the progessive movement of the early twentieth century, he advocated making city governments more professional by creating merit systems for hiring personnel. This was intended to replace the patronage or "spoils" system that was in place in most large cities in the United States at the turn of the twentieth century. Reprising a position that he took in his 1887 article, "The Study of Administration," Wilson advocated separating "politics from administration" by creating an administrative system that could operate without "interference" from political officials. This was intended to provide continuity of service to all residents in a city, rather than giving preference to those who supported the mayor in power. In strong mayor systems, corruption was often rampant, and those precincts in a city that did not offer sufficient support for the winning party or mayoral candidate during an election found themselves lacking city services such as fire or police protection.

Reform was meant to address specific problems associated with the strong mayor systems in place in the largest cities in the United States. To weaken the political machines that ran elections, many smaller cities opted for non-partisan elections where parties could not play a central role in selecting candidates. In addition, the position of city manager was created to formalize the separation of politics and administration. The city manager was a professional administrator who was responsible for managing all city services and personnel. Matters of policy were decided by the city council and the mayor, but the mayor's powers were not strong, as indicated in Chapter 3. This reformed type of government was meant to be more professional and less politically biased in service provision, and is currently the most common form of local government in the United States. But reform has come with a cost.

Voter turnout for local government elections in the United States is notoriously low. There has been much speculation on why this is the case, but it seems to plague reformed governments at a much higher rate than strong mayor governments. Turnout level in the United States for reformed governments is statistically lower than that for cities with strong mayor systems (approximately 10% fewer voters in reformed cities), and averages around 27% for all large cities over the past 25 years (Caren, 2007). So there is evidence that although strong mayor systems may have problems, low voter turnout is not one of them.

Reform, therefore, requires careful consideration of both current conditions and unintended consequences that might arise as a result of reform efforts. In the future, conditions such increased integration of technology into city functions may require reforming city structures, such as elections or service delivery, in ways that are difficult to foresee. This difficulty in forecasting is not unique to the public sector or government services. As advances in technology develop more rapidly and with increasing diversity, the ability to predict the future of services will become increasingly difficult.

11. 3　Future Challenges

11. 3. 1　Generation Flux

Today, there are multiple problems that did not exist twenty years ago. Cyber-warfare, hacking, blogging are all examples of activities that affect what people know, the importance of information to daily life, and the way in which individuals as well as governments communicate with each other. And yet, these are activities that people born prior to 1950 are far less likely to be aware of or give credence to than people born in the decades after that date (Safian, 2012). Future studies, which is an academic field that posits "alternative futures" that can be realized using methodologies that project a few variables twenty to fifty years into the future, is premised on the idea that the future is largely based on decisions we make today, and quite often, those decisions are not ones that we consider particularly important.

"Generation flux" is a term that has been used to describe a current field of entrepreneurs who focus on small pockets of technology development, mathematical modeling, or human service delivery (Safian, 2012). Key to the idea of generation flux is that models of organizations are increasingly obsolete. As Bob Greenberg, the CEO of R/GA, a digital advertising firm offers, old knowledge about what makes organizations successful is being rewritten (Safian, 2012). For example, Greenberg created 200 new positions in his firm in September of 2011, but had to hire 500 people to fill those positions. This was because the staff he hired was so technologically savvy, that he had turnover of 300 personnel because they were hired by other companies or started their own enterprises. He did not see this turnover as a problem, as most textbooks on organization theory would propose. This is because he recognized the reason behind the turnover as a skills issue in a fiercely competitive market. People weren't leaving because his company offered unsatisfying work; people left because their skill sets were in such high demand that they had more to gain by company-hopping than by staying with one position.

Generation flux is a generation of workers who move from one position to another with unprecedented frequency, and have portability across sectors, continents and cultures. Their skills change as needs arise in different industries across the globe, and although they may begin with training and education in a field, there is no way to predict how their career path will be affected by their chosen path of study. This is not a generation that plans to stay in the same position for their entire careers. It is estimated that Generation Flux workers will hold anywhere from ten to thirty full-time professional jobs over the course of their working lives. Stability is not what they seek, nor what the environment will demand.

How will such ideas and conditions affect cities of the future? As the cost of information declines, the ability of governments to provide and control information will become more difficult. But scale will still be important, as will technologies that move goods from one area of the world to another. Cities that remain trading hubs for goods and information will be the cities that become dominant in the future. But the kinds of goods and information will determine what sorts of residents will populate those cities. Predicting what the future city will be or what services it will provide requires predicting which aspects of human nature will manifest themselves over the next century. And as many of today's technologies demonstrate, such predictions are very difficult to make.

11. 3. 2　Cities of the Future and Natural Disasters

In 2007, the UNFPA looked at the vulnerability of cities to natural disasters, especially cities where widespread poverty persists (UNFPA, 2007). The report estimated that "between 1980 and 2000, seventy-five percent of the world's total population lived in areas affected by a natural disaster". Cities in poorer nations fare much worse, in general, since the problems caused by natural disasters such as flooding or mudslides are exacerbated by poor infrastructure and lack of planning or zoning enforcement.

However, even in developed nations, there are problems that cities will face as the global climate changes, and cities will have a role to play in either addressing the change and responding with adaptations, or ignoring their role and thus making the problems worse. As noted by the World Watch Institute in 2007: "It is particularly ironic that the battle to save the earth's remaining healthy ecosystems will be won or lost not in tropical forests or coral reefs that are threatened but on the streets of the most unnatural landscapes on the planet".

As humanity becomes increasingly concentrated in urban centers, the question of both planning for and response to natural disasters will grow in importance. Even cities with state-of-the-art planning and disaster management systems can be caught unprepared by large-scale disasters, as illustrated by the 2011 tsunami off the eastern coast of Japan. The tsunami and its aftermath caused huge upheavals. Takoyoshi Igarishi, who had been appointed to then-Prime Minister Kan's Cabinet to address rural region decline two days before the earthquake and tsunami, immediately proposed decentralizing operations from Tokyo. He argued that if a large earthquake hit Tokyo, it would cripple Japan because "everything is here" in the capital city (Ito, 2011). There would be such limited capacity to work around that loss that any recovery would take much longer, resulting in an increase in casualties, and a decline in public confidence. In the aftermath of the tsunami, the call to decentralize key emergency response functions became a mandate for the central government.

The planning for and response to natural disasters, often called "focusing events" in traditional city governments is not generally considered a core function. National governments are the only entities capable of mustering enough resources, both monetary and human, to address large-scale destruction. But as Igarishi points out, if there is overconcentration of resources in a national capital city, like Tokyo, a blow to the city can be devastating for the country as a whole. This is particularly true in older nations, where history has seen the slow accumulation of resources and expertise in city centers that have defined the identities of nation-states. This is not so true in younger countries, like the U. S. , where multiple cities can offer resources to assist during and after a disaster, as the aftermath of the September 11, 2001 attacks on New York City demonstrated.

The interconnectedness of cities of the future will determine whether they can survive such events or whether they will simply be left in isolation and desolation. It may also determine their ability to see their own activities as part of a larger system. If cities of the future do indeed compete and cooperate in the ways that are commonly seen today, the scale of shared information and, perhaps, governance, will increase in ways that may be difficult to envision today. Whatever the future may bring, cities will play a central role in the ways in which the generations to come experience life. For that reason alone, we should keep a watchful eye on the way in which our cities are governed, and how their administration affects present and future residents.

Questions

1. How might the functions of cities of the future differ from the functions they perform today?

2. What kinds of skills might be in high demand by city governments of the future?

3. How do city governments and nation-state governments differ?

Key Terms

focusing event

generation flux

global city

globalization

medical tourism

mega-city

smart city

technology

virtual shopping

References

［1］ Caren, Neal (2007). "Big City, Big Turnout? Electoral Participation in American Cities". *Journal of Urban Affairs*, 29 (1): 31 – 46.

［2］ Castells, Manuel (1985). *The City and the Grassroots: A Cross-Cultural Theory of Urban Social Movements.* Berkeley, CA: University of California Press.

［3］ Gopnik, Adam (2000). *Paris to the Moon.* New York: Random House.

［4］ Hales, Mike, King, Samantha, and Mendoza Pena, Andres (2010). *The Urban Elite: The A. T. Kearney Global Cities Index* 2010. Chicago, IL: A. T. Kearney, Chicago Council on Global Affairs and *Foreign Policy* Magazine.

［5］ Ito, Aki (March 28, 2011). "Kan Told to Decentralize Japan on Tokyo Annihilation Danger". Bloomberg News Services, New York.

［6］ Safian, Robert. Jan. 9, 2012. "This is Generation Flux: Meet the Pioneers of the New (and Chaotic) Frontier of Business". *Fast Company.* New York: Fast Company.

［7］ Sassen, Saskia (2001). *The Global City: New York, London, Tokyo.* 2nd ed. Princeton, NJ: Princeton University Press.

［8］ United Nations Population Fund (UNFPA) (2007). "Urbanization and Sustainability in the 21st Century". In *State of the World Population* 2007: *Unleashing the Potential of Urban Growth*, Chapter 5. online at: http://www.unfpa.org/swp/2007/english/chapter_5/poverty. html retrieved 5/6/2022.

［9］ United States Federal Bureau of Investigations (2011). "Cyber Crimes." online at: http://www. fbi.gov/aboutus/investigate/cyber/computer-intrusions retrieved 1/11/2021.

［10］ Woodman, Josef (2008). *Patients Beyond Borders: Everybody's Guide to Affordable*, *World-Class Medical Travel* 2nd ed. Chapel Hill, NC: Healthy Travel.